5/95

SANTA MARIA PUBLIC LIBRARY

Discarded by
Santa Maria Library

Discarded by
Santa Maria Library

629.22209
McConnell, Curt, 1959-
Great cars of the Great
Plains /
c1995.

D0768764

95   96   92   01

Great Cars of the Great Plains

Curt McConnell

University of Nebraska Press
Lincoln and London

© 1995 by the University of
Nebraska Press. All rights
reserved. Manufactured in
the United States of America.
The paper in this book meets
the minimum requirements
of American National Standard for Information Sciences –
Permanence of Paper for
Printed Library Materials,
ANSI Z39.48-1984. Library
of Congress Cataloging in
Publication Data. McConnell,
Curt, 1959–   Great Cars
of the Great Plains / by
Curt McConnell.   p.   cm.
Includes bibliographical
references and index.
ISBN 0-8032-3163-6 (alk.
paper) 1. Automobiles –
Middle West – History.
2. Automobile industry
and trade – United States –
History. I. Title.
TL4.M38   1995
629.222'0977 – dc20
94-3860 CIP

Contents

Photo Credits

BW   Betty Witham

CWB   Carl W. Burst III

DW   Doris Whithorn

FLP   Free Library of Philadelphia

GHM   Grinnell Historical Museum

HD   Harold Dunkle

JAC   John A. Conde Collection

JL   Jim Leicher

KSHS   Kansas State Historical Society

LB   Larry Bryan

LV   Lanna Vedvick

MHS   Missouri Historical Society

MNHS   Minnesota Historical Society

MTHS   Montana Historical Society, Library Collection

MS   Myhre Studio, Luverne, Minnesota

MSS   Miriam Spaulding Simms

NAHC   National Automotive History Collection, Detroit Public Library

NSHS   Nebraska State Historical Society

PW   F. Pace Woods II

RCHS   Rock County Historical Society, Luverne, Minnesota

SHSI   State Historical Society of Iowa–Des Moines

SLML   St. Louis Mercantile Library Association

SPPP   *Saint Paul Pioneer Press*

TCJ   *Topeka Capital-Journal*

TL   Tom Lutzi

TS   Townsend Studio, Lincoln, Nebraska

UNA   University of Nebraska Archives and Special Collections

Acknowledgments

For general research assistance I'd like to thank

Duane Ackerman, Kathy Adams, John Beers, Bob Boyce, Brenda Ealey, Sarah Samson, Scott Stewart, Barbara Rix, Bob Voelker, and others at Bennett Martin Public Library, Lincoln, Nebraska; Dianna Dean, Kate Kane, Joyce Melvin, and others at the University of Nebraska–Lincoln's Love Library; Ralph Dunwoodie; Jerry Falck; Louis G. Helverson, Automobile Reference Collection, Free Library of Philadelphia; Beverly Rae Kimes; Campbell R. McConnell; Kim Miller, Antique Automobile Club of America Library and Research Center, Hershey, Pennsylvania; and Mark Patrick and Ron Grantz, National Automotive History Collection, Detroit Public Library.

Luverne chapter

Nia Bagley; Tracey Baker, Alan Ominsky, and others, Minnesota Historical Society, St. Paul; Monica Barrett, Montana Secretary of State's office, Helena; Grace Bates and Phyllis Smith, Gallatin County Historical Society, Bozeman, Montana; Arlo Bierkamp; Buick Motor Division, General Motors Corporation; Eleanor Buzalsky and Patricia Virgil, Buffalo and Erie County Historical Society, Buffalo, New York; Isabel Chapman, Minnehaha County Historical Society, Sioux Falls, South Dakota; Barbara Clauson, Gallatin County Clerk and Recorder's Office, Bozeman, Montana; John A. Conde; George Dammann, Crestline Publishing, Sarasota, Florida; Norma DeJongh and Deb Fick, Luverne Chamber of Commerce, Luverne, Minnesota; Jack Down and Mick Potter, R. E. Olds Transportation Museum, Lansing, Michigan; Harold Dunkle; Hope Emerich, Antique Truck Club of America; Chad Fey and Bryan Green, Myhre Studio, Luverne, Minnesota; Kit Foster, Society of Automotive Historians; Gale Frost, Minnesota State Fair, St. Paul; Beat Glaus, Swiss Federal Institute of Technology Zurich, in Zurich, Switzerland; Ann Haller, Historical Society of Douglas County, Omaha, Nebraska; Jim Hoggatt, Indianapolis Motor Speedway Hall of Fame Museum, Indianapolis, Indiana; Ann Hollaren; Ann Jenks, South Dakota Historical Society, Pierre; George Jensen; Helen Jensen, Rock County Historical Society, Luverne, Minnesota; Elliott Kahn; Alan Kaiser, Ramsey County Historical Society, St. Paul, Minnesota; Paul Kelsey, Kelsey's Antique Cars, Camdenton, Missouri; Denyse Kraud; R. A.

Larson; Jim Leicher; Lyon County Historical Society, Marshall, Minnesota; Erhart Mueller, Sauk Prairie Historical Society, Sauk City, Wisconsin; David Nelson; Val V. Quandt, Hartford Heritage Auto Museum, Hartford, Wisconsin; David Rambow, Pipestone County Historical Society, Pipestone, Minnesota; Steve Reedy, Luverne Fire Apparatus Company, Brandon, South Dakota; Maurice Rendall; W. H. Rodman; Lou Sargent and Dave Smith, Tri-State Insurance Company of Minnesota, Luverne; Geraldine Strey, State Historical Society of Wisconsin, Madison; Kip Sundgaard; C. D. Tostenson, Emmet County Historical Society, Estherville, Iowa; Dave Walter, Montana Historical Society Library, Helena; Kathy Wark; David White, Alfred P. Sloan Museum, Flint, Michigan; Doris Whithorn; and Thomas Zishka, Nobles County Historical Society, Worthington, Minnesota.

Moon chapter

Dale Anderson, Hartford Heritage Auto Museum, Hartford, Wisconsin; Nia Bagley; Elizabeth Bailey and Laurel Boeckman, State Historical Society of Missouri, Columbia; Charles Brown, St. Louis Mercantile Library; Carl W. Burst III; Henry Austin Clark, Jr.; John A. Conde; Jack Donlan; Joe Egle; reference librarians at Ellis Library, University of Missouri–Columbia; Bob Johnson, Teledyne Total Power, Memphis, Tennessee; Denyse Kraud; Emily Miller and others, Missouri Historical Society, St. Louis; Muskegon County Museum, Muskegon, Michigan; Tom Pearson and Katherine Smith, St. Louis Public Library; reference librarians at Pius XII Memorial Library, St. Louis University; Robert Tuthill; Western Reserve Historical Society, Cleveland, Ohio; and Bill White.

Patriot chapter

Bob Bries; Tom Brownell and John Gunnell, *Old Cars Weekly News & Marketplace;* Jeff Caplan; Emily Clark, Chicago Historical Society; Jim Clark, Townsend Studio, Lincoln, Nebraska; Veda Clements, Franklin County Historical Society, Franklin, Nebraska; Betty Cook; Council Bluffs (Iowa) Public Library; Moe Carlton; John Carter, Emily Levine, Ane Hasselbalch McBride, Marty Vestecka-Miller, Randall Flagel, Linda Wagaman and others, Nebraska State Historical Society, Lincoln; Hope Emerich, Antique Truck Club of America; Jerry Finley; Jerry Gettman, Lincoln (Nebraska) Fire Department; Alan Gould, Engineering Library, University of Nebraska–Lincoln; Lillis Grassmick, North Platte Valley Museum, Gering, Nebraska; Betty Harnly, Woods Bros. Realty, Lincoln, Nebraska; Raymond Hebb; Roberta M. Hebb; Russell Hoppner, Hamilton County Superintendent of Schools, Aurora, Nebraska; William M. Johnson, State Historical Society of Iowa, Des Moines; Bill and Jo Jones; Matt Joseph, Society of Automotive Historians; Isabelle Lampshire; Pat Loos, *Journal-Star* Library, Lincoln, Nebraska; Tom and Judy Lutzi;

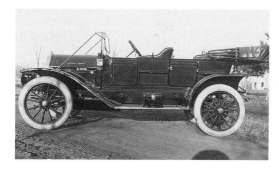

Marie and Ted Marshall; John B. Montville; David Nelson; Ohio Historical Society, Columbus; Denise Otto, Havelock Bank, Lincoln, Nebraska; Maureen Palmer and Larry Scheef, American Truck Historical Society; Plainsman Museum, Aurora, Nebraska; Public Records Division, Montpelier, Vermont; San Joaquin County Historical Museum at Micke Grove Park near Lodi, California; Randall Sawyers; Tammie Stofer, Lincoln (Nebraska) Convention and Visitors Bureau; Robert Thomas; Evelyn M. Timm; University of Nebraska Archives and Special Collections; Lloyd and Margaret Van Horn, Van Horn's Truck Museum, Mason City, Iowa; Lanna Vedvick; V. R. "Stub" Welch; Bill White; Betty Witham; F. Pace Woods, Sr., and F. Pace Woods II; and Wyuka Cemetery, Lincoln, Nebraska.

Smith chapter

Billie Aul, New York State Library, Albany; LeRoy Barnett, Michigan Department of State, Bureau of History, Lansing; Thomas Barr, Terry Harmon, Nancy Sherbert, and others, Kansas State Historical Society, Topeka; Ron Carey; Belinda Celis, Texas Historical Commission, Austin; George C. Curtis, Harry S. Truman Library, Independence, Missouri; Sims Firestone, Jr.; Patrick Fraker, Colorado Historical Society, Denver; Grand Rapids (Michigan) Public Library; Harold Irwin; Abigail Lavine, New-York Historical Society, New York City;

Edward Leach; Isabella Leach; Anne M. Marvin, Kansas Museum of History, Topeka; Debbie McCaffery, New York State Historical Association, Cooperstown; John C. Meyer III, *Horseless Carriage Gazette;* Denise Morrison, Kansas City (Missouri) Museum; James Mosher, Topeka Room, Topeka (Kansas) Public Library; National Automobile Museum, Reno, Nevada; Pearl A. O'Kieffe; Richard Petro; Tom Reese; Laura Saegert, Texas State Library, Austin; Murrell E. Smith; Richard Terry, California State Library, Sacramento; *Topeka (Kansas) Capital-Journal;* librarians, periodical room, Topeka (Kansas) Public Library; U.S. Commerce Department, Patent and Trademark Office; and Bill White.

Spaulding chapter

Sharon C. Avery and Beth Brannen, State Historical Society of Iowa, Des Moines; Jane Booth, San Diego Historical Society; Hans Brosig, Jasper County Museum, Newton, Iowa; Larry Bryan; John A. Conde; Crest Information Technologies, Cedar Rapids, Iowa; Betty Ernst, Grinnell (Iowa) Historical Museum; Nicholas Fintzelberg; Stan Francis; George Gagle; Iowa County Historical Society, Marengo, Iowa; Anne Kintner, Burling Library, Grinnell College, Grinnell, Iowa; John Kleinschmidt; William J. Lewis; Jeff Minard; Donna Sidney, Scott County Genealogical Society, Davenport, Iowa; Betty Sievers, Audubon County Historical Society, Exira, Iowa; Miriam Spaulding Simms and Ed Simms; Stewart Library, Grinnell, Iowa; Jim Valentine; and Irving Weber.

Introduction

One basic truth about automobiles is that they weren't made just in Detroit, New York, Indianapolis, or Cleveland – they were made everywhere. In the early days, nearly anyone with a good imagination and perhaps some mechanical experience – as a bicycle builder, blacksmith, or buggy maker – could make a horseless carriage. Thousands of people did it. The *Standard Catalog of American Cars, 1805–1942* documents more than 5,000 U.S. makes. Many of these were one-of-a-kind cars, but perhaps several hundred or more saw serious production. All but a few of these automakers disappeared or were absorbed in a natural consolidation of the industry during the 1920s and the ensuing Great Depression. This book details the stories of five Midwestern automobiles: the Luverne of Minnesota, Moon of Missouri, Patriot of Nebraska, Smith and Great Smith of Kansas, and Spaulding of Iowa.

By the most narrow definition of the term *success* – that is, "financial survival" – almost all of America's best-known cars were, ultimately, failures. Where is the Hudson, the Packard, the Pierce-Arrow today? Although the Midwestern automobiles in this book have likewise long since departed, they are neither "failures" nor are they presented as the awe-inspiring products of a few over-reaching eccentrics. Each was a good car, popular in its day and in its particular sales territory. Each company, as you shall see, had different strengths and weaknesses and performed accordingly.

Given their mission, the various automobile encyclopedias can devote only a few paragraphs to each smaller manufacturer. On the other hand, hundreds of writers have written millions of words about the Fords, Chryslers, and Studebakers of the industry.

Few of these works shed light on the day-to-day workings of the typical pioneer Midwestern automobile manufacturer. For instance: How did it succeed and fail? What did it do right and wrong? What contributions, technical or otherwise, did it make to the early-day art and latter-day science of making and selling automobiles? What special problems, if any, did this automaker face because of its Midwestern location? How did its cars and methods compare to the industry standard? Who were the people behind these Midwestern ventures and what qualifications did they have for such undertakings? How did they build and promote their cars, find financing, equip their factories? Where did they find buyers?

This is the time and place to make a few generalizations: First, a formal education was unnecessary for starting a small but successful automobile company in 1910, 1920, or even later. Of the five firms discussed in this volume, only A. G. Hebb of the Patriot company and the Smith brothers of Kansas got to high school or beyond. Rather, these entrepreneurs drew upon their experiences in other manufacturing fields. The creators of the Spaulding in Iowa, the Luverne in Minnesota, and the Moon in Missouri made carriages and wagons. The Smiths made artificial limbs and trusses in Kansas. Nebraska's Patriot Motors sprang from a company that manufactured truck bodies.

Second, more so than the ponderous giants, the smaller auto companies were leaders in making special cars for special needs. The Luverne company of Minnesota built a tough "Montana Special" automobile, a "Car for the Mountains," aimed at Montana drivers who needed a big, powerful automobile. In Iowa, the Spaulding company introduced a car equipped with a fold-down bed, its answer to "the most disagreeable question of touring – the hotel."

Third, early Midwestern auto manufacturers contributed to the growth of the industry in at least two ways. They helped boost the demand for autos: Horse-and-buggy owners were more comfortable buying their first car from a hometown factory rather than from a factory hundreds of miles distant. In addition, many small automakers evolved into parts suppliers after World War I. Thus during the 1920s, Ford ordered thousands of truck bodies from Iowa's Spaulding plant. Similarly, Chevrolet bought truck bodies from Patriot in Nebraska.

All the automakers included in this book fought a perceived prejudice against Midwestern products – though Moon, situated in industrial St. Louis, to a lesser degree. They attacked the notion by advertising that Midwestern manufacturers, better than their New York rivals, knew the condition of country roads and could build a vehicle correspondingly rugged. They also argued that Midwestern automakers offered Midwestern buyers a car priced to reflect cheaper labor and lower freight rates. The Midwestern factories also supplied repair parts quickly and often dealt directly with customers, instead of through sales agencies.

Every company in this book made its contributions. The Luverne company of Minnesota offered an unparalleled guarantee, free driving lessons, and such practical-minded improvements as headlights that could burn acetylene gas if the electrical system failed. The Moon company ultimately appealed to the middle class by selling cars that looked more expensive than they actually were. Moon was also among the most famous assembled cars of the 1920s and achieved production levels unknown to most other Midwestern companies. The Patriot company reversed the usual progression by first offering trucks – among the earliest to make a strong appeal to farmers – and only later planning to enter the automobile market. Long before Ford had a better idea, the Smith company challenged convention by offering a semi-automatic transmission and a half-dozen other patented designs. The luxurious Great Smith offered a built-in icebox. The Spaulding company proved that manufacturing can be an entertaining proposition. It staged some of the most colorful of the industry's early publicity stunts.

A word about my researching methods: I used automobile trade journals, factory catalogs, local newspapers – great chroniclers of a company's day-to-day evolution – a variety of government records, and, where possible, personal interviews, company correspondence, and corporate financial records. For background information about people or companies who crossed paths with these five automakers, I frequently consulted the *Standard Catalog of American Cars, 1805–1942*, second edition, by Beverly

Rae Kimes and Henry Austin Clark, Jr., which has an amazing depth and breadth. I used three books to document the trends and norms of the U.S. auto industry at a given point, against which I compared these five Midwestern manufacturers: *Automobiles of America* and its companion, *Motor Trucks of America,* both published by the Motor Vehicle Manufacturers Association of America; and *The Modern Gasoline Automobile,* published in 1913 by Victor M. Page, considered among the finest early automobile writers.

Undiscovered photos, articles, ads, factory catalogs, and the surviving cars themselves undoubtedly hold more clues to the past. If you have information to add or stories to share about these automobiles in which I've developed a lifelong interest, please feel free to write me in care of the University of Nebraska Press, P. O. Box 880484, Lincoln, Nebraska 68588–0484.

For four of the five auto companies, I present a specifications chart – an at-a-glance guide to technical changes over the life of a car. This was impractical for the Moon company, which put out as many as 25 models yearly, so I list the annual technical changes in a "Moon Chronicle" table. The charts and table appear as appendixes at the end of the book. I've tried to make the index as all-encompassing as possible. Each chapter has endnotes. In citing sources, I tried to walk the fine line between not saying enough and saying too much. I would be happy to provide additional source information to researchers who write to request it.

Two final observations: Automobile manufacturing has become a very serious business. Early companies, to their credit, were willing and even eager to let their cars advertise themselves. In classic Timex fashion, they gave their cars a licking in hopes they'd keep on ticking. The companies in this book staged publicity stunts ranging from driving up Pikes Peak on an abandoned wagon trail to racing across Iowa against the fast mail train. The stunts represent historic milestones for the companies involved, but are also entertaining in and of themselves.

Finally, as this project took shape, I had the opportunity to talk with grandsons and granddaughters of the company founders. Even standing two rungs down on the generational ladder, they offered many personal memories that helped to flesh out the dry bones of history. For them, these cars are a living memory. May retelling the exploits of a few pioneer Midwestern automakers keep alive the memory of them all.

It is a creative challenge to imagine how, in the early days, a slight change here and a minor difference there might have forever altered the face of the U.S. automobile industry. In such musing, it is but another small step to picture today's Americans driving Great Smiths instead of Grand Ams, Luvernes instead of Lincolns, Moons instead of Mustangs, Patriots instead of Pontiacs, and Spauldings instead of Subarus.

Happy wanderings. Oh, and next time you walk to your car – check the name tag, just to be sure.

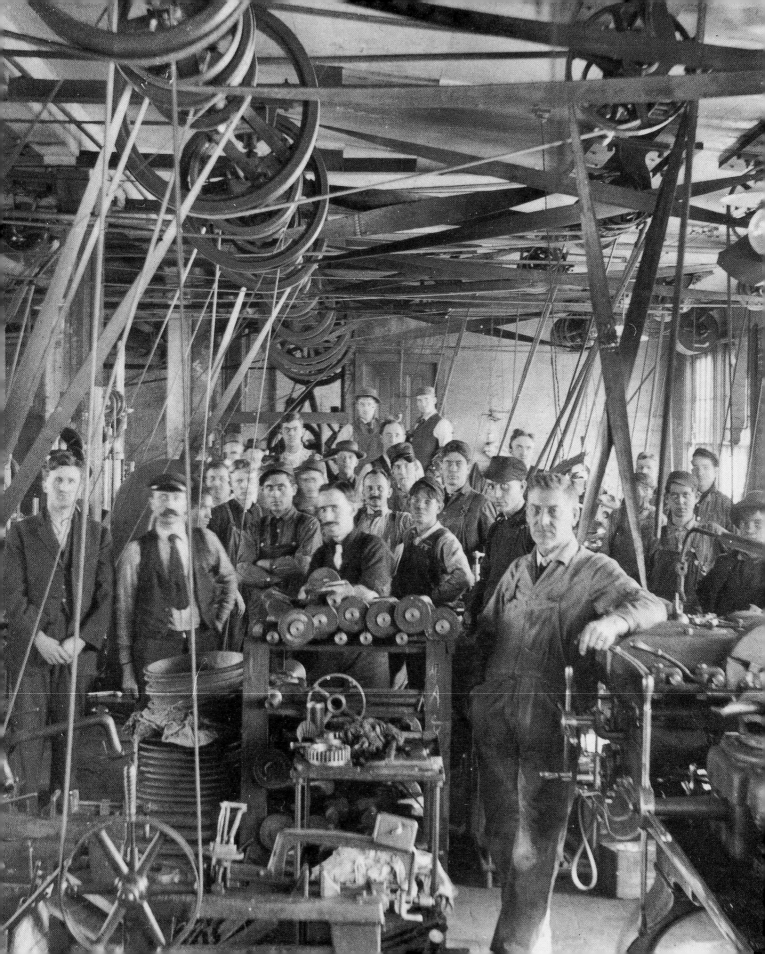

Great Smith of Kansas
The World's Greatest $2,500 Car

1

A model of self-sufficiency, the Smith Automobile Company of Topeka, Kansas, made virtually every piece that went into its Veracity, Smith, and Great Smith automobiles – from engines, transmissions, and steering gears to many nuts and bolts. Precision was the watchword; brothers Clement and Lucius Anton Smith spent $7,000 to build their first automobile factory, then paid twice that amount to fill it with the best machinery available.

Already nationally known to doctors and hernia patients for their Smith Truss Company products, the Smiths approached their new venture with this motto: "Build an Automobile at the lowest possible price at which it can be done well, make it light and strong, and put out no inferior grade."[1]

The brothers' varied manufacturing background included making artificial limbs, bows and arrows, and concert grand harps. Clement Smith, as mechanically adept as brother Anton was business-minded, owned or shared in owning eight automotive patents for Smith cars, including three for carburetors.

The Smiths, however, were miserly in extending the credit due Topeka inventor Terry Stafford, engineer of the Smith auto works until 1908. Stafford built a 2-cylinder motor carriage in his bicycle shop during 1899 and the first half of 1900, and with the Smith brothers, he won patents on the brakes, drive train, steering gear, and transmissions used in the Smith cars.

The Smith brothers, who began manufacturing autos in 1902 when a wholesale grocer ordered 10 runabouts for its salesmen, owned Smith cars. And by 1904, so did nearly half the motorists in Topeka. To earn broader acclaim, tantalize the public, and build a reputation for its cars, the brothers set out looking for challenges.

A stock 1908 Great Smith car placed third in a 320-mile Colorado mountain endurance race so grueling that five of the eight starters dropped out with broken axles, cracked engine cylinders, and a variety of other mechanical problems. A 1908 Great Smith set a round-trip speed record between San Diego and Los Angeles; a 1909 Great Smith beat every other car in its price class during a 700-mile Midwestern endurance contest. The company in 1910 ran a Great Smith touring car in a six-day non-stop circuit between Dallas and Fort Worth to promote the car to Southwestern buyers.

The car's most famous conquest came late in 1908, when a five-man team battled a blizzard in driving a Great Smith car up an abandoned stagecoach trail to the top of Pikes Peak.

Like automaking, automotive advertising was a wide-open field in the early 1900s, and the brothers showed a flair for both. The car factory's print shop turned out snappy, well-designed car catalogs with multicolored covers as early as 1904. The catalogs and endurance stunts helped stimulate sales in Kansas, the East, Southwest, and West.

Smith Auto Company offered an early semi-automatic transmission and telescoping steering wheel, as well as a steady stream of thoughtful touches. These made life as easy as possible for drivers of the early open motorcars and the mechanics who repaired them. For owners, these innovations included a front fold-up jump seat on the Veracity – "as an emergency seat for picking up a chance friend on the street" – to the picnicker's delight, a metal- and felt-lined icebox on the running board of the later Great Smith.

Smith 4-cylinder engines had crankcase peepholes so mechanics could simply remove a cover to inspect the crankshaft and connecting rods. Many cars needed new camshafts if a cam lobe wore out; the later Smith-made cars had camshafts with replaceable lobes.

Unable to afford mass-production techniques, the factory could turn out only about 100 cars a year with 150 employees. Ordering backlogs also kept willing buyers waiting weeks and months to receive their cars. It all came down to economics: As Ford and other large automakers flooded the market with no-frills $800 cars, the Great Smith, though undeniably a solid and more luxurious car, sold for three times that amount. As the American auto industry began a consolidation trend that would culminate in the Big Three, the Smith company was crowded out.

Barefoot Boys from Batavia

Inside a 1905 biography on the Smith brothers an inscription reads: "On the broad highway of American possibility, the barefoot boy may, and often does, outrun the golden-wheeled chariot of ancestral wealth." When Clement and Anton Smith left Batavia, Iowa, bound for Topeka in 1877, they may well have had shoes. But the two sons of Lucius Van Rensellaer Smith and Elizabeth (Leeson) Smith apparently had little else.

The Smiths' "queer, little, attractive house . . . was built from dry goods boxes by two young men who came to Topeka with no money in their pockets and who were consequently not able to buy lumber to build a home," Llewellyn Kiene, managing editor of the *Topeka State Journal,* wrote in a 23-page 1905 biography titled *The Story of Two Brothers.*[2]

In a shop on West Sixth Avenue, the brothers began making artificial limbs and bows and arrows, Kiene said. "They also filed butchers' saws and did any odd jobs that came their way," which included mounting birds that were displayed in the State Capitol Building in the 1870s. "The blowing of the six o'clock whistle did not mean a closing of the doors" at the Smith shop. "They had no money to spend for entertainment. When they had managed to save a few dollars, they invested in dry goods boxes which were knocked apart and from which the odd, little six room house, which was to be their home, was constructed."

The brothers' business of making artificial limbs began growing, "for no imperfect article left their shop," biographer Kiene said. They had made trusses for years but enrolled in the new Kansas Medical College to learn more. "Long before they had completed their course they agreed that all trusses were constructed upon a wrong principle, and set out to invent one which would coincide with their ideas."

The result was the "Honest John" truss in 1891. Before 1900, the brothers had three patents for trusses – including a "Smithsonian" truss – and had built up the self-proclaimed "biggest Truss business in America."[3] By 1896, the Smiths moved their 40 employees to a larger truss factory. Their classes at Kansas Medical College earned the Smith brothers "doctor" titles, but apparently neither one ever started a medical practice.

Clement Smith (see fig. 1.1), the younger of the two brothers, had an "inventive mind . . . which is ever reaching out and forward, in an attempt to grasp new things." Smith "intrenched himself in the hearts of his playmates by the manufacture of pipes, carts, boats, coffins, sleds and even miniature steam engines, and it was he who constructed the second bicycle in Topeka," Kiene said. He left readers to wonder if it was bicycle-shop owner Terry Stafford (see fig. 1.2) who built the first.

In September 1885, Clement Smith received two typewriter patents, the rights to which he assigned to another Topeka man. But Smith made another finger-operated instrument on his own. Concert grand harps, "though they appear simple in structure, [are] among the most complicated instruments in use. But as in other things, when the harp left Mr. Smith's hands it was perfect. The Smith harps gave out no discordant note," Kiene said.[4]

Clement Smith had a blueprint-filled office in the factory, but "he is more apt to be found in the blacksmith shop, watching the forging of a crank shaft, or standing beside the monster steam hammer while masses of iron are being pounded into shape for future use," Kiene said.

His older brother, Anton Smith (see fig. 1.3), "is one of humanity's sterner kind," with "a firm chin and well moulded mouth, such as one remembers in Bismarck, the Iron Chancellor. His is a face that indicates determination and fixedness of purpose, and an ability to bring to a successful termination any enterprise, in which he becomes engaged," Kiene wrote. "He keeps his large firm hand on the throttle of the enormous business of the Smith Company."

First "Smith" Actually a "Stafford"

A division of the Smith Truss Company first sold cars to the public in 1902. As early as 1905, however, the firm was advertising its year of origin as 1898. By 1910, the company had so overextended the truth that even a Smith truss couldn't contain it, claiming to be makers of the "Fourth Oldest Car in the U.S.A." By 1899, there were already 30 automakers in the United States, "practically all of them miniscule . . . [and] divided among New England, the Middle Atlantic states, and the Middle West," one authority contends.[5] In fact, there were scores – if not hundreds – of different makes of cars built by 1902, though many were one-of-a-kind vehicles. Those that were still in production included the Duryea, which appeared in 1893. The first Haynes (a Haynes-Apperson) can be traced to 1894, the first Winton and Ford to 1896, the first Oldsmobile and Rambler to 1897, the first Locomobile to 1899, and so on.

The Smiths could not even correctly claim to be the fourth-oldest surviving automaker, since many companies had followed the Duryea Motor Wagon Company, which in September 1895 became the first American company created to manufacture gas-powered cars.[6]

Still, to its credit, the Smith Truss Company was manufacturing cars before some of today's best-known cars appeared, including Cadillac, which tested its first car in October 1902; Buick (1903); Oakland, which in the 1930s became Pontiac (1907); Chevrolet (1912); Dodge (1914); Chrysler (1924); and Plymouth (1928).

Clement Smith, in a 1906 *Catalogue-Treatise upon the Automobile*, claimed that the Terry Stafford machine nicknamed "Old Bill" was "our first car" in 1898, that a two-

1.1 Clement Smith. (KSHS)

1.2 Terry Stafford in later years. (KSHS)

1.3 L. Anton Smith. (KSHS)

seat surrey dubbed "Christine" followed in 1899, and that the so-named "World Beater" became the third Smith car in 1901. Intrigued by the emerging technology, Smith wrote to many early automakers. A Kansas State Historical Society collection includes a May 21, 1898, response from the Pope Manufacturing Company of Hartford, Connecticut, makers of the Columbia electric carriage.

Exactly when Stafford finished his first car, Old Bill, is open to speculation, but it assuredly was later than 1898. The Kansas State Historical Society places the date at 1900. A 1907 *Topeka Daily Capital* article said Stafford "built the first automobile made in Topeka in his shop on East Fifth street in 1899." The same newspaper later dates the car's origins to spring 1900.[7]

Stafford may have been building his automobile in 1899, but he began testing his car early the following year. "Terry Stafford, a Topeka (Kan.) mechanic, has about finished a gasoline carriage," noted the *Horseless Age* of February 21, 1900. Nearly four months later, "Terry Stafford's automobile is nearing completion," reported the *Topeka State Journal* of June 8, 1900. "The engine and running gear are completed and set up, and the levers and finishing are to be done." The July 9 edition of the *Journal* said, "Terry Stafford ran his automobile half way to Silver Lake [about 17 miles from Topeka] and back through the sand as easily as it runs on the pavement."

The *Topeka State Journal* of August 11, 1900, said Stafford's car "has made several successful trips to Silver Lake, through the sand, and to Rossville, over hills as steep and rough as can be found in this part of the state. And the trip was made in four hours each way without trouble." The Stafford car also ran a nearly 20-mile circuit on the flatlands from the Topeka post office south to Pauline, Kansas, and back in 1 hour 21 minutes "carrying two people," the newspaper said.[8]

Stafford "has seen but one automobile

and that was of the storage battery type, while the one he constructed is propelled by a compound gasoline engine of seven horse power," the *State Journal* said. Stafford apparently did his homework, however, as he "was intrigued by accounts in the magazine *Scientific American* of the new horseless carriage. . . . He decided that he would like to build one, following descriptions in the magazine," according to a Kansas State Historical Society article. The *State Journal* said every part of Stafford's car "except rubber tires" was made in Topeka. A local carriage manufacturer, Rehkopf Bros., supplied the body and upholstery for the car, some accounts say.[9]

Car Rides "Smoothly As a Bicycle"

Stafford's motor buggy "can be geared to a speed of fifty miles an hour, but that is too much like a flying machine. On the pavement the machine runs at twenty-five miles an hour as smoothly as a bicycle and . . . the neckties of the passengers stand straight out behind like a pennant and felt hat rims lie flat," the August 11, 1900, *Topeka State Journal* account continued. Despite such speeds, "five gallons of gasoline will run over 100 miles."

Information is sketchy about the first engine Stafford built. All Smith cars since the first public sale in 1902 had 4-cycle engines. But in a 1906 Smith factory publication, Clement Smith reveals that "our earlier experiments" – perhaps meaning Stafford's Old Bill – used a 2-cycle engine. It had "the advantages of being an engine without valves, of giving an impulse for every down stroke of the piston, and as we built them[,] a twin engine side by side[,] they gave the stroke result of a four cylinder of the common type; but we were forced to abandon this construction . . . [because] the mixed gasoline vapor, air and dust from the road had to be drawn into the crank-base, where it mixed with the lubricating oil to make a cutting compound that rapidly ruined the

1.4 An early Terry Stafford auto by the Kansas State Capitol Building, about 1900. (KSHS)

bearings," Clement Smith wrote.[10] An air filter would have kept dust out of the engine, but the use of such filters was years away.

Old Bill "was an ordinary buggy, with solid rubber tired wheels," recounted the February 28, 1909, *Topeka Daily Capital*. "The engine was placed beneath the seat and sprocket chains comprised the driving apparatus. A steering lever projected in front of the seat, and on the lever was an ordinary bicycle bell to warn pedestrians."

After his success with Old Bill, "Mr. Stafford was induced to engage in the manufacture of autos by Drs. Clem and L. Anton Smith, at that time engaged in the making of trusses. They furnished their plant and the necessary capital, while Mr. Stafford took charge of the mechanical end of the business," the newspaper said.[11]

Stafford reportedly sold Old Bill to a firm called Giddings & Stevens of Rockford, Illinois, for $640. "It served the new owners as a working model for the production of more 'Old Bills,'" one historical account says. According to the *Standard Catalog of American Cars, 1805–1942*, Giddings &

Stevens displayed a 2-cylinder runabout at the 1900 Chicago automobile show, though there is little evidence to suggest that the Illinois company made more Old Bills.[12] Stafford's subsequent four-passenger 2-cylinder surrey, nicknamed "Christine," became the first car to climb Mount Oread on the University of Kansas campus at Lawrence. (See fig. 1.4.)

First Smiths "Capable of Hard Usage"

The June 1902 *Automobile and Motor Review* carried an article saying the Smith company of Topeka planned to build a factory for manufacturing steam automobiles. One source indicates that two steam autos were built. As a youth, Clement Smith amused his playmates by constructing "miniature steam engines," according to Llewellyn Kiene's *The Story of Two Brothers*. But neither that 1905 biography nor the many factory catalogs to follow ever mentioned a Smith steamer.

The first public sale of a Smith automobile came in late August 1902, according to the *Merchants Journal* of August 30, 1902.[13]

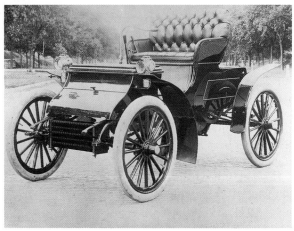

As the headline of the Topeka newspaper revealed, the car was the first of 10 such vehicles "Bought by the Parkhurst-Davis Mercantile Company for the Use of their Traveling Salesmen." The runabout-style car, with a bore and stroke of 4 x 5 inches, could hold four passengers with a folding two-passenger front jump seat, and sold for $1,300. (See fig.1.5.) The Smith company was so new to auto manufacturing that the newspaper felt compelled to point out "they have taken up the making of automobiles as an extension of their manufacturing business which has heretofore been devoted to trusses."

The 10-car purchase was an experiment for the wholesale grocery house, acknowledged Frank Parkhurst. If pleased with their 10-car fleet of Smith cars, Parkhurst-Davis officials would order 10 more, he said. The cars offered distinct advantages over trains and rented livery rigs.

"The Parkhurst-Davis salesman will no longer be that discontented animal that haunts the platform of these way stations waiting wearing hours for the local passenger train, but when he has finished his business according to his own and the merchants' best convenience, he will assemble his samples, board his horseless carriage and promptly speed away," the *Merchants Journal* said.

The first car's 4-cycle 8-horsepower engine had two opposed cylinders and rawhide gears to drive the camshaft, possibly to keep the engine quieter. By 1904, a steel crankshaft gear and phosphor bronze camshaft gear had replaced the rawhide. "Staunch in every part," the cars had 34-inch-diameter wood-spoke wheels, "3-inch double tube Dunlop pneumatic clincher tires," and a 78-inch wheelbase. Salesmen could store their samples in a 12-by-32-inch cargo area in the front of the car, which steered with a tiller from the right side.

The first 1902 Parkhurst-Davis car reportedly performed well during a three-hour, 60-mile trip from Topeka to St. Marys and back, averaging 20 miles per hour in the face of sandy roads and hills – a credible feat for the day. The chain-drive car weighed 1,400 pounds when loaded with 80 pounds of water and 60 pounds of gasoline. The remaining nine cars were delivered by mid-November 1902, press accounts reveal.

"The engines are entirely odorless and make but little more racket than an ordinary sewing machine. This statement, though absolutely the fact, will hardly be believable to persons who have heard the dreadful 'tuff-tuff' and experienced the frightful odor and trail of smoke that follows some machines that have been sold in the West," the *Merchants Journal* said. These early cars may have been nameless, as the article does not refer to them as Veracity autos.

At least one of the Parkhurst-Davis cars survives in the hands of a Canadian collector. Ron Carey of Calgary, Alberta, said a

1.5 The Smith auto pictured in the August 30, 1902, *Merchants Journal*. (KSHS)

1.6 What appears to be a 1903 Veracity runabout with the jump seat closed. (KSHS)

Smith workman signed his name and wrote the date August 22, 1902, under the seat. This suggests Carey's car could be the first Parkhurst-Davis car delivered, as described in the August 30, 1902, *Merchants Journal*. His car uses both a brake on the differential and an exhaust brake, Carey said. Moving a lever closes both exhaust valves so that the engine's compression slows the car.[14]

News of the 10-car sale earned the Smith company an early reputation for building commercial vehicles. "They have made a feature of a type of automobile suitable for the commercial traveler, capable of hard usage on rough roads, and of carrying heavy baggage," said the *Automobile and Motor Review* of November 22, 1902.[15]

"A machine is given about the severest test imaginable when used by a traveling man, but these have given excellent satisfaction," the March 22, 1903, *Topeka Daily Capital* confided. Less than two years after receiving its first car, the mercantile house offered its Smith cars for sale at prices ranging from $500 to $600 per car, presumably to send its sales staff back to the train stations, according to a Topeka historian.[16] Researchers, however, have been unable to document a reason for the sale. If it was because Parkhurst-Davis replaced its Smith cars with those of a different make, the Topeka newspapers – eager boosters of the local factory – may well have been reluctant to report the fact.

Demand for Smith Autos "Growing Like Alfalfa"

In 1903 and 1904, Terry Stafford and Clement Smith filed for five patents, replaced the tiller on the new Smith cars with a steering wheel, and steadily improved the 2-cylinder car they called Veracity.

Technical information is lacking on the Smith cars of 1903. (See fig. 1.6.) But the Smiths spent $7,000 to construct a building at 10th and Jefferson and in late February or early March 1903 moved into the new plant. "Prior to that time the work was car-

1.7 Chassis view of a 2-cylinder 1903 or early 1904 Veracity auto with tiller steering, before the switch to a steering wheel. The tiller is visible on the left, bolted to the middle of the frame. (KSHS)

ried on in the truss factory. But that business was growing rapidly, and it became necessary to seek new quarters for the auto plant, which was also growing like alfalfa under the most favorable conditions," the *Topeka Daily Capital* said.

Clement and Anton Smith spent $15,000 – more than twice the cost of the structure itself – to fill the factory with equipment, the newspaper said. "Automobile work requires the best of machinists and the best of machinery. The operations are very exact, and come as near perfection as watchwork."[17]

The company issued a second edition of its 1904 Veracity catalog to introduce a companion to its smaller Veracity Runabout, the Veracity Observation Car. Between the first and second editions of its 1904 Veracity catalogs, the Smith company switched to a right-side steering wheel (see fig. 1.7), which was kept through its last model in 1912.[18]

Also between catalog editions, the company scrapped its throttle lever so that "engine control is obtained by one simple lever attached to the spark and one foot pedal to the throttle." The company had also introduced a 2-speed planetary transmission with which "all changes are obtained by one lever only," as the lever also opened and closed the clutch. All Smith and Great Smith cars to follow would likewise have a semi-automatic transmission.

Similar to a touring car, the new Observation Car had a tonneau, or back seat, for three people, who entered from the rear of the car through a small door in the back of the seat. With a two-person front jump seat, the Observation Car could carry seven people.

The 1,800-pound Observation Car, with its 2-cylinder 18-horsepower engine, cost $1,500. The rear tonneau cost an extra $100, but "regular equipment includes a pair of kerosene lamps, fenders, wrenches, oil cans, screw driver, tire repair outfit, book of instructions, etc."

"This [is] a more powerful engine than is used in any other car upon the market selling for less than $2,500.00," the company claimed, although the engine was similar in size to many other 1904 automobile engines. "It is built wholly for practical purposes, but if occasion requires, can show its heels to anything else in the market, with the exception, of course, of a specially constructed racing car."

Removing the rear tonneau converted the Observation Car into "an exceeding handsome and high powered runabout." The first Veracity catalog, before the Observation Car came along, gave the 10-horsepower Runabout's top speed as 30 miles per hour. The second catalog, covering both the 10- and new 18-horsepower model, listed the Veracity's speed as from zero "to the maximum speed of the car."

With its trim 1,390 pounds reflected in a lower price of $1,250, the 1904 Veracity Runabout or Travelers' Car – an updated version of the Parkhurst-Davis commercial car – retained the folding front seat of its predecessor. The runabout engine had a bore of 4½ inches, a half-inch increase that would account for its 2-horsepower advantage over the 8-horsepower 1902 commercial car. Both chain-driven, the Observation Car and runabout had fenders of laminated wood, a "carrying box" under the front seat for tools or other cargo, and 34-inch wood-spoke wheels.

Made Where All Roads Are Poor Roads

The 14 Smith employees who moved to the new auto factory in early 1903 included Terry Stafford, "the mechanical expert in charge, and Jim Nicholas, long known as one of the very best men in the Santa Fe shops, [who] is the foreman of the machine room," a newspaper said. The Atchison, Topeka & Santa Fe Railway's large locomotive factory in town meant Topeka was well supplied with skilled machinists, a distinct advantage for Smith Automobile Company.

But a Topeka location also had its disadvantages over the heavily populated East Coast, the early automobile center of the United States. "It makes no matter if your Automobile is made in France or Topeka," the Smiths said, attacking the problem directly. Having said that it didn't matter, however, the company boasted that its cars were "developed in a country where all roads are poor roads," and urged buyers to avoid the freight cost of shipping an Eastern car into Kansas.[19]

By April 1904, the car factory's workforce had tripled to 50 "skilled men," and "the demand for the vehicles made at this factory is so great that work is carried on both day and night," the *Topeka Daily Capital* reported. In November 1904, Clement Smith, president of the newly formed Smith Automobile Company, raised $50,000 through a mortgage deed to double the factory's floor space and triple its output. Topeka motor-

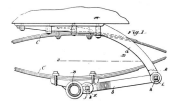

1.8 Clement Smith's second front-axle "leader iron" design, No. 761,857, filed September 17, 1903, and patented June 7, 1904.

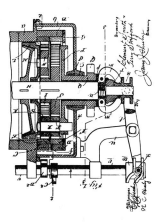

1.9 Clement Smith and Terry Stafford's clutch and planetary transmission, No. 760,160, filed December 26, 1903, and patented May 17, 1904.

ists cheerfully supported the bustling local factory. By early 1904, 13 of the first 31 cars in Topeka were Smith cars.[20]

Surviving photos indicate that the Smith company's early manufacturing process was basic: Workers would lay out a certain number of frames, and the machinists would begin turning out parts to build up a car out of each frame. "Work is now in progress on the first lot of ten machines [in the new factory], and this will keep the plant busy between sixty and ninety days," the March 22, 1903, *Topeka Daily Capital* reported. "Those in course of construction are all practically spoken for." Depending on which of the two production rates the workers achieved, the company could thus have made between 40 and 60 cars during 1903.

Clement Smith was granted his first automobile patent (No. 740,051) in late September 1903 for the use of a rod to connect the frame and front axle of the Smith car. "[The] front axle is pulled by our patented 'leader irons,' leaving the springs free to play and twist as they need, without subjecting them to any strain other than the carrying of their apportioned weight," the 1904 Veracity catalog explained. Clement Smith later received a patent (No. 761,857) for an improved leader-bar system. (See fig.1.8.)

During the last week of 1903, Smith and Terry Stafford filed for a patent (No. 760,160) on the Veracity's 2-speed planetary transmission and clutch. (See figs. 1.9, 1.10, and 1.11.) Almost a year later, Smith filed for two patents, one for a steering gear (No.

1.10 The Smith-Stafford planetary transmission. (KSHS)

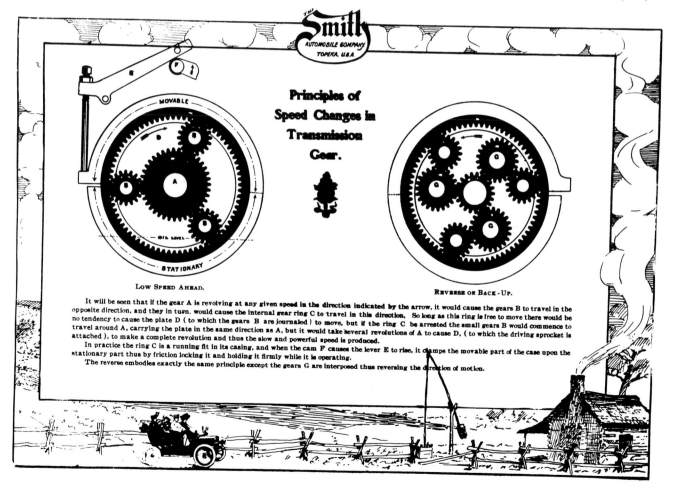

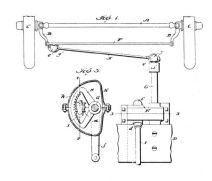

781,238) in which a worm gear meshed with an internal – rather than the more common external – sector. (See fig.1.12.) "The consequence is that whatever wear may occur between the threads of the worm and the teeth of the sector is less annoying to the operator, as it causes less lost motion to the steering wheel."[21] Smith's other 1904 patent filing (No. 784,636) was for an air-cooled engine cylinder that was apparently never used on the water-cooled Smith cars.

On the 1903 and 1904 Veracity engines (see fig.1.13), a belt-driven water pump ran off a pulley near an exposed 135-pound flywheel. Cylinder-head fins also promoted air cooling. In the clipped prose of the Veracity catalog: "Engine cooled by water around fire tract and valves. Head, air cooled by radiating flanges." Water cooling was "almost universal" at the National Automobile Show in New York as early as 1901, but many cars, even years later, still lacked pumps. Except for the first few Model Ts in 1908, Ford made Tin Lizzies without water pumps until 1928.[22]

On the 1904 Smith 2-cylinder engine, adjustable rocker arms opened the intake and exhaust valves, which were the same size and thereby interchangeable. To reduce

friction, valve lifters in Smith engines had tool-steel rollers riding on the camshaft – a design that carried over to the later Smith 4-cylinder engines. This was undoubtedly a good idea in an age when the Smiths and others were making engines with drip oilers and splash oiling systems instead of oil pumps. Most engine makers eventually adopted a solid lifter design. The Veracity engine's enclosed valve stems and springs were protected from dirt, which wasn't true of all 1904 automobile engines. But the later Smith 4-cylinder engines had exposed valve stems and springs that had to be cleaned "occasionally" with a squirt or two of kerosene.[23]

In Frame-Building, Do As the Railroads Do

The 1903 and 1904 Veracity cars had several nice touches: The 1904 Veracity steering wheel would tilt out of the way as the driver got in or out of the car; the commutator, an early spark distributor, had a glass top for easy inspection; and because the engine was mounted under the seat with a crank handle on the right side, a driver could start the right-hand-drive car from

1.11 A Veracity engine and partially dismantled transmission. (KSHS)

1.12 Clement Smith's steering gear and linkage, No. 781,238, filed September 7, 1904, and patented January 31, 1905.

1.13 Smith 2-cylinder engine; visible are the words "Veracity Automobile," cast into the top of each cylinder, and the Smith lubricator and commutator. (KSHS)

1.14 Smith wooden chassis with king posts for strength, compared to the typical steel chassis. (KSHS)

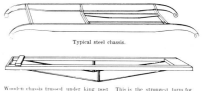

Typical steel chassis.

Wooden chassis trussed under king post. This is the strongest form for the same weight – it also allows for more springing as it cannot crystallize as a steel chassis can.

inside the car. An easy-starting cam "allows the escape of half the compression, thus allowing the engine to be turned over easily for starting." Designed for women, the starting crank "makes two revolutions to one of the engine so that a man seldom uses the easy starting attachment."

The company was also a pioneer in selling cars to women. Early Smith Auto brochures pictured women behind the wheel – driving both male and female passengers – and women are shown driving Smith cars in half of six Smith company catalogs from 1904 to 1906. But no such illustrations of women appear in any of 11 pieces of factory literature from 1906 to 1911.

Despite many creative touches and advanced designs, the Smith company steadfastly refused to use a steel frame. Other automakers gradually fell in line after Peerless introduced the pressed-steel frame in America with its 1903 car. Until the end in 1912, Smith cars were built on frames of second-growth ash. More expensive but as strong as a comparable steel chassis, a wood frame was also more flexible, was about 100 pounds lighter, and had one other important advantage, Clement Smith argued.

"Ash will not crystalize, and if it stands the strain of testing out, it is reasonably certain that it will not give out in service. On the other hand, steel may stand this work perfectly for weeks, months, or maybe years, and all of the time be gradually crystallizing. . . . We have repeatedly seen steel frames crystallize and break, but have never known such a thing to happen to one of our wooden frames," he said. The Smith frames were braced with metal truss rods and king pins to prevent sagging in the middle (see fig.1.14), "a very simple mechanical form and one which can be seen any day upon the passenger and freight cars of our railroads," Clement Smith said.

"Many of the best foreign cars are coming to our ideas, and it is our opinion that the steel frame will be practically, if not entirely, abandoned within the next few years in favor of a better, lighter and safer design of wood frame," he predicted.[24] The Franklin company of Syracuse, New York, which made wood-frame Franklin cars into the late 1920s, was about the only other American automaker to resist using a steel frame.

The Veracities were brightly colored: "Running gear is a rich red, outlined with black. Panels, seat, and fenders a lighter shade of red, also outlined with black.

Wheels and panels delicately striped with white. Cushions red, harmonizing with body. Under side of fenders, black. Radiator, dead black, and portions of machinery that show, are black. The engine is covered with aluminum bronze, except polished parts and brass and copper parts which are left natural color." The non-Smith parts mentioned in the 1904 Veracity catalog were a Brown-Lipe spur differential, Kingston float-feed carburetor, Timken roller bearings for the wheels, and a Splitdorf safety switch and duplex coils.

"Every part of our vehicle is designed, and the parts made, for the individual vehicle upon which they are used. They are not in any way to be compared to the many 'assembled' machines upon the market, where one piece is made at one factory, and another piece made somewhere else and so on, and the whole collection of various odds and ends are brought together, and 'made to do,'" the Smiths said.

"We offer a vehicle practically without vibration; practically without noise – only a slight rattle of the chain, and an inspiring little 'chuff' of exhaust, just enough to tell you how nicely your engine is working; with every part that is at all apt to need adjusting where it is easy to get at, and easy to adjust . . . with all cushions elegantly made and covered with genuine leather of a very fine quality . . . with all the conveniences and perfections of any practical vehicle with only a small per cent of the usual disadvantages."

Smiths Incorporate Auto Venture

The Smith brothers and Terry Stafford represented half the investors who filed incorporation papers in Kansas on October 15, 1904, creating the Smith Automobile Company. The stated purpose was to make and sell automobiles and parts, and "for the transaction of a printing and publishing business" to promote the Smith cars. The six incorporators – Stafford, the Smith

1.15 A Smith surrey, pictured in a 1905 Smith catalog. (KSHS)

1.16 A Smith truck, pictured in a 1905 Smith catalog. (KSHS)

brothers, Leni L. Smith, Adele A. Smith (Clement's wife), and Laura A. Strait—held 1,000 total shares of stock in the new $100,000 company. Clement and Anton Smith each held 498 of the $100 shares to account for 996 shares. The four remaining incorporators owned one share apiece. The company held property worth an estimated $50,000.

Business was good, Clement Smith said in 1905. "The business has been so prosperous that our company would be justified in investing a million dollars, if we could command it, in the enterprise, instead of the one hundred thousand dollars now represented." On August 26, 1905, the firm doubled its capitalization to $200,000 in reincorporating as Smith Automobile Company of Kansas City, Missouri. The Smiths retained control but let in two investors who bought most of the 4,000 shares of preferred stock. The other half of the total 8,000 shares—at $25 a share—was in common stock. Annual dividends were six percent for preferred stock but were unspecified for common stock.

L. Anton and Clement Smith held a combined $103,100 in stock, or just more than half the $200,000 total. J. W. O'Neill of Topeka, the new secretary and manager of the Smith Automobile Company, invested $50,150 in 2,006 shares. Clay H. Alexander, a lawyer from Kansas City, Missouri, bought 1,864 shares worth $46,600. Terry Stafford held three of the remaining six shares. Three Kansas City, Missouri, investors held one share apiece. Thus three of the company's four biggest investors lived in Topeka, but four of the eight incorporators were from Missouri.[25]

Smiths Unveil Fast 1905 Surrey

The Smith company stopped using the Veracity name and offered two distinctively different models with the introduction of its Smith Surrey in 1905. (See fig. 1.15.) It further emphasized the distinction by painting its runabout red and its new surrey blue. A drawing or airbrushed photo of a canvas-sided Smith light delivery truck appears, inexplicably, in the company's *March Brochure, 1905.* (See fig. 1.16.) No other information has surfaced on such a vehicle, and it is open to speculation how many, if any, Smith trucks were produced.[26]

The previous year's Observation Car was merely a stretched Veracity runabout, but the Smiths in 1905 scrapped the stub-nose front of the runabout for a hood and upright radiator. As in 1904, the 1905 runabout sold for $1,250 and had a 10-horsepower engine, so presumably it retained the same engine of 4½- x 4½-inch bore and stroke. The 18-horsepower surrey had a larger 5½- x 5½-inch bore and stroke and had gained 100 pounds to weigh in at 1,900 pounds. It sold for $1,600 equipped with a khaki-cloth extension top, leather front seat, and cloth rear seat.

Mostly ornamental, the hood of the 1905 Smith Surrey covered only the gas tank and such electrical parts as a duplex coil, vibrator, and eight dry cell batteries to fire the spark plugs. The surrey still had its engine under the driver's seat and its crank handle within easy reach of the driver's right hand.

Those who wanted a two-in-one car could buy the surrey. Removing its back seat converted the 18-horsepower car into "a stylish, powerful runabout type which is indeed ideal for cross country travel, since it certainly has the power to maintain a satisfactory speed on almost any road," according to factory literature.

Styling changes aside, Terry Stafford and Clement Smith had further refined the car. The two inventors were doubtless hard at work in early 1905 finishing the design of the 40-horsepower in-line 4-cylinder engine they would introduce in mid-1905. The surrey—and presumably the runabout—continued to use the Kingston carburetor. But in 1905 the carburetor was placed in an accessible "little cabinet" on the car's right running board. "This simply has to be unhooked, leaving the carburetor entirely exposed."

The carburetor box was one way the company made it simple to drive and repair the car. "Extreme simplicity of construction eliminates the difficulties experienced by the man who owns a machine with complicated mechanism which is frequently out of adjustment and[,] when out of adjustment, is hard to get at." Not long afterward, the company advertised "we . . . accomplish our results with about a third less parts than our nearest competitor; this means simplicity of construction which in turn means ease of maintenance and of understanding."[27]

As always, Smith Automobile Company in 1905 made most of its own parts. "We do not use the stock cap screws of commerce in any important place, wherever we need accurate, reliable screws (and it is nearly everywhere throughout the machinery), we make them ourselves of a special tough, fine grained steel that we have found the best for the purpose."

The 1905 Smith autos continued to use a throttle pedal that stayed in any position until moved. A driver's left foot rests "naturally on the throttle pedal[,] which perfectly controls the powerful engine underneath the car," the company explained. "With this form of control one can in case of emergency steer the car with the left hand, release the clutch or even apply the reverse with the right hand, put on the brake with the right foot, and instinctively the left [throttle foot] will have slowed the engine down."[28]

The 1905 Smith cars combined the water reservoir and radiator – separate units in 1904 – to create a modern-style radiator "fully ample" to cool the engine without need of a water pump. The top speed of the 1904 Veracity runabout was 30 miles per hour. But the Smith-Stafford 2-speed planetary transmission and bigger engine allowed the 1905 2-cylinder Smith Surrey to go even faster, the factory claimed. "This transmission is operated with one lever and

with our type of engine gives every possible variation of speed to the vehicle from naught to 40 miles per hour."

The Smith 4-cylinder engine, introduced in mid-1905, provided even more power. Harold Irwin of Rossville, Kansas, in 1973 bought a 1910 Great Smith (see fig. 1.17) from the grandson of Anton Smith. In driving the car, "the vibration kind of leaves it at about a certain point," which is 50 miles per hour, Irwin's preferred cruising speed. Papers that came with the new car indicate that a factory driver road-tested it at 57 miles per hour."[29]

"One of the Foremost Automobile Factories"

"The Smith Automobile Company . . . was early successful in bringing out many new inventions and valuable patents, and it stands to-day as one of the foremost automobile factories in the United States, if not in the world," the automaker said in a 1905 catalog describing its Topeka factory. (See fig. 1.18.) "These vehicles are of unusually high power, superior in workmanship, and with their graceful curves, attractive angles,

artistic mountings and beautifully finished trappings, they are without a doubt the finest, handsomest and best automobiles ever offered to the public."

The autos were being built in a main factory building of stone, brick, and steel, originally 130 feet long but measuring 45 by 185 feet after an expansion. "Within the last few months two buildings and an addition have been added . . . and the increasing and unprecedented demand for the 'Smith Auto' renders it imperative that it enlarge its already commodious factory to about four times its original capacity," the Smith catalog said.

One of the new buildings was a 35-by-70-foot structure for painting, varnishing, and upholstering. "At one end of the paint shop is the finishing rooms, which is as near air tight as a room can be made," a *Topeka Daily Capital* reporter wrote in 1908. "Here the sightseer must pause at the outer door . . . for not even a particle of dust or even a housefly can be tolerated." Workmen needed days to brush on and sand off paint, allowing drying time between coats. Each Smith car received "about fourteen coats of paint and varnish. . . . In between every

coat all the inequalities are glazed with a white-lead putty, and after each coat of varnish, except the final one, it is carefully ground down with pumice-stone by experienced workmen," Clement Smith said. In the upholstery department, "great piles of curled hair, with which the cushions are stuffed, are everywhere and a dozen or more upholsterers are busy. The seats are here lined with leather and carefully padded," said the newspaper.

The other new structure was a 35-by-50-foot storeroom "in which is carried a large stock of steel, iron, and all material used in the manufacture of Automobiles." The storeroom contained "all the component parts of the car in the rough," waiting to be machined to size, according to the *Topeka Daily Capital* account. "The blacksmith shop is up-to-date in every respect, and contains the best forges, steam hammer, power punch and shears, a gas forge, as well as a complete and modern equipment of small tools," the company said. In the machine shop (see fig. 1.19), "crank shafts are ground with a thousandth-part-of-an-inch accuracy; there cylinders are bored and gears cut; there fly wheels are trimmed and fitted;

1.17 Harold Irwin and his 1910 Great Smith roadster. (TCJ)

1.18 A drawing of the Smith Automobile Company factory, from a 1906 catalog. (KSHS)

in short, every bit of mechanism which goes in the car is here fashioned." Smith machinists used a tool room "plentifully supplied with jigs, dies, templets, etc."

In the woodworking department, "the bodies of the cars are built. The frames are set up and tested and the designers' plans are carried out. The Smith company buys no car bodies as many factories do. Every piece of timber is fitted to its place in the factory by the Smith workmen," the newspaper said. (See fig. 1.20.) In its 1905 factory catalog, the company described one additional

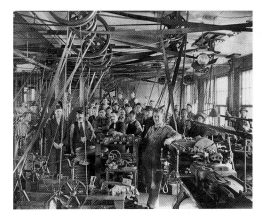

1.19 Undated photo of workmen in Smith machine shop. (KSHS)

1.20 Smith woodworking shop as pictured in a 1905 company catalog. Note the scale-model body on the table near the man inspecting plans. (KSHS)

1.21 Shop scene from 1905 or early 1906, with workmen building or repairing at least seven Smith cars. (KSHS)

building as "a very large iron shed used for out-of-door work in the summer-time and protection from snow, etc., in the winter."[30]

No Shoddy or Careless Work Is Tolerated

By early 1906, the automaker was completing "a new building with a floor space of 3,500 square feet which will be used as an erecting and assembling room," the *Topeka Daily Capital* reported.[31] Smith photos reveal that workmen in 1905 were assembling and

repairing 2- and 4-cylinder cars in cramped quarters at one end of the machine shop. (See fig. 1.21.)

In that completed assembly area, the 1908 *Daily Capital* article said, "the engine is brought from the machine shop and fitted to its place, the radiator is bolted in front and the water turned on. The frame with the engine and radiator in place is run out of the assembling room onto the streets for a severe and thorough test, which includes trips over rough country roads, hill climbing and every possible trial that a car may

have in actual service. The chassis is then returned to the shop, the body is put on, new tires are placed on the wheels and the car is ready for its purchaser."

In 1903, the factory's "electric light plant" was powered by a Veracity 2-cylinder engine. By 1906 the factory had switched to natural gas for its light, heat, and power. The machine shop in 1907, however, was powered by a Smith 6-cylinder engine.

The factory's northeast Topeka location placed it with "paved streets on two sides, and with two railroads, the Atchison, Topeka & Santa Fe and the Missouri Pacific[,] within one hundred feet." In a broader sense, "We are situated where living is cheap, health is free, men are contented and the maximum of good results from labor certain," the company said. "It is much easier to get good, industrious, reliable mechanics without labor troubles, than in the large Eastern cities. The wages are from 15 per cent. to 25 per cent. less than in the ordinary manufacturing districts, this being on account of living expenses being less than in the larger centers." In addition:

Tributary to this factory are the states of Iowa, Nebraska, Missouri, Colorado, Oklahoma, Indian Territory, and Arkansas, together with the Gulf States immediately south. We are, therefore, from 500 to 1000 miles nearer to any of these states than most of the automobile factories, and are fifteen hundred miles nearer the coast states, – closer to Chicago and all of Illinois, Wisconsin, and the states west of them, than any of the Eastern factories. In all this vast district there is a saving in the item of freight alone of from $75.00 to $100.00 on each auto.[32]

Based on press accounts, it appears the number of Smith Auto employees climbed from 14 in early 1903 to a peak of 150 by summertime 1908. The number fell to 100 by January 1910 before swelling again to 150 shortly after a new owner stepped in the following month. The workforce shrank to just 25 workers in December 1910 when the company was in receivership.[33]

Though they didn't call it "quality control" in 1908, the Smith car factory practiced it just the same, since "no car is permitted to leave the factory until every piece of machinery is in perfect working order," the *Topeka Daily Capital* said. "If it should be found that a valve does not work well another is put in. If the carburetor fails in any particular it is replaced. This fact has naturally had much to do with the success of the Great Smith. It is built throughout by workmen right here in the Topeka factory under careful supervision and no shoddy or careless work is tolerated."[34]

Introducing the Smith 4-Cylinder

In mid-1905, the Smith brothers – too impatient to wait for the next model year – started producing their 4-cylinder shaft-drive automobiles. The factory did not mention the new engine in its *March Brochure,* and local press accounts left readers to wonder if the new Smith cars were 1905 or early 1906 models.

The July 22, 1905, *Topeka Daily Herald* said Smith Automobile the previous week "shipped one of its beautiful gear-drive, 4-cylinder cars to Mr. Wm. Kennard of Phil-

1.22 Left side of the new 1906 Smith 4-cylinder engine. (KSHS)

1.23 1906 engine parts. (KSHS)

1.24 Drawing of the Smith 1906 4-cylinder engine, right side. (KSHS)

Plan of the cylinder and water jacket.

Cylinder. These are cast out of close grained grey iron, are ground out with microscopical accuracy. The working head is cast integral, the water head is of aluminum and separate to allow for cleaning the water space.

Exhaust valve, stem, nut and lock nut. The valve and stem are all one piece. The stems are machined and then ground, the seats are ground in place, the nut forms one bearing for the valve spring and the lock nut also forms the lifting staff.

Lubricator. This is entirely automatic and oils every bearing upon the motor, it requires no attention except to see that it is filled with oil.

Piston. This is a hollow shell that fits the ground out bore of the cylinder within two thousandths of an inch — picture shows the piston rings in place.

Piston ring. There are three of these on each piston, they are made a little larger than the bore of the cylinder and are cut in two, so that they can be sprung together enough to enter the cylinder, they therefore keep a pressure outward on the cylinder wall and their sides fit the grooves in the piston, they cork up all possible leak.

Connecting-rod. Made of steel the body portion being in "H" section the capping flanges being too wide to be called an "I" section. The wrist pin bearing is of Phosphor-bronze 1" diam. by 2¼" long, the crank pin bearing being of swaged babbit made extra hard and is the most durable bearing we have seen. The caps are held on with fine thread castle-head screws and a cotter pin through to keep them from unscrewing.

adelphia," who was planning a long trip through the Pennsylvania mountains. "The East has been for years sending its product into the West and the greatest competition western manufacturers had to meet was from the thickly-settled coast states. The Smith Automobile company, of Topeka, is reversing the rule," the *Herald* said.[35]

Smith Auto thus offered both 2- and 4-cylinder engines in 1905 but in 1906 began the exclusive use of the new 4-cylinder engine (see figs. 1.22, 1.23, and 1.24), equipped with a water pump. It was wise to develop the new engine. Four years earlier, Locomobile became the first American water-cooled gasoline car with a 4-cylinder, front-mounted engine. By 1909, some 71 percent of American gasoline cars had followed suit, though Buick and some other large automakers were still producing 2-cylinder cars.

A contemporary design, Smith engines had cylinders cast separately without removable heads, so it was necessary to remove a cylinder to inspect the combustion chamber. But special access plugs made it easy to remove the valves from the top of each cylinder. The advantage of casting single cylinders was "should one wear out with years of hard wear a new one can be put on in an hour's time and at a cost of twenty dollars for the cylinder," or one-third the cost

of replacing a twin-cylinder casting, the automaker said.

New Smith engines developed cylinder pressures of 75 pounds per square inch, nearly double the 40 psi of its first engines but barely half the pressure of modern auto engines. "This is not nearly so high as theory would indicate," Clement Smith said, "but a higher compression tends to cause premature explosions," a problem that lasted until anti-knock additives were discovered in the 1920s.[36]

Nonetheless, the new 4-cylinder engine in the Smith "Side Door Tonneau" developed 24 horsepower at 1,200 revolutions and 40 horsepower at 2,000 revolutions, the company claimed. Comparable figures for the "Side Entrance Surrey" were 20 and 32 horsepower. Factory literature neglects to reveal the formula by which the company calculated horsepower.

Smith Confronts "Confusion in the Popular Mind"

Smith Auto designers determinedly walked the fence as other automakers scrapped automatic-opening intake valves for mechanically operated ones. Automatic intake valves are held by light springs and open by suction as the piston moves downward on its intake stroke. With the other system, a camshaft or other mechanical device opens and closes the valves at the proper time.

"There is a confusion in the popular mind as to which are better . . . and after years of experience in building engines both ways and running them under all imaginable conditions, the writer must confess that he is in much the same situation," Clement Smith wrote in 1906. "They are each equally quiet-working as made by us [and] are equal as to engine speed and power." So until the engine was redesigned for 1907, a simple adjustment would allow the intake valves to open either automatically or mechanically, as the driver preferred.[37]

The 1905–1906 Smith 4-cylinder engines

thus had upside-down intake valves positioned over each piston, the valve stems and springs visible on top of the cylinders. Two springs held each intake valve for automatic operation: a "steady tension spring" to allow the valve to open 3/32 inch, then a heavier spring to catch it and prevent "the undue flapping of the valves," the company said. The exhaust valves ran in guides on the left side of each cylinder.

Engine bearings "must be of as great an area as practical," and "they must also be channeled through, so that a flood of oil can have easy access to all parts of them," Smith argued. Consequently, the crankshaft had generous end bearings 4 inches long, a central bearing 3 1/4 inches long, and connecting-rod bearings 2 1/2 inches long.

The new 4-cylinder engine continued to use the automatic lubricator that had been on Smith cars from nearly the beginning. "It is situated on top of the engine where it is kept warm and the oil made to flow certainly and regularly" through a ratchet and rod keyed to the opening of an exhaust valve. It automatically dispensed oil through tubes to lubricate the cylinder walls and the crankshaft front and rear bearings. "We have sold this instrument repeatedly to users of other makes of cars who substituted it for complicated and finely made lubricating devices with great satisfaction to themselves. The tank has capacity for about three hundred miles," more than the 225-mile cruising range allowed by the 15-gallon gas tank of the 1907 Great Smith car.

Smith Auto "Diverges from Other Builders"

In December 1905, Terry Stafford received Smith Auto's only patent for the year (No. 806,933). It was for the connection between his 3-speed semi-automatic sliding-gear transmission and the Smith car's rear axle, the solid unit being offered in the Smith 4-cylinder cars. (See fig. 1.25.) "We now arrive at a point where we again diverge from

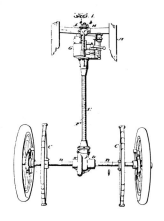

1.25 Terry Stafford's solid-unit drive train, No. 806,933, filed April 5, 1905, and patented December 12, 1905.

1.26 Terry Stafford's 3-speed progressive transmission, No. 830,460, filed April 4, 1906, and patented September 4, 1906.

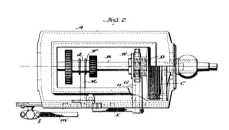

other builders, with a result of simplifying and strengthening the entire rear axle structure," Clement Smith said. Most shaft-driven cars of the day used two universal joints and a propeller shaft between the transmission and rear axle. The setup allowed the transmission to remain stationary and the rear axle to move up and down as the rear wheels bounced over road bumps.

But the early universal joints were open to road dust and therefore hard to keep lubricated, Smith said. Another drawback was that designers were forced to install a rod between the differential case and frame of the car. This rod acted as a "crowbar" to resist the natural upward pressure exerted against the propeller shaft as it propelled the rear-axle gears, Smith contended. "In place of a rod we carried a long tube from the casing of the rear axle forward" and held the propeller shaft in place with roller bearings at each end of the tube. So unlike traditional universal joints, bearings in the Smith design ran in oil inside the hollow torsion tube, isolated from road dust and moisture.

In addition, "the strain of hill climbing is taken by the solid propeller shaft" instead of being shared by the universal joints, rear springs, and frame, which allowed the Smith car to continue using its weight-saving wood frame, Smith added.

Stafford replaced the traditional two uni-

versal joints behind the transmission with a double universal joint and "a large ball" between the engine and clutch, sealed and protected from the elements. (This ball is clearly visible on the right side of the transmission in fig.1.26.) According to a 1907 description, the malleable-iron ball pivoted in a leather-lined socket joint. Thus the engine could remain stationary while the transmission, propeller shaft, and rear axle – a solid unit – moved up and down as the car's rear wheels encountered bumps.

"This you will notice gives absolute freedom and at the same time eliminates the necessity of very much motion, as the travel of the [rear] springs creates very little motion at this ball, which is about five feet from the center of the rear axle. . . . All that is needed is for the seat of the spring to be placed upon the axle in such a manner as to allow it a slight amount of rotational travel."

The rear axle was very much like a modern one. "The two live axles [shafts inside the axle tubes] are driven by being squared upon one end and the end inserted into a square hole in one of the differential gears; their other end is tapered and keyed into a taper hole in the pressed steel hubs of the driving wheel," Clement Smith said. Scattered mentions in Smith catalogs through the years suggest the Brown-Lipe company supplied the main differential gears for most, if not all, of the automaker's cars. But Smith machinists apparently made some of the differential gears, as well.

The Smith Blacksmith Shop

Clement Smith in 1906 succinctly summarized the challenges facing gas-engine designers: "While the actual operation of the gas engine is exceedingly simple, the physics involved in its action are very complex, as in its operation it uses fire, water, and electricity; compression, expansion, vaporization and condensation of gases; and it must have perfect mechanical freedom and balance, absolute closure of the valves, making an inappreciable leak of the hot gases while under enormous pressure. Concurrent with all this must be perfect lubrication of all moving parts, and some of these moving parts are subjected to intense heat."

Here is how Smith blacksmith and machine-shop workers, in building the 1908 Great Smith 4-cylinder power plant (see fig. 1.27), sought to overcome the complex physics of the internal-combustion engine:

Camshafts: "driven by 66 tooth, ten pitch, ¾ inch face gray iron gears, running from a steel gear of 33 teeth, ⅞ inch face upon the crankshaft. All cams are made of hardened and drawn tool steel."

Connecting rods: made of steel with a piston-pin bearing of phosphor bronze and a crankshaft bearing of "roll swaged white metal made extra hard." Fine-thread screws and cotter pins held the bearing caps in place.

Crankbase: lower half is a light aluminum casting "and serves only as an oil retainer and dust cap." Upper half is a heavy aluminum casting "with a heavy vertical wall dividing the two center engines [cylinders] and forming a support for the large center bearing of the crankshaft." Ribs between cylinders "stiffen the entire structure" of the crankbase, "and every joint is carefully filleted [and] all stud bases are reinforced with ample bosses." The crankshaft bearing caps were cast iron.

Crankshaft: drop-forged from high-carbon open-hearth steel "with the grain running around the bends" for strength. Diameter held to .001-inch tolerance.

Cylinders: cast separately using "close grained grey iron" and the crucible casting process. "The cylinder bore is machined and allowed to stand some days, when it is again machined, facing cuts being made at the same mountings to insure alignment; after this it is ground upon a special machine, the cylinder being revolved and a high speed emery wheel traveling up and down through it." Top of cylinder is crowned, cast solid with the side walls. Four studs hold each cylinder to the crankbase.

Exhaust manifold: "made of a very light seamless steel tubing in order to reduce its weight as much as possible."

Flywheel: weighing 85 pounds and cast of gray iron, it is "carefully balanced and machined over rim and bolting flange at one setting."

Pistons, rings, and piston pins: pistons are "made of high grade of grey iron, with ample reinforcement under wrist pin and head; outer surfaces ground to accurate diameter and with four oil grooves below wrist pin; above wrist pin there are three piston rings, also of grey iron, ground upon their edges while held in a magnetic chuck. . . . The entire piston is turned while held by a heavy ring which is cast upon the end of the piston for this purpose. After the piston is turned this is cut off, thereby relieving the portion used, of all clamping strain or warp from chucking." Tubular-steel piston pin "is held rigid in piston, the bronze bearing of the connecting rod working upon it."

Valves: "heads of nickel steel to avoid pitting, stems of special steel. The stems are machined and then heated to a low red, to relieve them of all strain from previous working. They are then remachined and ground," and the valve seats are ground.

Valve lifters: "the plunger casings [valve guides] are of cast iron," and the camshaft strikes "on large hardened steel rollers to lift the valves."

1.27 1908 Great Smith engine and engine parts. (KSHS)

MOTOR FROM LEFT SIDE

MOTOR FROM RIGHT SIDE

The Motor

The motor of the 1908 Great Smith car is of the four-cylinder vertical type, 4½ inches bore and 5-inch stroke, with the crankbase resting on three

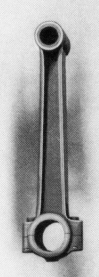

STEEL
CONNECTING ROD

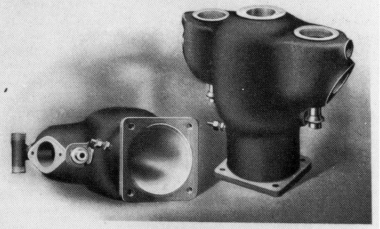

CYLINDERS

1906 Smiths: So Much Car for "So Little Money"

Despite a price increase, the Topeka factory was expecting to have its entire 1906 output spoken for by early summer. The 1905 2-cylinder Smiths cost $1,250 for the runabout and $1,600 for the surrey. The 4-cylinder cars introduced in mid-1905 carried over for 1906 (see figs. 1.28 and 1.29), and 1906 prices were $2,400 for the side-entrance surrey and $2,600 for the side-door tonneau.

Orders poured in from across Kansas. Clement Smith nonetheless took pains to justify the higher price to the "large class of the community who honestly believe that there is no sense in an automobile costing over three or four hundred dollars." The stationary engines commonly used in machine shops cost what some people wanted to pay for an entire car, Smith said. Putting a buggy chassis under an automobile was a foolish way to cut the price of a car, he added. "The finest carriage construction . . . would not last in an automobile much longer than a white shirt would stay clean on a coal-heaver.

"Now, as to the body: It is necessarily somewhat expensive; the cushions are very large; the materials must be the very best; and the finish on the outside should not be slighted when one has to go to all the expense necessary in other places about the car." After adding the expense of making or buying the transmission, rear axle, radiator, electrical system, lamps, horn, and other items, "we believe that anyone giving the matter calm consideration will no longer be surprised at the cost, but will wonder how so much can be put together so well for so little money."

Perhaps because its cars nearly doubled in price, Smith Auto wanted buyers to be able to make repairs cheaply. "For this reason we have adopted the use of standard bolts, nuts, screws, studs, etc., generally, and never depart from their use if we can possibly avoid doing so."[38]

Though phasing out its 2-cylinder engine, the company for a time offered buyers a choice of either the old Smith 2-speed planetary transmission or the new sliding-gear, 3-speed progressive transmission. A progressive transmission required shifting gears in sequence – you couldn't jump from third back to first gear without going through second. At the time, selective shift-at-will transmissions were becoming popular.

Because of a patented innovation, moving the Smith gearshift lever momentarily disengaged the clutch to permit shifting gears without using the clutch pedal, creating a one-lever control that was "simple, unique, grand," the company advertised.

1.28 Dr. Sam Lyman of Topeka with his 1906 Smith auto. (KSHS)

1.29 A 1906 Smith Side Door Tonneau. (KSHS)

"This is accomplished by means of two slides upon the right hand side of the case . . . one of the slides being able to move a distance before the other is engaged, which movement causes the clutch to open. As soon as the clutch is opened, the other slide moves until the gear wanted is in the proper position, when the clutch is again automatically closed. . . . At all times, changes can be made without the objectional burr-r-r-r of the gears, which is so common in other transmissions, except when handled by the highest grade of experts." It was "an absolute impossibility to engage the clutch unless the gears are entirely in mesh, and this makes the breakage of gears an impossibility." The 1909 instruction book confided that "the gear lever works tolerably hard when throwing from one speed to another, but this is entirely proper."[39]

"It is utterly inexcusable to have more than one thing to change when shifting from one gear combination to another. . . . The natural thing to do is to push this [gearshift] lever forward if you want to go faster, and to pull it farther back if you want to go slower. The natural way to make a car back up is to pull back on this selfsame lever. This action is instinctive, and it is therefore very easy of acquisition," Smith said.

Since mid-1905, Smith Auto had also been using a new multiple-disk clutch, running in oil, that Terry Stafford developed. It "takes a soft and easy hold of the car, starting it off smoothly, without jerks, jars or chatter." In addition, "The clutch being normally closed by a heavy coiled spring, it automatically takes care of any slight wear that may occur to it, in its action. Therefore, adjusting the clutch is something practically unknown with our cars."[40]

Smith Auto Goes Big Apple

Even a slight presence of oil could cause early commutators or circuit breakers – now called distributors – to deliver a weak spark to the spark plugs. Whereas a little bit of oil was bad, a lot of it was very good indeed, Clement Smith contended.

"We introduced a radical change in principle for circuit-breakers by designing one that could take advantage of the electro-condensative properties of oil," he said. The oil actually acted as a condenser by absorbing the self-induction of the circuit, "and in place of the contacts burning and carbonizing over they stayed clean and maintained their efficiency," he said in his 1906 *Catalogue-Treatise upon the Automobile*.

Smith Auto had replaced its seamless-tubing front axle with a more elastic square axle, first cast of manganese bronze but later drop-forged of steel. An advantage of the square front axle was "any first-class wagon-maker can repair it in event of its ever receiving injury."

Some automakers were apparently adopting smaller wheels in 1906, but Clement Smith justified his choice of 34-inch-diameter wood-spoke wheels. "Larger wheels roll over obstructions more easily than small ones, and so do not subject the tires to so much 'jamming' when going over stones and bumps; they do not drop so deeply into ditches, so do not subject the tires to the 'hammering' that small wheels give them," he said. "They admit of slower axle speed, as they revolve less times in a mile of travel."

One final thoughtful touch on the new front-engine Smith cars was that the starting crank – in harm's way on the front of the bumperless car – was automatically "held in a vertical position when not in use if desired, doing away with all straps, etc., to hold it up."[41]

In summer 1905, Smith Auto began taking orders for its 1906 cars. Factory Manager J. W. O'Neill told the January 1, 1906, *Topeka Daily Capital* that all 1906 cars would be spoken for by the end of spring – possibly by the end of January. Workmen began the new year assembling the first of 100 Smith 4-cylinder touring cars. Four months later, a newspaper reported the company was "working a night and day force of men,

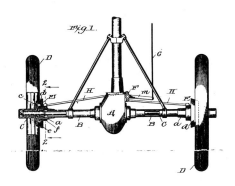

but still have not caught up with their orders."[42]

To add to the frantic pace, representatives of the Zim-Rock Motor Car Company, a New York City auto distributor, visited the factory in mid-May 1906 and contracted to buy 130 Smith cars. "They were greatly pleased with the Smith car and could not close the contract quick enough," the *Topeka Daily Capital* said. The total retail value of the 130 $2,600 cars was $338,000, though Zim-Rock undoubtedly paid a lower wholesale price. The factory was unable to meet a request to deliver 50 of the cars immediately, so "the first car of the lot will be shipped this week and the others will be sent at the rate of four and five a week or as fast as they can be completed," the newspaper said.

"By the middle of the automobiling season next year, the streets of New York city, the automobiling center of the country, will present the unique spectacle of 130 automobiles, manufactured by a firm in a city 1,500 miles away," the newspaper chortled. "They will all wear the brand of the Smith Auto company, and 'Made in Topeka, U.S.A.'" The Topeka autos were no strangers to Eastern cities, the newspaper added. "Several were sold to Philadelphia parties last year and gave satisfaction."[43]

The bodies of the 1906 Smith saw many refinements over the 1905 models, and were built to exacting standards, the company said.[44] Seat cushions were built from "the best curled hair" and "the best oil-tempered springs," the company said. Harold Irwin of Kansas said the seats of his 1910 Great Smith are stuffed with their original horse hair.

"It is our practice to build these spring frames out of as many springs as can be put into them – the front row of springs being one inch longer and one gauge heavier than the remaining springs," the Smith company said. "This accomplishes the purpose of throwing one back in the seat." Unusual for the times, the 1906 Smith hoods eschewed the side-hood louvers of the previous year because louvers "do not tend to create a current . . . along the cylinders which is useful in absorbing the surplus heat that is generated."

Except for the hoods and fenders, the bodies of the 1906 Smith cars were mostly wood, with aluminum door skins on the Side Door Tonneau. "All the panels of our Side Door Tonneaus are made of three thicknesses of wood glued under pressure and the grains crossing," the company said. Kerosene-burning side lamps on the Smith were fitted with bales, or handles, "so that they may be used as lanterns to look about the vehicle after night."

Terry Stafford in mid-March 1906 filed patent documents for his friction-cone rear brakes. (See fig. 1.30.) Three weeks later, he filed for patent protection on his new 3-speed sliding-gear transmission, with a multiple-disk clutch built into the transmission case (fig. 1.26). Both applications, his last while employed at Smith Auto, were approved (Nos. 839,222 and 830,460).

Automobile magazine of May 10, 1906, reported that Kansas City machinist W. C. Brooks "has patented a carbureter which he says shows a considerable fuel economy. . . . The Smith Automobile Company, of Topeka, is fitting it to its cars this year and the Olds Motor Works is conducting tests with it." The carburetor pictured in the 1906 Smith *Catalogue-Treatise upon the Automobile*, however, is the Schebler brand. Regardless, by mid-October 1906 Clement Smith filed for and later received his last patent (No. 844,900) while at Smith Auto for a carburetor that the 1907 Great Smiths would adopt.

1.30 Terry Stafford's rear brakes, No. 839,222, filed March 14, 1906, and patented December 25, 1906.

1.31 A Clement Smith–designed carburetor, as pictured in the 1909 Great Smith instruction book. (KSHS)

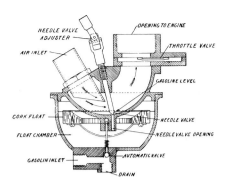

Onward Comes the Great Smith

When he first became interested in automobiles, Clement Smith wrote to Buffalo, New York, for information about the early Pierce cars. He was perhaps impressed enough with the 1904 debut of the Pierce "Great Arrow" that he decided to apply the same adjective to Smith cars. The company's 1906 publication, *Catalogue of Automobile Accessories, Supplies and Parts,* contains an ad for "The Great Smith Car." But the illustration is exactly the same one that, earlier in 1906, was identified as the 1906 Smith Side Door Tonneau. So instead of representing some grand mechanical advance, the first Great Smiths were nothing greater than renamed Smith tonneaus.

Following its May 1906 auto sale to the Zim-Rock company of New York City, the Smith firm for the first time displayed a car at New York's annual Grand Central Palace auto show. "The car possesses many novelties, one of the first being the quick method of valve removal," the December 6, 1906, *Motor Age* said of the 1907 Great Smith on display in New York. The valve stems rested on the end of a "horizontal foot" that was screwed to the top of each valve lifter or push rod, the magazine explained. "In removing a valve it is only necessary to loosen a screw holding the horizontal foot on the push rod and turn the foot through a part revolution, when the lift rod can be pushed out of position and the valve removed." *Motor Age* also praised the Smith-designed lubricator.

The 1907 Great Smith embodies "a few ideas that suggest some interesting possibilities of the up-to-date automobile engineer," said *Automobile,* another national journal. "The most interesting feature is the single-lever controller of the sliding-gear type, the lever being so arranged that it automatically engages the multiple-disk clutch prior to dropping in the speed that is sought."[45]

The Smith company displayed its cars at a number of other automobile shows, including the 1907 Grand Central Palace show, the 1906 and 1907 Chicago shows, and the 1909 Kansas City show.

The 1907 Great Smith had a Clement Smith-designed carburetor (see fig. 1.31) in place of a purchased Schebler carburetor. "It contains no springs, nor moving parts except the throttle, therefore there is nothing about it to change its adjustment. There is but one adjusting screw to be used, and if it is set for the proper amount of gasoline for the highest engine speed, all other speeds of the engine are automatically taken care of," the factory said. It was a self-priming carburetor that delivered the richest air-fuel mixture at idle, when the fuel pool was at its highest level, noted the January 1907 *Cycle and Automobile Trade Journal.* The size of fuel puddle shrank as the engine accelerated, "thus making the [air-fuel] charge poorest [leanest] at highest speed, all with no adjustments of mechanism, either automatic or hand-made," the magazine said.[46]

1907 Great Smith: "The Extreme of Style"

Except for a new valve arrangement, the 1907 Great Smith was mechanically similar to the 1906 car, as were all 4-cylinder cars to follow. The company claimed, however, that its 1907 engine developed an actual 45 horsepower – up from 40 horsepower in 1906 – possibly due to a longer stroke. The company freely broadcast that its 1907 car "embodies the well tried out machinery of our 1906 line."[47]

Clement Smith, however, overcame his self-described "confusion" of the previous

year to opt for mechanically operated intake valves in the 1907 Great Smith. The modified 4-cylinder engine adopted the popular T-head valve arrangement (visible in fig. 1.32), where the cylinder represents the base of a T and a valve on each side forms the top of a T. A left-side camshaft ran the exhaust valves, and a right-side camshaft ran the intake valves. The tool-steel cams on the camshaft "have a tapered hole and a pin to press them to their seat, and are keyed also." So a damaged cam lobe could be replaced for $1.25 instead of buying a new camshaft for $7 at 1907 prices.

In contrast to the minor mechanical changes, the Smith Automobile Company described its 1907 Great Smith as "a radical change in style of body from anything we have heretofore built. . . . The French Type body is the extreme of style, all its mouldings and panels being in a straight line, giving the car a very 'snappy' and artistic effect." (See fig. 1.33 and plate 4.) The company also installed an icebox, which it called "a very efficient refrigerator, in the step box at the right of the car [on the running board] and having a capacity of 1,200 cubic inches with provision for drawing off the water from the melted ice."

The company in 1907 became "Makers of the World's Greatest $2500 Car," that price including a mahogany dashboard, as well as one of three standard color schemes, described by the company as:

• "Rich red, gear and all, black and gold stripes"

• "Lake body with lighter red belt panel and gear, and striped black and gold"

1.32 A new 1907 Great Smith that overturned during a test drive in the country. (KSHS)

1.33 Right-side view of a 1907 Great Smith. (KSHS)

• "Smith Auto green with coach green belt panel and gear, black and gold striping"

For an extra $125, a buyer could have "an extension top made by us," which included "a large sheet of celluloid" that stretched between the top and dashboard to act as a windshield, the 1907 Smith catalog said.

Other features of the 1907 Great Smith were a telescoping steering column that adjusted to the height of the driver, and a change back to a throttle lever. The Smiths made a logical decision in adopting a throttle pedal in late 1904: Drivers' hands were already busy steering, shifting gears, adjusting the spark lever, and perhaps honking the horn or signaling a turn. But customers apparently didn't like the pedal. The Smiths were engineering leaders, as the company's 1908 catalog explained, but "nevertheless, where their ideas have proven at variance with the popular demand and where that popular demand did not go towards injuring the car, they have always been willing to adopt that which seemed favored."

The manufacturer stressed that the 1907 model was "unusually well supplied with carrying space, as all the room under the immense rear seat can be so utilized as well as the room under the tonneau floor, both of which compartments are easy of access through a large door opening from the back of the car, as well as by lifting the tonneau floor and raising the rear cushion."

The Smith factory in August 1907 turned out a special 6-cylinder car that, with a 4½ x 4½ bore and stroke, developed 60 horsepower. It was "the largest and most powerful automobile between Kansas City and Denver," according to the *Topeka Daily Capital*. "Placed in a racing auto and properly geared, this engine would probably make ninety or a hundred miles an hour."

The car was built for Arthur Capper of Topeka, who happened to be publisher of the *Daily Capital* and would later become a Kansas governor and U.S. senator. The red seven-passenger touring car was built on a stretched Great Smith chassis – 132 inches

compared to the normal 107. The car had a magneto, storage battery, and dry cells, so "if one fails the others can be called into use," the newspaper said. "It is the most magnificent running car I ever had anything to do with," Clement Smith told the *Daily Capital*. "It starts smoothly and gathers speed without a jerk. The engine runs so quietly you would hardly know there was an engine in it."[48]

Observers at the 1906 National Automobile Show in New York took notice of the few automobiles with 6-cylinder engines. They included Franklin, National, Pierce-Arrow, and Stevens-Duryea. A January 1907 article in *Cycle and Automobile Trade Journal* said that the Smith Automobile Company's 1907 production estimates were for 10 6-cylinder cars and 140 4-cylinder cars. How many 6-cylinder cars the factory actually made and sold remains a mystery. Four-cylinder cars remained the primary Smith product.

The Smith company scored another first in 1907 by exporting a Great Smith to South Africa. "One Smith car is running over the veldt of the Transvaal. It is owned by C. J. Price, a mining engineer, who purchased it during a visit to Kansas a few months ago," the *Topeka Daily Capital* said.[49]

In Kansas City, Missouri, Hollister Motor Car Company was a Smith agent. For a time the automaker distributed its cars through the Zim-Rock company of New York. Perhaps Smith Auto took too long in filling Zim-Rock's mid-1906 130-car order. Regardless, the December 5, 1906, *Horseless Age* says Zim-Rock was showing Pungs-Finch cars at a New York show in late 1906, and made no mention of Zim-Rock distributing any Great Smith vehicles. In Dallas, the Imperial Garage handled Great Smith cars. Smith Auto also had agents in Mexico City; Cheyenne, Wyoming; Chicago; Denver; Los Angeles, where the Renton Motor Car Company claimed to be distributors for California, Arizona, and Nevada; Philadelphia; and San Francisco.

Driving and Caring for Your Smith Car

Using instruction manuals and other factory literature, Smith Auto dispensed advice ranging from how to grip the starting crank to how to cross small mudholes. One piece of advice suggests that an automobile was still a novelty on some Kansas roads before 1910:

The average horse frightens because he thinks you are going to run into him. . . . Thus, when approaching a horse that appears frightened you can advance toward him as far as is safe and then turn away from him as if the machine itself is afraid of the horse, and it will nearly always quiet him down. Speaking to a horse from the automobile often has more effect upon him than if his driver himself speaks to him, as it gives him a sense of security upon hearing a voice coming from the machine.

The generous supply of tools and spare parts that came with the 1906 Smith suggest how much maintenance drivers were expected to perform on their own: 8-inch screwdriver, pliers, oil can, oil gun, tire pump, repair kit, wrenches, extra spark plug, crowfoot wrench (with planetary transmission), connecting rod wrench, roller-bearing wrench, extra valve springs, spanner wrench, cold chisel, hammer, punch, extra nuts, extra cotter pins, carburetor book, and book of instructions.

One regular maintenance chore was "to wash the engine out with kerosene once a month, if convenient. This removes carbon deposits in cylinder valves, and loosens up the piston rings." Close valves by swinging their lifter clips out of position. "Take out spark plugs and put about a pint of kerosene in each cylinder, put back plugs and turn engine over a few times by hand, allow kerosene to remain in cylinders over night." Reposition valve clips. "In morning start Motor, the usual way. This will cause a lot of smoke, and should be done out of doors."[50]

In the Valley of the Kaw

Dr. Clement Smith took a 1907 Great Smith on an overnight 150-mile jaunt from Topeka to Kansas City "to show the possibilities for enjoyment offered by the automobile almost in sight of one's home."[51] Llewellyn Kiene, who wrote the 1905 *Story of Two Brothers* booklet, accompanied Smith on his ride through the Kaw River valley, along with Smith's wife, Adele, Topeka photographer John F. Strickrott, and a New Jersey man named T. C. King.

The country roads of 1907 offered some surprising challenges for the early autos that ventured upon them. (See fig. 1.34.) "Now we can understand why auto drivers talk in whispers about 'Zarah hill,'" wrote Kiene. "But the incline has no terrors for Dr. Smith. . . . Just beyond the ascent we come upon a member of the Kansas City contingent [going to Lawrence, Kansas, on a good-roads campaign] in distress. His automobile, like a balky horse, has refused to go farther. . . . It may be cruel, but the truth must be told – he was not driving a Great Smith car."

1.34 A 1907 Great Smith on a trip through the Kansas countryside. (KSHS)

The occasional animosity between city dwellers with cars and country dwellers without them shows in Kiene's anecdote of the touring party stopping "at the foot of an ivy-covered cliff" near DeSoto, Kansas. "A few hundred yards away is a farm house and a dozen people are sitting in the doorway. They watch us a few moments and then shouts and laughter are heard as they point toward our car as it stands silent by the roadside. They . . . have concluded that we are in trouble and are laughing at our discomfiture and, no doubt, the farmer is wondering how much he will ask us to take us to the station in his farm wagon.

"Their laughter is stilled as we re-enter the car and Dr. Smith shows them a burst of speed as we pass the house. They are treated to a deluge of dust as a punishment for their bad manners."

On this journey through the valley of the Kaw in an open car, the auto tourists stop from time to time to dust themselves off. Another drawback, Kiene says, is "our faces have been slightly sunburned, but an application of cold cream soon enables us to forget that."

Stafford Leaves Smith Auto

Factory Superintendent Terry Stafford and Sales Manager J. F. Billings both resigned from Smith Auto Company in late December 1907, effective January 1, 1908. Stafford "has had offers from other automobile companies but has not decided what he will do," said the December 29, 1907, *Topeka Daily Capital*.

The newspaper credited Stafford with building "the first automobile made in Topeka." Stafford made two more cars, "then joined the Smiths and many of his patents and ideas are embodied in the Smith cars. . . . Mr. Stafford is recognized as an automobile expert and an expert mechanic."

Press accounts don't say why Stafford quit. One reason could be that Smith Auto

gave him far less credit than the local newspaper did for his role in designing Smith cars. In a collection of 17 Smith Auto publications issued from 1904 to 1911, Stafford's name is mentioned only twice – that in a single sentence from a 1907 Great Smith specifications sheet: "Clutch. – Our 'Stafford' patent multiple disc, encased oil and dust tight, with our 'Stafford' patent transmission is operated by pedal. . . ."[52]

In the 1905 *Story of Two Brothers,* the Smiths detailed their automotive beginnings without so much as mentioning Stafford. The same booklet presents a fictionalized account of the construction of Stafford's first car, Old Bill, with Clement Smith – not Stafford – portraying the inventor:

His friends were not surprised when they heard that Clement Smith had set out to build an Automobile. . . . No horseless carriage had been seen on the streets of Topeka. They were known only through the newspaper columns. . . . There were no beaten paths for him to follow. His success or failure depended entirely upon his own efforts, and it was only after weeks and months of patient toil and careful planning that an Automobile which would actually run was taken out of the Smith Truss Factory, with Dr. Clement Smith at the steering lever. . . . Years after, this vehicle was christened "Old Bill," and "Old Bill" is still on duty. The inventor speaks of it as fondly as a father does of his first born.

Local press accounts say Stafford built his first car alone; none of the articles credit Clement Smith as either the builder or an assistant.

In spring 1908, the former Smith factory superintendent bought a local business, the Mulvane Garage, and began making Stafford cars in competition with the Smith plant. On December 3, 1909, Stafford formed Stafford Motor Car Company, a Missouri business capitalized at $100,000 with seven stockholders. The capital authorization rose to $400,000 on October 15, 1910. Stafford bought the Kansas City Manufacturing Company and moved his plant to Kansas City, Missouri, in February 1910. The overhead camshaft and hemispherical combustion chambers in Stafford's own 30-horsepower 4-cylinder engine were two of the car's several "advanced engineering features," one authority wrote.

Three decades before moving into the White House, Harry S. Truman in 1913 paid Terry Stafford $600 for a used Stafford car, according to the Harry S. Truman Library in Independence, Missouri. Truman variously referred to the car as a 1910, 1911, or 1913 Stafford, but a research paper says it was most likely a 1910 or 1911. Truman, who drove his Stafford as fast as 60 miles per hour, sold the car in March 1918 as he prepared for World War I military service.[53] At that, Truman's Stafford car lasted longer than the company did. The last Stafford cars were produced in 1914; Stafford ran an auto garage and machine shop in Kansas City until his death in 1925.

1908: Year of the "Little Things"

Mechanically and visually, the 1908 Great Smith was only slightly improved, but the company's inspired ad-writers made the most of it, saying the 1908 model "is just as dependable as ever, it looks just as good, and it behaves just as well. . . .

"Then come the little things, and this is where we have made improvements that have materially increased the general efficiency of our 1908 model. The addition of roller bearings on the [transmission] auxiliary shaft makes far less noise and more power. The tonneau door has been made two inches wider, and a quadrant has been placed over the steering wheel giving better control of the throttle and spark levers."[54] A larger steering wheel for 1908 undoubtedly helped make the car easier to steer.

The company acted through its "Smith Motor Car Company" as the sole distributor of the 1908 Great Smith, which climbed

$150 in price to $2,650 for both the touring and runabout models. Undaunted by the price increase, the Smiths' Los Angeles agent simply replaced the "$2500" in the old slogan to create an updated version: "The World's Greatest $2650 Car." Back in Topeka, the Smith ad-writers elected to puff up their earlier claim without naming a price: "Always has been, is now, and always will be the best automobile at any price."

Two drive belts on the cooling fan provided an extra margin of safety for the 1908 car, which also had an improved steering gear and rear brakes with twice the previous surface area, "which feature alone is of inestimable value to the users of the car in mountainous and hilly districts." The company also improved the application of the brakes so that they "will hold the car with only a light pressure of the foot." In other changes, "the radiator is deeper in front and presents a greater radiating surface," "a beautiful brass coat rail has been added to the back of the front seat," and between the two front seats "is a neat little covered receptacle for goggles, gauntlets, maps and so forth." The touring car had a red chassis and body with black and gold stripes. The runabout was painted gray "with blue and gold leaf stripe."[55]

Clement Smith's 1905 assertion that it was easier in the Midwest than in the East "to get good, industrious, reliable mechanics without labor troubles" seemed naive by mid-1908. "The machinists of the Smith Automobile Company, Topeka, Kan., have been on strike for some time, the cause of the strike being said to be the dismissal of a machinist for refusal to instruct a helper in skilled work," reported the July 22, 1908, *Horseless Age*.

Great Smith Heads for the Hills

The best advertising is free and available in the news columns of the large daily newspapers, Smith Automobile Company officers learned. Los Angeles agent Paul A.

Renton won an open-class race during a Thanksgiving Day 1907 hill-climbing contest in Riverside, California. In the race for touring cars only, Renton beat a Thomas, an Oldsmobile, a Marmon, a Premier, a Pope-Hartford, and a Tourist car, the December 1, 1907, *Topeka Daily Capital* said.

The factory entered a 1908 Great Smith in the 320-mile Rocky Mountain Endurance Run near Denver on May 30, 1908. Some 10,000 spectators viewed a race in which five of the eight starters dropped out with mechanical problems. A distributor of Thomas cars in Denver, E. Linn Mathewson, driving a "Blue Bird" Thomas 40, was the only racer to finish the 10-lap race. Earlier in the year, Mathewson drove from Cheyenne, Wyoming, to Ogden, Utah, in the Thomas Flyer car that went on to win the New York-to-Paris race of 1908.[56]

As the number of contestants dwindled in the Denver mountain race, the judges called off the contest, awarding second prize to a Locomobile that had finished nine laps and third prize to the Great Smith, which had finished seven laps. "Around curves that threatened to tear the right front wheel from the axle . . . up hills that reduced all the force that could be mustered to make the high gears do their work, down hills that gave momentum . . . that was the course of the eight automobiles," the *Denver Post* recounted.

"This race was run over the roughest road ever traveled by any set of cars in any motor car endurance race ever promoted by the United States," according to *Motor Age*. "Fourteen miles of one leg of the course was a constant succession of bumps — it is a marvel how the driver and his mechanic in each car held their places." Great Smith driver G. A. Clark ran "a conservative race," the Denver newspaper said. He "did not push his car, but endeavored to keep it in shape for the finish."

Clark's best time of 55 minutes for a 32-mile lap tied him for first place in lap five. But that speed was 13 minutes off the 41:56

one-lap record pace set by one of three Thomas cars entered. Linn Mathewson's Thomas averaged 38 miles per hour to win the race in 8 hours, 26 minutes. Clark's strategy paid off, however, as a Thomas 60 hit a ditch and wrecked, another Thomas 60 cracked a cylinder, a Colburn 30 broke its front axle, a Colburn 40 suffered a "burst radiator feed pipe on [the] third lap," and a Studebaker went out with carburetor trouble.

The Great Smith "jarred its magneto loose in finishing the seventh lap," according to the *Post. Motor Age* said the Great Smith was "put out of commission after finishing the seventh lap." The *Post*, however, did not count it among the five dropout cars, implying that the Great Smith was receiving magneto repairs when judges halted the race.

It was perhaps still running, as a *Topeka Daily Capital* story revealed that the Great Smith "was the only one that was able to appear on the streets the day following the race. . . . Though every other car in the contest was a higher priced car, some of them costing twice as much, not one of them could leave the garage the day following the race and some of them were complete wrecks. The Smith car was sold a few days after the race to a wealthy Denver man, who watched its performance and it is in everyday use as a pleasure vehicle."[57]

The following September, Clark drove a Great Smith to a fifth-place finish out of 10 cars that competed in a 295-mile Labor Day road race near Denver. A Thomas Flyer completed 20 laps around the 14¾-mile course to win in 6 hours 26 minutes, followed by a Chalmers-Detroit, Colburn, Studebaker, and the Great Smith. The Smith car beat a Peerless, a White steamer, and three cars that dropped out – a Corbin, a Colburn, and a White steamer.[58]

Great Runs for Great Smiths

In a "Great Auto Run Made by Renton," the
Los Angeles Great Smith agent, Paul
Renton, drove a 1908 Great Smith roadster
to a Los Angeles–San Diego round-trip
speed record. (See fig. 1.35.) According to
the *San Diego Union*, Renton made the 320-
mile dash in 12 hours 28 minutes on June
20, 1908. Renton left Los Angeles at 4:05
A.M. Saturday on the coastal route south and
at 9:34 reached the offices of the *San Diego
Union*. He spent 13 minutes taking on fuel
and checking the car and apparently made
no stops on the return trip. His average
speed over the route was thus 25.7 miles per
hour for the elapsed time and 26.1 miles
per hour for the actual running time.

Returning north on an inland highway,
"through Escondido, San Marcos, and over
the red mountain grade the little machine
fairly flew," the newspaper said. "Renton
drove the car the 320 miles himself and not
once during the long journey was any serious trouble experienced. Taking into consideration the poor condition of the roads,
particularly the coast route, this performance is considered a remarkable one."

Renton's Great Smith shaved 2 hours 36
minutes off the Los Angeles–San Diego record that "Capt. H. D. Ryus," the Los Angeles agent for White, set May 22, 1908, in a
White steamer, the San Diego newspaper
said. On September 23, 1908, L. B. Harvey
of San Francisco in a Rambler car lowered
the Great Smith's record by 67 minutes.
Late in the year, driving a Rambler roadster,
Harvey again lowered the mark – to 10
hours 32 minutes.[59]

A Great Smith entered by agent J. H. Hollister of Kansas City won its price class in the
Kansas City Star's September 1909 five-day
endurance contest through Kansas and Nebraska. Hollister entered two Great Smiths
and drove the winning car. Private owner
W. W. Guthrie of Atchison, Kansas, drove a
third Great Smith in the amateur's division.
The contest attracted some of the country's
best drivers, among them C. S. Carris in a
Franklin, the same make of auto in which he
set transcontinental speed records in 1904
and 1906. Fifty-five contesting vehicles in
the *Kansas City Star* run followed a 700-mile
route from Kansas City to Junction City,
Kansas; to Lincoln and Omaha, Nebraska;
to St. Joseph, Missouri; and back to Kansas
City.

The reliability contest was hard on all the
cars. During the second day's run from
Junction City to Lincoln, "a Pennsylvania,
Maxwell and Great Smith had a three-cor-
nered collision while the Pennsylvania was
trying to pass. Each of the cars was damaged
but no one was hurt," according to the *Motor
Age* account, which fails to identify which of
the three Smith autos was damaged. It was
possibly the winning Great Smith, which led
its division despite being docked 23.5 points
for a loose fan belt and pulley, two bent
steering knuckles, and the labor required
for repairs. Also on the second day, Guthrie
stopped to help after a Buick smashed into
and toppled a telephone pole near Junction
City. He loaded two injured men into his
Great Smith and rushed them to a hospital
in Lawrence, Kansas, then turned around
to continue in the contest.[60]

1.35 The 1908 Great Smith
roadster "which recently
broke San Diego–Los Angeles
round trip record." *Motor
Field's* August 1908 issue identifies the occupants as Paul A.
Renton, at the wheel, Bert
Smith, and George L.
Thompson. (NAHC)

1.36 The January 1909 *Motor
Field* pictured four members
of the five-man group that
climbed Pikes Peak in a 1908
Great Smith touring car.
(KSHS)

At the Top

Again, the publicity took care of itself when the Topeka automaker orchestrated a mountain-climbing stunt in the Rocky Mountains and started a Great Smith on a grueling six-day endurance run on the Texas flatlands. The stunts blazed a trail into new sales territory and also provided fodder for the automaker's promotional catalogs.[61]

Five men in a red 1908 Great Smith touring car climbed Pikes Peak in October 1908 (see fig. 1.36) on a road "used only by burros and an occasional wood hauler," recalls a member of the party, F. C. Nessley. He wrote a January 1909 *Motor Field* account of the 11-day, 26-mile journey from the resort town of Manitou to the top of the 14,147-foot peak. The car was "an ordinary Great Smith touring car that had been used all season by the Denver Motor Car company for demonstration purposes."

According to Nessley, he was joined on the trip by E. L. Aiken, the Smith company's Denver distributor, and three others. The motoring mountaineers battled 40 percent grades, six-foot snowdrifts, errant boulders, temperatures of eight degrees below zero, frozen ears and hands, and a blizzard that forced them to abandon the Great Smith for eight of their 11 days on the mountain.

So narrow in spots that boulders grazed the car's hubcaps, the trail elsewhere clung so precariously to the mountainside that "a slight mistake would send us crashing to the rocks hundreds of feet below," Nessley recounted. On the first two days of the climb, October 15 and 16, 1908, the men spent hours building bridges by rolling boulders into two washed-out sections of trail. On October 16, the Great Smith encountered deep snow and 40 percent grades. "The car takes the grades without difficulty and the party attached to snow-shovel handles make short work of the drifts," but the narrow trail remained icy, Nessley said.

Day two came to a frustrating halt behind

two boulders "weighing several tons each." Hours of work with picks and shovels allowed the motorists to undercut the boulders and roll them aside. "Two members of the party are quite ill as a result of the elevation and the extreme cold," however, and the five men walked an estimated three miles to the summit hotel for the night. A "terrific snow storm" forced them to spend the next seven nights there.

As the snowfall dwindled on the fourth morning of the storm, four climbers hiked back to the car to find "nothing is visible but the top of the steering wheel and the backs of the seats." The storm blew up again before they could dig out the car. Finally, on October 25, or 11 days after starting their trip, the storm passed, and the travelers again struck out from the summit hotel for the snowbound Great Smith.

"When we reach the car and lift the hood, the engine is found to be incased in a mass of ice. Pieces of waste are saturated in gasoline and placed around the cylinders and the match applied. After about thirty minutes the ice is melted sufficiently to permit of the engine being turned over. The current is switched on and the engine starts off as though it had been reposing in a steam heated garage," Nessley wrote.

The drive to the summit was "a nightmare of snow shoveling. . . . The bright spot in that period is the fact that the car never fails us for a moment. No matter how long it has been standing in the freezing wind, waiting for a way to be cleared, a turn of the starting crank is all that is required to start the engine buzzing as merrily as on the day we left the hotel in Colorado Springs."

They completed their Pikes Peak climb late in the afternoon. "Each one of the four cylinders is responding without miss or protest. No repairs are made on the trip and only an occasional adjustment of the carburetor is necessary to adapt the mixture to the rarefied atmosphere of the mountain," Nessley said.

The Great Smith tore up two sets of Weed tire chains, 40 feet of trace chains, and 300 feet of hemp rope on the rocky road to the top. But the car's Goodrich tires held up, "which proves that the Great Smith car is exceedingly easy on tires," Nessley said. The party took an easier route back to Denver, then paraded through the streets of the Mile High City on October 27 "at the earnest solicitation of the Denver agent for the Great Smith."

In 1900, a year after organizing the Mobile Company of America in Tarrytown, New York, John Brisben Walker drove a Mobile steamer up Pikes Peak to 10,000 feet, the timberline. Denverites Charles A. Yont and W. B. Felker became the first to climb the mountain by auto when they did so on August 12, 1901, in an 1899 Locomobile steamer, according to one source. In autumn 1907, J. D. Hollingshead of Chicago, in a Stearns car driven by F. W. Leland, claimed his was "the first touring car ever to make the ascent and the only machine which ever turned the trick unaided." At the end of a factory-sponsored endurance run from Detroit to Denver, F. A. Trinkle of Denver drove a tiny 1-cylinder Brush runabout to the summit in seven hours in September 1908. The Great Smith followed in October, but was undoubtedly the first car to climb Pikes Peak during a blizzard.[62]

Capitalizing on the publicity value of the sensational climb, Anton Smith fired off a

AT THE TOP

GREAT SMITH "45"

Equal to the occasion—The only Touring Car with a

Pikes Peak Record

Space H, Balcony

Hollister Motor Car Co.

Selling Agents

KANSAS CITY

Both Phones 402 Main   209 Commerce Building

1.37 Great Smith ad in the official program of the auto show in Kansas City, Missouri, March 8–14, 1909.

telegram to Nessley: "Congratulations to yourself and party for having climbed Pikes peak in a Great Smith car in the face of a blinding snow storm, thereby accomplishing a feat greater than has ever before been accomplished in any automobile."[63] It was valuable publicity (see fig.1.37), and the Topeka manufacturer played on the Jackson car's "No Hill Too Steep, No Sand Too Deep" jingle with its own slogan: "No Road Too Rough – No Hill Too Tough." Another later Smith Auto slogan was "A Western Car for Western Roads."

Six Days on the Road

In Texas, "there were no mountains to climb so a six day non-stop run between Dallas and Ft. Worth was decided upon," in which the car's engine would run continuously for the six-day drive covering 1,400 miles. By this time, May 1910, such stunts were part of the Smith corporate policy. "A long and gruelling run or difficult feat is usually chosen which will prove conclusively that the car is mechanically right, will stand road abuse and prove its dependability," the Topeka manufacturer said.[64]

A crowd gathered outside the Oriental Hotel in Dallas Monday morning, May 16, 1910, to see the start of the non-stop run by the Great Smith touring car, shipped from Topeka for the endurance run, the company said. "No special adjustments were made and no other equipment than that of the regular stock car was put on." Local auto dealers were invited to join in the fun but declined, the Smiths claimed in their account of the endurance run.

Drivers H. E. Anderson, L. G. Carter, and K. C. Grimes planned to drive in eight-hour shifts from the Oriental Hotel, through Grand Prairie and Arlington to the Worth Hotel, their Fort Worth check-in station, and then back again. But on Monday night "a terrific storm raged and there was a heavy fall of rain," followed by more showers Tuesday. "The worst weather conditions of the week" arrived Wednesday night with "another heavy downpour of rain, accompanied by one of the most violent electrical storms of the season."

"Regardless of this, the car still steadily plugged over its assigned route until late in the evening the roads became inundated in the low country along the Trinity River," with standing water more than a foot deep in spots. "Indications were that it would wash out a part of the road bed," so the Great Smith was driven on the streets of Dallas Wednesday night and early Thursday morning.

"It almost takes actual experience to fully understand the severe test to which a machine is put in night driving over deep rutted muddy roads that are built high and so narrow that the slightest miscalculation would put the car into a deep ditch and completely out of the running," the Smith company said.

Thursday morning, "the car was placed in front of the Southland Hotel for a short time, the hood thrown back and the large crowd which gathered around was given an opportunity to see how the motor was working. The car was detained considerably longer than was intended on account of the continual crowds but shortly before noon was started on the circuit between the two cities." The Great Smith, in clocking 1,000 miles by Thursday, "had been raced through water covered roads, had been jammed and jerked up and down hills, through chuck holes, and had steadily plowed through deep mud for hours at a stretch, yet it showed not the least sign of mechanical derangement. The motor worked as well as when starting."

With Carter at the wheel Thursday afternoon, however, the Great Smith drivers took on an added risk by rescuing a five-passenger Buick mired in a mudhole. "The Smith plowed through the mud, passed a tow-line to the Buick and pulled it out to solid ground," repeating the feat Friday in pulling a Firestone-Columbus car out of the mire, the company said.

"A New Mark in Non-Stop Runs"

Driving bad roads was "rather unusual for a car which had so much at stake as did the 'Great Smith,'" noted the May 22, 1910, *Dallas Daily Times Herald*. "Usually, the drivers seek out the good roads and carefully drive over them. In this case, it was exactly opposite, as the drivers vied with each other in successfully taking the car through precarious places."

Both accidents of the six-day trip occurred Friday. Just after midnight, driver Carter was speeding up to cross a mud hole at the end of a plank bridge. When the Great Smith plunged into the mud, its hand crank broke off on a rock, "causing the car to veer and nearly overturn." Later Friday morning, a horse shied in front of the Great Smith, which was traveling at 25 miles per hour. "Driver Grimes chose the more hazardous course of boldly steering the car completely into the ditch, which was partially filled with water and caused the car to skid into the bank and narrowly escape overturning," the *Times Herald* reported.

A violent rainstorm Saturday night slowed the car as it began its last lap from Fort Worth to Dallas. "The heavy fall of rain again turned the low roads into a quagmire covered with water, all semblance of the track being obliterated. Through this long stretch of road on the last trip alone there was [a] sufficient amount of straining, jerking and jamming to put the average automobile in the repair shop. The car plugged steadily through this trying ordeal of rain, wind, muck and mire and though a little behind schedule, reached Dallas in perfect condition" at midnight to end the six-day run.

During the trip, neither the car nor its Goodrich tires needed any repairs, the company said. The Great Smith used 96 gallons of gas to average 15 miles per gallon. The oil consumption of eight gallons, or 175 miles per gallon of oil, "was something phenomenal . . . admittedly a very low figure for such a distance over the sort of roads which the 'Great Smith' traveled," the company boasted.

"Figuring fuel, amount of oil used in lubrication, tire trouble and mileage, the 'Great Smith' has established a new mark in non-stop runs. It was without doubt one of the most successful endurance contests ever held in the west," according to the *Dallas Daily Times Herald*.

The non-stop run sparked so much interest that Smith Auto's Dallas agent wired the factory "to send him 100 cars as soon as possible," the *Topeka Daily Capital* said. "The order was followed by a guaranty deposit on 25 of the cars." How many cars were actually delivered is open to speculation. In the same issue, however, the newspaper reported that "the Smith Automobile company shipped two carloads of machines to

the real wild west country of Wyoming the last week."

The Great Smith had apparently been taking on other challenges, including "a number of hill climbing and sand pulling tests in Texas," the newspaper added. "This week in Kansas City, the city agent for the Smith car has entered it in a hill climbing contest and a good record is expected of the famous climber."

It was perhaps the Smith company's flair for the dramatic that earned the Great Smith a leading role in *Those Miller Girls!* by children's author Alberta Wilson Constant. At one point in the book, a tardy Professor Cyrus Miller races his 1909 Great Smith to the train depot to welcome Chautauqua speaker William Jennings Bryan to Gloriosa, Kansas. "The Great Smith tore through the dust, rounding corners on two wheels. . . . With brakes screaming, the Great Smith slewed to a stop as the Santa Fe steamed up to the depot. A crowd was gathered to see Mr. Bryan, but they stared instead at the throbbing red auto and the wind-whipped quartet in it," Constant wrote.[65] The Great Smith is a leading character in another of her books, *Those Motoring Millers*.

Clement Smith Sells, Buyers Plan "Cruiser"

Clement Smith sold his interest in the auto factory in 1908, for reasons that went unrecorded, leaving his brother, Anton, to become president of Smith Auto. Under Anton Smith, the Smith Automobile Company in autumn 1909 said it would "erect an assembling plant in Kansas City," reported the September 29, 1909, *Horseless Age*. "The parts are to be manufactured in the Topeka plant, shipped to Kansas City and assembled there. This leads to a savings in transportation expenses, as parts can be shipped much cheaper than assembled cars."

In January 1910, 17 Grand Rapids, Michigan, investors paid Anton Smith $25,000 for his controlling interest in the car company. Under new President Otto H. L. Wernicke of Grand Rapids, the reorganized Smith Auto Company increased its capitalization to $300,000 from $200,000. "The intention of the new management is to retain the old heads of the departments and the present clerical force as far as this may be found practical," said Wernicke, a manufacturer of office furniture.

"The Great Smith car itself will not be changed radically," according to the January 8, 1910, *Topeka State Journal*. "It is now a standard car in every detail and is a most popular car in the market. . . . With the increased working capital and output the car will go rapidly to the front of the rank of cars for 1910."

Representatives of the Smith company "are practically sure of securing a site in Monroe, Mich., for a plant," reported *Motor Age* on December 30, 1909. The January 13, 1910, *Automobile* magazine reported that Wernicke and his investors' group would move the Smith factory to Grand Rapids. According to the *Standard Catalog of American Cars, 1805–1942*, the Association of Licensed Automobile Manufacturers (A.L.A.M.) – seeking a geographical distribu-

tion of automakers – threatened to withhold licensing if the company moved. The factory stayed in Kansas.

Many of the Topeka automaker's 1910 ads say the Great Smith was "Licensed under Selden Patent." Companies so licensed paid royalties to the A.L.A.M. and thereby avoided the lawsuits that the association was filing against non-members. Harold Irwin's 1910 Great Smith has a Selden tag on the base of the driver's seat, bearing the number 220938. The A.L.A.M.'s *Hand Book of Gasoline Automobiles, 1911* lists two Great Smith models, the touring car and the new Great Smith Cruiser.[66]

In February 1910, the reorganized firm announced plans to construct a 25-by-50-foot building in Topeka for the crowded woodworking department. New Smith managers installed $10,000 in machinery, and "they have lots more on the way that will be placed in the plant as soon as it arrives," the local press reported. The company said a full night shift and doubling the workforce to 300 would boost the annual production from 150 to 400 cars.

The company would offer a new car (see fig. 1.38) that "is almost like that great Italian car the Fiat," said the February 19, 1910,

1.38 An unpainted 1911 Great Smith Cruiser. (KSHS)

Topeka State Journal. "It will be torpedo shape[d] – the front seats enclosed as well as the back seats and the front end narrower than the rear." Passengers would sit lower than in tonneau cars. The Great Smith Cruiser would be "a fast, classy, air-splitting, graceful car of unusual foreign lines and hidden power," the newspaper said.

The new Smith officers, unable to move the factory to Michigan, began moving it piece by piece to Kansas City. The Hollister Motor Car Company, Great Smith agent for the Kansas City area, "has been made general factory distributor of the output of the Smith Automobile Co.," the March 3, 1910, *Motor Age* announced. The magazine's March 24, 1910, issue reported that "the sales department of the Smith Motor Car Co. has been moved from Topeka to the Smith Auto Company, 3116 Main street, Kansas City."

Despite such changes, financial troubles mounted for Grand Rapids investors, who called a November 5 meeting attended by "most of the creditors." The firm's total indebtedness was given as $196,000 – including $55,000 to three Topeka banks – with nearly identical tangible assets. Wernicke and others promoted a variety of plans to revive the company. But growing restlessness among the Smith company's 200 stockholders and two small lawsuits of about $2,000 apiece prompted the company in late November 1910 to voluntarily request a receiver "to preserve the property as a going concern," said the *Topeka State Journal.* Officers and creditors both cited "the lack of a sufficiently large working capital."[67]

Though no longer connected with the auto factory, Clement Smith was still designing parts. The same month Smith Auto went into receivership, Smith sought and would later receive patents (Nos. 995,919 and 1,020,931) for carburetors far more sophisticated than his 1906 design. Smith Auto equipped its 1910 and later cars with Schebler carburetors.

"Company Is Not Insolvent"

Some 125 of the factory's 150 employees were laid off after the receiver was appointed, but "it is declared that the company is not insolvent," said the December 3, 1910, *Topeka Daily Capital.* Auditor F. E. Whitney and General Sales Agent W. B. Morris were organizing a $1 million company to manufacture the Great Smith plus "a popular priced auto to compete with other lower priced cars . . . an auto truck and a light delivery wagon." But they were unable to sell the idea.[68]

By the 1911 model year, Great Smiths came with a warranty "against defective material and workmanship for one year from date of factory shipment, to the extent that all defective parts will be replaced, provided they are returned to factory, charges prepaid, and subject to our inspection." The 1911 Great Smiths (see figs. 1.39 and 1.40) also offered more standard equipment than ever before: lights, horn, tool kit, tire-repair outfit, jack, and tire pump. Once extras, a speedometer, clock, windshield, top, side curtains, and dust cover were included in the purchase price of $2,500 for the Cruiser and toy tonneau and $2,650 for the touring car. The company in 1911 also offered a "Special Tourabout," equipped with a 25-gallon gas tank, a four-gallon oil tank, and a detachable trunk, for $2,250.[69]

The Smith company "will move its plant from Topeka, Kan., to Denver if the proper inducements to make the change are offered to F. B. Clark, receiver and trustee for the company," reported *Motor Age* on September 21, 1911. Instead, Topeka engraver Charles A. Southwick eventually bought the factory in late 1911 or early 1912 "after several false alarms and several abortive efforts to effect a reorganization," according to the January 11, 1912, *Motor World.* The plant had been idle for "several months," the magazine said. Charles A. and George A. Southwick, who described themselves in ads

1.39 A 1911 Great Smith with an unpainted body. (KSHS)

1.40 A 1911 Great Smith. (KSHS)

as "Purchasers of Smith Auto Co. Plant," advertised locally in February 1912 that "$1400 Buys This New $2650 'Great Smith 45.'" The Southwicks said the special low price would apply to only 21 cars – apparently the last Great Smith cars that could be assembled from surplus parts. Five of the cars were ready then, and 16 were slated for a March 20, 1912, delivery. A big improvement for 1912 was an early self-starter, though company literature doesn't say what kind. Harold Irwin said his 1910 Great Smith was returned to the factory for the installation of a North East brand electric starter.

Then in April, with the first spring breezes, came the news that the Southwicks had big plans in store. "The Westerner is the name adopted for the new roadster and truck to be turned out in Topeka, Kan., this spring at the old Smith automobile plant which is now being operated by Charles and George Southwick," *Automobile* magazine announced. "Work on the new machines has not been started as yet, but all the specifications have been completed and the parts for the experimental cars ordered. A force of sixteen men are now busy at the plant assembling the Great Smith touring cars, a number of which will be ready to market by the time the roads are in condition for traveling."

In reality, automobile manufacturing soon came to a halt because the Southwicks were unable to attract enough investors, according to a May 1912 issue of *Motor Age*. The plant was sold on May 29, 1912, to the Perfection Metal Silo Company of Kansas City, which paid $27,500 for the Topeka factory, equipment, and "several automobiles." The buyer planned to make metal silos, culverts, and other products in the former car factory. That venture lasted just a few months, according to the *Automobile* magazine of September 5, 1912. "The Smith automobile plant was purchased at a bankrupt sale by C. E. Gault and J. D. Mulvane, who will maintain the parts and do a general repair business, but have discontinued the manufacture of cars."[70]

A 1902 Smith survives in the hands of collector Ron Carey of Alberta, Canada. Surviving Great Smith cars include Harold Irwin's 1910 roadster. The Kansas Museum of History has a 1908 touring car that belonged to Clement Smith. A Baltimore collector owns a 1906 Great Smith that was pulled from a barn near Lost Cabin, Wyoming, in 1959.

Before Failure, Success

Perhaps it is an American trait to dwell more on a company's financial failure than on its successes in reaching more subjective goals, such as those of designing a simple, rugged, and pretty car that met a particular need at a particular time. Discontent to copy existing machines, Clement Smith and Terry Stafford pioneered ingeniously direct and durable designs for brakes, carburetors, and drive trains, winning eight patents for the Smith car. Through its endurance runs and racing, the company succeeded in proving the worth not only of its marque but of the automobile in general. The company's publicity stunts and literature successfully added to the automobile's emerging aura of freedom, romance, speed, and thrills.

The Great Smith's unique designs and luxurious touches undoubtedly influenced automakers who read about the cars or saw them at auto shows. Such advertised features as a side-mounted icebox may have also helped shape what buyers wanted in their cars.

The Smith company had an opportunity to change as the market began favoring assembled cars made with suppliers' parts. But the company could not assemble a car and still meet its corporate goals. Assembling automobiles from suppliers' parts "may be a cheaper way of producing a car, but common sense dictates that it cannot produce so good a job as to have each individual part carefully calculated, and made for the place it is to occupy," the Topeka automaker contended.[71]

The flood of cheaper cars into Kansas made the Great Smith expensive in comparison. To compound the problem, the Smith factory kept well-to-do buyers waiting weeks or months to take delivery of a new Great Smith. Backlogs had been common since at least 1905, when "many unfilled orders for Automobiles [were] upon the books awaiting delivery, and much of the time they are sold months ahead."[72] Low production, delivery delays, and high prices all stemmed from the limited finances of the Smith company from the beginning.

Except for the introduction of the torpedo body style in 1911, the cars changed little after 1907, which may have discouraged some buyers. Freed up from inventing new and better ways to design their cars, Smith officers perhaps might have devoted their time to inventing a more efficient assembling procedure. When the Otto H. L. Wernicke group bought the factory, Auditor F. E. Whitney's comments to a Topeka newspaper suggest that the company needed stricter accounting procedures: "The proposed new company plans to install modern systems in the conduct of all departments of the plant. The absolute cost of every operation will be tabulated and every effort will be made for all reasonable economy in the management of the company. The company's cars can be produced at a cost that will make it possible to pay a good dividend . . . and leave a good surplus at the end of the year besides," Whitney said.[73]

No company records are available on Smith production levels. But press accounts and the company's own advertising claims through the years suggest that the total was about 1,000 to 1,200 cars – sold in Kansas, other parts of the Midwest, some Eastern cities, the West Coast, and the Southwest.

In its early years, company sales were limited to surrounding states. An early registration list shows that a "Smith runabout" was registered in July 1905 and a 16-horsepower "Smith-Veracity runabout" was registered in October 1906, both in southeast Nebraska. The years of the cars were not given. Some later Great Smiths found homes far from Topeka, however. Two Oregon residents owned Great Smith cars in 1914, according to an Oregon registration list. And Colorado's first-half 1915 registration list included 14 Smiths and 13 Great Smiths.[74]

By their own definition, the Smith brothers may have met their goals. They were still actively running their truss business when the Parkhurst-Davis Mercantile Company ordered 10 cars in 1902, and the truss business outlived the automobile venture. There is little evidence that Anton and Clement Smith ever entertained thoughts of mass-producing automobiles, as Henry Ford was doing.

Rather, producing automobiles represented an expansion of their product line, which previously had included only trusses. A plug for both products in one of the Smiths' automobile catalogs suggests that the brothers in 1905 were already having trouble keeping the two enterprises separate: "We invite your careful perusal of these pages, and if you contemplate the purchase of an Automobile (or truss) kindly favor us with your inquiries and orders. We have the handsomest and best Auto Cars on the market, and we have the fastest growing business on earth."[75]

Luverne of Minnesota
Cars That Last a Lifetime

2

Though it came completely and luxuriously equipped, the $2,850 seven-passenger 1913 Big Brown Luverne was "rather expensive to buy," brothers Al and Ed Leicher acknowledged. But "we believe that there will always be a large number of buyers who want a good car and are willing to pay a fair price for it, providing they are satisfied that 'It Is Worth The Money.'"

They were right. Orders from across the West, Midwest, and Northwest kept Luverne Automobile Company busy making hundreds of hand-built, high-priced luxury cars as late as 1917. That marked the first year the Leichers changed over to the full-time production of trucks and custom fire engines.

The Big Brown Luverne's "complete equipment" included double-step running boards, overbuilt 16-spoke rear wheels, brown Spanish leather, a two-tone deep-brown paint job, a gas-electric double-lighting system, and one of the earliest front bumpers in the industry. "Everything, in fact, but the license, and all of the very best quality," the company insisted.

But to the former carriage makers, "complete equipment" also meant a generous guarantee – 10 years on engines, five years on springs, one year on transmission and differential gears; free driving lessons; free delivery; a chance to learn about your new car as you helped build it; and a pledge against the "unfair" practice of annual style changes.

It also meant the company vowed "to keep in close touch with its customers[,] to study their requirements, to heed their suggestions for betterment. . . ." As a result, not long after the Leichers finished their first car in 1904, they began building a variety of special-order vehicles: sleeper cars, an aluminum-bodied race car, automobile hearses, heavy roadsters for state scale inspectors, a police car, and a rugged 50-horsepower "Car for the Mountains" – the Montana Special.

In Minnesota and surrounding states, contractors, farmers, ranchers, wealthy landowners, lawyers, doctors, and bank presidents owned Luvernes. The Luverne Automobile Company's customers included "a millionaire stove manufacturer," a former governor and presidential candidate from Missouri, and a Chicago inventor who counted Henry Ford and Thomas Edison among his powerful friends.

The automaker's 2-cylinder high-wheelers gave way to the 4-cylinder Luverne Forty of 1909, which evolved into the 1912 and later 6-cylinder cars – and at least one 8-cylinder roadster – that were "Big and Long and Brown and Strong." Along the way, the company assembled a loyal fan club whose members eagerly provided fodder for Luverne Auto's favorite advertising tool, the testimonial ad.

A. L. Brown took his Luverne out for an antelope hunt on the snow-covered buttes of the Black Hills during a 10-below-zero January day in 1911. "I doubt if there is another car made that will take the punishment that my Luverne has," commented Ben Austin, who bought Brown's car and raced it on dirt tracks in Nebraska and South Dakota.

A. H. Osborne's Luverne beat a $4,000 Peerless in a Southwestern cross-country grudge race. Harry Rodman loaded up the family and drove his Big Brown Luverne east to New York, south to Florida, and then back home to Minnesota 11,000 miles later. One man gave up a Packard to buy a Luverne. A South Dakota man would not give up his four-year-old 1910 Luverne for a Packard or any other car: "This car has . . . worked roads pulling a king drag, worked as a road tractor hauling [a] wagon loaded with grain, and for switching freight cars loaded with 85,000 pounds of corn. Unlike most old cars, My Car is Not For Sale, for I use it every day."

Even while they were making automobiles, the Leichers' versatile factory took on a variety of other jobs, from painting signs and sharpening saws to upholstering furniture. The brothers knew they would have to take on yet another line of work as the open automobile became outdated. Equipping the small factory to build modern closed cars simply would have cost too much, Al Leicher said. So the company wisely turned its attention elsewhere. Luverne fire engines were still being built in the 1990s.

Wagon-Making a "Gone Goose"

Born March 20, 1873, to Adam and Mariette (Kendall) Leicher, Fenton Alfred Leicher at age 13 began a five-year apprenticeship in his father's Loganville, Wisconsin, wagon-making shop.[1]

"I had just finished grade school, and my father wasn't very enthusiastic about the future of wagonmaking," Al Leicher said in a 1950 interview. "That was in 1886. He said wagonmaking by hand was a 'gone goose.' I told him it wouldn't hurt me any to become a good mechanic like he was. So he taught me," and later taught Al's younger brothers, Edward, Bert, and Frank.

In 1891 at age 18, Al Leicher moved to Luverne, Minnesota, to work in his Uncle William "Fent" Kendall's carriage shop. Leicher worked two years for Kendall and his successor, Elias Kreps, then set up his

2.1 Al Leicher, left, and brother Ed on the front page of the March 15, 1953, *St. Paul Pioneer Press* Sunday Magazine. (SPPP)

2.2 Al Leicher's drawing of a Luverne Forty or Fifty, complete with double running boards. (MS)

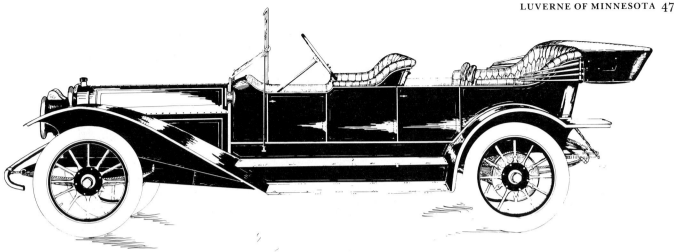

own carriage shop in Trosky, 17 miles north. "He established that business on a shoe string and, as he once put it[,] 'left there a richer and wiser man' in 1894 to buy his uncle's former shop" in Luverne, in partnership with his brother, Edward L. Leicher, according to a local newspaper account.

Born in September 1876, Ed Leicher, like his older brother, began building carriages right out of grade school. Ed "also had some blacksmithing experience which proved to be of great value to them in later years." The Leicher brothers (see fig.2.1) "soon turn[ed] to the manufacture of buggies, one known as the Luverne Buggy, selling for $35. Extra workers were needed to keep up with increasing business."

F. A. or "Al" Leicher would become both the designer and a salesman of Luverne autos, according to granddaughter Ann (Leicher) Hollaren. "F. A. was the front . . . which is why you'll hear more about him than you will about Ed, because Ed was the doer," she said. "Grandpa [F. A.] dreamt and . . . he would sit there for hours, drawing out these cars." (See fig.2.2.) Grandson Jim Leicher was designing rescue vehicles in Sumner, Iowa, in the 1990s with some of the same drafting tools that Al Leicher, a self-taught draftsman, had used to create

Luverne automobiles 80 years earlier.[2]

Ed and Al Leicher were "exceptionally well equipped to handle a business of this kind, both being expert mechanics and having a broad business experience," according to a 1912 Luverne Auto booklet.[3] In truth, "I wasn't much good at the crank," Al confessed years later. "Often when I was out demonstrating a car for a prospective buyer I didn't dare let it stop running for fear I wouldn't be able to start it again. Whenever that happened I'd have to leave the car where it was, get back to Luverne as best I could, and send my brother Ed out to bring back the car. He could always get them started."

"Foxy Enough to Please the Youngsters"

The Leichers built top-line carriages and wagons, according to Jim Leicher. "I don't have anywhere near the photographs that I can remember seeing in my grandmother's collection, but they built very fancy horse-drawn coaches and phaetons," he said.

"The brothers recall that they tried to embody in their buggies the better features of various other buggies. That way, they were able to satisfy the most particular buggy customers. 'We tried to make 'em foxy enough to please the youngsters, yet sedate enough to please the older folks,' they said," according to a *Rock County Star-Herald* retrospective article.

"Perhaps their most lavish creation was the 'Tally-ho' coach they built for Jay Kennicott. It was a 16 passenger affair, built something on the order of a double decker bus. It was upholstered in an imported fabric, and was drawn by four horses. A bugle was standard equipment on the 'Tally-ho,' Ed Leicher recalled. 'We'd hear the sound of the bugle, and we could look for Jay Kennicott to come down the street in the big rig, with a coach dog running ahead of the two teams which always pulled it.'"

Besides building new carriages, the factory painted and repaired old ones, made tops and side curtains, and sold tires, paint, and other buggy supplies. The shop upholstered furniture and even built a "Leicher Bros. Patent Clothes Reel," which sold for $4.50 in 1903. "They are a solidly built reel, nicely painted, and large enough to hold a good big washing," the brothers claimed.

The Leichers continued building carriages in diminishing numbers as the automobile company grew. The buggy factory was gone by 1916, apparently. That year, ironically, it fell to the auto company to make "a very fine horse drawn casket wagon" for a local undertaker who was afraid bad roads might stop his automobile hearse. Ann Hollaren and Jim Leicher said they are unaware of any surviving Leicher-made carriages.

"We Shall Build Automobiles"

The idea for building automobiles arose from a conversation between Al Leicher and one of the buggy factory's good customers, Henry Bierkamp, a local farmer and prominent landowner. "He was very particular about his buggy and periodically brought it into our shop for refurbishing. About 1903, I think, he had it in our shop and I suggested that he'd better be buying a new one," Al Leicher recalled in a 1953 St. Paul newspaper interview. "He astounded me by saying that it was his last buggy. He'd been reading about the new fangled gas buggies and had decided to buy one. It started me thinking. Maybe we should get in on the ground floor building cars."[4]

The local *Rock County Herald* reported in late October 1903 that "Henry Bierkamp will be the first of Luverne's citizens to own an automobile. He has ordered a machine from Leicher Bros. and expects to have it in use in about two weeks." It was on the morning of November 18 that Bierkamp's new Overland car arrived from Terre Haute, Indiana. "By noon he was running it on the streets," as the *Herald* described it. "It is one of the 'Red Fellows' and makes a handsome rig. . . . The machine was purchased from Leicher Bros., who are agents for southern Minnesota."[5]

When Bierkamp's Overland arrived, the Leichers "studied it from end to end, then purchased an auto in kit form from a St. Louis manufacturer and assembled it in their shop," according to the 1953 article. A *Rock County Herald* article in early December 1903 reported that Bierkamp and Ed Leicher had left Luverne for a three-week trip to St. Louis. There, they planned to buy "engines, gears and other parts of the vehicles and they expect to have the goods here by the fore part of January."

Their most likely source for a kit car in St. Louis was the A. L. Dyke Automobile Supply Company, which sold its own engines in kits that contained all parts necessary to assemble a car. Several retrospective articles have identified one photograph as the first Luverne car. (See fig.2.3.) The automobile shares similarities with the "A. L. Dyke No. 1 Outfit" of 1902 and 1903.

This so-called first Luverne contains many parts sold by Dyke or made by the St. Louis Motor Carriage Company, a Dyke supplier, according to Chuck Rhoads, who has had a longtime interest in the history of St. Louis automobiles. Dyke parts on the

2.3 A 1904 rear-entrance surrey, photographed near the Luverne Automobile Company factory; though made from parts supplied by A. L. Dyke of St. Louis, this car is often identified as the first Luverne. (JAC)

first Luverne include the hubs, hubcaps, wheels, front spring reaches, fenders, hood, and body, Rhoads said. "I really have no way of telling just how much of the auto in your picture was Dyke-furnished but with all the items I mentioned, I would think probably the whole thing was assembled from parts bought from Dyke," according to Rhoads.[6]

The Bierkamp-Leicher partnership was "organized to manufacture, repair, sell and store automobiles and do a general business of that character," according to the *Rock County Herald*. The Leichers noted the change with a casual, one-sentence announcement in their carriage factory's regular ad for December 18, 1903: "We Shall Build Automobiles the coming season and shall build machines that are right."

"An Especial Effort to Eliminate Noise"

The first Luverne car is often mistakenly dated to 1903. But it was 1904 before parts would arrive at the newly christened Luverne Automobile Company, so that in early 1904 the automakers were "rapidly pushing the work on the two automobiles they now have under construction in their

shops," reported the *Rock County Herald* of March 11, 1904. "Both machines will be equipped with a ten-horse power gasoline engine, although a different type of engine will be used in each." The first of the two touring cars, which would be "practically completed in about ten days," had a 2-cylinder engine, while the second had a 1-cylinder engine, the *Herald* said.

Perhaps to appease their buggy customers, the Leichers were "making an especial effort to eliminate noise to the greatest degree and to produce a machine as nearly noiseless as possible in an engine-power automobile," the *Herald* said. Eastern cars were fine for Eastern roads, but traveling men of Minnesota and other Northwestern areas "need a machine built for special purposes, to run on country roads, and as all large manufacturers refuse to make machines of other than the regular styles, it falls to the small factories to get out the specials," the newspaper said.

"To begin with, it was largely a matter of copying existing makes," Al Leicher recalled years later. For example, he made a June 1904 buying trip to St. Louis, after which the *Herald* revealed that "the company has secured a number of new patterns of machines in addition to those already possessed and will endeavor to build a machine that will meet the general demand." That was the beginning. In later years, Leicher said in a 1950 interview, "we made improvements of our own, and we always put emphasis on sturdiness."

The Leichers in March 1904 traveled to the twin cities of Minneapolis and St. Paul "for the purpose of studying the different automobiles in the shops there." Upon returning to Luverne, they completed the testing of their first car and sent it to their paint shop, the April 1, 1904, *Herald* said.

As Fast as the Trains

By early May, the Leichers had taken "several trips into the country and about town with their new touring car . . . giving the car a general test. The tests have proven very satisfactory to the makers and have also greatly stimulated interest in autos. . . . The second car which the company is building, is now nearly completed and will soon be given a road test."

It took them four months to build the first car; it took five more months to name the new vehicles. Finally, on September 30, 1904, the local newspaper announced "the machines built by the company will be called 'Luverne.'" Henry Bierkamp owned the first Luverne car, which he later sold to E. A. Brown, a grain dealer and Luverne's mayor.

By the end of 1904, Luverne Auto had installed a 2-cylinder 16-horsepower replacement engine in Brown's car. The first Luverne automobile received an even more powerful 2-cylinder 20-horsepower engine early the following summer, the *Herald* noted. "Mr. Brown will use his machine for travelling through the country on his visits to his line of elevators, and wanted ample power to make any trip regardless of the condition of the roads. This will now be possible and he will be able to make nearly as

good time as the trains without any waits between trains." In the summer of 1907, Brown closed a deal to trade his "old Luverne automobile, the first machine manufactured by the Luverne Automobile company, to a party at Humboldt, S.D., for a quantity of machinery," the newspaper wrote.

In late May 1904, Ed Leicher and Henry Bierkamp's son, Otto, drove the 34-mile round trip between Luverne and Rock Rapids, Iowa, "in one of the new automobiles recently completed by the Luverne Automobile Co." A month later, Otto Bierkamp was accompanied by banker A. D. LaDue and lawyer Jay A. Kennicott on "a trip of nearly fifty miles through the country northeast of here," the Luverne newspaper said. They made a 21-mile non-stop return trip in 1 hour 35 minutes against a strong headwind, "and in view of the fact that the roads were quite rough it was remarkably good time."

On two separate trips a few days later, Ed Leicher drove one of the company's touring cars to nearby towns so civic boosters could tack up posters advertising Luverne's July Fourth celebration. The second of the two trips took the new car on a 95-mile circuit through nearby Kenneth, Hardwick, Garretson, Booge, Beaver Creek, and Hills, with no reported problems. Luverne's two most important Independence Day visitors, Governor Samuel R. Van Sant and his wife, toured the town and a large nearby park in a Luverne automobile.

In June 1904, Al Leicher visited St. Louis, where he "thoroughly investigated the merits of the different engines manufactured for automobile purposes and placed orders for some of the most reliable makes, which will be used by the Luverne Automobile company in the machines they are building."

The Car for the Mountains
MONTANA SPECIAL

50 HORSE POWER

PRICE: $3,000
Completely Equipped (as shown in cut) and Delivered to You

126 inch Wheel Base   36 x 4 1-2 inch Non-Skid Tires   Plenty of Clearance

A Strictly High Class, High Powered Car
Embodying all that has proven best in high class Auto construction, combined with the most up-to-date design, finish and equipment. It is designed to meet the requirements of those that want the best, and that appreciate value when they see it.

An Established Reputation For Merit
That has been gained by actually making good at the most severe work in all parts of the country, during the past three years, during which time there have been no changes made in construction of these cars, except the addition of up-to-date features as they have developed.

Especially Designed and Equipped For The Montana Trade
We are perfectly familiar with conditions in Montana, and know from actual experience what the requirements are, and we also know from actual experience that our car will meet these requirements. We specialize in building Automobiles for the hardest kind of service, and naturally have to seek our market in the localities where they need such cars.

Springs That Are Positively Guaranteed For Five Years
Our springs are EASY RIDING and will not break. Easy springs mean comfort to passengers, a big saving on the machinery, and especially on tire wear, and remember, THEY ARE GUARANTEED FOR FIVE YEARS.

Good For A Life Time—No Wear Possible on Permanent Parts
Every bearing and working part in this car is of ample proportion, and so arranged that no wear comes on the permanent parts.

Handsome Design, Luxurious Finish and Equipment
The Body, Upholstering, Painting, etc., are all of the very best. Lamps are finished in Silver and Black, making a rich and lasting finish.

Tremendously Powerful Motor With Perfect Lubrication
Our 50 H. P. Rutenber motor, with its heavy bearings and general staunch construction, together with its perfect lubricating system, and ample cooling apparatus, and the complete double independent Ignition system, provides a POWER PLANT that can be depended upon at all times to not only furnish the power, but stand up to the work.

Heavy Frame and Long Wheel Base
Our splendid POWER PLANT would be wasted, were it not backed up by a FRAME that was proportionally strong and of sufficient length to give a LONG WHEEL BASE. Long wheel base is very essential in a high powered car and our FRAMES are made for BIG POWER, LONG WHEEL BASE, HEAVY LOADS and MOUNTAIN ROADS if necessary.

High Wheels, Big Tires, Ample Clearance
High wheels provide for CLEARANCE UNDER THE CAR which is absolutely necessary on Western roads. Our special DOVE TAIL, TENON SPOKE CONSTRUCTION makes our wheels practically indestructible. BIG TIRES with EXTRA HEAVY NON-SKID TREAD form the only practical means of providing against tire trouble.

Equipped To Last Detail With Every Necessary Accessory
When this car is delivered to buyer, it is ready for business, with all necessary attachments and duplicate parts included.

We Pay The Freight and Deliver The Car To The Buyer
Remember, that in addition to our including with this car, several hundred dollars worth of equipment, which other concerns bill at extra price, we also pay the Freight, and deliver the car to you in perfect condition.

We Want You to See and Compare This Car With Any In Existence
If you are in the market for a car that will give you satisfaction all the time, it will pay you to find out all about the MONTANA SPECIAL.

MANUFACTURED BY
THE LUVERNE AUTOMOBILE CO.
LUVERNE, MINNESOTA

Plate 1 In 1911, the Luverne Automobile Company of Minnesota began marketing a car for the mountains, the 50-horsepower, Montana Special. (MTHS)

PATRIOT
PERFORMANCE

Plate 2 Cover of a 1920 folder issued by the Lincoln, Nebraska, manufacturer of Patriot trucks. (NSHS)

Plate 3 This painting shows Hal Wells at the wheel of the brightly colored Spaulding racer that set an Iowa transstate speed record in 1913. (GHM)

Plate 4 "The 1907 Great Smith Car," color drawing. (from K 629.2 Sm5 cat. at KSHS)

One of the Moon innovations of the year is this new Cabriolet roadster.
The deck lid opens up a fully upholstered rear seat "a deux." With the
lid down the car is a closed roadster. Concealed compartment for golf
bag and other luggage. Rear window may be lowered for communica-
tion between passengers. (Patents applied for)

A HEAD of its day with a distinct and different
smartness, Moon enjoys an amazing preference
wherever smartness is a *sine qua non*.

For pride of possession is the chief satisfaction of the
Moon family. Pride in its dauntless performance.
Pride in its distinguished appearance. And as the
miles roll up, a feeling almost of affection for its clock-
like regularity.

So, in the metropolitan style centers, where most of
the motor-wise live, you find Moon selling away
ahead of its price class, outranking in registrations
many of the makers who build more cars than Moon.

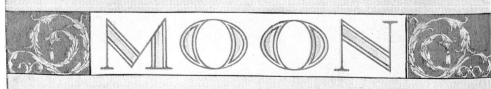

MOON MOTOR CAR COMPANY , ST. LOUIS , U. S. A.

Plate 5 Moon advertisement from *Century Magazine* (April 1925).

"Not Necessary to Be an Expert"

Less than a year after forming the auto venture, Henry Bierkamp sold his interest in August 1904. The buyers, A. D. LaDue of the First National Bank and lawyer Jay A. Kennicott, had apparently been impressed by their 50-mile Luverne test drive six weeks earlier. LaDue became president of the Luverne Automobile Company; Kennicott, secretary-treasurer; Al Leicher, "manager"; and Ed Leicher, "foreman."

The same *Herald* article that reported Bierkamp's departure said the auto company had just finished testing its second car. It "has just been placed in the paint shop for its finishing touches and will be ready for the market in about two weeks," the August 5, 1904, *Herald* said.

In mid-September, the auto company made its first public sale. No purchase price was disclosed, but, in partial payment, Dr. C. O. Wright traded in the used 6-horsepower Oldsmobile he had bought that spring for making emergency calls. The new car's perfection was obvious, according to the *Herald*. "It was unnecessary to make the slightest change after it was assembled and that throughout all of the tests it worked with a smoothness and precision impossible to excel."

Wright's four-passenger Luverne tonneau, capable of 25 miles per hour, soon proved its utility when the doctor made a run to visit a patient in nearby Garretson, South Dakota. "The roads were very heavy and badly cut-up but he made the run in remarkably quick time, averaging fourteen miles an hour," the newspaper said.

Wright's auto, the third Luverne, was "somewhat shorter than the other two and the lines have been materially changed which gives the machine a more compact appearance. Larger wheels are also used and by this change the speed has been increased, while the gearing has been so arranged that the machine runs with very little noise." Luverne Automobile Company decided to pattern its regular models after Wright's car "and now [has] four machines of that size and style under course of construction," said the September 30, 1904, *Rock County Herald*. Plans also called for building a "light runabout" of 5 or 6 horsepower.

The firm's two new officers, Jay A. Kennicott and A. D. LaDue, became Luverne owners during the latter half of 1904, apparently buying the company's second and fourth machines. In November, with just a few minutes' driving practice under his belt, Kennicott and three passengers left for a Sunday drive to Beaver Creek and Hills, returning unscathed. Such a feat demonstrated that "it is not necessary to be an expert in order to run a Luverne automobile," the newspaper observed.

In mid-November 1904, Al Leicher left on a two-week trip to Detroit to study "improvements made in the 1905 model automobiles in the large factories in that city. He will also close a contract to insure the prompt delivery of the engines the Luverne company will require in their operations during the coming year," the *Herald* said, without identifying the engines.

First-Year Output: Four Cars

In a year-end article, the *Herald* placed Luverne Auto's 1904 output at four cars, owned by Brown the grain trader, Kennicott the lawyer, LaDue the banker, and Wright the physician. Thus the town's leading citizens were already showing support for the local automobile factory, even if three of the four were company officers.

Over the winter, the company planned to build 10 cars – all touring cars and runabouts (see fig.2.4) with 2-cylinder 16-

2.4 A 1905 bulldog-nose 16-horsepower Luverne runabout, from the letterhead of a Luverne Automobile Company invoice dated October 1, 1905. (JL) horsepower engines. Al Leicher returned from Detroit "convinced that there is no room for improvement in the design of the 1904 model of the Luverne company," the *Herald* said. "The only change, therefore, that will be made for the 1905 models will be . . . the use of sixteen instead of ten horse-power engines, and the fitting of the new machines with appliances for a top, so that one may be attached at any time after the machine leaves the shop, should the owner desire, without any changes being necessary."

Later, however, the Leichers did find room for improvement in their 2-cylinder, chain-driven Luverne cars, which they made through the 1909 model year. For one thing, they discovered that their first cars had a tendency to lose their driving chains. Dr. C. O. Wright had that experience often, Ed Leicher recalled in a *Rock County Star-Herald* interview years later. Despite his troubles, Wright later invested in the company. As Ed Leicher told it:

I believe Doc Wright and I have had our backs on nearly every square foot of ground in this town some time or other. It seemed we were lying down putting on the drive chain most of the time. Every so often I'd have to go out in the country at night to do the same thing. I'd get a telephone call from Doc telling me to get Tom, his house man, to hitch up "Billy" the horse, and drive out to a certain place where the car had broken down. Chances are, he'd gotten the nearest farmer to take him by team to his destination. When the repairs were made, I'd pick him up at the farm place, and we'd head back to town.

Six local businessmen joined the venture in autumn 1906, forming a new $50,000 stock company to "develop the business on the large scale which the success of the machines warrant," the *Rock County Herald* said. They paid in $25,000 and filed incorporation documents January 9, 1907. Joining the Leichers, Kennicott, and LaDue were grain dealer E. A. Brown, still driving the first Luverne car; S. B. Nelson of the Nelson

2.5 A late 1907 or early 1908 view of the Luverne company's newly finished three-story brick factory building. (JAC)

Brothers' "mammoth mercantile establishment"; lawyer S. C. Rea; William Jacobsen, Jr., cashier of the city's First National Bank; Dr. C. O. Wright, owner of the first publicly sold Luverne car; and hardware-man J. W. Gerber.

Al Leicher kept his title of "manager," but Ed became "mechanical engineer" and, later, "factory superintendent." LaDue was named president; Kennicott, treasurer; Rea, secretary; and Brown, vice president. A 1912 factory booklet names three other early stockholders, among them blacksmith George W. Cottrell. In 1908, the auto company built its factory across the street south of Cottrell's two-story wooden shop building, which would become the backdrop for many photographs of new Luverne cars.

A $5,000 Automobile Factory

"A large building for the purpose of storing machines [automobiles] is now being built adjoining the [carriage] factory," a late 1905 *Herald* article said. "The building will be so arranged as to display the machines readily and will be well lighted." Chronic space problems persisted, so the new company in

February 1907 bought three lots on the southeast corner of McKenzie and Maple streets, just east across McKenzie Street from the Leichers' buggy factory.

Plans called for erecting a $5,000 three-level brick steam-heated factory "equipped with elevators and other modern appliances," the Luverne newspaper said. (See fig.2.5.) The 40-by-76-foot factory could be ready by "early summer." Several Luverne Auto investors also had money in the newly formed Luverne Pressed Brick Company, which presented a dilemma whereby a delay in starting up the new brick company postponed the factory project. Consequently, the Leichers in April were forced to rent a building for painting their carriages. "The demands for room in their present quarters have become so great that additional room is imperative," the Herald said.

When the first kiln-load of gray sand-lime bricks arrived late in 1907, "every available brick layer in the city" took advantage of an unusually warm December to build the auto factory. Luverne Auto moved out of the Leicher's carriage factory and across the street into its new factory in mid-January 1908. With a walkout south entrance, the basement "is the machine shop and construction room. In this department the steel chassis frames, the forgings, the copper and steel work, etc., are gotten out and the cars assembled," the Rock County Herald said. The basement was shallow "to permit of numerous large windows" for natural lighting.

After assembly, each bare chassis was "fitted with a rough testing body outfit and set of wheels and given a road test of about fifty miles, which includes various tests at hill climbing, pulling, speed, etc. After satisfactorily passing these tests the cars are returned to the [basement] construction department and thoroughly cleaned, and then hoisted on a large elevator to the third floor, on which is the painting and trimming department.

"Here the cars are painted and the bodies upholstered, the tops fitted, etc., and when

all [is] completed are again run on to the elevator and lowered to the show room on the second floor," which had a ground-level entrance on the north. Four men operated the hand-pull elevator to raise each car, recalls Jim Leicher, who worked in the factory from 1932 to 1970. He said the elevator was still there when he left.

The factory's second or ground-level floor also housed offices and Luverne Auto's accessory department, where "'everything for the automobile' is kept, and is arranged and displayed in glass show cases," the Herald said. In the carriage factory that the young auto company just vacated, "the bodies and wheels for the machines are built. The repair department is also contained in this building."[7]

Suitors Woo Luverne

Luverne Auto always gave its cars long road tests. A driver took out the prototype Luverne Forty in March 1909 on roads that were "in good condition to give the car a most severe test, being very rough and muddy. Despite the rough and slippery condition of the roads the car negotiated the longest and steepest hills in this section on the high speed clutch and with an apparent abundance of reserve power, showing . . . that there is no hill in the country it can't 'eat up,'" the Herald recounted. "We aim to drive a car from 400 to 600 miles before it is put into the paint shop," a 1910 Luverne catalog says. "After this try out it receives final inspection, and is ready to be painted, and when turned over to the buyer, it is in shape to give him the very best of results at the outset."

Later, the factory acquired a Mitchell car in trade for a new Luverne and used the Mitchell for breaking in Luverne engines, according to Jim Leicher. "They'd get these engines from Rutenber or whoever they happened to be using, and, of course, in those days [the engines] were very tight . . . so they'd install them in the old Mitchell and drive them for 400 or 500 miles, so when the Luverne was delivered to the customer it was ready to go."

The auto factory generated its own power until late 1913, when it put a $50 price tag on its 6-horsepower stationary gas engine. "Since we put in Electric Power, we have no further use for the Engine and want to get it out of the way, hence, this very low price." Occasional disruptions at the municipal power plant forced the auto plant to improvise, as it did in June 1914 by "using a four cylinder automobile engine for power . . . pending the resumption of electric power service."

Other cities began making overtures to the promising young Luverne company. "It is true that we have figured some with Sioux Falls [South Dakota] as well as other cities regarding the matter of changing our location," Al Leicher wrote in a December 1910 ad titled "Luverne Automobile Factory Will Not Move To Sioux Falls." But "so far we have found no good reason for so doing," he added coyly, leaving the door open to further offers. What followed was an all-out bidding war.

"We have had propositions made us from several large cities throughout the Northwest," Leicher revealed more than a year later. One offer came from Duluth, Minnesota, many times larger than Luverne's 1910 population of 2,540. But the company wanted to stay in Luverne, which offered it skilled workers, "unlimited room for expansion," and "good railroad facilities in every direction, making it easy for people from all over the Northwest to visit us and giving us good shipping rates."

But "for a time it seemed as if it was going to be impossible for us to reach the outside trade, for there seemed to be a natural prejudice against any car made in a small town so far West," Leicher said. The company also found it difficult persuading buyers that "brains and money were just as productive on the prairies of Minnesota as among the sand hills of Michigan."

Is That a French Car?

Leicher personally encountered such prejudice at the 1910 Minneapolis Automobile Show – Luverne Auto's first show. "Many that visited our exhibit from the northern parts of the state and from the Dakotas and Montana, had never heard of Luverne, either as a car or a city," he said. Other viewers, believing the car could not be a local product, "would come along and after sizing up the name would say 'That must be a French car from the name,' and we would immediately proceed to convince them that it was strictly an American product." Those who had heard of the cars but had never seen them "were usually very much surprised, as they said they had expected to see a rather cheap looking car," he said.

The Leichers' auto-supply business reached the outside trade before Luverne automobiles did. In 1910, the factory's woodworking department received an order from Long Island, New York, for a Cadillac wheel. "They have the material on hand and are able to make these parts without delay," the *Herald* noted. Also in 1910 the company received an order "from a large automobile garage in Baltimore, Md., for garage equipment which the local company manufactures here in Luverne. The order was accompanied by a draft covering the full amount, showing that the Eastern people do not hesitate to send their money out West, when it is necessary to do so to secure what they want."

The situation improved greatly for automobiles in 1911. "We have been able to make such rapid strides in the way of reaching the outside trade, and breaking down the prejudices that have existed against a Western product, that we have decided to give up all thoughts of leaving Luverne," Leicher said. "We are now doing a nice business with Eastern buyers, but it is due to the fact that they have been shown and they have come to us." Late in 1911, the company announced that its cars would be "advertised extensively" across the country.

In November 1911, stockholders doubled Luverne Auto's capitalization to $100,000 and discussed building a five-story factory building. Some of the new issue was "sold in Luverne and to outside parties, who have already expressed a desire to be identified with this concern," the *Herald* said. Early in 1912, however, the automaker began publicly advertising its stock as a "good solid investment" opportunity, sweetened by the offer of investors' discounts on auto accessories and Luverne cars.

"We are now increasing our capitalization, and are arranging for a much larger output, which will mean a larger Factory, and larger and better facilities all around," the growing company advertised. The Luverne car's reputation "enables us to secure the very cream of the business at a price that gives us a good profit." The idea for a new five-story factory somehow got lost in the shuffle. Nevertheless, Luverne Automobile Company sold enough stock to add a 28-by-74-foot extension to its factory late in 1912.

Never More Than 20 Employees

Like many early automakers, the Minnesota company built its own bodies, frames, seats, tops, and the like but sent to suppliers for engines, transmissions, and other mechanical parts. The Luverne Automobile Company aimed its early cars at the increasingly crowded low-price market. Its $650 2-cylinder runabout for 1906 was "strictly a two-passenger rig, designed to take the place of a team and single buggy," the *Herald* said. Beginning with its $2,000 1909 Luverne Forty, however, the automaker shifted its focus to wealthier buyers.

Apparently seeking to become more self-sufficient, Luverne Auto in early 1908 equipped its new factory with "the necessary machinery, tools and stock to enable it to make all of its own copper tubing, copper plate radiators, tanks, hoods, etc.," the *Her-*

ald said. The company sold some of its weight-saving radiators to other automakers, whom the local newspaper did not identify, but the radiator department was seldom mentioned thereafter.

By 1913, the company was at peace with its assembly methods. "We manufacture all parts which we believe we can make better than anyone else, and . . . we buy such parts as we know are better than we or any other automobile manufacturer can make them," as a factory booklet put it.

During the late fall–early winter production lull, Al Leicher would travel to Chicago, Cincinnati, Detroit, Indianapolis, Milwaukee, and what the *Rock County Herald* was fond of calling "other points in the East." At each stop he contracted for the coming season's supplies, paying the same prices as larger automakers because "we buy on yearly contracts, paying spot cash, thus getting the very lowest quantity prices."

The 1907 Luvernes used Hyatt roller bearings, Schebler carburetors, Diamond chains, Weston-Mott rear axles, and Brown-Lipe differentials, according to the 1907 Luverne catalog. The factory also bought engines and other heavy parts, including springs "made after our own designs and specifications." Luverne Auto's workers made bodies and tops, upholstery, wheels, and, in 1907, the angle-iron frames. By 1912, the Leichers were buying Schwartz wheels and Smith frames. At least some Luverne models that year were using B.T.K. 3-speed selective transmissions, Spicer universal joints, Weston-Mott axles, Harvey springs, and Gemmer steering gears.

In the winter, the factory "worked its full force making bodies, seats, leather tops, forging and sheet steel parts, and getting these parts painted and finished, and as a consequence these parts, which require the greatest amount of time and labor, are ready in large quantities" for assembly as customers placed orders for spring or summer delivery. The result of buying from

suppliers was that "our plant never had more than about 20 employes [*sic*]," Al Leicher said in a 1950 interview. (See figs. 2.6 and 2.7.)

Luverne cars were known for their hand-crafted bodies, hand-rubbed paint jobs, brown Spanish leather upholstery, and a long list of standard equipment. The 1912 and 1913 model Luverne 760 – seven-passenger and 60-horsepower – cost $2,850, nearly the most expensive stock model. The company at one point advertised its Montana Special for $3,000, which included freight charges. That price, according to a 1912 factory booklet, included as standard features a mohair top with curtains and boot, adjustable windshield, speedometer, clock, auxiliary seats, foot rest, robe rail, double Prest-O-Lite outfit, electric dash lighter for headlights, self-starter, electric horn with storage battery, auto-chime exhaust horn, trunk rack, spare-tire carrier, front bumper, shock absorbers, tire chains, extra inner tube, blow-out shoe, tire-repair outfit, tire pump, lifting jack, tool roll with hand tools, luggage boxes, folding pail, and funnel.

The Original "Luverne" Bumpers

By using 2-cylinder amidships engines through 1909 and wooden bodies through 1913, Luverne Automobile Company appeared to be settling into its own peaceful backwater, well out of the automotive mainstream. Such was not the case.

The automaker put 4-cylinder front-mount engines in all its 1910 cars and began using some 6-cylinder engines in 1912. From 1914 on, Luvernes also used standard bodies of metal over a framework of wood. In later years, Ed and Al Leicher played the spoilers, leading the way in adopting front bumpers and self-starters, for instance. They also pioneered the use of "double" running boards and double-duty gas-electric headlights of their own design. From midyear 1912 onward, Luverne cars were easy to recognize for their extraordinarily strong 16-spoke wooden driving wheels.

The company would steer clear of fads, however, the Leichers promised their customers in 1912. "Our claims for superiority are all based upon plain, common sense features, the value of which will at once be appreciated by any practical person, for while we employ and carry out many distinctive ideas and features, none of them are 'freaks,' but on the contrary, are the result of our ten years of experience at building cars that will sell themselves at a good price."

The Minnesota automaker was years ahead of the big names in mounting a bumper to protect the radiator and headlights. The first bumpers were round plated bars, spring-loaded to absorb an impact. (See figs. 2.8 and 2.9.) Later bumpers had a

This page:

2.6 A dozen Luverne Automobile Company workers pose on the north side of the factory; Al Leicher's son, Robert, is standing with his head against the window ledge. (JL)

2.7 Two workers beside a hoodless later-model Luverne in the factory, probably 1915 or 1916. (JL)

2.8 A 1912 Big Brown Luverne, photographed in front of the Nelson Mansion in Luverne, Minnesota. (MS)

Next page:

2.9 A 1914 seven-passenger Big Brown Luverne. (JL)

2.10 A 1917 Big Brown Luverne touring car photographed on a snowy street in front of Cameron's Cash Grocery, Luverne, Minnesota. (HD)

square cross-section and – in photos where such detail is visible – appear to be more rigidly mounted. (See fig.2.10.) Though a standard feature since 1912, the Luverne's front bumper still stood out in *Motor Age*'s January 4, 1917, new-model specifications issue. A Big Brown Luverne was pictured on a page with 12 other new cars – including the Chalmers, Overland, and Saxon – but was the only car with a bumper.

Not an "Ought to Start Her"

Hand-cranking an engine was hard work, so for years inventors had been experimenting with self-starters powered by springs, exhaust gases, compressed air, acetylene, electricity, and other means. Many large American automakers unveiled starters on their 1912 models, and Luverne Auto was riding the crest of the wave. "All Luverne cars will be equipped with self-starters for 1912," the company announced in October

1911. It promised to publish full details later. "In the meantime, you may rest assured that our Self-Starter will be as far superior to other self-starters as Luverne cars are superior to other cars."

The automaker equipped one of its demonstrator cars with the new starter, claiming that it "can be operated by a child, and that it can be depended upon to start the motor under all conditions," the *Rock County Herald* said. An ad illustrating the new 1912 models said, "they are equipped with an Auto Starter, not an 'Ought to Start Her.'" Later factory ads, newspaper articles, and even a 1912 factory booklet fail to name the starter brand. One retrospective piece identifies it as an acetylene starter, however.[8]

According to factory literature, the local newspaper, and national trade journals, Luverne Auto experimented with Gray & Davis electric starters in late 1912 and used a Bijur electric on the 1913 Luverne 760. But for 1913 and 1914 cars, the company settled upon the Kellogg compressed-air starter, made in Rochester, New York. The Kellogg starter used an engine-driven air compressor to fill a chassis-mounted steel storage tank; a timer released air into the cylinders through special air valves to spin the engine for starting.

"This motor driven compressor may be started or stopped at will by the driver by pushing a button or releasing it with his foot," the 1914 Luverne instruction book explains. "A gauge on the dash shows the amount of air pressure at all times. Any pressure from 80 to 200 pounds is sufficient for starting the motor, and usually from 3 to 5 pounds is consumed at each start." Running the pump for just "five or six blocks" was enough to fill the air tank to 200 pounds per square inch. Then the driver "can throw the pump out of gear, and has sufficient air to start his car as many times as he wants during the day."

The system also provided "an inexhaustible supply" of compressed air for inflating tires. A special nozzle allowed Luverne

owners to clean the engine or other greasy parts with a mixture of compressed air and gasoline. "Anyone who has ever used a six cylinder car properly equipped with compressed air will not be satisfied with any other equipment," the automaker claimed. At the February 1913 Chicago auto show, Al Leicher was "much pleased" to discover so many well-known 6-cylinder cars using compressed-air starters, the *Herald* said.

The national trade press agrees that Luverne returned to an electric starter in 1915, but there is no consensus on what brand the company used. The makers listed are Bosch, Jesco, Jones, and Splitdorf-Apelco. Possibly, Luverne Auto tested all four.

"Lighting Problem Solved"

An October 1913 *Minneapolis Tribune* article on the Luverne's new double-lighting system proclaimed: "Lighting Problem Solved." The Luverne system allowed a single pair of headlamps to run off either electricity or acetylene gas, surely a comfort to motorists who shared the Leichers' distrust of early auto electric systems.

The 1914 Luverne used a Vesta generator and Willard storage battery. "It is quite possible, however, for any one of a thousand reasons, for electric lights to fail, and such failures are sure to happen at the most inconvenient time," the car's instruction book confides. "To provide against such emergencies the Luverne headlights are equipped with gas burners as well as electric bulbs," with the gas provided by a Prest-O-Lite tank hidden in one of the car's double running boards. "This feature is a very important one for the man who is looking for reliability."

The electric bulbs and gas tips were mounted on a triangular fixture, "so that either bulb or gas tip may be placed in front of the reflector, with the other out of the way entirely. The change in lights can be made in an instant, and a snap lock holds them securely in place," the *Minneapolis Tribune* said.

"So far as we know, we are the originators of the double lighting system for automobiles," the company said. "We have no patent on the system, so can't hinder other concerns who are willing to pay the extra cost from using it nor do we care to do so, but we simply ask you to remember that we claim the credit for having been the first concern to equip with a double lighting system."

Pinning down any "first" is difficult, but it appears that Gray & Davis, a well-known lamp manufacturer, had a similar combination lamp on the market as early as 1909. Other brands of combination lamps developed before 1913 include those made by Badger Brass Manufacturing Company, C. T. Ham Manufacturing Company, and Witherbee.[9]

In the midst of the 1912 model year, the Leichers replaced their industry-standard 12-spoke rear wheels with stronger 16-spoke drive wheels. "They just felt they were necessary to handle all that torque," according to Jim Leicher. "These are the Schwartz Patent Wheels Having Interlocking Spoke Construction," factory literature reveals. "Note the Number of Spokes and Large Flange Diameter."

Wouldn't You Rather Buy a Buick (Engine)?

Two-cylinder Luvernes used Beilfuss and Buick engines, as well as an engine the company claimed was made to its own designs. Unfortunately, early Luverne ads and literature generally fail to reveal when the company used each engine. It was in November 1906, however, that Luverne Auto became the exclusive dealer in the Dakotas, Iowa, and Minnesota for Beilfuss automobile engines. "It is the engine used by the Luverne Automobile company in its machines," the November 30, 1906, *Herald* notes. Later, the Luverne company sold many Beilfuss sta-

tionery engines, mostly for running corn shellers or for other farm work.

In 1905, Beilfuss Motor Company of Lansing, Michigan, was advertising an opposed 2-cylinder "go-and-get-back" 16-horsepower engine – the same size as the engines used in the 1905 Luvernes. Beilfuss later produced a 2-cylinder 20-horsepower engine that likewise corresponded to an engine size that Luverne autos used in 1906, 1907, and 1908. Harold Dunkle of Luverne owned what was either a 1905 or 1906 Luverne with a Beilfuss engine.

For its 1908 cars, Luverne Auto was also buying some Buick 2-cylinder engines, according to Al Leicher in a 1950 *Minneapolis Tribune* interview. Leicher recalled getting a letter from David Buick "saying he couldn't supply us with any more." Jim Leicher confirms the story, and adds that his grandfather took the train to Michigan to talk with Buick: "Mr. Buick said, 'Well, Mr. Leicher, I guess this is probably the last engine I'll be able to supply you because a bunch of the fellows here in Detroit – a guy by the name of [Billy] Durant – has organized these people together as a group and they're going to call themselves General Motors.'" An *Automobile Quarterly* article confirms that after the Buick company's move to Flint, Michigan, the sale of Buick engines to Luverne Auto and several other small auto companies "was abruptly cut off around 1908." The reason was that Durant and his associates "wanted the entire production and were planning to organize another new company to take over Buick."[10]

Luverne Twos "Are Mighty Smooth"

At the end of 1908, the Luverne company advertised that "the two cylinder motors which we shall use as power for three of our '09 Models, will be the Luverne Motor, made entirely after our own design and specifications. This motor is of about the same size and weight as the Beilfuss motor, which we have used in the past, and we have retained all the best points of the Beilfuss design." The new Luverne engine had removable white-bronze bearings throughout, "which makes [it] probably the highest priced two-cylinder motor in use."

"A trial spin in one of our '09 Two Cylinder cars will do your heart good, for they certainly are mighty smooth," the company invited in July 1909. "We are . . . making Two Cylinder cars as fast as we can get them out, and selling them as fast as we can make them." The Leichers, however, discontinued their 2-cylinder cars in October 1909, citing the popularity of their first 4-cylinder product – the 1909 Luverne Forty (see fig.2.11), named for its horsepower rating. The Luverne Forty used a Rutenber, the same engine brand the company would buy in 1912 for its first regular 6-cylinder model. As early as March 1911,

however, the automaker equipped one of its special-order cars with a 6-cylinder Rutenber 60-horsepower engine.

In its smaller 1912 models, the company used two sizes of Beaver 4-cylinder engines. Its experience with Beaver engines dated to the 1910 Luverne 535 model, named for its five-passenger capacity and 35-horsepower rating. Luverne advertising failed to identify the make of its 1913 engines. Press accounts and factory literature indicate that for 1914, 1915, and 1916 the Big Brown Luvernes used 6-cylinder Beaver engines (see fig.2.12) of 4 x 5 bore and stroke. As an industry pioneer, the Milwaukee-based Beaver Manufacturing Company enjoyed "a national reputation for high class motors," the Luverne company said.

The 1917 6-cylinder Luvernes would use Continental engines, according to an *Auto-*

mobile Trade Journal article dated December 1916. That same month, the company took an order from "Dr. Kartrude" of Jasper, Minnesota, for "a Brown four-passenger roadster with a small eight-cylinder motor," the *Herald* said. Kartrude's 8-cylinder Luverne sold for $1,200.

Antique Automobile magazine says Luverne Auto ordered four Ferro V-8 engines at some unspecified date after Cadillac unveiled its V-8 in 1915 models. As designed by the Ferro Machine & Foundry Company of Cleveland, the 3¼ x 4 overhead-valve V-8 weighed 580 pounds and was just 26 inches wide.[11] Jim Leicher failed to recognize the Ferro name, "and it's unusual because I would have, I'm sure, heard someplace along the line Ed [Leicher] talking about it or my Dad [Robert Leicher] talking about it." Few company records remain to either prove or disprove the use of Ferro engines.

"Fast Enough over a Country Road"

Dr. C. O. Wright's 1904 Luverne surrey could hit 25 miles per hour. The *Rock County Herald* gives the top speed of the 1906 models as 25 for the runabout, 30 for the touring car, and 40 for the surrey. The 1909 Luverne Thirty friction-drive car had an advertised top speed of 50 miles per hour, and S. L. Chapin matched that on a two-mile stretch of dirt road near Luverne. He was convinced he could have gone faster, "but fifty mile an hour is fast enough over a country road."

In a 1912 testimonial letter, Luverne Forty owner W. A. Taylor of Rapid City, South Dakota, declared "my speedometer isn't geared high enough to record how fast it will go." Assuming his car used the same 60-mile-per-hour Stewart speedometer that came on later Luvernes, Taylor was driving at least 10 miles per hour over Chapin's preferred cruising speed.

One night in December 1911, Al Leicher's son, Robert, and five friends took out a Luverne Sixty test car that slid off the road at a slight curve, rolled twice, and threw everybody out. The young men "had a miraculous escape from death," especially considering how fast they were going, the *Herald* reported. "The car is geared to a speed of eighty miles an hour and when Mr. [Ed] Leicher went out to get it he found the throttle wide open."

Seven was the greatest number of advertised Luverne models offered during a single year – 1909. Four of the models were 2-cylinder cars: Model A touring ($1,250), Model B touring ($900), Model C surrey ($800), and Model D runabout ($750). The remaining three were 4-cylinder cars: the Luverne Thirty friction-drive ($1,000), Luverne Thirty shaft-drive ($1,400), and the Luverne Forty ($2,000). Despite contrary claims, Luverne Auto in later years offered two or more body styles each year. "In the $2,500 class only three makers specialize on the touring car alone. These are Luverne, Lyons-Knight and Speedwell," claimed the December 31, 1914, *Automobile* magazine. Actually, Luverne offered a roadster model in both 1914 and 1915.

2.11 A 1909 Luverne Forty on the muddy street in front of Luverne's Manitou Livery. (MS)

2.12 Right side of the 1915 Luverne's 6-cylinder engine; visible on the firewall, upper left, are an oil can and the vacuum tank, which draws fuel from the gas tank to the carburetor.

Friction-Drive: A Greasy Mess

By all appearances, the Luverne Automobile Company didn't know which way to
jump in 1909, hence the seven models. It
was out with a few of its new 4-cylinder
Luverne Forty cars, though output had
been "seriously handicapped . . . on account of not being able to promptly get the
Rutenber motors," the *Herald* said. The automaker was offering four models of 2-cyl-
inder mid-engined cars. (See fig.2.13.) It
was building a shaft-drive Luverne Thirty
(see fig.2.14) and the prototype for a short-
lived Luverne Thirty in which a 4-cylinder
Rutenber powered a "gearless" friction-
drive transmission.

The friction-drive car "has many adher-
ents because of its simple design and easy
operation [that] employs two friction disks
which are held together by sufficient pressure to cause one of these members to turn
the other," Victor W. Page said in his 1913
book, *The Modern Gasoline Automobile*. A
shaft connected to the second, or driven,
disk turned the car's rear wheels through
one or more chains. The friction-drive
Luverne Thirty used a center drive chain.

"This form of gearing has the advantage
that it is easily handled by the novice and it
is difficult to injure it by careless manipula-
tion. The number of forward speeds provided are infinite, as the driven member
may be moved across the driving face very
gradually. . . . The surfaces must be kept
clean and free from grease or the gearing
will slip, and for this reason this form is not
so generally used as one might suppose,"
Page said. The early transmission design
was enjoying a comeback, he added.[12]

Luverne Auto, naturally, promoted the
very advantages Page mentioned. "There is
absolutely nothing about it that can be broken, and it gives the car the ability to travel
on any kind of roads at any speed desired,
from three to fifty miles per hour," an April
1909 ad claimed. The company also billed
its new $1,000 car as both "The simplest and

most reliable Car in existence" (see fig.2.15) and "The Car That Has Them All Skinned." During testing in April 1909, the "Luverne Gearless" prototype "was found to have positively unlimited power and speed," according to the April 30, 1909, *Rock County Herald*. "Its operation is so simple that a little child could run it."

Jim Leicher recalls it differently. "I can remember Ed [Leicher] talking about those sliding-disk transmissions and the problems they had with them. It's friction . . . and if you got any grease on there, or picked up any road grease, that was it." Jim Leicher said the company didn't produce the friction-drive car for long. Press accounts and ads suggest the Luverne Gearless was built just in 1909.

Angle Iron, Wood, and Steel

The 1907 Luvernes used frames of "angle steel, re-inforced with adjustable truss rods which pass under the motor," a factory catalog says. "This is admittedly the most practical type of frame, affording the greatest amount of strength and rigidity in proportion to its weight." The 1911 shaft-drive Luverne Thirty had a frame of "Combination Wood and Steel. Same as used on the Franklin Cars. This construction gives great strength and flexibility and light weight."

If the wood-and-steel frames were homemade, they were among the last. In late 1911, the factory received "a big carload of pressed steel chassis frames. . . . These frames came direct from the steel mill, where they were manufactured expressly for Luverne cars," the *Herald* said. Later Big Brown Luvernes used a "Smith Frame," according to the 1914 instruction book.

"Our pressed-steel frame differs from the usual type of frame . . . [by its] main frame and a sub-frame. The sub-frame is tied to [the] main frame by cross girders making a very rigid as well as a very flexible frame, with the strength and carrying capacity distributed over a large portion of the

THE "LUVERNE THIRTY"

The simplest and most reliable Car in existence.

Four Cylinder Motor -- Contact Drive

This Cut shows a top view of the Running Gear or Chassis of our "Luverne Thirty" Model, and below we give a description and explanation of same.

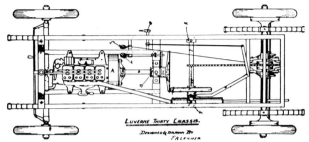

The Motor shown at front end of Car **is** a 30 H. P.

Four Cylinder Rutenber Motor.
Fly wheel of Motor is marked letter A
Connected to this Fly Wheel, by a Sliding Socket, is Shaft marked B, and attached to Shaft B is a Disc marked C.
Now when the Motor is running, the Shaft B and Disc C revolve with the Motor. By pressing forward on Foot Pedal, marked E, the Disc and Shaft are moved a slight distance away from Motor and the Disc comes in contact with the Drive Wheel marked F, which is a wheel with a Wood Fibre Rim. This Drive Wheel F is fitted on a Sliding Key in the Cross Shaft, marked I. so that as the Drive Wheel revolves the shaft must also revolve. On this Shaft is keyed a Sprocket, connecting by roller chain to rear Axle, consequently the act of pressing forward on Foot Pedal E immediately starts the car in motion, and by releasing the pressure on this Foot Pedal E the contact between Disc C and Drive Wheel F is broken, and the car stops.
To get different speeds, the drive Wheel F is slid on Shaft I to any position required.
As shown in Cut Drive Wheel F is placed for highest speed, as it is in contact with the outside edge of the Disc C. By pulling back on Hand Lever H, this Drive Wheel F is slid towards the center of the Car, and the nearer to the center, the slower the car is driven and the greater the power.
When Drive Wheel F reaches the exact center it does not revolve at all. As it is slid on past the center, it begins to revolve in the opposite direction, and thus drives the car backwards.

Luverne Automobile Company

Luverne, - - - Minnesota

frame. . . . Another advantage we get with our sub frame construction is being able to secure a double bearing mounting for the steering gear," which was mounted between the frame and subframe. (The sub-frame construction is visible in fig.2.16.)

"The normal procedure was to mount the engine and support it from the frame," said Jim Leicher, Al's grandson. "That was kind of a distinct feature, an identifying feature, of a Luverne automobile."

Wooden Bodies "Practically Indestructible"

Luverne Auto built its bodies entirely of wood long after most automakers had

2.13 A 2-cylinder 1909 Luverne Model A, carrying a full load of well-dressed passengers. (RCHS)

2.14 A Luverne Thirty shaft-drive touring car. (MS)

2.15 A promotional card explains the workings of the friction-drive transmission in the short-lived 1909 Luverne Thirty. (JL)

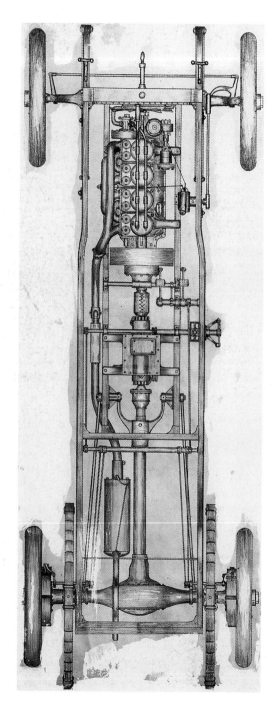

switched to steel or aluminum. "Bodies are hand made throughout, of the best quality of poplar and ash, as experience has shown that sheet metal of any kind is not suitable for body construction," the company's 1907 catalog advised. By 1910, the all-wood bodies were "re-inforced on the inside by canvas glued to the panels, making them practically indestructible." Some 1906 Luvernes lacked fenders and running boards. (See fig. 2.17.) The 1907 cars, however, had fenders "of laminated wood, very light and entirely free from rattle." (See fig. 2.18.)

All three 1907 Luverne models – the runabout, surrey, and touring car – had bodies hinged in the rear. An owner could thus tilt the body upward to expose the amidships 2-cylinder engine. "This . . . makes these parts more easily accessible than in any other car, not even excepting those with engine under the hood. This is a decided advantage and pertains alone to the Luverne Car."

The 1907 wooden-bodied cars did have metal hoods, trimmed with polished brass. For an extra $100, the 1907 touring car came with side curtains and a top, "light, durable and strong, made in our own factory, insuring perfect fit." Tops "are made on the cars, and are carefully fitted, with specially designed, closely fitting Limousine type side curtains. All tops are made of heavy Brown Silk Mohair," a 1913 factory booklet says.

"By the standards then for a wood shop, it was able to do things that an ordinary wood shop wouldn't," Jim Leicher said of Luverne Auto's body-building department. "In other words, the Leicher Brothers carriage works – and this evolved from it – was considered top notch. It wasn't run-of-the-mill carriages; they were quality carriages."

A surviving photo of two Luverne bodies under construction in about 1915 (see fig. 2.19) also pictures a workbench and tool board. In the photo, Jim Leicher spotted a "very elaborate, very sophisticated" Stanley universal plane. "They'd use it for rabbit-

This page:
2.16 An overhead view of the 1912 4-cylinder Luverne Fifty chassis, undoubtedly drawn by Al Leicher. (MS)

Next page:
2.17 A 1906 high-wheeled Luverne surrey or touring car with solid tires but lacking fenders and running boards. (HD)

2.18 A 1907 Luverne Model A touring car with its top up. (HD)

2.19 Woodworker Charlie Larson and two Luverne auto bodies, probably 1915 or 1916. (JAC)

2.20 A new 1911 Luverne Forty, photographed on a country road. (MS)

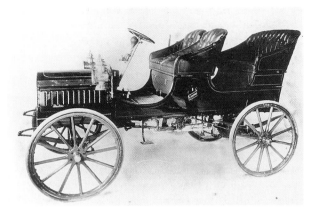

ing," he said. He also identified a flame-heated glue pot, which supplied glue for fastening wooden body panels.

The 1909 Luverne Forty had rear doors but an open front compartment. That would last until October 1910, when the company unveiled the four-door "vestibuled body" it would use on its 1911 models (see fig. 2.20), which were also the first Luvernes with windshields as standard equipment. The Minnesota automaker thus switched to four doors at the same time as many other American automakers. "This style of body has made a hit, and has come to stay, not only because it looks better, but because it really is better."

According to its advertising, the company tried using metal on its 1912 cars but switched back to all-wood bodies for 1913. "We make our bodies of wood and genuine aluminum, and we take especial pains to secure strength with the least possible weight," a 1912 company publication said. The next year, however, a factory specifications booklet said "we manufacture our bodies entirely of wood, thereby securing the lightest, strongest body obtainable, and one which will hold paint, and not dent up or rattle and come apart at the joints and corners."

The manufacturer switched back to using metal over a wooden framework for 1914 and later Big Brown Luvernes. "In the upper construction where weight is a great

hindrance to the car we save every possible ounce of weight, by making our bodies of aluminum and light woodwork, instead of sheet steel."

1912 Luverne: "An Appearance of Quality"

The 1912 Luverne was a breakthrough automobile, exhibiting the clean lines that, with some changes, would distinguish the car until its demise in 1917. "The plain and simple straight line design, with all proportions absolutely correct, gives the car an appearance of Quality that is always there," the company advertised. Designer Al Leicher eventually refined the streamlining idea by eliminating outside door handles and hinges. It was an open car so motorists simply reached over to use the inside door handles. With its new longer wheelbase – up to 130 inches from 122 inches in 1911 – the first 6-cylinder Luverne earned its nickname: "Big Six."

The 1912 model year also saw Luverne Auto introduce its double-step running boards. (See fig.2.8 and photos of later Luvernes.) The top step was actually a latched covering for the battery, acetylene tank, tools, and other items that cluttered the open running boards of many other cars.

Luvernes adopted left-hand steering for their 1913 models. In October 1913, the factory began turning out 1914 Big Brown Luvernes with top rolls – a piece of brown leather rolled over the tops of the doors and side panels, extending the length of the body. It was a fashion touch that, like double-step running boards, helped identify Luverne cars. The 1914 and earlier Luvernes had hoods that butted into the cowl board. During 1915, in step with its competitors, Luverne Auto adopted a smooth, flowing cowl and a hood that turned downward with a soft curve, rather than a sharp edge.

Photos reveal that upholstery work on Luverne autos (see fig.2.21) changed little over the years, undoubtedly because the factory's upholsterers simply transferred their carriage-trimming skills to automobiles. "Upholstering is of the finest quality of hand buffed leather in a special shade of tan, made expressly for our use," the 1907 catalog said. "A Luverne Car can always be recognized by the color of the upholstering. The best grade of curled hair is used for filling and both cushions and backs are softened by oil tempered coil springs."

In 1912, Luverne buyers could order black or Spanish brown leather on all but the cheapest Model 540. "All tufting and sewing is done by hand, insuring a smooth, perfect finish and lasting quality. Both cushions and backs are very thick, and are backed by rows of carefully tempered and graduated springs." What's more, "We use great care to cut the leather so that the strong portion of the hide will come where the wear is greatest, and the fitting is all done by hand. This is expensive, but it is high class construction, and whoever saw shoddy upholstering in a Luverne car?" a 1908 ad asked.

2.21 Jump seats allow this 1915 Luverne touring car to carry seven passengers.

Painters Use "Old Formula"

In painting as in trimming, Luverne workmen applied to automobiles the techniques that had worked so well with carriages. "Our method of painting is the old formula of two coats primed, fifteen coats rough stuff, three coats color and three coats varnish, requiring two months for the complete operation," the 1907 Luverne catalog reveals. "We realize that there are a number of quicker and cheaper ways of painting in vogue, but Quality is our standard and the watchword in all our departments."

The "rough stuff" was apparently the "dull finish color coats" that the company referred to elsewhere. Even in 1913, after 10 years of automobile manufacturing, the company advertised proudly that "Luverne cars are painted by the old fashioned carriage method." Hand rubbing between coats produced "a very, very deep, luxurious brown" on the later Luvernes of that color, Jim Leicher recalls.

Each winter and spring, the Leichers' carriage factory ran ads urging people to "Bring in Your Buggies" for their yearly painting. As late as 1915 the Luverne Automobile Company likewise suggested that "it is a good plan to have the car varnished every year. The cost isn't very great, and it means saving in the end."

The earliest Luverne cars may well have been the "deep red" that the Leichers' 1903 advertising claimed was their "speciality" color for wagons, buggies, and machinery. In addition, the brothers' first experience with an automobile involved Henry Bierkamp's red Overland. Early ads do not reveal the colors of the first Luvernes. But according to the 1907 catalog, Luverne cars had "automobile yellow running gear [springs, frame, and other chassis parts] with black fine line. Aluminum on metal parts. Brewster green on body with gold fine lines. Genuine gold leaf ornamentation."

The 1908 colors included olive green and deep red. In 1909, the company first advertised "onyx brown," also called "Luverne brown," from which the Big Brown Luverne would take its nickname. Brown and brewster green were 1910 colors. The 1911 Luverne Thirty was "finished in plain black" with a gold stripe. A 1911 "Black Hills Special" special-order four-passenger roadster received a "gray combination" finish. The Duluth Commercial Club's special 1912 Luverne Fifty was "to be painted a golden tan and have all bright nickel mountings." The smallest 1912 model came in a battleship gray; the larger 1912 models came in either a dark blue or dark brown.

"We got to painting ours brown so they'd look nice for the Minneapolis [auto] show," Al Leicher said in a September 17, 1950, *Minneapolis Tribune* interview. "We upholstered them with brown Spanish leather and put on brown tops. Our later models were all big and sturdy. People got to referring to them as 'Big Brown Luvernes,' so we just adopted the name."

Visitors to the September 1912 Minnesota State Fair coined the name "Big Brown Beauty" – "and it's a name that's going to stick, too," Al Leicher predicted after his return from the fair that year. The name that stuck, however, was a derived nickname that Luverne Auto began using just a few weeks later: "Big Brown Luverne." No one at the auto factory was paying attention when the *Rock County Herald* editor stumbled upon the "Big Brown" epithet in a September 22, 1911, short news item: "George Wolf . . . is the latest buyer of a big brown seven-passenger 'Luverne Forty.'" One retrospective account says the automaker actually asked State Fair visitors to cast ballots in a name contest.[13]

Factory literature from 1913 refers to a two-tone brown paint job. "The standard finish of Luverne cars is in two shades of brown, with all nickel trimmings," the 1914 instruction book confirms. "The shades of paint are dark Luverne Brown trimmed with light Luverne Brown, and the same shades run through the leather upholstering and top material." Even the tire cover was brown. "We do build cars finished in other colors," the 1914 book added, "but only to order."

Luverne Company Thinks Big

In late 1909, because of the strong demand for the larger 4-cylinder Luverne Forty, "we have decided to discontinue the manufacture of Runabouts and small cars," the company announced. "To supply the demand for such cars we have secured the Agency for Southwestern Minnesota, for the famous Brush Car," a light 1-cylinder Detroit product. (See fig.2.22.)

Early in 1910 the automaker also began selling the Reo. "For some time past we have realized the necessity of securing the agency for a line of medium-priced cars to handle in connection with our Luverne Cars." The company's full-range lineup for 1910 was thus the low-price Brush at $485, the medium-price Reo Thirty at $1,250 and the higher-priced Luverne 30-, 35-, and 40-horsepower models, ranging from $1,400 to $2,250.

The 1910 Luverne 740 sold for $2,250, completely equipped, "and when we would explain that 'Complete Equipment' meant everything that is needed with the car, and included delivery to buyer, the usual comment was, 'Now that is the way to buy an automobile,'" Al Leicher said.

Constructing a Luverne car cost 10 percent more than "most of the large concerns for the simple reason that we do a different class of work." But unlike larger companies, Luverne cars sold at "a price that is based upon actual cost of construction, with no allowance for commission, high freight rates, elaborate advertising, etc." Luverne cars "are rather expensive to buy, but very economical to own." As a result, the staunch, well-appointed Luverne car was "the best investment in the long run."

At $650, the company's 1906 runabout

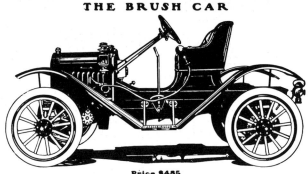

THE BRUSH CAR

Price $485
LUVERNE AUTOMOBILE CO.
Agents for Southwestern Minnesota.   Luverne, Minn.

was a bargain. But prices grew with the cars to reach a 1912–1913 peak of $2,850 – higher for some special-order cars and as high as $3,000 for the Montana Special – before falling to $2,500 for the Big Brown Luverne Sixty models of 1914–1916. "Any car that can by pure merit alone, without the assistance of expensive advertising or publicity stunts, push itself to the front as has the Big Brown Luverne has a good reason for being a 'little high priced,'" the company declared.

By 1913, several locally owned four- and five-year-old Luverne cars had traveled 50,000 to 100,000 miles. "The owners paid in the neighborhood of $2000 for these cars, but when you consider the immense amount of service they have had, and that their cars are worth practically as much now as they were when new, it proves that the Luverne is a good investment, and really is 'worth the money.'"

"Wish You and Klim Would Come Right Down"

At a big auto factory, officers rarely saw or even spoke to a customer. Ed and Al Leicher, on the other hand, invited buyers to drop by the factory and lend a hand as their new cars took shape. During one week in August 1908, three Luverne buyers were in the factory helping to build their own automobiles "on account of the practical experience to be gained by so doing," the *Herald* reported. "It gives the buyer an opportunity to thoroughly understand his car through-

2.22 When Luverne Automobile Company stopped making its own small cars in late 1909, it became an agent for the 1-cylinder Brush. (HD)

2.23 A 1908 2-cylinder Luverne Model A touring car. (MS)

out, and puts him in position to secure the best results from it."

A number of other policies – free driving lessons and perhaps the best guarantee in the industry – attracted and held customers in what was fast becoming a very competitive market. Of course, building a good product is a sales strategy in itself. Thus the factory equipped the Big Brown Luverne with emergency ignition and lighting systems, as well as a starter that worked even if the electrical system failed.

The Leichers' open-door policy undoubtedly led to many sales. It also encouraged people to take an interest in the Luverne car. Upon receiving the Rutenber engine for its first 1909 4-cylinder car, the auto factory – like a kid with a new toy – invited "any one interested to call and see it."

By 1912, people were beginning to "take notice and make comment upon" the number of Luverne owners in Minneapolis and St. Paul. "City buyers fully appreciate the advantage of being able to come to the factory and spend a day or so studying the details of their cars, and then driving them home, accompanied by an expert, as the trip home teaches them a great deal about the operation of the car, and is much cheaper than to ship, besides being a very pleasant trip," the Luverne newspaper noted.

"We are always glad to have prospective automobile buyers visit our factory, as we know by experience that every visitor either buys a Luverne car or goes away with the firm determination of having one some day," the company said. After several weeks

looking elsewhere, a prospective buyer from St. Paul visited the Luverne Automobile plant and apparently liked what he saw – so much so that he sent an urgent telegram to his car-shopping friends back home: "Don't close deal for ——— Car or any other kind. The Luverne is the best we have considered. Wish you and Klim would come right down."

We Make It Right – Guaranteed

For the first three seasons, Luverne cars sold only to buyers living within 25 miles of the factory, the company said. "When we sold a car to a man living in our home town, we had to do so, of course, with the understanding that if anything about the car was not right we would make it right, and, as may readily be imagined, with a guarantee of this kind the user did not hesitate in the least to give us every opportunity to make things right." The brothers "fully realized that before we could ever expect to make any money under the 'make good' plan . . . we would first have to eliminate every weakness" in the Luverne car.

During the fourth season, buyers began coming from greater distances but received the same guarantee "regardless of expense to ourselves, with the result that every customer was satisfied and always ready to recommend the Luverne cars."

The 2-cylinder engine broke in one of the 32 Model A touring cars the company made for 1908 (see fig.2.23), "and that was an accident pure and simple, and no fault of the motor, yet we replaced the breakage and did the work absolutely free of charge." Undaunted, the automaker offered to "replace free of charge all breakage on '09 motors (except where caused by carelessness of operator or accident)." Engines in 1911 Luvernes were "Guaranteed by the Rutenber Motor Co., and by ourselves[,] for 10 years."

"You will find that no other Automobile Manufacturers (except us) will give any Guarantee on Tires," the Leichers advertised in 1909. Buying tires in lots worth $3,000 or $4,000 meant tire manufacturers "are willing to grant us all possible favors in order to hold our business." So the automaker promised to get a quick replacement for Luverne owners who received a defective tire, thus saving them "a great deal of expense and annoyance."

Under its 1913 guarantee, the Minnesota automaker made free adjustments and replaced free any broken transmission or differential gears during the first year. It would eventually guarantee its springs for five years. "If we had the least idea in the world that they would break, we wouldn't guarantee them for so long, but Luverne springs won't break. Of course they are somewhat heavy; but they made the Luverne the easiest riding car on the market."

"Pleasant Feelings and Friendly Relations"

"When cars are sold we send an expert with the car to instruct the owner," the automaker pledged in 1910. "It has been our experience that if a buyer is properly instructed in regard to operating and care of [the] car at the outset, he will get much better results and will be better satisfied." It was usually Ed Leicher who did the instructing.

The Leichers kept track of their cars. Luverne cars were "backed by a concern that is solid as a rock and whose aim has al-

ways been to keep in close touch with its customers to study their requirements, to heed their suggestions for betterment, and to do everything possible to insure pleasant feelings and friendly relations with the customer," they said. Doing so meant keeping "an accurate record of all sales, so that we know the name and occupation of every user of a Luverne car and the factory number of his car, when he bought it and all about it."

Recording the mechanical details of each Luverne car would have been especially important, as "each car was an individual thing," says Ann Hollaren, Al Leicher's granddaughter. "You have your specifications listed for the Big Brown and yet you can bet that if you could line up three or four of them, each one would have some different specification to it that the individual [buyer] wanted."

By referring to the record book, factory workers could fill parts orders quickly, "for we believed that this one item would add greatly to the value and desirably of The Big Brown Luverne in the minds of that class of buyers who buy high grade cars, and such has proven the case." Speedy parts deliveries were even guaranteed to owners of used Luvernes. "Those who have bought used Luverne cars . . . we ask to advise us at once the number of car, from whom purchased, and the home address of the new owner."

Because few companies today will assume any moral obligation, the Leichers' 1912 parts pledge is especially refreshing: "We feel that when we sell a man a Luverne car we assume a moral obligation . . . to furnish him with any repairs or duplicate parts he may require without delay and at a reasonable price. . . . It is a certainty that when a customer needs a new part he wants it quick."

Such was J. L. White's predicament in 1915 when he "ground out" two transmission gears while returning north to end an 8,000-mile trip in his 1910 Luverne Forty.

He managed to limp into Laredo, Texas, where a smirking mechanic predicted a 30-day wait for parts. "With the confidence I had in your promptness and being familiar with the railroad connections from Luverne clear across the United States, I said to him that the repairs would be there next Sunday morning," White said in a testimonial letter. "He smiled again and said, 'Maybe.' Well, they arrived Sunday morning, not having missed a single connection, and within one hour after their arrival we broke camp and started north."

In autumn 1910 the factory went so far as to mail letters to its owners, asking "exactly what results you have had from your Luverne Car, and whether or not same has been satisfactory to you. We shall not publish these letters, but want them for our files." Shortly thereafter the company said, "we have received answers from nearly every man, and these answers certainly settle the matter that Luverne Cars satisfy the users."

Ed Leicher spent three weeks traveling through Montana in late 1911, visiting owners of the Luverne company's rugged new Montana Special model. "He found them very well pleased with their cars, and particularly well pleased when they found that he was a representative of the company and had gone to the trouble and expense of hunting them up for no other purpose than to find out whether everything was all right and if not to make it so," the *Herald* said.

Annual Changes "Ridiculous, Unfair"

In making "Cars That Last A Lifetime," the Luverne company sought a car heavy enough – 3,700 pounds in 1917 – to tackle bad country highways yet designed to look stylish for years. Makers of low- and medium-priced cars make annual style changes so a buyer "finds it necessary to buy a new car to keep from being hopelessly out of date," the automaker said.

"As improvements come out, we arrange to put them on Luverne cars in use, as well as on new cars, so that it isn't necessary to buy a new car every year to keep up to date." The Big Brown Luverne "seems to suit people" with its shape, features, and color, the company added. "It is very gratifying . . . to continue year after year to make cars that all look alike, and it obviates the necessity of yearly models, which in our estimation is not only ridiculous, but unfair to the customer."

A Luverne car has "a big motor, heavy gears, and big tires, backed up with the best possible construction and material throughout," the company claimed. But "if it isn't dependable it's a failure," so the 1914 Luverne had a Bosch magneto for ignition, plus backup batteries; a generator and storage battery for lights with a backup acetylene system; a compressed-air starter that worked independently of the ignition and lighting systems; and an unspecified "fuel reserve." The car also had a power tire pump and an acetylene engine-priming device. "The above items of ignition, lighting, starting, tire inflation, priming and fuel system, five of the leading causes of trouble on any car, are each taken care of independently and every source has a reserve provided for it."

Another reason behind the success of the Luverne Automobile Company is that, despite its name, it was diversified. In addition to making cars, the company sold and installed 2-cylinder engines on corn shellers; carved mahogany bars for local saloons; stitched tops and side curtains for both buggies and automobiles; sold auto and upholstery supplies, paint supplies, varnish, lumber, steel, and fire extinguishers; painted signs and cars (any Ford, $25); upholstered furniture and cars; filed saws; and repaired automobiles. At various times the company was an agent for new Brush, Dodge, Overland, and Reo automobiles. It also resold the used cars that were traded in on new Luvernes. In 1909 and 1910, the Luverne Automobile Company ran an "auto livery" business that rented Luverne cars equipped with "careful and experienced drivers."

"They did anything to make a buck in those days," said Al's grandson, Jim Leicher. "You know, this was a small town and these people were the craftsmen of the town. You wanted something done nobody else did, go to the Leicher brothers."

In December 1909, the company advertised unfinished cars – "Automobiles In The White" – to would-be automakers. "We manufacture a line of high-grade cars, which we sell ready to paint and trim, with or without body," read their ad in *The Carriage Dealers' Journal*.

In 1913, the company assembled and "placed upon the market a four-cylinder unit power plant (see fig.2.24) completely equipped and with electric generator and self-starter if desired," *Motor Age* reported. The compact unit used much weight-saving aluminum and could be supplied for right-hand or the newer left-hand-drive cars. It came complete with gearshift, hand-brake lever, and clutch and brake pedals "to meet the demand for a dependable self-starting motor, that can be installed in cars having out-of-date or inefficient motors," *Automobile Trade Journal* said.[14]

Special Cars for Special Needs

Bigger automobile companies rarely made special-order cars, which left a fertile field for the smaller manufacturers. Ed and Al Leicher, who knew most of their customers personally, listened to their requests and built a variety of cars for special needs.

One of Luverne Auto's special orders was a 100-mile-per-hour racer, which sparked the persistent myth that a Luverne raced in the Indianapolis 500. Customers ordered a variety of other special cars, beginning as early as 1906. Special orders for a mountain-climbing Montana Special, hearses, fire engines, and a variety of trucks prompted the company to expand its line.

In late July 1915, Luverne Auto bid on and won a contract to construct two special cars for the Minnesota Department of Weights and Measures. (See fig.2.25.) Built with the new Luverne streamlined cowl and hood, the resulting sporty two-passenger roadsters had large trunks – accessible through a side door – for 1,000 pounds of test weights.

"It is now more than one year since the State Department of Weights and Measures received from you the two inspectors' cars which you built specially to our order," agency Commissioner Charles C. Neale wrote in a letter dated September 27, 1916. "These machines have given . . . excellent satisfaction in the very hard service to which they have been put. . . . When I speak of hard service I mean that these cars have been used constantly under the full load of 1,000 pounds of standard test weights, 2 men and light equipment, or about 1500 pounds in all, in all kinds of weather, and last winter was certainly severe enough to try out any car."

2.24 Two Luverne workmen display a unit power plant in the machine-shop area of the factory. (JL)

2.25 In 1915 Luverne Automobile Company made two special roadsters for the Minnesota Department of Weights and Measures. This one is parked in front of the old State Capitol Building, 10th and Cedar streets in St. Paul, which is no longer standing; St. Louis Church, far left, survives today. (JAC)

2.26 Ed Leicher, at the wheel, with son Larry in the cherry-red roadster that the Luverne company built for inventor Charles A. Balton, 1915. (JL)

Balton's Cherry-Red "Special Speed Roadster"

In early September 1915, the company started work on an aluminum "Special Speed Roadster" (see fig. 2.26) for inventor Charles A. Balton, who designed the car and its 4-cylinder 110-horsepower engine. During an unspecified series of road tests in late October, the car "more than fulfilled all requirements as to speed, power and general roadability," the *Rock County Herald* said. Balton, an independent consultant from Chicago as well as "an aviator and racing driver," would race the car, the *Herald* said. But it later reversed itself, saying Balton would use the roadster "entirely as a pleasure car."

By its description of the car, the newspaper may have been correct the first time. "The transmission, clutch, steering gear, axles and speedometer, etc., are standard Luverne equipment with the exception that the gear ratio in the rear axle is special and the speedometer is designed to register up to 150 miles per hour," the *Herald* said. Al Leicher's son, Robert, helped test the racer. "He said the car would go over 100 miles an hour. He personally had it up that high

many times," according to Robert Leicher's son, Jim.

Special equipment included Houk wire wheels, painted white enamel, "a pair of bucket seats built very low . . . and two tanks back of the seat. One of these tanks, holding 34 gallons, is for gasoline and the other, with a capacity of 16 gallons, is for oil. Aluminum is used throughout the body construction. The entire chassis and under side of fenders is painted ivory white and the body is painted cherry red, trimmed with white," the *Herald* said.

Jim Leicher said the story passed down to him was that a ban on large engines prevented Balton from entering his car in the

Indianapolis 500. The Indianapolis Motor Speedway Hall of Fame Museum has no record of Balton attempting to qualify in the car. The Luverne racer's engine size of over 800 cubic inches would have far exceeded the Indy 500's 300-cubic-inch limit of 1915, according to museum researcher Jim Hoggatt.[15]

Born in Athens, Greece, Balton co-designed an early radial airplane engine and did experimental engineering work on Hispano-Suiza airplane engines, according to Buffalo, New York, newspaper accounts. They add that Balton associated with Henry Ford, Albert Einstein, and Thomas Edison. In Oakland, California, Balton designed a Fageol automobile chassis using a 6-cylinder Hall-Scott airplane engine, family documents indicate. How Balton met the Leichers remains a mystery, but "he always liked people who built quality," according to the inventor's daughter, Denyse Kraud of Michigan. Balton also favored such cars as the Franklin, Hupmobile, and Marmon, she recalled.

In 1919, his Charles A. Balton Engineering Corporation of Buffalo, New York, announced plans to build "the World's Fastest and Most Efficient Stock Car." Balton's 4-cylinder 187-horsepower engine would make the Diana a 100-mile-per-hour car "built far above the ordinary engineering standards," the Buffalo press reported. In a 1920 article titled "The Car of Tomorrow," Balton lauded the "natural static and dynamic balance" of the 4-cylinder racing engine.

The Luverne special speed roadster built for Charles Balton may have been the Diana prototype: A full-page photo of the Luverne racer appeared in a stock prospectus promoting Balton's new Diana. Kraud said a lack of financing kept Balton's car out of production, however. Balton also parted with his Luverne racer. A Greek restaurant owner in Sioux Falls bought the car, which later became the fire chief's car in St. Cloud, Minnesota, according to Jim

Leicher. "It disappeared during the years of World War Two," he said. "It apparently ended up on a scrap drive."[16]

Sleepers, Police Car, "Black Hills Special"

Numerous stories in the *Rock County Herald* recorded other special Luverne cars made over the years, including the following:

• August 31, 1906: The company delivers to C. A. Kinsey of Adrian "a special model designed for use by Mr. Kinsey in his photographic work. The mechanical equipment is the same as that used in the regular cars, and the wheels are fitted with solid rubber tires."

• May 14, 1909: "Mr. Packard" of Redfield, South Dakota, "has several ideas of his own as to how he wants a car, and is placing his order accordingly" for a special Luverne 30-horsepower automobile.

• July 1, 1910: O. P. Huntington of Luverne orders "a special built Luverne Forty having a closed body of the torpedo type," a feature that "his long experience as an auto driver has shown to be desirable."

• September 9, 1910: Al Leicher travels to Superior, Wisconsin, "to arrange for a sale of a Luverne Forty to the police department of that city." The car undoubtedly carried special equipment, but the newspaper neglects to specify it. During its first year the car was driven 16,000 miles day and night "under the most trying conditions, but it has never failed us," the police department reported.

• March 31, 1911: J. L. White of Sioux Falls picks up a special Luverne Forty "arranged with folding seats, so that it can be converted into a sleeping car at night. Mr. White is on the road constantly during the summer months and . . . his latest [Luverne] car makes him independent of poor hotels."

• March 31, 1911: J. E. Goltra of Adrian picks up the 60-horsepower touring car that Luverne Auto "made to his order" using one of the first Rutenber 6-cylinder engines, from "a large Racer that took in many of the early races, and for several years this motor held the world's record for twenty-four hours performance."

• May 26, 1911: The company ships "a very handsome car to a customer in the Black Hills. It is of special design, being in the shape of a four passenger Roadster, with body on 50 H.P. chassis. The whole car is finished in a gray combination, and the name, 'Black Hills Special,' is painted on the hood in black and gold letters."

• August 11, 1911: Luverne Auto sells the Duluth Commercial Club a 50-horsepower car, with special paint and equipped to tackle "the famous Duluth hills. . . . The fact that this car will be used by the Commercial Club partly for entertaining club visitors, who consist largely of eastern capitalists, will place the Luverne car where its merits will be appreciated by men who buy cars of quality, regardless of price."

• March 6, 1914: Luverne Auto sells to C. R. Hildred of Los Angeles a Luverne Forty having a body "arranged so that it could be converted into a sleeping car, and a tent which extended over the car with wing extensions on each side, was a part of the equipment."

"The Car for the Mountains"

The Luverne company saw the need for a mountain car and thus created "The Car for the Mountains," namely the Montana Special. (See color plate 1.) In 1915, the year it built the Charles Balton racer and the two Weights and Measures roadsters, the Minnesota automaker finished its first hearse and first fire engine – both commercial cars that would become part of its expanding line.

In November 1910, J. A. Bean of Bozeman, Montana, contracted with the Luverne company to buy 25 heavy-duty Montana Special cars equipped with 40- and 50-horsepower engines. Luverne Auto quickly settled upon the 6-cylinder 50-horsepower

Rutenber engine for all the cars, which Bean planned to distribute through his newly formed Montana Special Auto Company. The automaker would sell the same or a similar car as the Model 750, or Luverne Fifty. Luverne Auto was vague about what special equipment it installed to make this a hard-service model. One ad put the Montana Special's price at $3,000, which included delivery costs.

"It has the power to do our work, and the fine appearance that a high grade car should have," rancher Louis Siefert of Belgrade, Montana, wrote in late 1911. "You can rest assured that the Luverne has a big future here." He was right. By 1913, the *Herald* could report that "the company is having a splendid demand for this model, and has been forced to refuse orders for immediate delivery."

Cars for Fires and Funerals

In an October 30, 1914, article, the *Rock County Herald* said Luverne Auto "would place upon the market in the near future a fire apparatus car, combining chemical, hose, hook and ladder and squad wagon all in one car." The following March, the automaker began building the first Luverne hearse for County Commissioner G. A. Hagedorn of Beaver Creek, who had secured "the business of the local undertakers and those of surrounding towns, so that he feels warranted in making the expenditure."

At least since October 1914, Luverne Auto had been supplying a special Luverne hearse chassis to the Northwestern Casket Company of Minneapolis and continued the practice while it built its own hearses. Funeral cars "will hereafter be a standard product of the Luverne factory," the company announced in June 1915. "There is a constantly increasing demand for such hearses."

Though it used a lower gear ratio, the Luverne hearse came on a stretched 150-

inch Big Brown Luverne chassis and used the Luverne's standard 60-horsepower 6-cylinder self-starting engine. Al Leicher said he designed the funeral car with "fixtures and fittings [of] genuine silver finish" and such ornate woodwork that "each one of these jobs that we turn out means several months' employment to Luverne workmen."

Making a wooden-body hearse was a logical move for Luverne Auto since "they were basically and primarily woodworkers, skilled woodworkers, and all this ornate column work and carving and so forth on this old hearse, they did that themselves," recalled Jim Leicher, Al's grandson. "They made several of the mahogany bars that the saloons in the area had."

The Big Brown Luverne's double running boards apparently inspired what the *Herald* termed an "ingeniously concealed" side box for undertakers' equipment. Most hearses had awkward-looking utility boxes bolted to their running boards. The book *American Funeral Cars & Ambulances Since 1900* reveals that the only other funeral car of the period with something close to a built-in side box was a 1914 White, and the

1915 Luverne hearse (see fig.2.27) was an improvement on that design.[17]

The Luverne hearse built for G. A. Hagedorn got its first job in September 1915, making a 45-mile round trip over hilly, rough roads on "one of those long distance funerals for which an automobile hearse is practically a necessity," according to the *Herald*. A flood of query letters from across the United States "goes to show that the design is meeting with marked favor," the *Herald* noted.

As with its hearse, the company used a 150-inch-wheelbase 6-cylinder Luverne chassis when, in the summer of 1915, it began building its first fire truck (see fig.2.28), painted vermillion red, striped in white, and lettered in gold. In November 1915, the Luverne Fire Department took delivery of a fire engine having a "large chemical tank" under the driver's seat and a steel body to carry 1,000 feet of hose. The siren was electric. As it looked like a Big Brown Luverne automobile from the cowl forward, the fire engine was "a very handsome vehicle," the *Herald* said.

The truck's $3,500 price was $1,500 cheaper than similar rigs and thus ideal for

2.27 The 1915 Luverne hearse built for G. A. Hagedorn of Beaver Creek, Minnesota. (JAC)

2.28 Luverne's first fire truck, 1915; the handwritten date in the lower right-hand corner of this photo is incorrect. (JL)

medium-size Northwestern cities, Luverne Auto claimed. "This Fire Truck is designed as a complete fire apparatus in itself, having the chemical outfit, water hose, ladders, pike poles, axes, lanterns, hand extinguishers, siren and gong signals, and all fire fighting equipment, with standing room for eight or ten men."

Testimonials Offer "Unanswerable Arguments"

Factory open houses, demonstrations, newspaper ads, posters, buttons, postcards, factory catalogs, and displays at Minneapolis–St. Paul auto shows all helped to sell Luverne cars. Testimonial ads perhaps gave the Luverne more exposure than any other sales tool. Luverne owners who found a variety of ingenious ways to punish their cars often wrote to the factory to report on the results. Al Leicher liked testimonials because "they are unanswerable arguments in proof of our claims that the Luverne cars, backed up by our methods of doing business, give a man more genuine satisfaction for his money than he can secure from any other Concern."

The Paxton-Eckman Chemical Company of South Omaha, Nebraska, ordered six 1909 Model D runabouts. The company, which sold "stock powder, stock dip and chicken powder," wanted a fleet of sturdy cars for its salesmen. "From our experience with the Ford, and from our investigation of the Luverne, we are satisfied that after three or four years' usage there will be considerable salvage in a Luverne car and that the Ford, if it should run that long, would not be fit for anything but the scrap pile," the buyers wrote.

A South Dakota customer sent in a photo of his four-year-old Luverne with a belt attached to one of its jacked-up rear wheels. "The photograph shows my 1910 model Luverne sawing wood, and it certainly makes a wood saw hum," the unnamed buyer wrote. "This car has traveled over

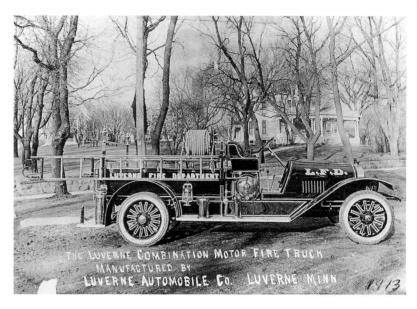

40,000 miles over all kinds of roads and fields, has forded rivers, bucked snow, worked roads pulling a king drag, worked as a road tractor hauling [a] wagon loaded with grain, and for switching freight cars loaded with 85,000 pounds of corn. Unlike most old cars, My Car is Not For Sale, for I use it every day."

The following summer, E. L. Morris of Fargo, North Dakota, visited the Luverne factory. Morris "had fully decided to buy a Packard car, but after a very thorough test of the Luverne fifty . . . he placed his order with the Luverne company for a $3200 car."

Luverne to the Rescue

The September 20, 1912, *Minneapolis Tribune* carried two front-page stories of Luverne automobiles coming to the rescue. A Minnesota State Fair 6-cylinder Luverne display car belonging to a staff member rushed Governor Adolph Eberhart from Anoka to a Twin Cities train station, arriving three minutes before Eberhart's train departed.

"The other item had reference to the street car riot in Superior [Wisconsin] where several street cars were demolished [by strikers] and over thirty people in-jured," the Luverne newspaper reported. "The mob had surrounded a street car and were stoning the car and crew, when the po-lice auto charged the mob and rescued the crew. While the auto was stopped the wind shield was smashed and the driver was struck on the head by a rock, and the strikers placed a plank through the spokes of the rear wheels, but . . . it made a quick get-a-way in spite of all obstacles. This car was a Luverne Forty which has been in con-stant service by the police department night and day, winter and summer[,] for over two years."[18]

W. B. "Ben" Austin and mechanic Red Thompson, both of Deadwood, South Da-kota, raced Austin's three-year-old Luverne Forty at the September 1913 Dawes County Fair in Chadron, Nebraska. "During the past six years I have driven several makes of high powered cars, but the Luverne is the best car I have ever driven, and I doubt if there is another car made that will take the punishment that my Luverne has, and be in as good shape as it is," Austin wrote to the factory.

The second entry in a five-mile timed race, Austin crashed his stripped Luverne car through a fence when the cracker box that he was using for a seat slipped, accord-ing to the *Deadwood Herald*. "When I drove up to the Judges stand after the accident the Judge asked if the car was damaged much and I said – 'The people that make the Luverne build them so that it takes more than hitting a plank fence at 60 miles per hour to put them out of business.' The peo-ple in the grand stand cheered in great shape," Austin wrote.[19]

"Up in the Air, Down Ker-Chunk"

This same storied racer "gained consider-able notoriety during the winter of 1911 on account of being used in an antelope hunt in the Black Hills," the automaker disclosed in an ad. A. L. Brown of Belle Fourche, South Dakota, and fellow notoriety seekers Lou Tunley, Glen Sebree, and Earl Wilson left Belle Fourche "at 10 below zero in a Luverne automobile, 40 h.p., for an ante-lope hunt about fifty miles north," accord-ing to the *Belle Fourche Post*. While patrolling the Two Top Butte area in their Luverne Forty the next morning, the men spotted a herd of 100 antelope. "But wild was no name for it; no sooner did we see them than they saw us, and then the fun started," said the unsigned article, apparently written by one of the hunters.

"Brown at the throttle opened the ma-chine wide and took down the ridge after the antelope. After a run of about three miles he overtakes them, runs in ahead, slams on the brakes and stops the machine and the firing commences. One killed, an-other wounded at a distance of about 300 yards, then after the wounded one in the auto, across the bad lands country, over ditches, draws, hills and snowbanks for about five miles," the *Post* article said.

"Next morning the wind was blowing a gale. Out again for more game, and after about thirty miles' run around the rough country and sagebrush, we spotted a small bunch of six being pursued by a man on horseback. The boys at once took in behind the antlers and after a short run something happened. Up in the air, down ker-chunk. The machine hit a ditch at about thirty miles per hour. The ditch being level full of snow, looked o.k., but nit – Wilson left the ma-chine about thirty feet behind, coming down into the snow. The boys spent some time getting him out and finding the guns. Upon looking the machine over we found everything O.K. except the front axel [*sic*], which was slightly sprung[,] and a broken wind-shield, through which Sebree took a header. Biggest wonder in the world that the machine was not all smashed to pieces. If it hadn't been a Luverne, no doubt it would have been. . . . Brown certainly has one of the best cars in the Hills, or this trip could not have been taken."[20]

On his three-week swing through Montana in late 1911, Ed Leicher stopped to inquire about the Luverne car owned by the Chico Hot Springs resort hotel, perched on the edge of Yellowstone Park. It was performing taxi service by meeting passengers at the Emigrant, Montana, railroad station to drive them the four miles to the hotel. "It is a constant climb every foot of the way and the car is usually loaded with from six to ten passengers and all their baggage," as the *Rock County Herald* recounted the tale. Ed Leicher met the Luverne car at Emigrant and, before revealing his identity, asked the driver about his car.

"When that driver began talking about that car one would have thought he was trying to make a sale right there," the *Herald* related. "He said they had tried several cars at that work and had decided to go back to horses, when their attention had been called to the Montana Special, and they bought one, and since then their troubles were over." The resort bought a second Luverne, according to a January 1915 ad. A booklet about the resort, "Photo History of Chico Lodge," pictures a 6-cylinder Luverne that crashed off a low wooden bridge spanning the Yellowstone River near Emigrant. (See fig.2.29.)[21]

The Trip That Rodman Made

Harry S. Rodman and family left Luverne in June 1914 for a grueling 11,000-mile trip to New York City and Washington, D.C., and then south along the coast to spend the winter in Florida. He drove a 6-cylinder Big Brown Luverne with suitcases lashed to the running boards.

"When we left New York City there was such a crowd around the car that we could hardly get away," Rodman wrote. "Everybody likes the car, and the fact that it is made in Minnesota and came all the distance makes it quite a curiosity." On the trip, "I drove over all kinds of roads that are made, and some that were not made. The most dangerous roads and the hardest on tires were in Virginia, between Alexandria and Fredericksburg, and the hardest pulling was in Florida, between Kissimmee and Bartow, which was very sandy. . . . . In the whole drive the only mishap was the slipping off of one front wheel from a small grade in southern Georgia, and it was very little trouble to get back. . . . My wife says it is some credit to the driver and the rest goes to the Luverne, for it certainly took us through in fine shape.

"In regard to the condition of the car: With a little 'currying' it would be ready to make the same trip over again. Have one valve that clicks a little, but it doesn't affect the running of the motor any. One of the air plugs for the starter leaked and I stopped at the Kellogg factory at Rochester, N.Y., and they put in a new one. . . . Aside from the plug, I made no adjustments nor spent a cent on the car on the entire trip," he said upon reaching Florida. When the family returned to Luverne in June 1915, Rodman reported that, aside from the air plug, the car had needed no repairs or adjustments during the entire trip.

Luverne Auto published a map "Showing The Trip That Rodman Made and the principal cities he went through," and otherwise capitalized on the long trip: "We often read of remarkable cross continent auto trips made by experts for advertising purposes, but this trip was a demonstration of what a

2.29 Owned by the resort hotel at Chico Hot Springs, Montana, this 1914 Big Brown Luverne ran off the approach to the Yellowstone River bridge near Emigrant, Montana; damage to the car appears minor. (DW)

plain every day citizen, accompanied by his entire family, can accomplish, providing he has a Big Brown Luverne. It is probably the most remarkably successful trip ever made under the same circumstances and conditions."

W. H. "Shorty" Rodman of Luverne, nine months old when the trip started, said a tent covering both sides of the Luverne car allowed the family to camp out along the road. Afterward, Luverne Auto modified the Rodman car with a newer body and a 90-horsepower Continental fire-truck engine. Harry Rodman drove the Big Brown Luverne into the 1930s. When Shorty Rodman returned from World War II duty, "I went out to see the old Luverne car. Dad had torn the body off of it and stripped it down and they made a corn sheller out of it. I had tears in my eyes, you can believe me."

"The Last I Saw of Him . . ."

On a long-distance trip in 1914, A. H. Osborne of Springfield, Missouri, fell in with a 6-cylinder Peerless and a third car for the trek from Tulsa, Oklahoma, south to Denison, Texas. "After a few hours of the worst going I ever saw, the driver of the third car weakened and suggested that we turn back," said Osborne, who concurred. "But the boys with the big $4000 Peerless gave us the laugh, and said: if you expected to have paved streets going, we should have stayed in the City. That made me sore; for having pulled the Big Brown Luverne over 7500 miles of all kinds of going without a single slip, I knew what I could do with it, and I declared myself right there. I says, old man, you hit right down the road; and if you can get out of my sight between here and Dennison [sic], I will, hereafter stay on paved streets. I followed him for about ten miles with the whistle in his ear at every jump until he pulled over and gave me the road. That was the last I saw of him until noon the following day."

In 1913 and 1914, the auto factory urged

Luverne visitors to the Minnesota State Fair to "wear a Luverne button. It will do us both good," since the buttons advertised the city as well as the cars. The company in 1908 began giving out black-and-white postcards of Luverne cars. Other postcards had similar photos "in natural colors." Local merchants sold the cards for the cost of the one-cent stamp affixed to each. "We are anxious to have these cards sent all over the U.S.," the company said.

In late 1911, Luverne Auto distributed a postcard map of Minnesota and other Northwestern states. The only city named was Luverne – in red ink. The factory issued a variety of full-line catalogs, specifications booklets, and instruction manuals. For 1912, at least, the factory issued what the *Duluth Herald* called "one of the most beautiful automobile posters" it had ever seen.

Starting with its first auto ads in 1908, the company used nearly two dozen slogans. Three saw sustained use: "Cars That Are Worth The Money," "The Best Investment in the Long Run," and "They Look Good, They Are Good, and They Stay Good." Here are a few of the many other slogans that saw some use:

• Strictly High Grade and Moderate in Price
• The Big Brown Luverne/Eventually You Will Want One (and the variation in fig. 2.30)
• Good for a Lifetime
• Cars With the Doubt Left Out
• The car that is always right, and on time
• They are Big and Long and Brown and Strong

2.30 The Luverne company's slogan for a brief time in 1915, here reproduced from a purple-and-white sticker.

2.31 Charcoal rubbing of the script identification tag used on Luverne cars.

"None Showed Prettier Lines"

Although the company never displayed cars there, Al Leicher attended the Chicago auto show from 1907 to 1913, when he declared that Northwestern motorists were traveling to the increasingly prominent Minneapolis show. He returned from the 1909 Chicago show lamenting that the cost of an auto display "is something enormous, and must be added to the price of these cars, although adding no actual value to them."

Later in the year, however, the automaker decided to make its debut on the show circuit at the 1910 Minneapolis event. The company had resisted such displays because of their "big expense . . . but it feels that in justice to all concerned it cannot longer delay in the matter." The Leichers frowned at the way other makers gave their show cars special painting and plating treatments. "We have found . . . it is advisable to exhibit a stock car just exactly as it is to be delivered to the customer."

The *St. Paul Pioneer Press* noted the popularity of the new Big Six displayed at the 1912 Minneapolis show: "The 'Pride of Minnesota' is the epithet applied to the Luverne cars, the first to be met with at the entrance of the Auditorium. The machines are attracting a great deal of attention among the visitors."

Reporting on that city's 1914 auto show, the *Minneapolis Sunday Tribune* said "the honor of selling the first car at the show was made by the Luverne company and was well sustained all week. Dozens of the people stopped and admired the Big Brown Luverne for minutes at a time. Almost without exception their first question was: 'Where is that car made?' Then swelling with pride the answer would come, 'At Luverne, Minnesota.' And incredulity was written all over the face of the questioner. The Luverne was the only Minnesota made car on the floor and none showed prettier lines, equipment nor got more exclamations of admiration," the *Tribune* said.[22] (Fig. 2.31

shows the prominent mention of Luverne, Minnesota, on the identification tag used on Luverne cars.)

Despite such showings, the annual late-summer Minnesota State Fair at St. Paul gave Luverne cars their best exposure, Al Leicher said. "As an advertising medium, and a means of getting in touch with customers, the Minnesota State Fair has no equal in our estimation," he wrote in a 1915 ad. The Luverne company was no longer complaining about the cost of displaying cars. Quite to the contrary, "We booked a few orders," Leicher said after the 1914 state fair show, "and did advertising that would probably cost a million dollars through any other medium."

Instead of traveling to the Twin City auto shows, many Rock County residents simply stopped in at the Luverne Auto factory beforehand. The automaker capitalized on such local interest by hosting its first pre-show factory open house in early February 1912. Bad weather disrupted the train schedule, but Al Leicher "recorded visitors from eighteen different towns outside of Rock county," the *Herald* reported.

"The cars were arranged in rows on the second floor of the factory, with carpeted aisles on both sides, while along the walls were exhibited parts and materials that are used in the cars, all of which proved very interesting to the visitors," according to the newspaper. "The machine shop, the paint shop and the finishing department, in each of which work was under way during the show, also proved very interesting to the visitors, giving a clear illustration of how the work is done and showing what a lot of careful work is necessary to produce a high-class motor car."

The company opened its new factory for July Fourth tours in 1908. "There is lots of room in the building, and it is generally cool, and visitors to the city are invited to call and make that their resting place, if they wish," the company added, undoubtedly with an eye cocked toward future business.

Street-Car Crash "Good Advertising"

The Luverne Auto company also used demonstration cars to make sales. Unlike modern auto dealers, however, the Leichers drove their demonstrator cars out to meet potential buyers. In autumn 1907, for instance, Ed and Al Leicher and two company investors piled in a Model A touring car for a weekday 16-hour 165-mile demonstration tour to eight towns surrounding Luverne. "The purpose of the trip was to advertise the cars and they therefore made quite lengthy stops at each place and gave interested parties rides about their respective towns and explained the merits of the machine," the *Herald* said.

Twenty-four autos took part in Luverne's 1908 July Fourth parade, "and it is a noteworthy fact that all but seven of the machines were manufactured by the Luverne Automobile company," the *Herald* reported. The owners of 24 Luverne cars organized a Sunday run to Madison, South Dakota, in spring 1912. That fall, a Luverne resident "witnessed a carnival parade at St. Paul, and in this parade he counted seven Luverne automobiles."

Even the company's practice of delivering cars by road instead of by rail constituted advertising. In April 1913, factory driver Walter Port drove a Luverne Fifty to a customer in St. Peter, Minnesota. He was accompanied for a distance by two older Fifties that had been left at the factory "to be equipped with the latest features," the *Her-*

ald said. "All three cars were exactly alike and Mr. Port states that they attracted a great deal of attention all along the route."

Ever one to seize the moment, Al Leicher "expects to secure a lot of good advertising out of the accident" in which a street car hit a Luverne Forty police car in Superior, Wisconsin, according to the June 9, 1911, *Rock County Herald*. Onlookers believed the car was a total loss, according to Leicher, who witnessed the accident. But he told the crowd that the Luverne car would be back on the street in 10 days; then he hustled back to Luverne "and began getting out the new parts that are needed, with the intention of fully carrying out his promise," the newspaper said.

Branching Out through Agents

An important ingredient in Luverne Auto's formula for success was direct sales to the customer. Such a policy allowed it to brag in a February 1909 ad: "Remember our cars are sold on their merits, and when you hear them recommended, you may be certain that it is not on account of any prospective commission."

But by summer 1909, the company's territory was expanding rapidly. Demand was strong for its new 4-cylinder Luverne Forty, and it was planning a July 1 delivery date for its first shaft-drive Luverne Thirty, a smaller 4-cylinder car. "It is our intention to make this car our Leader as it is of the popular size, style and price, and we have arranged to manufacture these cars in quantities, and sell them through the regular agency method at distant points," the company announced in early June 1909.

In August, Luverne Auto named an agent in nearby Hospers, Iowa, closing a deal "which involves a large order for Luverne cars, and gives to the purchasers the exclusive right in O'Brien and Sioux counties, Iowa." In November 1910 the company signed a Montana agent. Kenneth Kennicott, son of Luverne Auto's treasurer, returned to spend Christmas 1912 in Luverne, having spent "the last few months looking after the interests of the Luverne Automobile company" in Duluth.

The company "closed contracts with several agents" at the February 1911 Minneapolis auto show, the *Herald* reported. St. Paul auto dealer A. G. Bauer (see fig.2.32) eventually dropped his other car lines to handle only Luvernes and took charge of the Luverne display at the Minneapolis and St. Paul auto shows in February 1912. That month, the factory announced "Luverne cars will be advertised extensively all over the country; live agents are handling them in several large Cities."

The company was ambivalent about the use of agents, however. "While we have our agents to look after sales for us at distant points, our main business is and always will be with the individual buyer, most of whom come to the factory," a 1912 booklet asserts. And "if the local agent can not or will not give the buyer the attention required, we consider it our duty to do so."

The company opened its showrooms at 1210 Hennepin Avenue in Minneapolis in mid-March 1914 and at Sixth and Nebraska streets in Sioux City, Iowa, that August. The Rud Motor Car Company of Sioux Falls later became a Luverne agent. No record of all Luverne Auto agents is known to exist. The November 28, 1912, issue of *Automobile*, however, lists six new Luverne agencies – four in surrounding states and the other two in North Yakima, Washington, and Portland, Oregon. A 1914 state registration list shows two Luvernes registered in Oregon.[23]

"Known to the Ends of the Earth"

Luverne cars sold only in the Luverne vicinity for the first three seasons, but "the fourth year our cars began attracting considerable attention . . . and we were occasionally very much surprised to receive inquiries from distant points regarding our

The LUVERNE
High Grade Motor Cars

Model 760—Six Cylinder, Seven Passenger Car

For the Man who wants a Good Car and is willing to pay what it is actually worth

CATALOG OR DEMONSTRATION ON REQUEST

A. G. BAUER AUTO CO.

TELEPHONES: N. W. Dale 3556 / Tri-State 474 **1107 W. 7th St., ST. PAUL, MINN.**

2.32 A. G. Bauer, the Luverne's St. Paul dealer, advertised in the *Minnesota Auto Guide Book* of 1912. (MNHS)

cars, for up to this time the idea had never occurred to us to go after business outside our home locality," a 1912 company booklet said. "The demand for Luverne cars has gradually extended over the entire West from the Mississippi to the Pacific coast."

In July 1906, real-estate agent John Newell of Pierre, South Dakota, made a 300-mile trip to drive home a Luverne. In February 1907, Luverne Auto President A. D. LaDue sold his nearly two-year-old 20-horsepower touring car to a buyer in South Haven, Michigan, and then bought a new model.

"The demand for our cars from distant points is steadily increasing," a mid-1908 ad asserts. In the next few years buyers came from as far east as Sheffield, Illinois, and as far west as Belle Fourche, South Dakota, near the Montana border, to purchase Luverne cars. "They are in use all over the country, in Chicago, Minneapolis, St. Paul, Mitchell, and other cities, and wherever they are used, they are in the lead," the company claimed in 1910. Orders came from Portland, Oregon; North Yakima, Washington; and Los Angeles. A query from the Philippines in 1911 and England and Japan in 1915 prompted the company to exclaim:

"They Are Known to the Ends of the Earth."

Despite a few distant sales, however, the company's main sales territory was within a 450-mile-diameter circle that included parts of Iowa, Minnesota, Nebraska, North Dakota, and South Dakota, according to a January 1915 ad. "If you live in this territory, you will find it greatly to your interest to patronize your home Automobile Factory."

In early April 1913, the company delivered "a very handsome six cylinder, 60-horsepower Luverne touring car made for F. H. Joesting, the millionaire stove manufacturer of St. Paul," the *Herald* said. "It was of the regular equipment . . . with the exception that it was painted blue-black instead of brown."

Herbert S. Hadley of Kansas City, Missouri, former Missouri governor "and possibly the next president of the United States, will hereafter travel about his home city in a 'Luverne' automobile," reported the July 25, 1913, *Rock County Herald*. "When Governor Hadley was in Luverne last summer he became very favorably impressed with the cars" and while in the area a second time had arranged for Ed and Al Leicher to drive him to Worthington, Minnesota, for a chautauqua engagement. "On the trip Mr. Hadley was still further impressed with the beauty and character of the car, and before he reached Worthington he placed his order for a car."

The "ladies of the Catholic church" in Pipestone, Minnesota, bought a Luverne car for Father Mangan that "is now at the command of the reverend gentleman," the *Pipestone Leader* wrote in summer 1913. "It is a late model of the five passenger Luverne 40 and is a very classy looking vehicle."

How Many?

Missing records make it guesswork to arrive at production figures. Though certainly an incomplete count, ads and news items in the *Rock County Herald* from 1904 to 1917 tell of the sale of at least 273 Luverne autos to more than 195 buyers. Orders such as one from a company that bought "a number of model C two-seated runabouts" were too indefinite to include in the 273 total. There were at least 21 repeat buyers, the biggest being the Paxton-Eckman Chemical Company of South Omaha, Nebraska, which bought at least seven Luverne runabouts for its traveling salesmen.

Company President A. D. LaDue, eligible for an investors' discount, bought six Luvernes, starting with a 1904 side-entrance tonneau and ending with a brown 4-cylinder 1913 Luverne Thirty-Five roadster. Nearly as faithful was D. A. Mc-Cullough, president of the First National Bank at Howard, South Dakota, who owned five Luvernes from 1910 to 1916. Another South Dakota man, contractor J. L. White of Sioux Falls, who criss-crossed South Dakota and Minnesota installing municipal water systems, owned four Luvernes from 1905 to 1911. O. P. Huntington of Luverne also bought four Luvernes.

Ninety percent of the 273 cars went to buyers in four states: Minnesota (136 cars, 49.8%), South Dakota (54 cars, 19.8%), Montana (33 cars, 12.1%), and Iowa (23 cars, 8.4%). The remaining 27 cars, representing 9.9% of the 273-car total, were sold in Nebraska (7), Illinois (6), North Dakota (6), and Wisconsin (3). One car apiece went to California, Missouri, Oregon, Washington, and to an unidentified state. The *Rock County Herald* frequently neglected to date the cars, making it impossible to provide a year-by-year production breakdown. Ads and press accounts both reveal that the company sold only a few autos in 1916, when Luverne Auto's truck-related sales took off. The newspaper mentions the sale of just three 1917 Big Brown Luverne cars.

This newspaper-based total undoubtedly understates the total production, but only slightly, according to a September 17, 1950, *Minneapolis Tribune* story. "All told, we turned out about 300 automobiles," Al

Leicher told the newspaper. A November-December 1969 *Antique Automobile* feature story on Luvernes seems to confirm that number: "No exact records remain, but it is known that about 750 cars, trucks and hearses were built through 1916 and an educated guess would be that less than half of these were cars."

A 1911 county history book published in Luverne, however, said: "From the plant of the Luverne Automobile company are now turned out seventy-five cars annually." Six 75-car years from 1910 to 1915 would have produced 450 cars, in addition to the many Luvernes made before 1910. Such a production rate would lend credence to a *Rock County Star-Herald* retrospective piece that contends "they built in all about 600 of these cars, which were driven by some of the leading men in the northwest."

Could Luverne Auto's production have reached a thousand? "No, no, never a thousand. It's impossible," says Jim Leicher, Al Leicher's grandson, who puts the total at a few hundred, if that. "With a small crew of people working by hand on these things, there was no volume to it."

Sold for Scrap

After auto production ceased, the Leichers stored some Luverne cars and early trucks in the dirt-floor basement of a building they owned west of the factory. "As a kid I used to spend hours and hours down there, playing in those old cars," Jim Leicher recalls. Al's Big Brown Luverne was stored there, as was his brother's Luverne roadster, nicknamed the "Chummy." Other cars filled the basement, such as brass-shell Model T Fords and "a Pierce-Arrow with the big streamlined headlights," Jim Leicher said. "In 1936, during the height of the Depression, they had to let loose of the building. They sold the cars to the junk heap and I still have a vivid memory of the junk man pulling those cars out, the old Luvernes and so forth, and with a torch cutting them right

in two, right out in front, and hauling them off. They sold them for scrap metal and in '36 that's all they were worth. I still have dreams about it once in awhile."

Surviving Luvernes include a 1909 touring car owned by a St. Paul man, a 1915 Big Brown Luverne touring car on display at Kelsey's Antique Cars in Camdenton, Missouri (see fig. 2.33), and at least three 2-cylinder Luverne cars, privately owned.

"Cars for Every Requirement"

Luverne Auto began its move toward making commercial vehicles in a small way as early as March 1912, when a St. Paul man ordered a 40-horsepower truck. The April 15, 1912, *Commercial Car Journal* described a new Luverne one-ton truck that "will be equipped with a 40 horse-power engine and a heavy duty clutch and transmission." A year later, local merchant J. W. Gerber, a Luverne Auto investor, had "an attachment put onto the rear part of his Luverne touring car which makes it adaptable for delivery work and at the same time does not impair its usefulness as a touring car." The device was probably a product of the Luverne factory since a factory photo collage shows several touring cars equipped with two-wheeled attachments that could be lowered to haul extra loads.

2.33 Kelsey's Antique Cars of Camdenton, Missouri, is displaying this seven-passenger 1915 Big Brown Luverne.

In June 1913, the automaker shipped a 35-horsepower delivery car chassis to Mich & Heck Carriage and Wagon Company of St. Paul, which planned to equip it with "any style of body to suit the customer's requirements." The June 27, 1913, *Herald* also documented a number of later sales. "The opening up of this business will mean that . . . Luverne business cars as well as Luverne pleasure cars will be found on the streets of many of the leading cities of the Northwest," it said.

By autumn 1915, the company was advertising "Minnesota Made Motorcars To Meet Every Requirement." Those "motorcars" included Luverne autos, fire trucks, hearses, "motor service trucks" – early tow trucks, by the sound of it – and chassis for commercial cars.

In 1916, the company began making and selling a "Luverne Truckgear" – essentially the back half of a truck chassis, including a driveshaft, rear axle, springs, and wheels. "Any old car combined with a Luverne Truckgear makes a practical two-ton farm truck," the company advertised. Truckgears began selling across the United States. A Milwaukee firm placed a single order for 100 Luverne Truckgears in 1917, a year that saw Luverne fire trucks sell to fire departments as far away as Poughkeepsie, New York; Mechanicsburg, Pennsylvania; and Baird, Texas. The Luverne company's future was in trucks, not cars.

After switching from automobile to truck production, Ed and Al Leicher on July 23, 1919, filed incorporation documents to create the Luverne Motor Truck Company and in 1922 formed the Luverne Fire Apparatus Company. Al Leicher's son, Robert, and Ed Leicher's son, Larry, became partners in the business, from which Ed and Al Leicher retired in 1959. The company was in family hands until purchased by the A. R. Wood Manufacturing Company in the early 1970s. Luverne Truck Equipment Company, which manufactures "Luverne" bumpers and other after-market items for trucks and vans, bought the company in 1985. Luverne Fire Apparatus was relocated across the border in nearby Brandon, South Dakota.

"The Best I Ever Owned"

The handmade techniques that created the Big Brown Luverne were becoming outdated, and modern assembly methods were out of reach for the small company, Ed and Al Leicher recalled. "'We couldn't see such things as assembly lines and mass production,' the brothers declared, 'even though we had heard there were manufacturers contemplating such a move,'" according to a March 15, 1953, *St. Paul Pioneer Press* article. "To make closed bodies we would have needed a lot of new machinery," Al Leicher said. "We would have needed more skilled workmen and, most of all, almost unlimited financial backing. We just couldn't make the grade."

Not everyone heard the news, however, and many Luverne cars far outlived the Luverne Automobile Company, as the 1953 *St. Paul Pioneer Press* story reveals. "There used to be a saying, 'once a Luverne owner always a Luverne owner,' and a recent letter received by the Leicher brothers attests the affection owners had for the Minnesota car. The letter, from a dude ranch owner in Arizona, included an order for a new car. He wrote, 'My old one has finally broken down. Although I bought it second hand it's the best I ever owned. Please ship me a new car.' He was 37 years late."

Patriot of Nebraska
Every Farmer Needs One

3

A farmer's son with a diverse background of selling hog insurance, picture frames, wallpaper paste, animal feed, and coal, A. G. Hebb had a sense of what would sell and what would not. In 1913, Hebb acted upon his sense that selling feed for horses had, at best, a mediocre future. He began selling Ford cars and Chase trucks.

Viewed from today's perspective, the move seems obvious, even belated. Some contemporaries, however, would have found fault with Hebb's reasoning. After all, despite the rise of the automobile, most businesses began the second decade of the 1900s relying on horse-drawn wagons for local deliveries and railroads for long-distance shipments. Farmers may have owned automobiles, but they plowed with horses. The truck and tractor, as they are known today, were still new ideas.

Chevrolet in 1913, for instance, was five years away from introducing its first truck. Ford flirted with trucks earlier, offering a lightweight "delivery car" in 1905 and a similar vehicle in 1912 and early 1913. Still, the company didn't make trucks a regular part of its lineup until 1917, though many Ford owners – a innovative lot – made their own truck bodies to fit the Model T chassis.

Noting that trend, Hebb (see fig. 3.1) started a compatible sideline business: building wooden delivery bodies for the increasing number of buyers who wanted a new Ford for making business deliveries. Soon Hebb had more carpenters on his payroll than he had Ford mechanics, office workers, and salesmen. And the demand for the Hebb truck bodies came not just from Ford buyers. It seemed everyone else wanted delivery bodies, as well as the special-order bus, hearse, and ambulance bodies that the big automakers were slow to supply.

3.1 A. G. Hebb, 1919. (TS)

Ahead of the annual wheat and corn harvest, Hebb filled warehouses from Texas to Canada with special grain bodies for trucks. Farmers responded cheerfully, snapping up the inventories. Some early independent truck makers were topping off their vehicles with Hebb-built bodies. His success with farmers in a dirt-road America that was still more rural than urban prompted Hebb to design a truck for the ripening farm market. His advantage, of course, was that he could build his own bodies. In addition, few automakers were offering farmers a truck designed just for their needs.

As the country's World War I transportation demands overloaded the railroads and speeded both the acceptance and development of the motor truck, 1917 looked like a good year to get into the truck business. Thus was born Hebb Motors Company, the maker of Patriot trucks, buses, and fire engines. It was reincorporated as Patriot Motors Company in 1920 – employing as many as 500 people – was reincarnated in 1921 as Patriot Manufacturing, and by World War II evolved into Patriot Body Company.

Making similar calculations after the war, Hebb seized the opportunity – along with hundreds of cheap government-owned surplus biplanes – to pioneer a new way to move people and products: the commercial airplane.

In the Beginning

Born on July 26, 1880, in Vermont, Arthur Grainger Hebb at age five moved with his family to Bloomington, Nebraska, a town of 524 people in south-central Nebraska near the Kansas border. In 1892, young Arthur's father, Cresser "Crit" Hebb, a farmer, moved the family northeast to Aurora, a town of more than 1,200 people about 70 miles west of Lincoln. The oldest of four children, Arthur Hebb attended rural Aurora schools and spent his early years on the farm, taking up farming by 1900. He later became a district agent in Aurora for the Lincoln Insurance Company, selling insurance to protect hog farmers against cholera losses.

"He did well for awhile," recalled his son, Grainger Hebb, "until there was a terrible epidemic of it. This caused the failure of several hog-insurance companies" and sent A. G. Hebb to Lincoln to seek a job in the city that was both capital of the state and second in size only to Omaha.

There, Hebb met Daisy Roberta Jones, the daughter of a Lincoln farmer, and they married in January 1901. The two opened up a picture-framing business in a small downtown Lincoln shop. In 1903, A. G. Hebb and the future superintendent of Hebb's truck factory, King W. Gillespie, teamed up to open Lincoln Corn Food Company in downtown Lincoln. The enterprise continued for about one year under that name. A carpenter and homebuilder, Gillespie by 1904 had moved on into that line of work.

From about 1904 to 1913, A. G. and Daisy Hebb – along with Hebb's father, Cresser, and other Hebb family members – operated Lincoln Steam Paste Company and Lincoln Feed and Fuel Company at 315 S. 9th Street. The companies that A. G. Hebb ran made steam paste flour – a wallpaper glue – in 55-gallon drums, and also sold hay, grain, and coal. Hebb built up the businesses until he had 2,200 active accounts.[1]

In time, Hebb would lead a company that built a 4½-acre truck-manufacturing plant. During his early years in the hay and feed business, however, his livelihood depended on – and he got daily experience in working with – the mode of transportation that motor trucks would replace: the horse.

A Change in Business

In 1912, Hebb "detected a significant change in the business," according to an article April 8, 1917, in the *Sunday State Journal* of Lincoln. "The growth of the pleasure motor car had cut down the sale of feed to private barns to an amazing extent," the newspaper said. "Noticing the quickness and comparative economy of the light delivery car over the old-fashioned horse delivery[,] he made up his mind that as great changes would take place in the delivery business as had taken place in pleasure riding," the article said.

According to the *Motorist* magazine, based in Omaha, Hebb sold the Lincoln Steam Paste and Lincoln Feed and Fuel companies against the advice of his friends: "His friends were amazed when he told them he was going to sell his feed, grain and coal business and enter the automobile field. 'The automobile is a fad,' his friends cautioned him, 'and will pass away in a few years, after the novelty has worn off, while the horse is here to stay.'"

But "nobody replaces a horse with another animal," Hebb told the *Sunday State Journal*. "The argument is now so completely on the side of the automobile delivery vehicle that the debate is ended. The cost of equipping and maintaining a horse delivery and a motor delivery is practically the same, but on account of the superior speed of the motor delivery the amount of service given is two or three times as much. Therefore there is no possible chance that the horse will remain in the business. He cannot come back," Hebb said.[2]

Hebb sold his feed and fuel business to form the A. G. Hebb Auto Company on April 1, 1913, taking over the E. L. Pratt Automobile Company's Ford agency. Situated along the east edge of downtown along O Street, Lincoln's main commercial avenue, the new Ford agency's territory included Lincoln and Lancaster County, as well as parts of three adjacent rural counties.

By late spring 1913, Hebb announced that in addition to his Ford cars he would also sell Chase trucks, made in Syracuse, New York, from about 1907 to 1917 in ¾-ton and heavier models. Hebb advertised "the wonderfully simple, powerful and economical" 3-cylinder, 2-cycle, air-cooled engine of 20 horsepower in the solid-tired Chase truck:

Just a personal word in regard to Chase Trucks. I have had a number of years experience in the coal and feed business and during the last three or four years used motor trucks. It is my candid opinion that the Chase, because of its extreme simplicity, doing away with water jacket, superfluous valves, cam shafts, oilers and a hundred or more of other unnecessary parts – the sensible tires adapted to all roads and weathers – is the best motor truck on the market today. We are always pleased to show business men the Chase and prove to them that it pays to use the motor truck for deliveries.[3]

By early 1914, Chase trucks – which by then had engines supplied by Continental Motors – cost $1,000 for the 1½-ton model and $3,000 for the 3-ton model. The heavier truck used a transmission made by Brown-Lipe, a company that would later supply parts for the Patriot truck.

Ford Business Accelerates

About the same time that he bought the Ford agency, Hebb applied to buy more life insurance and was required to see a doctor for a routine physical examination. The family received what son Grainger Hebb called "a terrible shock" in learning that he had diabetes – an untreatable disease in the days before insulin injections. Hebb's request for more life insurance was denied. "Dieting was the only way to help control it and special food with no sugar and little starch made up the things he could eat. He . . . was able to fight it for about 10 years," Grainger said.

On January 1, 1916, Hebb moved the Ford agency to a newly constructed 80-by-150-foot two-story brick building in the north downtown business district at 12th and Q streets. There, the A. G. Hebb Auto Company had 24,000 square feet of working space on two floors – a so-called daylight building lighted primarily through large multi-pane windows. Joining Hebb at about this time was a partner, Frederick Ray Hussong.

Fifty people – including about 20 salesmen – worked in the new building, which housed the Ford dealer's offices, salesrooms, garage, repair shop, and paint shop. Hebb's local advertising singled out "expert tire service" as a specialty, but the company also sold a wide variety of general auto accessories.

The demand for more Fords prompted Hebb to travel to the Highland Park, Michigan, Ford plant in mid-September 1915 "and attempt to secure more cars for his territory," a newspaper reported. Hebb sold some 2,000 Fords from April 1913 to April 1917, according to one press account. To appeal to wealthier buyers, Hebb in 1916 began selling the higher-priced Mitchell car, made in Racine, Wisconsin, from 1903 to 1923. A 1916 Ford, built on the world's first moving automobile assembly line, cost as little as $390 for a two-door runabout. The 1916 Mitchell – with its 22 coats of paint, French-finished upholstery, and power tire pump – cost from $1,325 for a roadster to $2,650 for a limousine, according to one of Hebb's November 1916 Lincoln newspaper ads.

Hebb Buys, Then Builds Bodies

Since about one-fifth of the Fords he was selling were used for delivery vehicles and the demand was increasing, Hebb began buying delivery bodies from a Pennsylvania factory that went unnamed in local press accounts. From 1913 to 1917, as Ford took a break from making trucks, Ford agencies and oftentimes buyers had to supply their own truck bodies to fit on Ford car frames. As 1915 began, there were only four Ford delivery cars in Lincoln, Hebb told the April 8, 1917, *Sunday State Journal*. By mid-1917, the number approached 400.

High shipping costs and delays in receiving custom bodies from Pennsylvania prompted Hebb in 1915 to begin building his own delivery bodies. Though Hebb had formed the A. G. Hebb Auto Company in

3.2 E. C. Hammond, 1916. (TS)

3.3 Artist's drawing of the A. G. Hebb Auto Company's body-building plant at 10th and Vine streets in Lincoln. (NSHS)

1913, he incorporated on February 2, 1916, with an authorized capital of $200,000. Its officers were Elmer C. Hammond (see fig.3.2), a former banker, vice president; F. R. Hussong, co-owner of the Ford business, secretary and treasurer; and King W. Gillespie, a carpenter and Hebb's business partner from the Lincoln Corn Food Company days of 1903, manager of the new body factory.

In the fall of 1915, Hebb entered the business of building delivery bodies by buying "at an advantageous figure" from Frank E. Folts the shop equipment of Folts Furniture Factory. Along with the deal came the carpenters who made the furniture, and Gillespie, who was supervisor of the Folts factory.

"The men formerly engaged in furniture making turned their attention to the making of bodies without loss of time or efficiency," a Lincoln newspaper said. "The buying connections of the furniture people in the hard wood fields of the south enabled the new company to secure fine material at a proper cost. . . . When the work of turning out delivery bodies began eighteen months ago three men were given regular employment. Now the number has reached seventy-five and there seems to be no limit to the expansion of the business."[4]

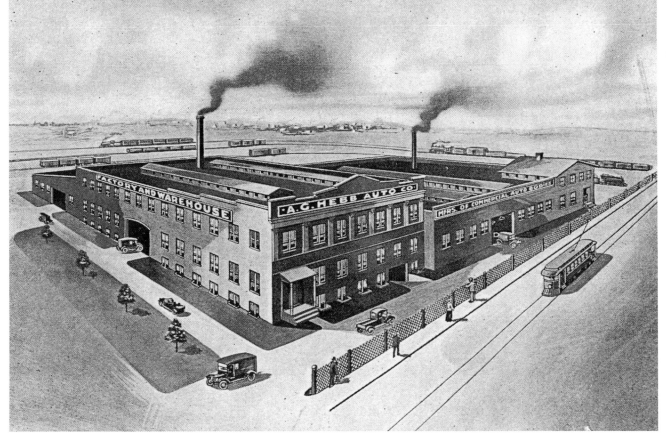

Body Business Booms

In December 1916, the A. G. Hebb Auto Company began making commercial bodies in "a fine new building erected for one of the transfer companies on North Tenth street," a newspaper said. (See fig.3.3.) To supplement this new location at 10th and Vine streets, the company two months later began making ambulance, bus, and hearse bodies in the former Harrison Cabinet & Mill Work Company building at 26th and X streets. For a time, Hebb operated these two outlets along with the Ford agency.

At the 10th and Vine facility, railcars loaded with wood were rolled directly into kilns, where the wood was dried. The dried wood was first cut into stock sizes for the various standard bodies Hebb offered. The pieces then went to a separate room where the bodies were assembled before being painted and polished.

"While the company makes a number of regular stock designs, a considerable part of its business consists of making special bodies to meet individual requirements. The average delivery vehicle is an ordinary Ford chassis with a light top either enclosed with panel sides or with curtains. The most popular form has the panel top. It makes a vehicle enclosed against the weather and also has the advantage of carrying the name of the firm in printed signs along the sides," according to a press account.[5]

A "large motor truck distributing concern in Seattle" in May 1918 placed a $207,000 order for "one type of auto body for truck purposes which the Hebb company has been most successful in manufacturing." The May 30, 1918, *Havelock Post* didn't name the body style, but it was likely Hebb's standard panel delivery body.

Hebb "was a very able man" in his sales strategy, recalled F. Pace Woods, Sr., whose father and uncle took over the manufacture of Patriot trucks in 1924. Woods said Hebb would begin shipping bodies to a Texas warehouse near the end of each year. He

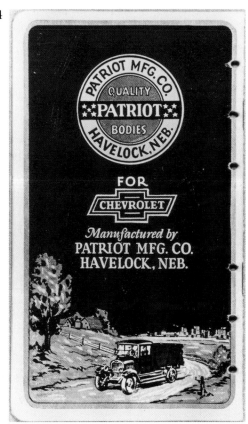

had 11 other warehouses, situated from Texas to Canada, and would stock each with one month's supply of bodies ahead of the harvest season, Woods said. Thus, Hebb would have a ready supply of merchandise from which to make sales of farm bodies as the corn and wheat harvest progressed from Texas northward to the Canadian border, Woods said.[6]

Hebb's body department also made wooden bodies for the Douglas Truck Manufacturing Company of Omaha, which made the Douglas truck (1917–1935), and sold bodies to other companies. After its revival in 1921 as Patriot Manufacturing Company, the factory made bodies for Chevrolet trucks.[7] (See fig.3.4 and 3.5.)

Patriot Born in Detroit

The strong demand for Ford cars in the late teens, noted a Lincoln newspaper article

about Hebb, was preventing Ford from moving ahead with its announced plans to build a 1-ton truck. That suggested a marketplace void that Hebb would seek to fill when, in 1917, he set up what the *Havelock Post* called a "small factory" in Detroit and hired engineers to design and test what would become the Patriot truck. "Mr. Hebb believes that the future of the automobile business will be in commercial cars to a larger extent than in pleasure cars," the *Lincoln Sunday Star* added.

"For a number of months past the company has been maintaining a small factory at Detroit, Mich., where a staff of competent engineers has been making blue prints, testing and assembling different units, and now, after a thoro test and investigation, have completed a line of motor trucks which will unquestionably be as fine and substantial a truck as there is produced in the United States," said the *Havelock Post* in early 1918.[8] The *Lincoln Daily Star* and *Lincoln Trade Review* agreed that the Michigan factory was a year old, with the *Star* saying Hebb had been operating in Detroit "since early in 1917."

"War conditions have pushed into the lime light the necessity for the fastest transportation facilities and an industry of this kind, which, although certain to come, has

3.4 Cover of the Patriot body section of *Chevrolet Sales Data: A Handbook of Sales Information for Chevrolet Salesmen*, 1925.

3.5 A Patriot "Combination Grain and Stock Body" for a Chevrolet truck, as illustrated in *Chevrolet Sales Data: A Handbook of Sales Information for Chevrolet Salesmen*, 1925.

been pushed ahead until the next year or two will see the adoption of the truck in all lines of mercantile and farming work," predicted the *Lincoln Trade Review*.

"The entire development work in the Patriot truck has been carefully carried out under the able engineering management of F. A. Kateley of New York with the cooperation of a corps of capable and well known engineers made up of such men as A. A. Gloetsner of the Covert gear company, formerly consulting engineer and production-workers manager of the Bour-Davis company and assistant engineer of the Chalmers company," the *Lincoln Daily Star* said. Hebb "kept in constant personal touch with developments in the Detroit plant, keeping foremost at all times the special truck needs of the western farmer."[9]

The company "has been manufacturing auto truck bodies for all makes of trucks and supplying a large trade now extending over eleven Western states," Hebb Motors said in announcing its truck-making plans. "This has resulted in the securing of an invaluable experience as to the types and kinds of trucks most needed and with this knowledge in possession, the services of a competent corps of mechanical engineers were secured last year to design a line of motor trucks to meet the greatest demand as we view it."[10]

A. G. Hebb filed incorporation papers January 10, 1918, to create Hebb Motors Company, capitalized at $1 million, later increased to $2.5 million. In ads announcing the new truck, Hebb Motors, which began advertising its Patriot trucks just a few weeks into 1918, said it would make its first truck deliveries about April 1.

New Truck a "True Patriot"

Naming the truck "Patriot" was appropriate, since America was fighting in the Great War. Not even the most decorated general could pull rank on a Patriot truck, whose logo contained two groupings of five stars.

"Be a Patriot, Buy a Patriot, Boost the Patriot," read the copy of an early Hebb Motors ad. "The Patriot Farm Truck is a true Patriot. It will serve the country by serving the farmer, giving him cheap, quick, certain transportation at all times of the year."

The U.S. government in 1917 issued a list of standards for trucks that would see wartime service. The first such "Liberty" trucks were completed and ready for testing in October 1917, in plenty of time for A. G. Hebb to study the government standards and modify his trucks accordingly. Hebb Motors advertised its trucks as being built to "the best standards of practice . . . especially those endorsed by our government."

"His real goal, of course, was to put trucks on the road, to haul freight," said Charles William Jones, Hebb's nephew. "He said it's a more convenient method than shipping by rail. . . . He was promoting the efficiency of being able to deliver direct to the door: stop all of this extra handling. You see, you have to load a freight car to start with, then you transport it, then you have to unload it and then [find] some other means of delivery, either a horse dray or a truck."[11]

Patriot Trucks "Will Help Win the War"

Hebb Motors' advertising suggested that its main sales territory would be "Nebraska and the west" or "the states west of the Missouri River." The company made a large number of sales in Oklahoma, Texas, California, and Washington, but also set up Patriot dealerships as far east as Connecticut and Florida.

One of the company's earliest truck ads was headlined "Patriot Trucks Will Help Win the War." The ad, in a Lincoln newspaper, quoted a member of the War Industries Board in Washington, D.C., who said: "The Motor Truck will win the war, because it will solve the almost overwhelming problem of transportation." Building Patriot trucks thus represented "an effort on the part of Lincoln business men to meet this urgent need and supply the tremendous demand developing all over the country for motor trucks," Hebb Motors said.

In a later ad, the company elaborated by saying "ours is not a hastily conceived proposition arising only from patriotic impulses, but is a logical outcome of several years of very successful manufacturing by men thoroughly experienced in the business. It is this most fortunate condition that is enabling us to render at this time a national service in the natural expansion of our chosen business." Another ad asserted that "the great demand for trucks, by our government, as well as every line of business, means that there MUST be a tremendous increase in the output."[12]

Officers and Gentlemen

A Hebb Motors' promotional sheet describes the company's namesake as "an ideal executive, a man of vision, whose sole aim and ambition is to make the company the largest and strongest in the great West. His heavy investment in the stock of the Company guarantees his fidelity and responsibility."

As he moved into his new truck-making venture in the second half of 1917, Hebb made a friendly break with F. R. Hussong, who continued to run the Ford agency. There were other changes in personnel.

Loyd A. Winship, who took charge of finances for the A. G. Hebb Auto Company in 1917, became secretary-treasurer of Hebb Motors. A lawyer, Winship also had a banking, real estate, and investment background. In addition, Winship became treasurer of Standard Securities Corporation, the stock agent for Hebb Motors and its successor, Patriot Motors.

Like Winship, Hebb Motors' Vice President Elmer C. Hammond had been a Nebraska banker. He later doubled as president of Standard Securities.

K. W. Gillespie, manager of the A. G.

Hebb Auto Company commercial body department, became superintendent of the new truck-manufacturing plant.

Laurence F. Seaton (see fig.3.6), chief engineer and production manager, had been an engineering teacher at the University of Nebraska. "For the past five years Professor Seaton was in charge of automobile and tractor instruction at the university, and during that time conducted hundreds of tractor and truck tests, many of which tended to bring about radical changes in the construction of these machines, in the line of improvements," the *Havelock Post* said. Seaton's own research included "a careful study of most all truck factories in the United States together with their products," according to the company's promotional piece.

"Three summers while in university work he spent in the east studying manufacturing methods as applied to the automobile industry," the *Havelock Post* reported. Seaton began work for Hebb Motors late in the summer of 1919, filling a post held earlier by Frank A. Kateley of New York, whom Hebb credits as the engineer primarily responsible for the Patriot truck.

John Fulton, assistant engineer and draftsman for Hebb Motors, helped create

3.6 L. F. Seaton, 1939. (UNA)

3.7 Cartoon from the July 1920 *Patriot Progress* magazine. (NSHS)

3.8 June 1920 cover of *Patriot Progress* Magazine. (NSHS)

the Stone tractor during the six years he worked as a designer and draftsman in the tractor division of the Electric Wheel Company of Quincy, Illinois.[13]

Home on the Range, Farm, Battlefield

During 1918 and early 1919, Hebb Motors referred to itself as the manufacturer of "Patriot Farm Trucks," often with the word "farm" set in a different type style. "Masters bad roads. Saves high-priced horses. Every farmer with 160 acres or more needs one," says a Patriot ad in the November 7, 1918, *Motor Age* magazine. "Body is built like a farm wagon body, except better." Its early ads used the slogan "Built for Country Roads, Built for Country Loads." By 1920, that had evolved into "Made in the West, Built for the World." The back cover of the July 1920 *Patriot Progress*, the company's pocket-sized magazine for dealers and others (see fig.3.7 and 3.8), introduced what was apparently another slogan: "Properly Built, Properly Priced."

America had a great many farmers. The 1920 U.S. census classified 48.6 percent of the population as rural. The 6.49 million farms of 1920 were nearly three times the 2.18 million farms of 1987. "But the farmers have not bought them [trucks] to any great extent," the company noted in an April 1918 ad.

"Why? The reason is that there has never been a real Farm Motor Truck on the market. Those that have been sold have been built for the paved street of the cities – not

the soft roads and fields of the country. Or – They have been mere cheap unit affairs – to combine with wornout, low-priced, low-powered cars – forming a makeshift truck that never was expected to deliver real farm service." In addition, the company noted in another ad, "The city demand so far has easily kept pace with motor truck production, and the war demand of the past year or two has prevented the established makers from even considering a special farm truck."[14]

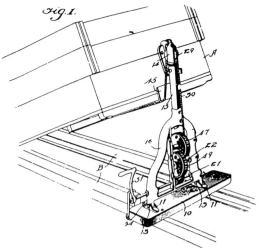

Patriot trucks were also popular in the oil fields of Oklahoma and Texas. "The business grew fast. The first world war was on, and an order for 50 trucks was received from the government. Farmers were anxious for trucks, too, as well as delivery companies," said Hebb's son, Grainger. The 1½-ton Lincoln model Patriot "seems to be the popular size in this immediate neighborhood, northern Kansas, Iowa, Nebraska and the Dakotas, according to company reports, while the east, south and extreme western states seem to favor the 'Washington Model,' two and one-half ton," said the *Lincoln Sunday Star* of September 1, 1918. The government's order of 50 trucks, apparently placed late in World War I, was canceled when the fighting ended, said Grainger Hebb. The family that donated a Patriot truck to the North Platte Valley Museum in Gering, Nebraska, claims it "was originally built by Hebb Motors in Lincoln to be used as a World War I Army truck" and was sold as surplus afterward.[15]

It is unclear how many Patriot trucks were delivered for wartime service. But Hebb Motors indirectly helped build "thousands" of truck bodies for the U.S. Army, press accounts reveal. "They [Hebb Motors] have already promised the government to furnish the material for manufacturing bodies and hoists and assembling trucks for teaching the boys who will be in training for the army at the university [of Nebraska] this summer," said a local newspaper article in May 1918.

L. F. Seaton, who became Hebb Motors' chief engineer in 1919, "was instrumental in securing the army mechanical laboratories for the university during the war where more than 400 soldiers received special training. Under his direction these student soldiers put out thousands of commercial truck bodies and hoists on a production basis," the *Havelock Post* said. These trucks were apparently built to include the special hand hoist patented by Hebb Motors.[16]

A Truck That Dumps

Hebb Motors found a strong selling point in what it called its No. 1055 Hebb farm body equipped with the Patriot Hand Hoist. Drivers using the geared hoist could crank up the front of the box to quickly dump its cargo. (See fig. 3.9.) "You have got the right idea about dumping the load," an unnamed Iowa farmer said in one late 1918 Hebb Motors testimonial ad. "It is what I have been looking for. The farmer wants a truck that he can dump at the country elevators."

King W. Gillespie, plant superintendent, was granted Patent No. 1,277,907 for the hoist on September 3, 1918. Hebb Motors first called it the King Hand Hoist but soon settled on the name Patriot Hand Hoist.

"The Hebb Farm Body . . . is the only successful standardized farm body ever put on the market, and it has become very popular among western truck dealers," the company advertised.[17]

"In the manufacturing and marketing of this body the maker has kept in mind the fact that usually the farmer is not willing to pay the price required to purchase the engine-driven hoist, since it is not in constant use as would be the case with the contractor," the July 1918 *Automobile Trade Journal* reported. The hoist, constructed of pure gray iron, lifted 7,600 pounds in tests and was guaranteed to hold 4,000 pounds, the journal said. "The distinguishing feature of it is the fact that it is hinged at the base, per-

3.9 Patriot Hand Hoist, patented in 1918.

3.10 Patriot factory, 1919. (*A Little Journey*, LV)

mitting it to tilt backward as the body is raised, thus insuring a straight pull on the cable at all times. The space required between body and cab is but 10 inches."

"The Patriot Farm Truck is the first motor truck built for farm work," the company said in a mid-1918 ad. "It will bring better markets within reach, for the farmer with a Patriot Truck can easily drive his loads to a market 50 or 100 miles distant. It will increase the value of his farm, for the value of a farm depends largely upon its distance from a good market, and distance is measured today in time, not in miles."[18]

Growing Pains: "A Modern Daylight Factory"

Between the former planing mill and the former warehouse, the company had a cramped 50,000 square feet of working space, company officials complained. And because the buildings were originally put up for other uses, "it was impossible to attain the efficiency that is possible in our new building," said an early 1920 promotional piece lauding the new Patriot truck factory.

Hebb Motors in early 1918 began constructing a "modern daylight factory," so called because of windows that contained – according to various press accounts – from 10,000 to 14,000 panes of glass. (See fig. 3.10.) The two-story reinforced concrete building with an exterior brick veneer mea-

sured 420 feet by 240 feet, producing a work area of about 180,000 square feet. The truck factory thus covered the equivalent of nearly 4½ acres or 3¼ football fields. For its boilers and lumber-drying kilns, Hebb Motors constructed on the site an 80-by-62-foot concrete building with a 155-foot-tall concrete smokestack. It also built a 20-by-160-foot wood-frame lumber shed.[19]

Costing "upward of half a million dollars to build," the new factory was "the largest truck and body plant west of the Mississippi River," the company claimed. Though it eventually set up dealers on both coasts, one early ad predicted that, despite the higher production a new factory would allow, Hebb Motors "has reason to expect that its entire output will be taken readily by the farmers of the states west of the Missouri River."

The U-shaped factory had an opening at its west end to allow a Burlington Railroad switch line to run into a narrow open area. The truck assembly line was on the building's second floor, said Hebb's son, Grainger.

"There were three large elevators, one located south of the base of the U, and the other two at each end of the U. The machine shop and assembly area was located on the south side main floor. Above this area was the paint shop and storage area for some parts. On the north lower end was the body building shop which was run by King Gillespie," Grainger wrote.

The new plant had at least 78 pieces of power equipment or large items other than hand tools. An early 1920 machinery and tool inventory listed three air compressors, a 20-ton press, an 8-foot-long metal-bending brake, a press for bending fenders, a Singer sewing machine for upholstery work, and a variety of lathes, drills, power saws, cutters, grinders, and sanders.[20]

The railroad switch track enabled freight cars to pull up to the plant to disgorge parts or load up finished trucks. Though Hebb's trucks were presumably taking business away from the railroads and he frequently advertised the advantages trucks had over the railroads, he nonetheless shipped many trucks by rail to his far-flung dealers.

"Congested railroad conditions have made necessary the use of the motor truck in hauls of many miles distance," the company said in a June 22, 1918, *Lincoln Trade Review* ad. "Entered into at first with more or less an experimental nature, but now not only quicker deliveries, but even less expensive transportation costs come from the use of the motor truck."

Some dealers took trains into Havelock to drive home their new trucks. "The Hebb Motors Company of Havelock, manufacturers of Patriot trucks, claim that so great is the demand for Patriot trucks that their distributors will not wait for delivery by railroad, but are coming to the factory and driving the trucks overland to the point of destination," the August 21, 1919, *Havelock Post* reported. The information accompanied a photo of two Patriot trucks, each carrying another Patriot, preparing to leave the Havelock factory for the 525-mile drive to Denver.

Hebb Home Has High Hopes

Involved in real estate, investments, and other ventures, the Woods Bros. Company was developing residential and commercial property in Havelock. The industrial city northeast of Lincoln, boasting a 1920 population of 3,602, already had one large industry: the Burlington Railroad shops, whose 1,200 employees built and repaired steam locomotives.

Brothers Mark and George Woods reasoned that giving Hebb Motors the land for its new factory would help create more demand for housing in Havelock. Their gift was a land parcel variously estimated in the press at between 12 and 17 acres. The brothers invested more directly in Hebb Motors by buying "a large slice of the stock that is being offered for sale," said the *Havelock Post*. The Woods Bros. Company would build between 50 and 75 Havelock houses to greet the influx of Hebb Motors workers, the newspaper estimated.

Hebb Motors' officials described their Havelock location as ideal, "located three blocks southwest of the Burlington station at Havelock, and between the transcontinental lines of the Burlington and the Rock Island railroads, and between the O.L.D. [Omaha-Lincoln-Denver] and Cornhusker highways, in full view of them all."

Hebb Motors and the *Havelock Post*, editorially, urged Havelock residents to support the local truck-making venture by buying stock. And the Havelock Commercial Club voted unanimously "to give its moral support to the Hebb Motors Co. and recommended to the business men and others that they should subscribe liberally to the stock of the corporation."[21]

Built in Havelock . . . or Detroit?

"Plans are already drawn and site selected for a large modern plant in Havelock. . . . In the meantime we will produce Patriot Trucks in our local factories," Hebb Motors said in an ad dated February 17, 1918, alluding to its body factories at 10th and Vine and 26th and X streets. But the company contradicted itself in another ad just a month later, when it announced: "We are building Patriot Trucks in Detroit, now, but will soon be building them in our new plant at Havelock. Deliveries will begin about April First."

In May, the *Sunday State Journal* reported yet another assembly site for the first Patriot trucks, noting Hebb Motors had arranged to temporarily use a cattle barn at the State Fairgrounds in Lincoln. "Crates and crates of motors and other parts of trucks are piled up in the stalls where the prize-winning cattle are on exhibition during the fair. It is here that the company will do its big work in assembling trucks during the next few months." Such confusion makes it difficult today to determine just where Hebb Motors built its first trucks – Detroit or Lincoln.

Regardless, the company was months late in meeting its April 1 deadline. "Patriot trucks will be ready for distribution in a very short time," the company said in late April. In late August, the company had at least some trucks ready to display at the Nebraska State Fair in Lincoln, announcing "we are now in production and have an article in which you should be interested." A month later, at the end of September, Hebb Motors was back-pedaling again. "These new sturdy Motor Trucks will be ready for service shortly and when you see one you will say 'here is a real truck.'"[22] According to ads and press accounts, production problems – probably stemming from wartime material shortages – were solved by October 1918.

Hebb Motors in early 1918 filed for trademark protection, claiming it had been using the name Patriot since October 1, 1917. One or two automobile encyclopedias now list October 1 as the date production started, but it's doubtful more than one or two prototypes were ready then.

Fire Levels One Body Factory

Workmen started pouring concrete for the foundation pilings of the new factory in late May 1918. Two months later, anyone passing through Havelock "cannot fail but notice the structural frame work that is now up for the great Hebb Motors Company's plant in that suburb," the *Lincoln Trade Review* said. "One section of the big building is being advanced as rapidly as possible, so that by September 1st, the firm hopes to have the section ready for occupancy."[23]

A *Lincoln Daily Star* headline on September 1, 1918, announced, "New Hebb Factory Now In Operation," though construction on part of the building was continuing. Hebb Motors had the entire factory at its disposal by early 1919.

The week Hebb Motors began the move into the completed section of its new reinforced-concrete factory in Havelock, its hearse, ambulance, and bus body factory at 26th and X streets was gutted in what a press account called "one of the most disastrous fires in the history of Lincoln." The fire, attributed to arson, started late Saturday night, September 7, 1918, leveling what was commonly known as Hebb Factory No. 2. Also destroyed was a nearby lumber yard and grain company.

Insurance would cover $25,000 of his company's estimated $30,000 loss, Hebb told the Lincoln newspapers. "The severest loss, however . . . was the stopping of this manufacturing plant and the difficulty that they will experience in replacing the machinery," the *Lincoln Trade Review* noted.[24]

German sympathizers perhaps set the fire to destroy essential industries, police and fire officials theorized. Another theory was that the fire was accidently or purposely set by burglars, since the lumber company's safe was found open. Witnesses saw two people fleeing the area minutes before the fire broke out, but press reports in the days following the fire make no mention of any arrests.

Trucks Named for Famous Americans

In keeping with its practice of naming its trucks after famous Americans, Hebb Motors during its first year introduced a Lincoln and a Washington model. The Lincoln was commonly regarded as a 1½-ton truck and the Washington as a 2½-ton truck. By 1920, Hebb Motors tacked the title "Rocky Mountain Special" onto its Lincoln and Washington model names.

The big trucks were made to haul timber, build roads, plow snow, work in the oil fields, and haul grain to market on the often muddy, rutted country roads of the day. Fitted with special bodies in the Hebb Motors woodworking shop, Patriot trucks were also used as school buses, moving vans, gasoline tankers, building movers, dump trucks, coal haulers, road graders, long-distance transporters, and fire engines, among other things.

The Lincoln model weighed less – 3,200 versus 4,200 pounds – than the Washington, and its 135-inch wheelbase was 21 inches shorter. The two had similar hand-cranked Continental-brand 4-cylinder engines, made in Detroit. Four-cylinder power plants were used in 99 percent of all trucks as late as 1921 but would gradually give way to the 6-cylinder engine in the mid-1920s. The 4-cylinder engines of about 1920 would generally turn at well below 2,000 rpm. With a 3¾-inch cylinder bore and a 5-inch stroke, the Lincoln's engine developed 22.5 horsepower under a formula attributed to the Society of Automotive Engineers. The Washington's bigger engine – a 4⅛-inch bore and 5¼-inch stroke – developed 27.2 SAE horsepower.

A centrifugal pump circulated water through the Washington's big engine, but the Lincoln model, which had no water pump, was cooled on the thermosiphon principle. The principle assumed that, as the water cooled, it would sink and exit the bottom of the radiator, displacing hot water, which would flow into the top of the radiator for cooling.

Both models used a Stewart vacuum system to draw gas from an under-seat tank to a Stromberg updraft carburetor with a 1-inch-diameter throat. They also both used a Bosch magneto to fire the spark plugs. A Prest-O-Lite tank on the left running board supplied acetylene to 10-inch headlamps. Electric-powered lights and a starter were an option on the two bigger trucks by 1920.

In 1918, each truck came equipped with a mechanical horn, a tool kit, and a jack. Standard equipment also included hard-rubber front tires measuring 36 x 4 inches for both models. The Lincoln had solid rear tires measuring 36 x 5 inches, compared to bigger 36 x 7-inch rear tires on the Washington model. Hebb Motors installed Russel rear axles and Covert transmissions in its early Lincoln models but Empire rear axles and Brown-Lipe transmissions in the bigger Washington models.[25]

Only the biggest companies could afford to make their own engines, transmissions, springs, brakes, axles, and similar parts. Hebb Motors made many of its own parts – frames, radiators, wood-spoked wheels, hoods, fenders, running boards, seats, bodies – but bought other components from national suppliers. Such purchases were a common practice. By 1920, for instance, 86 percent of the rear axles used on American trucks were made by suppliers rather than the truck manufacturers themselves. At the time there were more than 200 truck-part suppliers in the United States.[26]

Larger companies proudly advertised that they made their own parts. But "most of our best trucks are designed with a view of using standard parts which have been designed and tested out thoroughly by specialists along their line," Chief Engineer L. F. Seaton wrote in the company's June 1920 *Patriot Progress* magazine. "Carefully selected and thoroughly tested Standardized units throughout, make Patriot Trucks almost abuse-proof," trumpeted a March 10, 1918, *Lincoln Sunday Star* ad. "This Standardized construction means much in the long run. It means the maximum of Serviceability and the minimum cost of up-keep."

"Not the Cheapest to Buy"

The company billed its heavier Washington model as having "the power of a locomotive in a chassis famous for its strength, simplicity and accessibility." The Lincoln model was "*the* accepted truck for such extra hard service as ore hauling, timber handling, rural motor transport, oil fields, construction work, road building – where unfailing, continuous and economical heavy-duty truck operation is demanded."

Through the years, Hebb switched suppliers on some parts. By 1919, for example, the company was using Detroit-based Hinkley engines rather than Continental engines in its Lincoln and Washington models. But the new lightweight truck that Hebb Motors introduced in 1919 was using a Continental engine.

The Patriot truck "is the simplest, the strongest and while it is not the cheapest to buy it is by far the cheapest to own and to operate," the company claimed. "One Patriot on the farm replaces three men, six horses and three wagons."[27]

A farmer in one year could easily pay for the truck by driving to distant but more profitable markets, the company contended. For example, a Western Nebraska man farming 1,600 acres "produced 30,000 bushels of wheat last year," the company said in its July 1920 *Patriot Progress* magazine. "Through the use of a Lincoln Model Patriot Truck he was able to haul this wheat to a market fifteen miles away where he got 8c more per bushel, or a total of $2400.00 profit through the use of his Patriot truck."

A late 1918 Patriot chassis – minus the stock rack, grain box, or other wooden body – cost $2,150 for the Lincoln model and $3,150 for its bigger brother, the Washington model. There were cheaper trucks on the market, but even Hebb Motors' higher

prices were well in line with what other makers of heavy trucks were charging. Buying the Patriot truck cab, a body, and a Patriot Hand Hoist to raise and dump the truck bed cost an extra $165 to $195, depending on the length of the body. In 1918, bodies for Patriot trucks ranged in length from six to 10 feet.

In a testimonial letter, an unnamed Oklahoma farmer justified his new truck's purchase price by saying it cost him 35 cents per ton-mile to haul alfalfa hay and seed 3½ miles to the nearest rail station by wagon but just 15 cents per ton-mile by Patriot. "Our truck cost, complete, $3,500," the farmer wrote. "Some of our neighbors seemed troubled about this and asked, 'Why didn't you buy a so-and-so truck; they cost only $1200?' Our reason for buying the higher priced truck was that we knew beforehand what a truck would have to do on the farm, so we bought a truck that was especially built for country roads and country loads."[28]

A Patriot fire truck that the Havelock Volunteer Fire Department bought in the summer of 1919 "cost close to $4500, fully equipped with chemical apparatus, hose reels, ladders, etc.," the *Havelock Post* said.

By spring 1920, Patriot Motors was promoting two styles of bus bodies for use by schools, stage lines, and even hotels. It built a $600 15-passenger bus body for its new lightweight Revere chassis, which became the third truck in Hebb's lineup with its mid-1919 introduction. The company also made a $700 19-passenger body for the medium-weight Lincoln chassis. Consolidated school districts across Nebraska were using such specially equipped Patriots as school buses, the *Havelock Post* reported.[29]

The White Line Stage Company used at least one 15-passenger Patriot bus on its route through Potwin, Ferris City, Oil Valley, Elbing, and Burns in south-central Kansas. "The bus bodies . . . are equipped with plate glass, drop sash windows held in place by anti-rattlers. Entrance is made through a door at the front of the bus opposite the driver's seat. The outside over the flare [at the edge of the roof] is covered with sheet metal mounted over felt to prevent rattling. . . . A door in the rear also furnishes a quick means of exit for passengers in case of accident," the company said in its June 1920 *Patriot Progress* magazine.

Patriots Built on "Progressive" Assembly Line

Probably from the start – if not, at least by late 1919 – Hebb Motors used the progressive assembly method, which by 1917 had replaced the slower group-assembly process in many truck factories. Though not built like Henry Ford's Model Ts, which were in constant motion, Patriot trucks "progressed" from station to station, where they stopped to give workers time to attach parts.

Hebb knew well how Fords were manufactured. He traveled to Ford's Highland Park, Michigan, factory as early as mid-September 1915, and perhaps visited there earlier. Returning to Lincoln from a trip to the East Coast in August 1919, he and his future partner in an airplane venture again stopped in the Detroit area to tour a sprawling Ford assembly plant and also saw the Hinkley and Continental engine plants, said Hebb's nephew, Bill Jones.

That same month, L. F. Seaton, a University of Nebraska engineering professor, began working at Hebb Motors, bringing with him a vast knowledge of automobile factories. "Plans are now under way to organize the production of Patriot trucks on an efficient basis, as is done in the larger and . . . up-to-date truck factories in the United States," the August 21, 1919, *Havelock Post* quoted Seaton as saying. "I have just returned from a three weeks' trip thru the east, visiting practically all of the larger plants, where I made inspections and studied the most approved methods of efficiency and production. I don't mind saying that we have here at Havelock the most

modern factory that I found on my rounds; also one of the largest and best equipped."

Hebb Motors in December 1919 published a softbound book of photographs and descriptions titled *A Little Journey to the Home of Patriot Trucks*, a spinoff of the "Little Journeys in a Patriot Truck" advertising theme it was then using. The book describes the order of assembly in its factory.[30]

In one part of the factory's general machine shop, workers machined smaller parts that arrived from its Council Bluffs, Iowa, foundry.[31] Jigs ensured that "parts are exact duplicates. This is a very important feature from a service as well as manufacturing standpoint[,] making all parts interchangeable," the book said. Lathes in the Hebb Motors shop were able to machine bronze bushings to tolerances of one-thousandth of an inch. (See fig.3.11.)

Elsewhere in the machine shop, workers

3.11 "Section of machine shop where delicate work requiring exceptional skill on the part of the operator is done—such as machining bronze bushings which requires $\frac{1}{1000}$ of an inch accuracy." (*A Little Journey*, LV)

3.12 "Large multiple spindle drill. This machine is a great saver of time and labor and is capable of drilling thirty-eight holes in one operation. It was drilling thirty-eight holes in top and base of radiator core when photographed." (*A Little Journey*, LV)

3.13 "The first step in wheel assembly upon their arrival from the wood wheel department. As illustrated in this picture the hubs are first pressed in and bolted to the spokes of the wheel." (*A Little Journey*, LV)

used a 38-bit multiple-spindle drill to drill out radiator cores to fit its own cast-iron radiator top and bottom tanks. (See fig.3.12.) Machinists used stationary high-speed table grinders to smooth the mating surfaces of the radiator tanks.

A horizontal-stroke air compressor and 10-foot-tall storage tank delivered a generous 200 cubic feet of air per minute to a variety of machine-shop tools. It was one of three air compressors at the factory. In a riveting room, workmen with pneumatic hammers built frames from metal that was formed and cut to size inside the plant.

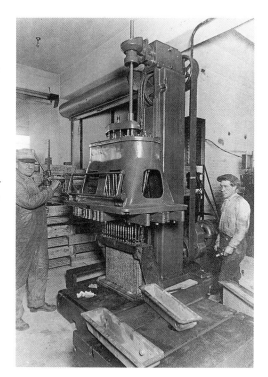

Design of Clutch, Brake Pedals a "Novelty"

Other workers received 14-spoke rear wheels and 12-spoke front wheels from a "wood wheel department" – suggesting that the spokes were made in the factory's woodworking shop. Workers would first press on and then bolt metal hubs to the wooden spokes. (See fig.3.13.) A hydraulic press with a working pressure limit of 200 tons pressed onto each wheel a solid rubber tire mounted to a metal rim.[32]

Automotive journals of the day report that Hebb from the beginning offered Goodyear pneumatic tires for its two heavy truck models. In 1920, equipping one of the two heavier Patriot models with pneumatic tires cost an extra $300 for the Lincoln model and $550 for the Washington model. The use of pneumatic truck tires had been steadily increasing before 1920, but it wasn't until 1926 that pneumatic tires surpassed solid rubber tires in popularity. Hard-rubber tires made for a bone-jarring ride, caused more damage to roads, and required heavier shock-resistant engines. "The hard rubber tires were not very comfortable to ride on unless the truck was loaded and, later, large pneumatic tires were put on as the smooth hard-rubber tires did not give sufficient traction," Grainger Hebb said.

Receiving the finished wheels and tires at another assembly station, workmen using hand tools bolted leaf springs and a pair of wheels onto each axle. (See fig.3.14.) Photographs show that torsion bars were added between rear springs. Steering tie rods were attached to front axles. The workers pushed each finished wheel-and-axle unit out to the main assembly line. To seal the wheel bearings, mechanics bolted dust covers – the first true "hubcaps" – to the front wheels. Similar hubcaps were either bolted or screwed onto the back wheels, depending on the model of the truck.

At the first stop on the assembly line, a riveted frame was lowered onto the assembled axles and bolted into place. Workers next lowered a transmission into place in the center of the frame and installed a previously assembled rear driveshaft, along with universal joints. Photos of the assembly line show precious few air-powered tools in use. Hanging near the work stations are many more hand tools: combination wrenches, long-handled wrenches, adjustable wrenches, speed-handle wrenches, and hammers.

At another station, more parts were added to the frame, including the brake and clutch pedals and mountings, the forward driveshaft, and the gearshift and hand-brake levers. (See fig.3.15.) Both *Automobile Trade Journal* and *Motor World* praised the design of the clutch and brake pedals. "A novelty in construction is the double linkage and bell cranks on the pedals which give both brake and clutch pedals additional leverage and decrease the amount of foot pressure necessary to throw out the clutch or apply the service brakes," *Motor World* said.[33]

Engines from outside suppliers were moved by an overhead track to an engine-assembly area. There, workers installed the clutch and clutch housing, magneto, carburetor, governor, fan, wiring, a crank handle where called for, and all accessories. The overhead track took each finished engine to the assembly line, where it was lowered onto a chassis that had already been fitted with a transmission, gearshift lever, driveshafts, and brake and clutch pedals. (See fig.3.16.)

This page:
3.14 "This picture illustrates the assembly of wheels and springs on the axle." (*A Little Journey*, LV)

Next page:
3.15 "The truck now moves along the main assembly aisle on its wheels and brake pedals with mountings, together with front section of propeller shaft and gear shift levers are connected to the chassis as illustrated." (*A Little Journey*, LV)

3.16 "The motor is then run out on overhead track and dropped in chassis as it comes along the main assembly aisle as shown in picture." (*A Little Journey*, LV)

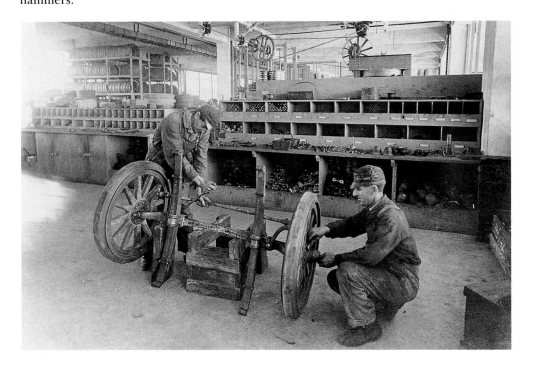

This page:
3.17 "The chassis moves on along the main assembly aisle and the dash, which comes from the dash manufacturing department, with vacuum tank and oil lights are added." (*A Little Journey,* LV)

3.18 "A corner of the sheet metal department. Here the fenders, hoods, etc., are made." (*A Little Journey,* LV)

Next page:
3.19 "A concrete block, representing a 25% overload[,] is placed on frame as shown in this picture." (*A Little Journey,* LV)

Farther down the assembly line, the iron-bound oak dashboards – made in a separate assembly area – were installed, along with a vacuum tank for drawing gasoline from the under-seat 20-gallon gas tank. Other parts added included the steering column and 18-inch-diameter wood-covered steering wheel. Kerosene-burning carriage lamps were bolted to the engine side of the dashboard, near the top. (See fig.3.17.) The painted fenders, made in the plant's sheet-metal shop (see fig.3.18), were also installed.

The next parts installed included the wooden one-half running boards, bound in iron like the dashboard. Workers mounted a Prest-O-Lite tank on the left-side running board to supply acetylene for the head-lamps on trucks so equipped. Also installed were radiators and finished hoods. Along the way, each truck also received floor-boards, a gas tank, exhaust system, head-lights, and a small oil-burning carriage lamp – like those on the front – that was mounted precariously from the lower left back frame rail. It served as a tail lamp. Some customers ordered trucks without headlights. In 1920, an acetylene tank and headlights cost an extra $40 for the Lincoln model, according to a May 24, 1920, letter from the Patriot Motors sales department.

Trucks Get Load, Road Tests

At the end of the assembly line, the trucks still lacked seats and paint. It appears from photos in the 1919 Hebb picture book that a driver simply perched on the gas tank to drive a finished truck off the line and onto the often-muddy grounds outside the factory. There, he backed the truck carefully under a homemade wooden chain hoist. Other workers lowered onto the rear frame of the truck a concrete block "representing a 25% overload." (See fig.3.19.) The truck was then "thoroughly road tested and after passing through the hands of the final inspectors, having been inspected by the head of each assembly division, is ready for paint." A company photograph shows marks where tires rubbed against the concrete block, indicating that the heavy weight was left straddling the frame while the trucks were road-tested.

Especially because of the rough dirt and gravel roads of the day, the trucks were as slow as their rear-axle ratios suggest. Many of the first paved rural roads in the United States were financed with federal money, but by October 1920 only 191 miles of federal-aid highways had been completed.[34] For 1920, the rear-axle ratio was 7.25:1 for the 1½-ton Lincoln model, a much higher ratio than for a modern truck of the same size. The ratio was 9.66:1 for the 2½-ton Washington model, meaning the driveshaft revolved nearly 10 times for each single revolution of the truck's rear wheels.

Like most other heavy trucks of the day, the Lincoln and Washington models of 1919 were unable to break the 20-mile-per-hour barrier, even if there had been enough good roads to allow it. Equipped with Pierce governors to thwart daredevil drivers, the Lincoln's top speed was 18 miles per hour, compared to 14 miles per hour for the heavier Washington model, though both trucks lacked speedometers. Hebb motors was not at all troubled by such low speeds. "A truck can be likened to a splendid draft team — built to pull loads and not for speed," the company said in an August 1919 press release.[35]

The Waverly, Nebraska, volunteer fire department called a special meeting for December 24, 1931, to buy a used Patriot fire truck, according to fire department records. The purchase price wasn't noted, but it cost $2.45 to equip the truck with a windshield in early 1933, records indicate. "I remember the Patriot. It wouldn't go very fast," recalled Aaron Johnson of rural Waverly, whose father and uncle were Waverly volunteer firefighters. "Some of the firemen would jump off and run to the fire to get to it before the truck if it was going uphill," Johnson said.[36]

In an April 21, 1918, *Lincoln Daily Star* ad showing how a Patriot truck could outwork a horse team, Hebb Motors made the undoubtedly honest, though certainly modest, claim that the Lincoln model Patriot farm truck "readily transports twice as much in weight with twice the speed of horse-drawn wagons." As perhaps some compensation, the Lincoln model could get up to 15 miles per gallon, according to a letter and photograph sent to Hebb Motors by its district manager in Fort Lauderdale, Florida. "This is the truck that run [*sic*] from Miami to West Palm Beach . . . a distance of 150 miles on 10 gallon [*sic*] of gas and 1 quart of oil," the Patriot representative wrote in the July 1920 *Patriot Progress* magazine.

Ready for Paint

Next after the road test in the assembly sequence, the trucks went to a vented paint booth, eight feet tall and open at one end so the trucks could be partly backed inside. (See fig. 3.20.) "Practically all painting is

3.20 "Practically all painting is done by compressed air as illustrated." (*A Little Journey,* LV)

done by compressed air," the company said. A line connected a spray gun to an overhead paint bucket of approximately five gallons. A separate air line attached to the spray gun. Painters sprayed the frame, springs, axles, and the outside edges of the floorboards. The fenders and hood, however, were painted before being bolted to the trucks.

Each truck received three coats of paint: a filler or primer coat, a color coat, and a varnish coat. "Previous to varnishing, two-color striping has been applied by hand, giving [an] unusually attractive finish to truck," said the company's softbound book, *A Little Journey to the Home of Patriot Trucks*. The headlamp stands and radiator, still bare metal, were apparently later painted by hand or sprayed after nearby parts were masked to catch overspray. When the painting was done, the seat was installed.

As A. G. Hebb's nephew, Bill Jones was allowed to wander through the Havelock factory in 1918, 1919, and 1920. He remembers seeing trucks with bright-red bodies, black frames, and jet-black radiators roll off the assembly line. "I don't think they painted all of them any one color. It is assumed that anyone buying trucks could say 'I'd like to have it painted so-and-so,'" Jones said.

By 1920, at least some Patriot bodies were finished in "brewster green" paint with yellow stripes, according to one automobile reference guide of the period.[37] A Patriot owner in Washington state has a Washington model Patriot with a red frame and black body, though he says the truck colors may not be original.

A "Patriot Performance" catalog of mid-1920 has a front-cover drawing of a heavy Patriot with a bright-red frame and wheels; gray or black fenders, hood, and radiator; and a green cab and stock rack. (See color plate 2.) A color folder from the same period shows all three models with bright-red frames and wheels. Even the springs,

driveshafts, transmissions, and what is visible of the engines were red. The hoods, radiators, fenders, and headlamps were a shade of gray that was perhaps intended to reproduce as black in the folder, and the wooden seat boxes and cowling were a medium green.

From the paint booth, the trucks were driven to an area where wooden bodies were installed, along with a cab, if so ordered. Unlike the truck chassis, "the bodies . . . are all hand painted," according to a Hebb press release carried in the July 1918 *Automobile Trade Journal*. However, one factory folder said painting with a spray gun "requires only a few minutes for each truck and body," suggesting that Hebb Motors later began spray-painting the wooden bodies, as well as the frames.

Some of the trucks – including most, if not all, of the fire trucks – had seats open to the elements, but Bill Jones said many of the trucks had cabs. By 1919, closed cabs "were evident and visibly popular" on trucks displayed at both the New York and Chicago truck shows.[38]

Patriot Fire Truck "Perfect in Construction"

To make the truck bodies, the factory used kilns to heat and dry the oak, poplar, redwood, ash, and hard pine woods that it bought from "one of the oldest and largest mills in the South," according to the Hebb Motors book. In a July 1918 article, the *Automobile Trade Journal* said, "the sills and frames of these bodies are of first-grade white ash, and the panels [are] of genuine yellow poplar. All the lumber used in the construction of these bodies is placed in dry kilns for several weeks at a temperature of 100 to 150 degrees, before being put to use."

In a mill room, woodworkers cut the lumber to standard sizes and forwarded the pieces to a general body assembly room.

(See fig.3.21.) From there, the finished bodies went to a blacksmith department, where metal fittings were added. The bodies were then ready to bolt onto the finished trucks.

In a special body construction room, workers fabricated custom bodies, such as "school busses, hotel busses, oil field equipment, sugar beet bodies, oil tanks, fire equipment and all such special bodies," the Hebb factory picture book said. (See fig.3.22 and 3.23.)

The Havelock Volunteer Fire Department bought, patriotically, a locally produced fire truck in the summer of 1919. "This truck was built by the Hebb Motors company of Havelock, and it is considered so perfect in construction and a model of its class that the Hebb company asked permission of the mayor and council to place it on exhibition at the [Nebraska] State Fair next week, as showing what can be produced in Havelock. The request was granted," reported the August 28, 1919, *Havelock Post*. "It is considered one of the finest in Nebraska and when placed on exhibition will do much to advertise this city," the newspaper added with a note of pride.

In addition to being a state-of-the-art factory, the Hebb Motors plant had a cafeteria that served some of the best food in the Lincoln area, said Isabelle Lampshire, daughter of Plant Superintendent King W. Gillespie. She said pies made by a cook named Sophie Armstrong – a former neighbor of the Hebb family – were much in demand.[39]

In a roped-off section of the cafeteria was the executive dining room, where company officers could get table service, Bill Jones said. In the clipped prose of a photo caption, the Hebb Motors' book describes the modern conveniences of the factory's cafeteria: "Workmen avail themselves of hot lunches from factory kitchen and for this purpose are provided double-sided lunch counter some 90 feet long."

Hebb Woos City Market

In summer 1919, Hebb Motors introduced the Revere, a ¾-ton light delivery truck named after yet another famous American, to appeal to businesses that needed vehicles for local deliveries. As early as April 1918, the company had acknowledged that "for city delivery work, where the merchant is called on to cover a wide radius in the shortest time, he can, with his motor truck, keep up the best of service demanded by his customers and do it in an economical way."

By early 1919, as Hebb Motors was developing its light city-delivery truck, its advertising began to appeal more and more to urban merchants. It did so, ironically, by citing the farm record of Patriot trucks. "A truck that will stand up and deliver under the rough-and-tumble conditions under which a truck must operate on the farm, usually in the hands of inexperienced operators, is a good truck for City service," one ad said.[40]

"We have featured Patriot Trucks for farm work, because 60% to 75% of the haulage west of the Mississippi is the transportation of farm products," the company said in an April 17, 1919, *Motor Age* ad. "However, Patriot Trucks are equally satisfactory for

3.21 "General body assembly room. Here the parts which have been cut in the mill are put together." (*A Little Journey*, LV)

3.22 Special body construction room. (*A Little Journey*, LV)

3.23 A flatbed body under construction at the Patriot factory. (TL)

every other kind of service where a high grade, reliable product is desired."

The most notable standard feature of the new Revere was pneumatic, rather than solid rubber, tires. Other features included an electric starter, horn, lights, and dimmer switch, along with a battery and ammeter, which were lacking in the two bigger trucks; a 129-inch wheelbase; and a shipping weight of 2,800 pounds. The Revere's Continental engine was smaller than the Hinkley engines in the heavier trucks. The bigger trucks also had longer wheelbases to match their size. Like the 1919 Lincoln, the

Revere model had a 3-speed transmission, compared to the Washington model's 4-speed transmission.

"Sturdy Truck engineers" at the Hebb Motors plant worked several months on the new truck, the *Lincoln Daily Star* recounted:

The only instruction they had from Mr. A. G. Hebb, president of the company, were: "We want to build the sturdiest and classiest three-quarter ton job on the American market. It must be 'more truck' for the money than anyone else has ever turned out."

Every truck on the market of the ¾-ton size was gone over very carefully. Many of these trucks were secured for experimental purposes at the Hebb factory, torn down, examined part by part, and put together again. The war-record of light trucks was consulted and the weak points which developed in them under the stress of unusual duty were charted. Many factories were visited and investigations relating to manufacture were made.[41]

Hebb Motors Makes 5,000 Bodies, 750 Trucks

The company had received orders for 3,000 trucks by January 1919, the *Havelock Post* reported. "It is confidently believed that at least 4,000 truck orders will be on the Hebb files by the first of March," the newspaper added. But company records show Hebb Motors delivered not 4,000 or 3,000 but just 750 trucks in 1919. The same records fail to provide production figures for 1918 but say that Hebb Motors' established body department in 1918 "turned out nearly 5,000 jobs" – each job presumably a body. Hebb Motors' 1918 production was undoubtedly less than the 750 trucks it made in 1919, so it's likely that 4,500 or more of the body department's 5,000 deliveries in 1918 were for outside orders. That's possible, because at the Hebb factory "stock models [of bodies] are built for thirty odd makes of trucks, besides Patriots," the company claimed.[42]

The government's wartime demands for standard parts – particularly engines – had made it difficult for Hebb Motors and other truck makers, Grainger Hebb said. "With the war in full bloom, engines were hard to get. Too, the railroads were under the control of the government, so goods were shipped to the advantage of the government," he said. The *Branham Automobile Reference Book* indicates that the company made no more than 200 Revere models, 300 Lincoln models, and 100 Washington models – or a total production of 600 or fewer trucks during the turbulent postwar year of 1920.

The company, however, had projected building 2,000 trucks in 1920; more than double that number, or 4,500, in 1921; 7,000 in 1922; and 10,000 in 1923. The financial projections assumed the company would make a $200 profit on each truck and a $100 profit on each body it sold.

Therefore, based on 310 working days per year, company officials had hoped to go from making fewer than 2½ trucks per day in 1919 to 32 trucks per day in 1923. The company may have speeded up production ahead of that schedule, however. An April 3, 1920, *Automobile Topics* article about the Patriot factory reported that "at present 12 trucks are being put out a day, but by midsummer production is expected to reach 25 trucks daily."

In making its production estimates for 1920 and beyond, the company noted that "1919 is no criterion for estimating future years. Like in many other manufacturing and construction lines of business, the buying public was in a 'watchful-waiting' frame of mind during the first half of the year, but[,] coming to a realization during the second half year that prices were bound to remain firm on account of general shortage of materials of every description, commenced to place buying orders for quick delivery. It was only this favorable reaction that made for volume in the Truck business during 1919."[43]

Shifting to High Gear: Patriot Motors

The future looked bright, however, at the dawning of 1920, the second full year following World War I. Though still coping with material shortages and postwar economic uncertainties, manufacturers were hoping for strong 1920 sales.

To finance its growth, Hebb Motors reincorporated effective March 13, 1920, offering current investors an exchange of stock. A letter to stockholders said that exchanging old Hebb Motors stock for the new Patriot Motors stock would mean holders of common stock would see "a further fifty per cent (50%) dividend or increase on their present holdings," receiving $150 of Patriot Motors stock for each $100 of Hebb Motors stock they held. The new Patriot Motors stock was priced at $10 a share, compared to $100 a share for old Hebb Motors stock – likely because the smaller denominations would make it easier to sell.[44]

"With the formation of the new corporation, Havelock will have the third largest exclusive truck manufacturing establishment in the United States, according to the statistics," said the *Havelock Post*'s March 25, 1920, edition. "The corporation has eight million dollars' worth of orders on the books at the present time and under the new arrangement it is planned to do at least $16,000,000 worth of truck business this year."

All the firm's officers kept their posts under the reorganization. But the change allowed Hebb Motors – authorized to issue $2.5 million worth of stock – to quadruple that amount. Holders of preferred stock were entitled to a quarterly dividend of 1¾ percent – an annual rate of 7 percent – from Patriot Motors' net profits. Standard Securities Corporation in mid-April 1920 announced the sale of the first $1 million in Patriot Motors' common stock.

Patriot Motors Plans to Build Cars

The reorganized Patriot Motors planned to build four new buildings: a 40,000-square-foot (100-by-400-foot) one-story plant for woodworking; a foundry and machine shop; a body factory; and a two-story office building. "All the wood that goes into a car or truck will be cut in this [woodworking] shop," said the March 25, 1920, *Havelock Post*. By March 1921, construction would start on the office building, which would contain "a gymnasium, kitchen and dining room for employees and other conveniences," the *Post* said.

The new Patriot Motors "owns a foundry in Council Bluffs, but this is said to be inadequate for their needs, and a new and larger institution of this nature is being sought to locate here," the *Havelock Post* had reported as early as October 2, 1919. Hebb already controlled the Badger Manufacturing Company of Council Bluffs, Iowa, but bought the plant outright in June 1920, possibly to move some of its foundry equipment to Havelock.

"The manufacture of passenger cars is expected to commence late this year or early in 1921. This will mean a duplicate of the present main [factory] building," reported the April 1, 1920, *Automobile Topics* magazine. The company put the cost of the new building at $700,000. Undoubtedly basing their information on a company press release, both the local and national press reported that Patriot Motors was expecting to employ between 2,000 and 3,000 people by the end of 1920.

The new Patriot Motors was authorized to issue up to $10 million in stock but applied to the state Bureau of Securities to sell $5 million in common and $2 million in preferred stock. The new company planned to place in its treasury "for future needs" $1 million of its $2 million in preferred stock. The other $1 million of preferred stock was being held by Hebb Motors investors. Of its

$5 million in common stock, Patriot Motors planned to set aside $2.25 million to issue to Hebb Motors' stockholders as part of the stock exchange.

That left $2.75 million in common stock to sell at large. Financial records show that Patriot Motors planned to set aside $1.3 million for increasing assets, paying stock-selling commissions and expenses, as well as paying off current liabilities. A $1 million share of the new common stock revenues would go toward building up the factory's inventory of parts "based on [the] abnormal material shortage situation experienced during the past two years," a company document indicates.

Of the remaining $450,000 in common stock, $300,000 was earmarked for building and equipping a factory for manufacturing bodies and $150,000 would be saved for new foundry equipment and other machinery for the truck factory.[45]

Various artist's conceptions of the finished factory complex had been circulating within the company for months. One such illustration was even part of the company letterhead. As early as July 10, 1919, the drawing appeared in a *Motor Age* ad that claimed Patriot trucks were built "in one of the largest factories in America" and backed by "a financial strength that is unusual in the truck business." (A similar drawing appears in fig. 3.24.)

Unfortunately, the company neglected to point out that the drawing in its ads and letterhead was only a vision of the future. Potential truck buyers and stockholders alike were left with the impression that the company was bigger – and correspondingly safer – than it actually was. The office building, foundry, and body plant that were pictured in the drawing never got built.

"Hitting the Low Spots"

To entice farmers and other potential buyers, Hebb Motors raised the level of tough-truck advertising almost to an art

form. (See fig. 3.25.) In a variety of sales literature, automotive journals, and magazines, Hebb Motors showed its trucks climbing mountains, grinding through muddy plowed fields (see fig. 3.26), and pushing through snow drifts. One truck is pictured pulling an eight-ton steel gasoline station on a trailer along a road in Stockton, California.

In an undated factory sales catalog about the Patriot truck, Hebb Motors claimed "its extra powerful motor can not be stalled and its extra powerful construction will endure the severest strains." The lively copy of an

3.24 The sprawling Hebb factory complex pictured in this ad never came to be. (November 1919 *Motorist*)

3.25 A loaded flatbed Patriot crests a hill in this ad. (June 1920 *Motorist*)

3.26 From a mid-1920 Patriot folder: "A Lincoln Model Patriot on the farm near Wellington, Kans." (NSHS)

April 3, 1920, ad in the *Literary Digest* contends that "good roads, bad roads, or no roads at all – it's 'all in the day's work' for the Patriot. This truck is always ready for trouble."

One ad in a series titled "Little Journeys in Patriot Motor Trucks" carried the subtitle "At the Crest of Berthoud Pass." The copy continued, "On its way over the Rockies, at the highest point on Berthoud Pass, 11,300 feet altitude, a Patriot Truck was stopped long enough to be photographed. Our Denver distributors tell us that the Patriot is a wonder for mountain hauling."[46]

Another ad in a later advertising series, "Hitting the Low Spots," shows a drawing of a loaded truck rounding a curve on a muddy country road. "One of the chief virtues of Patriot Motor Trucks is their ability to 'hit the low spots' as serenely and undisturbed as though the miles of mud holes were smooth-surfaced pavement. Patriot Motor Trucks are equally indifferent to conditions of road, load and weather. They do their work willingly and well, whether running on a paved highway or through sloughs of stiff, clinging mud."[47]

Hebb Ads Let Customers Do the Talking

But Hebb Motors and the renamed Patriot Motors got the most use out of testimonials. For instance, J. G. Uzzell of Lamar, Colorado, owned a trucking service that made daily runs between Lamar and Springfield, Colorado, using a 2½-ton Patriot. "I drove the fifty miles from Springfield to Lamar partly after dark through mud and snow 12 to 18 inches deep in places in three hours and thirty five minutes," Uzzell said in a testimonial letter. "Do not think that this load is anything out of the ordinary because I am hauling these kind [*sic*] of loads every day. Yesterday I had 7500# on my truck and towed a 6000# tractor thirty miles through mud hub deep in places," Uzzell said.

"You will be pleased to know that a two

Ship by Patriot

Patriot Motor Trucks were designed for use in districts where good roads are scarce.

They are built to conquer steep, slippery hills; boggy lowland roads; clinging clay; clogging gumbo and dragging sand.

The result is that every Patriot Truck gives matchless efficiency and economy on good roads and pavements.

Owners most appreciate the sterling worth of the Patriot Truck when they **do** face a hard climb with a heavy load; when they **do** find a stretch of bottomless mud, when they **have** to make the trip in weather that means impassable roads to trucks of less ability than the Patriot.

The Patriot franchise is one of the most valuable a progressive dealer can own. Wire or write for details.

Patriot Motors Company
MANUFACTURERS

1395 P STREET		LINCOLN, NEB.
Revere Model 1,500 to 2,000 Lbs. Capacity	Lincoln Model 3,000 to 5,000 Lbs. Capacity	Washington Model 5,000 to 7,500 Lbs. Capacity

PATRIOT

MOTOR TRUCKS

and one half ton Patriot truck has been operating daily for six months in Stockton Territory and during grain harvest worked twenty four hours per day averaging five tons a load and trailing four tons being operated by three drivers," read a telegram from California. "Same truck is now operating between Stockton and Sonora forty miles over mountain roads always carrying hundred percent overload and giving perfect satisfaction."

Hodgins Motor Company, a Patriot dealer in Spokane, Washington, wrote that logger P. A. Lundburg took delivery of a Patriot "at a time when it was thought that no truck of any capacity could make a trip. However, the Washington Model proved true and at one point in the road the entire truck was covered with water and mud with the exception of the frame, motor and carburetor. It caused such excitement at this point that an entire mill crew stopped their work to see the Patriot go through."

A. J. Edmondston, a Savannah, Georgia, Patriot dealer, told of a truck demonstration near Monteith, Georgia, that impressed a "Mr. Hillman." Hillman had three teams of mules and an unnamed brand of truck that he couldn't even turn around in his soft farm fields, Edmondston wrote. "He asked me if I could bring my truck on the field and turn it around empty. I told him I could do it loaded. He told me it was an impossibility; there wasn't a truck built could do it. . . . I told Mr. Hillman to get up and drive it himself, and he crossed and re-crossed the field, picking up a barrel [of potatoes] here and there, and going over furrows where the wheels were making 12 to 14 inch tracks. . . . He drove the truck out on high gear, then when he got on the road, he told me that if any body had told him a truck would do this, he would have told them they were liars."

"All My Meals at Home"

Farmer I. E. Thompson of Iona, South Dakota, wrote to the manufacturer about the

exploits of his 1½-ton Patriot. "I live 25 miles from the railroad, and it used to take me 2 days with 4 horses to get 70 bushels of wheat to the elevator and back home again, and the horses could only stand 2 trips a week and keep it up. So you can readily see I know how to appreciate making 2 trips in one day and get all my meals at home," Thompson wrote.

The Standard Oil Company – Patriot Motors called them "the world's largest users of Motor Trucks" – placed a large order for Patriot gasoline-tank trucks to be delivered before July 15, 1920, the manufacturer said in its advertising. According to a March 1920 Patriot ad, the order amounted to "more than 200 trucks."

Standard Oil "was having serious trouble with their motor trucks in a certain bad-roads section of the country" – identified elsewhere as Sandhills country around Sidney, Nebraska. A representative sent out to study the problem "reported favorably on the Patriot. Six trucks were ordered for trial. Five or six months later, the Standard Oil Company entered an order for a great many more, on which some 50 or 60 trucks have been delivered to date." A photo in a mid-1920 "Patriot Performance" catalog shows a row of 10 Lincoln-model Patriots ready for delivery to the Standard Oil Company. (See fig.3.27.)

One early 1920 ad gave a state-by-state rundown of Patriot's accomplishments:

In Washington, at the Walla Walla Farm Power Show, Patriot Trucks were the only rear-driven

3.27 Ten Lincoln-model Rocky Mountain Special Patriot tanker trucks for Standard Oil Company, from the mid-1920 *Patriot Performance* folder. (NSHS)

trucks that went over the hills in the plowed ground under capacity loads. Their performance was the talk of the Northwest.

In Kansas, a fleet of Patriot Trucks, heavily loaded, made a run of 350 miles last summer, through territory where there had been much rain for several weeks, some of the roads having practically no bottom – over 200 miles made in the rain – the entire trip of 350 miles being made in two days, each truck going through on its own power."[48]

Patriot Builds for the World

The number of Patriot truck dealers is more difficult to determine. *Patriot Progress,* the in-house magazine published for dealers and others, contained a page of dealer news called "Field Notes." The June and July 1920 issues of the magazine mentioned dealers in 12 states: California, Colorado, Connecticut, Florida, Georgia, Kansas, Missouri, Nebraska, Oklahoma, Texas, Washington, and Wyoming. Other sources indicate Patriot also had dealers in Sioux Falls, South Dakota, and Kansas City, Missouri.

Dealers abounded, however. For instance, Hebb Motors in late December 1919 brought to Havelock "more than 150 Patriot truck dealers" from Louisiana, Oklahoma, and Texas for a three-day get-acquainted session that included a tour of the factory and a banquet, according to the January 1, 1920, *Havelock Post* and the company's own promotional materials.

"Practically every state in the union is now reached by sales agencies of this company[,] and the Patriot truck is becoming known nationwide," said the *Havelock Post* of April 17, 1919. "They had sales offices all over the country because it was A. G.'s idea to really build a national sales organization," according to Hebb's nephew, Bill Jones.

"In the grain fields of Saskatchewan and the cotton fields of Alabama – in the forests of Washington and the oilfields of Texas – on the farms of the Middlewest and in the manufacturing centers of New England – wherever there is work for motor trucks to do you will find Patriot Trucks doing it, and doing it well," according to a mid-1920 Patriot sales catalog.[49] Patriot apparently was living up to its motto of "Made in the West, Built for the World," as the company had established an export office at 245 W. 55th Street in New York City, company documents indicate. "The company now has representatives in Canada, Mexico and almost every country in South America and contemplates the development of foreign markets for its trucks," *Automotive Industries* said in an April 1, 1920, article.

Aviation: The Flying Frontier

A. G. Hebb began experimenting with airplanes as early as autumn 1918, as revealed by a *Lincoln Daily Star* article headlined "$2,000,000 Aircraft Plant in Havelock; Build 1,000 Planes." With the financial backing of real-estate barons Mark and George Woods, Hebb was hoping to hire 1,000 workers to build 10 planes per day for America's war needs. But World War I – and the U.S. government's demand for warplanes – ended two months later, temporarily grounding Hebb's airplane plans.

Hebb and his wife's brother, William S. Jones, traveled to a military supply depot, Camp Holabird at Baltimore, Maryland, in August 1919. Thwarted in their attempts to buy the government's surplus Cadillac and Dodge cars, they instead struck a deal to pay $400,000 for 480 Standard J-1 training airplanes and Hispano-Suiza V-8 engines. They also bought enough parts to make an additional 120 planes, according to press accounts and to Hebb's son, Grainger, and Hebb's nephew, Charles William Jones. Hebb and brother-in-law William S. Jones filed articles of incorporation on October 4, 1919, forming the Nebraska Aircraft Corporation. Other incorporators were Patriot officers Loyd A. Winship and Elmer C. Hammond.

Among Nebraska Aircraft's early customers was Walter Varney of Los Angeles, a founder of United Airlines, who ordered 50 of the so-called Lincoln Standards for a pre-United aviation venture. Charles Lindbergh – who became internationally famous in May 1927 as the first person to fly solo across the Atlantic Ocean – arrived in Lincoln on April 1, 1922. He took his first flying lessons in a Lincoln Standard Tourabout airplane, though after Hebb had left the company. Nebraska Aircraft sold several Lincoln Standard airplanes to the Mexican government, Lincoln newspaper articles indicate.

In 1920, building wood-frame airplanes was surprisingly similar to building wooden-bodied trucks in that both enterprises needed large supplies of timber. One of Nebraska Aircraft's goals, according to its articles of incorporation, was "to buy and sell lumber, timber, (and) timber land" – wood likely destined for trucks as well as airplanes. Hebb may well have had in mind an eventual merger or close association of his aircraft and truck companies. Patriot Motors' incorporation documents state the truck company's purpose as "the purchase and manufacture and sale . . . of all kinds of motor propelled or operated vehicles and machinery and aircraft."

By 1920 the Nebraska Aircraft Corporation was beginning to feel the pinch as credit tightened across the nation – a situation also facing the manufacturers of Patriot trucks.[50]

Patriot Leads Drive for Motor-Freight Lines

To boost the demand for its trucks, Hebb Motors and the reorganized Patriot Motors promoted the benefits of trucks over trains. The motor truck "is now coming to the rescue of a system of railroad transportation that has cracked from the strain of the wartime overload. It picks up goods where railroads can't go. It delivers goods where steel rails are not. Even where railroads run the motor truck is more efficient on short hauls," the company said in an April 13, 1918, *Lincoln Trade Review* ad. The company also encouraged more entrepreneurs to set up motor-freight companies, no doubt with hopes they would buy Patriot trucks.

The October 6, 1919, *Kansas City Times* announced that the newly formed Patriot Motor Express Company of Kansas City, Missouri, and Wichita, Kansas, had ordered 250 Patriot trucks. The purchase was "said to be the biggest venture to date in highway transportation competing with railroads," according to a subsequent *Lincoln Daily Star* article. Among those spearheading the venture were officials with the Patriot Motor Company of Kansas City, Missouri, a Patriot sales agency. The companies shared the same address.

Patriot Motor Express Chief Engineer Robert G. Olson told the *Kansas City Times* that daily "truck trains" would run regular schedules between larger cities in Kansas and Missouri and that the company planned to build freight warehouses in Kansas City and St. Joseph, Missouri, and in Wichita. "The Patriot Motor Express Lines will take on shipments at the loading docks and warehouses of the wholesale houses in the cities, and, returning, will pick up shipments of grain, live stock and other products of the farms, along the route," Olson said.

But even the company's active promotion of motor-freight companies failed to generate the business volume Patriot officials needed in that tough business year of 1920.

"A Widespread Industrial Depression"

By late in 1920, U.S. manufacturers' recent intense "period of super-production" had lapsed into "a widespread industrial depression" that hit auto plants particularly hard, the *New York Times* reported. "Unemployment is widespread throughout the automobile centres" in Michigan and elsewhere, according to the National Industrial Conference Board. Detroit's mayor estimated that 100,000 manufacturing employees had lost their jobs. Ford's Highland Park, Michigan, plant shut down for a month due to slow orders.

Some 1,085 U.S. businesses worth $39.8 million failed in November 1920, making it the worst November on record, according to a Bradstreet's report. Triggering the downturn was what the *New York Times* called "the unwillingness of the public to buy goods and the consequent fall of prices." Bradstreet's said the total dollar loss of failed businesses since the start of 1920 "exceed those for any year except those periods of stress, 1914 and 1907, when great international or domestic disturbances were operative."

The Federal Reserve Board, which in October denied farm groups their request for more credit, blamed the depression on a "'consumers' strike' – an evident public determination to 'wait for prices to come down,'" the *New York Times* said. "The disturbances in price and demand . . . are inevitable and unavoidable circumstances of the economic derangements occasioned by the World War," the Fed said. The Chamber of Commerce of the State of New York surveyed more than 30 industrial and commercial groups, "and all report that cancellations this year have been on an unprecedentedly large scale, save in the oil and petroleum business."

Food producers went on strike, too, when the Wheat Growers' Association of the United States in autumn 1920 called a "wheat strike," which pinched banks in Kansas and other wheat states. The pressure intensified when the National Farmers' Union on November 18 called a nationwide producers' strike, urging farmers to hold onto their 1920 harvests because of "abnormal deflation in prices of farm products," the *New York Times* said.[51]

All in all, it was a very bad time to be building farm trucks in Nebraska.

Dealers Fail, Orders Fall

Company correspondence from 1920 indicates Patriot Motors, like its dealers, was beginning to have trouble.[52] As the economy worsened, the canceled orders that rolled into the factory prevented new trucks from rolling out. A. G. Hebb and other Patriot top officers went to Fort Worth, Texas, to repossess trucks from a Patriot agency that was apparently having trouble making sales to farmers and thus could not pay the factory for trucks taken on credit. The factory was having trouble paying its own bills. A Fort Worth hotel wrote to the truck manufacturer complaining about a $53.78 bill that a Patriot representative left unpaid. Perhaps as a last-ditch attempt to generate income, Patriot Motors sent Loyd A. Winship to Houston in October "to confer with the Chamber of Commerce of that city on the erection of a branch of its truck body building plant in that city," the October 14, 1920, *Automotive Industries* reported. The branch factory never came about.

Patriot Motor's vice president, Elmer C. Hammond, wrote an October 2, 1920, reply to a stockholder who had complained about late dividend payments:

If you are acquainted with the present financial situation all over the country, you will realize that it has been pretty hard for dealers in automobiles and trucks to secure sufficient finances from their banks to carry on their business.

Consequently, they could not send us money for trucks and naturally that would cause us to keep every cent in the business that could possibly be kept. We are confident that you will be willing to play the game along with the rest of the stockholders and be patient a little while until financial conditions change to such an extent that there would be justification in sending out the dividends.

Patriot Motors "Absolutely up against It"

In a November 6, 1920, letter, Hammond was effusive in thanking a Fremont, Nebraska, man who purchased 300 shares of preferred stock in the struggling company. "The English language is inadequate to express my appreciation," Hammond wrote. "We are absolutely up against it here.

"Materials, that in the last inventory showed up for an immense sum of money, have depreciated considerably in the present inventory on account of market conditions. We are doing our best to pull the thing thru and I have all the money at my command in the company, so you can see just how much we appreciate help from persons who are big enough to come to our rescue and big enough to try to help save what seems at times to be a sinking ship."

Because of the firm's precarious financial footing, the state of Nebraska on November 8 revoked Patriot Motors' authority to sell stock. With stock sales halted, about the only way left for the company to raise money was by selling trucks or truck bodies, and few people were buying.

"As per my letter a few days ago, I am enclosing you herewith certificate No. 459 for 300 shares of preferred stock in the Patriot Motors Company," Hammond wrote on November 16, 1920, to the new owner of those shares. "It is hard to tell how the thing will come out yet, but it certainly does not look very encouraging," he added.

Underscoring Hammond's gloomy assessment, the *Lincoln Daily Star* that same day ran an article titled "Action against Patriot Motors." A Chicago supplier of bus side panels, dashes, roofing materials, and waterproof plywood filed a "replevin" lawsuit. Haskelite Manufacturing Company sought to replevin, or repossess, $22,624 in materials and supplies it had advanced to the Lincoln manufacturer during the previous four months. Haskelite also asked for $30,000 in damages.

But perhaps more threatening to the firm's survival was the lawsuit's allegations that the company had outstanding bills exceeding $750,000 and that Patriot Motors falsified a May 1920 financial statement to inflate the value of its assets and understate its liabilities. Specifically, the lawsuit alleged that the "bills receivable" portion of Patriot Motors' listing of assets included $325,000 in notes from its stock agent, Standard Securities Corporation, that "were executed for the purpose of padding the assets. . . . They were returned to the Standard Securities company after the financial statement was made," according to the newspaper account.

The petition also contended that the new Patriot Motors failed to fully take over Hebb Motors, which it called a separate organization. The petitioners thus claimed that Patriot Motors was an illegally incorporated entity with no authority to issue stock.

Small Creditors Cry "Bankruptcy"

On November 17, 1920, three small creditors – one held an unpaid bill of just $20 for paint – filed a U.S. District Court petition in Lincoln, asking that Patriot Motors and Hebb Motors be declared bankrupt. The Patriot plant had shut down late the previous week, a local newspaper reported.

The bankruptcy petition forced Patriot Motors to cancel a creditors' meeting set for November 22 in Chicago, at which Patriot officials intended to "present an accurate statement of our condition with a view of reaching some plan of meeting at least as nearly as possible all claims against the company," according to a letter sent to creditors.

Federal Judge T. C. Munger appointed Joseph E. Rosenfeld of Omaha as receiver, or trustee, for both Hebb Motors and Patriot Motors, pending the outcome of the request for a bankruptcy declaration. Named as referee was Dan H. McClenahan, who would take testimony in the case and offer his recommendations to the court.

The truck manufacturer's attorney, Fred

C. Foster, "makes no denial of the claim that they are unable to pay their debts," said the *Lincoln Daily Star* of November 18, 1920. "He declares, however, that the bigger creditors were willing to mark time for a while in order to let conditions improve but were overridden by others who came in and began to replevin material and brought things to a climax. "He [Foster] believes that the men who were instrumental in organizing and promoting the company have invested practically all they have in the businesses and that they were fighting to the last minute to keep the business going," the newspaper said.

Isabelle Lampshire of Lincoln, daughter of Plant Superintendent King W. Gillespie, confirmed that the motor company's officers lost heavily. Her father, the former carpenter and homebuilder, owned his family's home and also owned four or five other houses that he had mortgaged to invest in Hebb Motors, Lampshire said. "He lost those places but he kept our family home when Hebb Motors went broke," Lampshire said. In 1918, A. G. Hebb could have sold out for $750,000 "but loved business so much he refused," remembered his son, Grainger Hebb. "As a result, he lost about everything except a mortgaged house."

Canceled Orders "Like Confetti"

"Bad business and market conditions are blamed in a large extent for the trouble in the company's finances," the *Lincoln Daily Star* reported on November 18, 1920. "Sales began to slacken last spring. . . . Large orders of material were received and the value of this fell rapidly. In August there was a slight boom in the truck business and it appeared that the company might pull out of its overload by winter, but market conditions went bad again and sales fell off," the *Star* said.

"Gee, it was a booming place. They were going great guns while they went," Lampshire remembers. Because of the credit pinch, "the cancellations of orders came in just like confetti in the mails for trucks and planes, as well," said Bill Jones, Hebb's nephew, who was also referring to the Lincoln Standard airplanes sold by Hebb's Nebraska Aircraft Corporation, which likewise failed.

After the war, Jones remembers, Federal Reserve Banks began to tighten lending to state and national banks. "This condition made it hard for people, and certain businesses, to borrow money. The farmer couldn't borrow on his next year's crop so had to cancel his order for that new Patriot truck. Businesses were in a similar condition for borrowing, and they too had to cancel. Orders all over the United States were being canceled."

In May 1920, the Kansas City Federal Reserve Bank "declined to discount any paper from member banks based on passenger car stocks. This action caused great concern within the automotive industry, for it meant a tightening of credit," according to a book chronicling the development of the U.S. auto industry.[53]

The poor business climate hurt the entire truck industry, though much of the effect carried over into 1921 production. Total 1920 U.S. sales of 321,789 trucks plummeted to just 148,052 in 1921. It would take truck makers until 1923 to top the 1920 production figure.

A "Silent" Auction

Since no reorganization plan was forthcoming, Referee Dan McClenahan ordered that the factory, grounds, and equipment be auctioned on June 23, 1921, to pay creditors. Appraisers, apparently hired by the bankruptcy trustee, put the value of the factory and assets at $569,806 while "the Hebb interests valued the plant at $1,575,000," reported the *Lincoln Star*. Claims against the truck manufacturer totaled $1.35 million.

With Trustee Joseph Rosenfeld acting as auctioneer "to save the expense of hiring a professional," some 150 onlookers packed the truck factory's dining room. "Benches piled up outside the windows furnished stands for many more," the *Lincoln Star* said.

Rosenfeld first asked for separate bids on items including the plant and real estate, service department, about 120 trucks in the factory, truck parts, truck bodies and body parts, office furniture and equipment, machinery, 29 trucks in various warehouses across the country, railroad sidings, lumber, hardware, and tools.

"But the pleas of the auctioneer were received in silence," the *Star* reported. When "the whole plant was then put under the hammer," William H. Ferguson, co-founder and president of Beatrice Creamery Company of Lincoln – today the Chicago-based Beatrice Companies – won the plant with a $110,000 bid. For another $5,000, he also bought the 29 warehoused trucks. Ferguson, who would become vice president of the reorganized Patriot Manufacturing Company, was acting for a group of creditors who planned to reopen the plant, the *Star* said.

Hearing no objections during a June 28 court hearing attended by all creditors, Referee Dan McClenahan confirmed what he called Ferguson's "very low" bid of $110,000 for the factory, rendering all outstanding Hebb and Patriot stock worthless. Creditors fared little better, receiving "about 10 percent of their claims," the *Havelock Post* said. The national banks that lost the most included National Bank of New York, $125,000; Omaha (Nebraska) National, $120,000; and First National of Council Bluffs (Iowa), $44,000. Three local nationally chartered banks carried a total Patriot debt of $162,000.

Swayed by 16 "prominent Lincoln businessmen" and by attorney Fred C. Foster, representing the truck maker in bankruptcy proceedings, the Lancaster County Board in July cut the factory building's $350,000 assessment to $125,000. "In making the as-

sessment reduction the board of equalization sought a fair and just assessment and yet one which will not burden the plant and prevent it from becoming a going concern again," the *Lincoln Star* said.[54]

Through its promotional materials and advertising, Hebb Motors gradually came to identify its home as Lincoln, rather than Havelock. But the two cities were no longer jostling for recognition by the time the court confirmed the factory's bankruptcy sale, grumbled the editor of the *Havelock Post*. "This confirmation . . . writes finis to the dreams of most of the stockholders in Havelock who invested their savings under the guise of 'helping a home concern,' which, while in its glory, was classed as a 'Lincoln industry,' but after its failure was referred to as 'a Havelock venture.' Now that it may be reorganized as a profitable concern[,] watch the Lincoln papers class it as 'a Lincoln industry' again."[55]

New Owners "Hard-Headed, Far-Seeing"

Local financier Charles C. Quiggle on July 23 began managing the factory for the group of creditors who paid $126,000 for the plant's assets at the auction. That amount is apparently the sum of the plant's purchase price of $110,000, the $5,000 paid for 29 warehoused trucks, and the $11,000 paid to assume accounts and notes receivable.

The creditor-owners, holding $700,000 worth of stock issued by the defunct truck manufacturer, were having new incorporation papers prepared. The group hoped "to purchase the interests of the eastern creditors and make the company an entirely local one," reported the July 27, 1921, *Lincoln Star*. The Havelock factory would again make trucks and truck bodies under the new name of Patriot Manufacturing Company. Its new officers were Hardy Furniture Company President William E. Hardy, president; William H. Ferguson, vice president;

and C. C. Quiggle, who as secretary-treasurer was to be the company's full-time financial manager.

Sixty-five employees had already begun making trucks in the factory again, the officers announced on August 6, 1921. Patriot Manufacturing had $300,000 paid in toward its authorized capitalization of $400,000 and the new company would sell no stock, said A. Reis Meyer, new general manager of manufacturing, who sounded a new theme of caution:

The new company will continue the making of both trucks and truck bodies, on a conservative scale to meet the needs of adjacent territory in surrounding states. The management will endeavor to create a permanent business for Lincoln, with the backing of hard-headed, far-seeing business men. Business will be conducted along moderate lines to meet only the needs of the territory. There will be no high-financing. . . . The company will probably concentrate on one model and that a model developed to suit the very particular needs of Nebraska farmers and those in adjoining states.[56]

The company, in fact, continued producing the light Revere truck and the heavier Lincoln and Washington models, names that lasted until the 1924 model year. Patriot Manufacturing also introduced an LS-800 model that, at 2 tons, fit between the 1½-ton Lincoln and 2½-ton Washington models, reported the September 28, 1922, *Motor Age* magazine.

Perhaps publicity-shy, the new company was seldom mentioned in the local press. But Charles Quiggle, the company's secretary-treasurer, told the *Lincoln Sunday Star* in April 1923 that "motor truck sales since the first of January have been more than double those for the same months of last year," as the newspaper put it. "Patriot dealers in Oklahoma, Wyoming, Colorado, Kansas, Minnesota and Nebraska also anticipate an even greater demand for the remainder of the year.

"To meet this increasing popularity of Patriot trucks, especially in the Oklahoma and Wyoming oil fields, the Patriot company have [*sic*] placed large orders of materials for the three standard models with their eastern parts manufacturers," the *Star* said. "Mr. Quiggle states that it has also been necessary to employ an additional force of men for machine and assembly work to increase production. The commercial body department is now operating on a volume not usually attained before mid-summer. Shipments are being made daily as far west as the Pacific coast, and to the extreme southwest."[57]

The new owners "believe that the plant can be operated to provide employment for 300 men," said the *Lincoln Star* of July 27, 1921. But the factory undoubtedly had a larger workforce under Hebb, who sold internationally, than under the new owners. Press accounts generally agree that Hebb Motors opened in the fall of 1918 with about 200 employees. The *Lincoln Star* put the workforce at 240 by mid-1919. By late March 1920, when business was booming and plans were set for constructing more factory space, the company was employing 500 workers, according to the *Havelock Post*.

Woods Brothers Buy Patriot

"Woods Bros. Now Control Patriot Plant," read a bold front-page headline in the January 11, 1924, *Lincoln Star*. "The Woods Brothers companies acquired controlling interest in the Patriot [Manufacturing] company Thursday [January 10], buying a majority of the stock from various banks and individuals who took over the assets and buildings when the original company" was forced into bankruptcy, the newspaper said.

Under Mark and George Woods, the company would reorganize with new officers and directors, but "the management and general policy of the company will not be radically changed and the business will

continue for the time being at least, along the same general conservative lines that have been followed since its organization," the newspaper said.

"The plant, one of the finest in the middle west, located near Havelock, has been owned since bankruptcy days by banks and individuals, and has continued to produce Patriot trucks and to enjoy good business. Woods Brothers had some interest in the business at the first re-organization but the recent transfer of stock gives them entire control," the *Star* said.

The Woods brothers continued to put out three or more Patriot models a year, bearing such designations as 7R, 9L, and 11W. The weights of the different models indicate that R, L, and W were letter codes for the former Revere, Lincoln, and Washington trucks.

In April 1925 on a Lincoln residential street, General John J. "Blackjack" Pershing and Mark and George Woods posed for photographs beside a Patriot truck. (See fig.3.28.) Pershing, a friend of the Woods brothers, in 1893 graduated with a bachelor of laws degree from the University of Nebraska in Lincoln, where he was also a military instructor. Mark Woods spearheaded a Nebraska-based "Pershing for President" movement in 1919, though Pershing – commander of the Allied Expeditionary Force during World War I – stayed out of the race, F. Pace Woods, Sr., Mark's son, said in an interview.

"They showed this truck to Pershing and Pershing was a great friend, a personal friend, of Dad's, so they got a picture of the truck in front of the house with Pershing standing near the truck and George on one end and Mark on the other end of the picture. That was a promotional deal. Pershing

3.28 From left, George Woods, General John J. Pershing, and Mark Woods by a Patriot truck, 1925. (PW)

3.29 This Woods truck with roll-down canvas side curtains was apparently used by a Nebraska state fish hatchery. (PW)

was interested in the type of truck. In those days, we used any damn thing we could to get a name in 'em."

Mark and George Woods kept the Patriot Manufacturing name but changed the name of the truck from Patriot to Woods, beginning with the 1927 model year. (See fig.3.29.) The bodies it built were still called Patriot bodies, however. As the 1930s dawned, the factory was producing eight different truck models, ranging from a 1½-ton 160-inch-wheelbase chassis for $1,995 to a 5½-ton 190-inch chassis priced at just under $7,000. Though complete trucks bearing the Patriot name were assembled for nine model years (1918–1926), Patriot bodies were built under various owners until 1948, for a total of 31 years.

Kenneth Latimer of Newton, Iowa, in 1970 bought from the original owner a 1927 Woods truck, which he has since sold. Equipped with a 6-cylinder Buda engine, the Woods truck was "very easy to start, taking only a few revolutions, even after sitting all winter," he said. But the 4-speed transmission was "fairly hard to shift," and the truck was "very hard to steer," so it is just as well its top speed was around 35 or 40 miles per hour – Latimer's best guess, since the truck came without a speedometer.[58]

In March 1927, shortly after the Woods had replaced the Patriot truck, the company filed for and, on September 3, received Patent No. 1,726,918 for an adjustable Highway Weed Cutter. Designed by Harry C. Ohler of Lincoln, a supervisor at Patriot Manufacturing, the cutter allowed a truck to do the job of a tractor in trimming roadside ditches.

Patriot Manufacturing by 1929 was a division of another Woods-owned company, Arrow Aircraft and Motors Corporation, both situated at the original Hebb Motors factory in Havelock. In the mid-1930s, Arrow would begin producing an Arrow airplane powered by an only slightly modified Ford V-8 engine.

Woods Truck Phased Out

The last Woods truck produced by the Patriot Motors division was made as late as 1932, the last year for which *Automotive Industries* magazine included the truck in its annual specifications issue. The directories issued by Lincoln Telephone & Telegraph Company, another company controlled by the Woods brothers, mentioned "Woods Trucks" as a Patriot Manufacturing product as late as the Winter 1931–32 telephone directory.

Competition, economic hard times in 1920, 1921, and later years – especially during the Great Depression of the 1930s – and the public's demand for low-priced, well-engineered cars and trucks forced automakers to build ever more expensive factories to mass-produce their vehicles. Only the strong survived, as reflected by the sharp drop in the number of truck manufacturers since 1920. Approximately 155 companies were making trucks for national distribution in 1920, though the ranks thinned to 91 by 1930 and to 25 by 1940, according to the annual specification editions of *Automotive Industries* magazine.

With new owners and under the new name Patriot Body Company – which it had adopted by 1941 – the firm by 1943 had moved from Havelock back to the 10th and Vine streets building in Lincoln that once housed the Hebb commercial body factory.

Granville A. Bishop, who joined Patriot Manufacturing in the early 1920s and was factory superintendent by 1940, designed many of the later bodies, according to his daughter, Betty Witham.[59] These later products included metal moving-van bodies, livestock racks for tractor-trailer trucks, and refrigerated bodies for local dairies. (See fig.3.30.)

A fire blamed on a faulty boiler blower motor leveled the Patriot Body Company's building at 10th and Vine on January 24, 1948, consuming 250,000 board feet of stored lumber and apparently spelling the end of a modest business that was then employing 25 people and shipping bodies to 15 states. The shell of the concrete Hebb Motors factory in Havelock, a state-of-the-art plant in 1918, was still being used in the 1990s by Goodyear Tire & Rubber Com-

pany, which bought the plant at the close of World War II.

The 1928 *Branham Automobile Reference Book* lists beginning serial numbers for Patriot Manufacturing's truck models for 1921 through 1924. Instead of giving specific ending serial numbers, the reference manual gives a range. Based on that information, all that can be said is that the company made no more – and likely less – than 250 trucks in 1921, 750 in 1922, 400 in 1923, and 300 in 1924. The manual doesn't provide enough information to estimate production for 1925 and 1926.

A Patriot historian near Lincoln, Tom Lutzi, has compiled a list of about 15 Patriots that he knows have survived into the 1990s. They are in various states of repair but at least five are driveable. Those available for public viewing include a Patriot owned by the North Platte Valley Historical Society in Gering, Nebraska. In addition, a booster club operates a 1918 Patriot that club members drive in parades to promote the Southeast Community College campus in Milford, Nebraska. Shoemaker's Truck

3.30 A mid-1930s Chevrolet straight truck at the Patriot body factory in Havelock. (BW)

Stop in Lincoln is displaying a Patriot fitted with a non-original tow truck body. Another Patriot, restored by county honor-farm inmates, is on display in the San Joaquin County Historical Museum at Micke Grove Park near Lodi, California. In nearby Woodland, California, Hays Antique Truck Museum has what it identifies as a 1920 Lincoln-model Patriot. Van Horn's Truck Museum near Mason City, Iowa, has an early Woods truck.

Hebb Was Idea Man, an Organizer

After Patriot Motors failed in late 1920, A. G. Hebb went back to selling cars in partnership with longtime Lincoln auto dealer Ebenezer E. Mockett, but died April 21, 1923, from diabetes complications. Bill Jones remembers his Uncle Arthur Hebb not as a Henry Ford – hands greasy from tinkering with machinery – but as an idea man, an organizer, and a consummate salesman.

"He was a very persuasive person and that's how he got associated with a lot of people and had a tremendous group of friends there in Lincoln," Jones said. "He made all these friends and got into all these different types of businesses. . . . He was so well liked and so well respected for his ability and judgment.

"He was the guy that had the good ideas but he also went out and hired good men to head those various departments. That was one of his abilities, to get good people, because no one man could single-handedly do all those things. And he had a good sales department," Jones said.

When Hebb Motors failed in late 1920, Grainger Hebb said, "Like normal, many figured the business had been run [i]n a crooked manner so many lawsuits were brought against father. Each time, he was found not guilty. After many court cases, and auditing of the books of the company, it was determined . . . that the business was

operated as it should have been, that it was a case of conditions that caused it to fail."

The Mysterious Patriot Car

One shrouded part of the Patriot legend is whether the company actually produced any of the cars that it planned to build. "Patriot had one little car one year. I don't remember what it was," said Marion Garcia of Havelock. "Somebody who worked over there had one. If I remember right, it was a touring car. I think the name of it was a Patriot," Garcia said in an interview at age 77. Garcia said the factory made the car – painted black – at the same time it was building trucks.[60]

Though Hebb's success story was marred by a plot twist in the closing chapter, his rise from selling hog-cholera insurance to manufacturing trucks bore all the marks of careful business planning. It is reasonable to assume that, before announcing his car plans, Hebb had prepared detailed design drawings for the car he envisioned, and possibly built one or more prototypes. What became of such plans or of any prototype cars is open to conjecture. Even before he moved to his new factory in 1918, Hebb foresaw the possibility of building cars in Havelock: In February 1918 he filed for a trademark on the name Patriot for both "Automobiles and Automobile-Trucks."

"It Might Have Been"

With his background of selling Fords and building commercial bodies, A. G. Hebb built a modern 4½-acre truck factory that in 1919 and 1920 produced about 1,350 heavy trucks under the worst possible economic conditions. Nationwide advertising helped the trucks sell across the Midwest, West, and Southwest and, selectively, in the East through a strong dealer network. The Havelock factory even exported some trucks.

Hebb Motors diversified – though still within the automotive industry – by supplying truck bodies to other manufacturers, building a variety of special-order bodies for its own trucks, and actively encouraging the development of motor-freight companies, such as the Patriot Motor Express Company. Under a separate corporate banner, Hebb tapped another promising transportation field by converting surplus biplanes to commercial uses after World War I. If the company's testimonial advertising is to be believed, the trucks were sturdy. The evidence suggests Hebb's well-planned enterprise had a rosy future. Then the already troubled economy took a nosedive. The company did continue making trucks under different managers, but not on the grand scale Hebb envisioned.

On behalf of Patriot Motors, Standard Securities Corporation in April 1920 had offered investors "an opportunity and an invitation" to buy the first $1 million in common stock issued by the expanded and renamed Patriot Motors. "Life is a progression – or the reverse; manufactories go ahead or go backward. Nature will harbor nothing stationary. . . . In 1918 a limited

number of investors were fortunate enough to secure stock of the original issue, although they knew not of their good fortune then and had to be urged to invest. One thousand dollars invested then represents a value today of $3,630.00," said the two-page newspaper ad, which went on to stress the safety of a new investment in Patriot Motors.

"In the history of the United States there has never been a general crop failure, and there never will be, because there is involved too wide a scope of territory. . . . On the same basis, the manufacturing concern, rightly directed, producing needed articles, and MARKETING IT IN THE ENTIRE COUNTRY, cannot fail, because too much territory is involved. There will be a market every month, somewhere between Canada and the Gulf; between New York and San Francisco."[61]

A more pointed prophesy came in an early 1920 stock notice offering "The Last of the Issue Of Hebb Motors Co." The upper right-hand corner of the ad carried this epigram: "Opportunity Ignored: 'Of all sad words of tongue or pen/'The saddest are these –/'It might have been.'"[62]

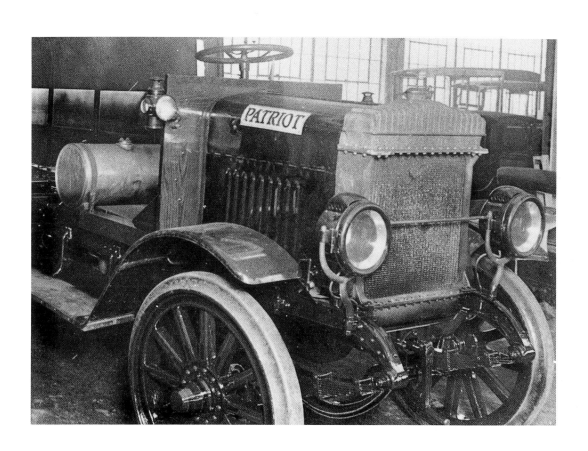

Spaulding of Iowa
Honestly Constructed of Honest Materials

4

Best known for the fold-down bed in its novel "Sleeping Car," a 1914 version of the recreational vehicle, the Spaulding Manufacturing Company of Grinnell, Iowa, made other headlines from 1909 to 1916.

The driver of a Spaulding car topped 80 miles per hour at times and rocketed past the Rock Island fast mail train to set a world's dirt-road speed record in a wild Iowa border-to-border race. A Spaulding car turned in a perfect road score during the June 1911 650-mile "Little Glidden" endurance run across Iowa. In a slow-speed stunt better suited to photography, Ernest H. Spaulding took the wheel to drive a loaded Spaulding touring car up the steps of the State Capitol in Des Moines.

San Diego promoters of the Panama-California Exposition of 1915 used a Spaulding touring car to shoot thousands of feet of movie film during a transcontinental mapping tour designed both to publicize the Expo and to promote an ocean-to-ocean highway. "I am writing you to let you know the success we are having with the Spaulding car in plowing through snow from one to three feet deep," a member of the transcontinental mapping crew wrote from Pennsylvania. "Ours was the only automobile that was able to come through. Even a Packard car could only go part way."

Within the state, the Iowa Publishing Company of Des Moines used a Spaulding 30 to map Iowa highways. Even loaded with nine people, a Spaulding 40 challenged and tamed a homegrown terror, Potato Knoll, a "freak formation in the center of a corn field" near Belmond, Iowa.

In addition to sales agents in Des Moines and across Iowa, the automaker had agents as far away as Fort Worth, Texas, and Los Angeles, where the Spaulding had performed well in a Riverside hill-climbing contest. Grinnell cars were poised to take the West Coast by storm: "300 Spaulding Cars Go to California," cried the headline over an August 1913 *Grinnell Herald* news story, but that turned out to be more fiction than fact.

In the midst of its 1912 model year, the Spaulding adopted an electric self-starter but didn't identify the brand. Likewise, the automaker was tight-lipped about its earliest engine supplier, though it later used Rutenber before a switch to Buda – all 4-cylinder engines. Spaulding used steel bodies, which it made in a new $150,000 factory constructed in Grinnell for that purpose.

In the best carriage-making tradition, Spauldings were trimmed in leather, and in 1912 the car sported "11-inch Turkish tilted spring cushions, making it ride like a rocking chair." The standard Spaulding color was a deep blue, but various models were painted light blue, green, gray, cream, red, and even orange.

Unlike some other carriage makers, Spaulding Manufacturing Company continued to prosper in its production of carriages and wagons at the same time it was making automobiles. As many as 500 men worked at the Grinnell factory when it was producing both horse-drawn and horseless carriages. Only about 30 were in the motorcar department. In the 1920s, long after it had closed the automobile chapter of its history, the company's woodworking department was busy making truck cabs and bodies for Ford.

"You Pay a Little More But You Pay Less Often" was a Spaulding slogan. The new automobiles supplemented a line of carriages and spring wagons – 10,000 a year by 1909 – that H. W. Spaulding had been making since 1876. By the time the company announced its automotive intentions in 1910, it was transacting $1.5 million in business annually on sales of carriages and wagons, according to one estimate. The company insisted that its longtime Spaulding diamond logo also "Signifies Motor Car Quality."

Though no great threat to Michigan, Ohio, or Indiana, Iowa was the scene of an active automotive industry. Grinnell, for instance, was already home to a nationally known manufacturer of leather driving gloves. The Meteor Motor Car Company was producing 4-cylinder 50-horsepower Meteor cars in Bettendorf. Fred and August Duesenberg were building 2-cylinder Mason cars in Des Moines, which, after a buyout, became the Maytag of Waterloo. The Colby car was poised to enter the market in Mason City.

The auto-manufacturing centers of the country considered Iowa as just a farm state. But it was the Spaulding car's main sales territory, and the Grinnell manufacturer took advantage of homegrown pride

in the state's agricultural might. To promote its display at the 1914 Des Moines auto show, the Grinnell automaker ran a cartoon ad (see fig.4.1) showing a cigar-chomping, grizzle-faced, grinning Iowan, holding aloft a Spaulding car: "You've seen the kind of corn and pigs I raise, well the auto I make is just as good."

Spaulding Manufacturing added a line of farm and general-delivery trucks in late 1912, its second full year of auto production. The demand for Spaulding cars pushed aside any plans to develop and promote trucks, however.

The company dropped its automobile line in 1916; during and after World War I it made products as varied as wagon parts,

4.1 A 1914 Spaulding ad. (March 8, 1914, *Des Moines Register and Leader*)

4.2 Henry W. Spaulding. (SHSI)

packing crates, and knitting needles. Later, Spaulding Manufacturing made truck cabs and bodies for other car and truck manufacturers, including Henry Ford, who was rebuffed in his attempt to buy out Spaulding. The family-owned Spaulding concern, unincorporated, foundered when Ford and other large automakers began making their own truck bodies. Creditors forced the company to cease operations in the late 1920s.

A Blacksmithing, Carriage-Making Politician

As a blacksmith, carriage maker, mayor, and state senator, Henry W. Spaulding (see fig.4.2) had a reputation for getting things done. Spaulding, a transplanted Vermonter who worked on neighbors' farms as a youth, left school after the eighth grade and by the age of 19 had opened a blacksmith shop in his hometown of Chelsea, making buggies as a sideline.[1]

Though a half-dozen biographical accounts of Spaulding's life differ widely in detailing it, all credit the carriage maker with developing the Spaulding "trailing system" of selling buggies. "This system,

Spaulding once pointed out, was brought about by a case of necessity," according to the version given in the January 21, 1937, *Des Moines Tribune*. "Shortly before coming to Grinnell, he had two or three finished buggies on hand and his creditors were pushing him for the money due on materials. . . . Spaulding promised his creditors he would settle within a few weeks. He hitched up his buggies one behind the other – trailer fashion – and started out to sell them. He did sell them and he returned and payed [*sic*] his debts." The trailer system was what one account called Spaulding's "greatest contribution to the science of selling."

Spaulding later sold his own shop to work as a mechanic in other shops, according to one account. Two versions in Grinnell newspapers suggest that Spaulding then either "traveled for" or "assisted in the manufacture" of organs for a Vermont organ manufacturer. All accounts agree, however, that in 1873 he began a three-year stint selling tools and screw-cutting machines for a Massachusetts wholesale manufacturer. He left that job in 1876 to move to Grinnell, a town he had perhaps visited on a sales trip, according to his granddaughter, Miriam Spaulding Simms.[2]

In Grinnell, Spaulding divided his time between blacksmithing and building carriages and wagons until 1882, when a devastating tornado destroyed his home – the *Des Moines Tribune* says "his factory was virtually demolished," as well – as was any hope for a career in blacksmithing. Simms says the tornado ripped through Spaulding's home, spun him through the air for "eight or 10 blocks" and set him down only after inflicting a permanent arm injury that prevented him from swinging a heavy blacksmith's hammer.

Despite the tornado and a March 1893 fire that reportedly caused $60,000 damage to a Spaulding factory building, production increased from 15 vehicles in 1876 to 350 by 1883, 6,000 by 1903, "and in 1909, 10,000 buggies, carriages and spring wagons a

If wanting any style vehicle that looks and wears better than many others, our Agent will call on you.

Happy as larks, and got engaged on their first trip, and now awfully stuck on each other, but not with Spaulding's glue, but because riding in this gem of a buggy built by

The Spaulding Mfg. Co.
GINNELL, IOWA, U.S.A.

If a Body meet a Body coming through the Rye
If a Body kiss a Body need a Body cry,

Card No. 1

The International Co., Bellefontaine, Ohio.

year, employing 300 men," according to the April 1937 edition of *Annals of Iowa* magazine. (See fig.4.3.) In a 1936 recounting of the Spaulding empire, the *Grinnell Herald-Register* put the peak carriage production at 20,000 annually with 500 employees. In light of such production figures, it's understandable that more Spaulding carriages than cars have survived. The collection of the Grinnell Historical Museum includes a Spaulding surrey and buggy.

"Work Hard, Save, Get a Good Wife"

"Naturally, a man of his driving energy and restless industry was concerned with many other things beside his own business," the *Grinnell Herald-Register* said following Spaulding's death on January 20, 1937, at the age of 90. A city councilman, Spaulding also served two terms as Grinnell mayor before being elected in 1910 for his first of two terms as a state senator. "For many years he was one of the state's most active Republicans," according to the *Des Moines Tribune*. Biographies recount his support for a variety of local causes, including paved city streets for Grinnell.

If he was active in politics, he was even more so in business. Spaulding was a founder of such local businesses as the Grinnell Washing Machine Company, Colonial Theatre, Citizens National Bank, and others. He helped nationally known aviator Billy Robinson start a Grinnell airplane factory that showed promise until Robinson died in a March 1916 plane crash while trying to set an altitude record.

"He was a hard worker himself so he worked everybody else," said Miriam Simms, who recalls her grandfather working his employees on New Year's Day. "H. W. Spaulding is fairly earning the name of being the most energetic man in Grinnell," the local paper wrote as early as August 1881. "He has built a barn this summer, has made a good addition to his residence, and is now adding a forty-foot rear extension to his brick carriage shop."

As a freshman senator in early 1911, Spaulding revealed his business philosophy to the writer of the *Des Moines Tribune*'s "Little Jaunts to the Statehouse" column: "Work twice as hard as you think you ought to, save something out of every piece of money you get, live quietly and regularly, don't buy any thing without seeing it, and get a good wife."

4.3 An undated advertising card for Spaulding carriages. (GHM)

4.4 Fred Spaulding as a young man. (MSS)

4.5 Ernest Spaulding, 1919. (MSS)

Though his company was making annual sales of $1.5 million, "the canny Senator Spaulding is not saying how much he is worth," the newspaper said. Its columnist added, however, that "Spaulding was rated in Bradstreet's fifteen years ago at $750,000. The company has given out no figures since. In the interim the Spaulding Manufacturing company at Grinnell has grown from a 'kid's size' concern to one of the most complete establishments in Iowa, and one of the largest carriage building concerns in the world. Spaulding has $300,000 invested outside of the firm."

Spaulding had three partners in the business at various times after 1876, but by 1903 both his sons had joined him – Frederick E. (see fig.4.4) as a bookkeeper and Ernest H. (see fig. 4.5) as a carriage salesman. They were all involved in the production of autos, which began with an auspicious announcement in 1909.

"Experiments Are Now Being Conducted"

"Spaulding Mfg. Co. May Make Autos," read the top of a four-deck headline in the June 11, 1909, *Grinnell Herald,* giving the first public hint of what was afoot. "The firm has been considering such a plan for some time, but not until recently has it appeared feasible," the article said. "Now, however, a room for experimenting has been fitted up and if all goes well, the Spaulding automobile may be expected to make its appearance on the market in due course of time."

Just two months later on August 17, the newspaper reported that "experiments are now being conducted at the factory and a model, made up at the Spaulding shops[,] has been seen frequently around the streets. Last Saturday it made a trip to Newburg [five or six miles distant] in fast time." The company called in an architect to draw up plans for adding a third floor and enlarging a brick building east across the street from the building that housed offices for the Spaulding carriage factory.

"It is planned now to place three different grades of automobiles upon the market; the most expensive, a $1,500 car with sliding gear [transmission] and 112-inch wheel base; one for $1,400, which will be a planetary [transmission] touring car[,] and a $1,250 roadster," the newspaper said.

Contrasting markedly with the detailed, almost breathless, accounts in the *Grinnell*

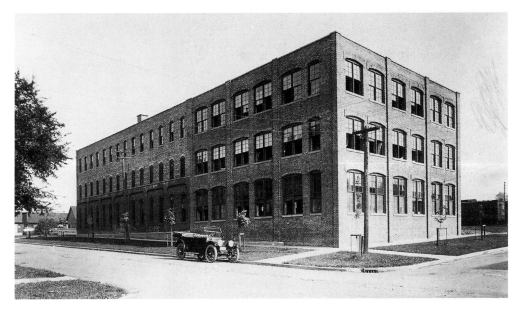

Herald's news columns, Ernest Spaulding matter-of-factly broke the news in a two-line letter to the Iowa Secretary of State's office on September 17, 1909: "We are about to manufacture motor cars. What arrangements could be made for numbers for our testers, etc." The company subsequently paid $10 for a dealer's permit and to receive the demonstration number D-419, which can be seen in the photos of new Spaulding cars being tested on the roads in and around Grinnell.[3]

Four months after its first article about the Spaulding plans, the October 5, 1909, *Grinnell Herald* reported that workmen were extending the west end and adding a third floor to the building that would "be devoted entirely to the manufacture of the Spaulding automobile." The completed structure would be 158 feet long by 60 feet wide, or about 28,000 square feet. (Fig. 4.6 shows the finished factory.)

Further, C. W. Miller, the new auto department foreman, who "comes from the works of the Carter Motor Car Co., in Pontiac, Mich.," was already in Grinnell to help with the car, which the newspaper called "a combination of the ideas of H. W., F. E. and E. H. Spaulding. All these gentlemen drive automobiles and all have been studying them for some time. Charles Cratty has given especially valuable aid in the experiments which have finally resulted in the evolution of a 30-horse power car which has surprised everyone who has ridden in it by its marvelous hill climbing ability." A company driver, Cratty drove a Spaulding in the 1911 Iowa Little Glidden tour and helped prepare the 1913 Spaulding cross-state racer.

Glove Factory a Happy Happenstance

Mild weather in January 1910 allowed work to resume on the new brick automobile factory at Fourth Avenue and Spring Street, where "already active manufacturing has been begun. A good sized force of men is now employed in the factory and automobiles in various stages of construction are to be seen there," reported the January 25, 1910, *Grinnell Herald*. Autos would be assembled on the first floor (see fig.4.7), painted on the third, and stored on the second – a standard arrangement for 1910 – and moved between floors via an elevator on the building's south side. Near the elevator would be a stock room on the first floor

4.6 A 1913 Spaulding 40 is parked on the north side of the Spaulding auto factory. (SHSI)

4.7 Spaulding cars under construction; the right-hand steering means the cars in this undated photo are 1912 or earlier models. (LB)

and a finish stock room on the second floor. Within the coming five years, the Spauldings hoped to add two 6,000-foot "feeder" additions to the south – extending from the east and west ends of the main factory – to boost production to 1,000 autos annually.[4]

As his father's company geared up to make cars, Ernest Spaulding was already cornering the market on local auto repairs with the purchase of a Grinnell garage. By 1915 he was one of several investors in a Spaulding agency, the Hawkeye Motor Sales Company, which was also selling Davis, Dodge, and Saxon autos. "Daddy [Ernest] has told me so many times that he had to not only sell the car, he had to sell the idea to the customer that they needed a car, because they were still driving horse and buggies," Miriam Simms said.

Ernest and his brother, Fred, were members of the Grinnell Automobile Club that in March 1910 pledged to support "the proposition for a river to a river road through the state of Iowa, to follow the line of the Rock Island railroad" and to pass through Grinnell. The resulting River-to-River Road was the route later followed by a Spaulding racer in the car company's most famous publicity stunt.

When a pathfinding car for the 1910 Glidden Tour reliability contest passed through Grinnell in early April 1910, a new Spaulding 30 acted as a pilot car for the next 35 miles along the newly designated River-to-River Road. It would be the first of the company's long string of publicity events. Charles Cratty drove the Spaulding car, and his passengers included two of the three Spaulding men, Henry and Ernest. Cratty was perhaps driving the Spaulding prototype car, since automobile production was two months away.

As the Spauldings prepared to make automobiles in central Iowa, it helped that auto enthusiasts across the United States knew their city as home to Grinnell brand leather driving gloves. Despite their hurry, members of the 1910 Glidden Tour pathfinding crew stopped at the Morrison-Ricker Manufacturing Company on their way through Grinnell. "Each of the party was fitted out with a pair of the firm's famous automobile gloves," according to the *Grinnell Herald.* "The party were already wearing Grinnell gloves, having purchased them at Dallas, Texas."[5]

"A Joy Unspeakable Forever"

Just a week later in mid-April 1910, Spaulding Manufacturing, "the oldest and largest manufacturers of vehicles west of the Mississippi, announced the debut of the Spaulding '30,' the 1910 model which is now ready for the market," according to the *Grinnell Herald.*[6] The car had been one year in coming to market, "the first year having been spent in giving the first model exhaustive tests and a thorough tryout," Henry Spaulding said. The 1910 lineup consisted of two models that shared the same chassis and engine but had different transmissions.

According to the *Grinnell Herald,* Model CP was equipped with a 2-speed planetary transmission, which was then fading in popularity, while the Model CS used a more modern 3-speed selective sliding-gear transmission. The three body styles were a five-passenger touring car, a pony tonneau, "and a roadster with a rumble seat mounted on a tool box."

A different model designation is used by both the February 1910 *MoTor* magazine and the March 1910 *Cycle and Automobile Trade Journal.* They list a Model C, equipped with the sliding-gear transmission, and a Model D, equipped with the planetary. The journals list the price as $1,500 for either model.

According to the June 1910 *Motor Print* magazine, "The car has been built with the intention of being particularly adapted for farmers and merchants, the frame and spring suspension construction being such as to meet the requirements of western roads."

Iowa roads of that period were among the worst in the West, according to the first woman to drive across the United States. The road from Jefferson to Vail in west-central Iowa "had one section composed of a veritable sea of chuck holes of varying sizes, most of them so filled with water that it was difficult to determine their depths," Alice Huyler Ramsey wrote of the 1909 trip she made with three female friends in a Maxwell car. "The people were so eager for us to like their state, to which they had great loyalty. And we really did like it; but – oh, those terrible roads!"[7]

None of this was news to Henry Spaulding, who had known Iowa roads for 35 years. He was undoubtedly very concerned about this aspect of the automobiles that would bear his name. "Particular attention has been given to the spring suspension, and a number of very severe tests, such as only Iowa roads afford," led the company to adopt softer full-scroll elliptic springs on the CP and firmer three-quarter scroll elliptics on the CS model, according to the *Grinnell Herald.* Both new Spaulding models had long, flat, semi-elliptic front springs. "Rubber bumpers set on the rear spring clip spacers preclude the possibility of sudden jolts from road shocks. As a result of this carefully tested spring suspension, there is a notable absence of side sway even at high speed over rough roads and a consequent ease in steering."

All cars came equipped with Rushmore-brand headlamps, Dietz sidelights and taillights, a Prest-O-Lite tank of compressed acetylene for the headlamps, horn, foot rail, robe rail, tire-repair outfit, tire pump, and a tool kit. The 30-horsepower 4-cylinder engine had a 4-inch bore and stroke with cylinders cast separately. The company neglected to identify the maker of the engine, which had a splash oiling system, magneto ignition with dry cells in reserve, and a leather-and-cork cone clutch. A driveshaft carried the power from the clutch to the rear axle. Both the planetary and sliding-gear transmissions were bolted to the rear-axle housing, a practice losing favor as

4.8 Fitted with a rough testing body and tire chains, a Spaulding car gets a workout on muddy Iowa roads. (SHSI)

many automakers were mounting transmissions directly to the rear of the engine or in the center of the car frame.

Both the touring car and pony tonneau had detachable tonneaus, or back seats, "affording an interchangeable car, a feature particularly desirable for farmers and merchants. When the tonneau is removed, a large deck space is left which is well adapted for the transportation of small produce and merchandise," the *Grinnell Herald* said. Prices were $1,550 for the touring car and $1,450 apiece for the pony tonneau and roadster bodies, or just slightly higher than the prices announced in August 1909. All three body styles were $50 cheaper if ordered with the planetary transmission.

The factory had a policy of testing not only the springs but the entire cars. (See fig.4.8.) "During a strenuous winter, tests of several thousand miles through mud and snow, the car showed itself to be quiet and powerful," the *Grinnell Herald* said in its April 1910 announcement of the new Spaulding line. A month later, the newspaper reported that factory test-driver Floyd Eichhorn had left in a Spaulding 30 for a trip to Chicago, about 275 miles by modern roads but probably longer on the meandering roads of 1910. The test drive would be "an excellent endurance test for the new car," the *Herald* said.

"Automobile men say the Spaulding car stands comparison with any car of the price ever put on the market, and that the new Iowa car is likely to prove a most popular one with purchasers of the middle class," according to the *Des Moines Register and Leader*. The writer of a May 1910 *Grinnell Herald* article "had the pleasure of riding in the Spaulding car and is free to claim it is a dandy, an easy, speedy runner, a great climber and in its finished form a thing of beauty, a joy unspeakable forever."

Each Car Receives "Individual Attention"

The mid-April debut announcement may have been premature. It wasn't until Friday, June 10, that a news article titled "First Finished Spaulding Car Makes Its Debut" reported that the first production car "flashed around the streets of Grinnell Tuesday afternoon." It sported a "very dark blue body and cream colored gear," the running gear being the frame, springs, axles, and wheels. The article said two machines had been shipped – both to Spaulding in-laws, with "one going to C. W. Brown, of Sibley, a brother of Mrs. F. E. Spaulding, and the other to N. Towne, of Des Moines, the father of Mrs. E. H. Spaulding. It is expected that four more machines will be ready to ship this week."

The *Des Moines Sunday Register and Leader* of June 26, 1910, pictured "the second Spaulding '30' touring car turned out of the shops of the Spaulding Manufacturing company at Grinnell," which it said had been delivered to "Mr. N. C. Towne" of Des Moines.

The first season's output, added the Des Moines newspaper, "will be several hundred cars, most of which will be used to supply the market in Iowa." Henry Spaulding's actual production plan, as revealed to the *Grinnell Herald* the previous October, was that "the output will not exceed 200 or 300 cars the first year. The first consideration, as in the Spaulding buggies, will be quality and this will be striven for rather than volume of output." In looking back later upon the first year of auto production, Henry Spaulding in mid-1911 said the output had been below his earlier projections:

We have built few cars, less than two hundred in fact, and for that very reason we have felt that each car leaving the factory to go to an owner had been the recipient of more careful and individual attention than is possible for any other American manufacturer to give his product. Our methods have more resembled those of European factories where quality, not quantity, is the keynote of the motor car industry. We realize that the future success of the motor car department is only to be attained by building absolutely dependable cars, and one unsuccessful car will completely efface a record of ninety-nine successful ones. You may be sure that we will put out no inferior product and you can readily understand why we have not attempted to build five hundred or five thousand cars the first year.

What's more, Spaulding seemed pleased at how closely his supply of cars matched the demand for them:

The motor car business is seasonal, the manufacturing being done in fall and winter to care for the heavy buying done in the spring and early summer. Thus, last winter [1910–1911] we ran full working force ten hours a day and constructed enough chassis to take care of this season's probable demand. How well we gauged the demand may be judged by visiting the factory and noting the few cars now left for present purchasers.

The Spaulding company as late as 1914 was producing cars at something less than a furious pace, judging by the tone of its catalog from that year. "After 38 years of manufacturing experience we believe that the buying public has vindicated our motto of 'Quality First.' If this were not so and people did not want good goods there would not be the ever increasing demand for our products." As the writer of a 1911 *Des Moines Register and Leader* article put it, "Their output is limited, as the firm has always allowed quality to take precedence over quantity."

Spaulding Factories "A Bee Hive of Industry"

At least five cars had been sold locally by the end of August 1910, when five Spauldings, four Overlands, a Moline 40, and a Glide, "all gaily decorated," drove to surrounding towns to spark interest in an upcoming Grinnell fair. Earlier in the month, the company broke ground on the west end of its block-and-a-half-wide complex to construct a new 74-by-206-foot factory built of paving blocks.[8] The Rock Island tracks abutted the south end of the new building, which would have four 150-horsepower boilers in the basement. "They will generate their own electricity, provide their own light and every bit of machinery in the entire plant will be power driven," the *Grinnell Herald* said. The rest of the basement would be occupied by a dry kiln; "a mill room will be on the first floor and the second and third floors will provide rooms for bench work."

This building would become home to what the company's automobile advertising later referred to as its new body plant, which one source valued at $150,000. A sign, "Vehicles and Motor Cars," atop the building in an artist's drawing suggests the new factory was also used for Spaulding carriages, however. For "despite the wail of many carriage men that the automobile business has ruined their trade, each year has seen the output of Spaulding vehicles increased," Henry Spaulding wrote in a June 1911 letter to the *Grinnell Herald*. He predicted a 1911 output of between 12,000 and 15,000 wagons and buggies.

The various Spaulding factories were "a veritable bee hive of industry," employing as many as 500 people during the years when the company was producing both automobiles and spring wagons, according to a retrospective piece in the local newspaper. Only a small number of those workers were in the motorcar department, however, according to a December 1912 Grinnell newspaper article that put the number at 30.

At 64 years of age, the already-busy company founder became a state senator in November 1910, carrying his own Poweshiek County by 1,050 votes and neighboring Keokuk County by 175 votes. Unusual for a first-year senator, Spaulding was named chairman "of the important committee on manufacturers" and would also serve on the highway committee – two fields in which the vehicle manufacturer presumably had some expertise.[9]

Testers Topple in Twos

During the start of its fall-winter production run of 1911 models, the Spaulding auto factory saw the first of two serious accidents involving its automobile test-drivers. Returning to town in a Spaulding car, Italio Berto, who had come to Grinnell two months earlier from the Maytag automobile factory at Waterloo, turned aside for a buggy he met. "He was running fast and very possibly the machine skidded and then struck a bump. At any rate, the car turned turtle and rolled over three times. . . . Berto had no chance to jump and was carried along with his car. The steering gear gashed him terribly in the abdomen, making an opening about 2½ inches long and cutting through the large intestine twice." The *Herald* said doctors gave the driver only a fighting chance to live.

"He is an expert engine tester and a fearless driver, so much so that the Spauldings have often warned him to be careful on the road and to stop whenever he passed a team, but it was hard for the young Italian to obey the orders, though he had shown improvement," the *Grinnell Herald* said. In a week's time, however, the newspaper could say that Berto "bids fair to recover from the terrible injuries which he received when his car turned turtle with him."

Four months after Berto's August 1910 smash-up, test-driver William Hamilton lost control of a 1911 Spaulding car on a slippery curve known as Sloan Corner, "a bad one to negotiate in an automobile, as the road slopes and an upset is easy," the *Grinnell Herald* said. Hamilton "was not running at any extravagant rate of speed" when he approached the turn in gathering dusk after a 65-mile test run to Marshalltown and back. But his car skidded anyway and then rolled twice before crashing into a telephone pole.

"Hamilton was thrown clear of the wreckage and was picked up unconscious. He regained his senses in about half an hour and aside from a few bruises appears

SPAULDING "30" TOURING CAR
SLIDING GEAR $1550 } WITHOUT
PLANETARY $1500 } TOP

none the worse for his experience," his first wreck in six years as a test-driver, the *Herald* said. Though "the machine was pretty well smashed up as a result of its roll," it was taken to the factory for repairs, according to the *Grinnell Register*'s account of the mishap. Ernest Spaulding and Charles Cratty from the factory "hurried out in an automobile" to rescue Hamilton.[10]

Spaulding Shows Big New Car

Its first full year of production, 1911, saw Spaulding Manufacturing continue its Spaulding 30 and unveil a Spaulding 40, appropriately named for its advertised horsepower rating. (Figs. 4.9, 4.10, and 4.11 show 1911 models.) The company, however, insisted on confusing buyers by also calling its new car the Model D – a one-letter promotion from the Model C (Spaulding 30) of 1910. More correctly, the Spaulding 30 was also known as either the CP (with planetary transmission) or CS (with selective transmission). The CP and CS offerings of 1910 were continued largely unchanged for 1911 and 1912, after which the Spaulding 30 was dropped. The bigger Spaulding 40 would

graduate from its Model D designation in 1911 to become Model E in 1912, Model G in 1913, and Model H in 1914, 1915, and 1916.

"All the bodies are of sheet steel heavily reinforced and beaded, with tonneaus permanent or detachable at the purchaser's option," the October 1910 *Automobile Trade Journal* said. In addition, the 1911 Spaulding frame was "of pressed steel, channel section, securely held together by four pressed steel cross members which are widened at the points of attachment to the side rails."

Aside from its new Spaulding 40 model, most other 1911 design changes were "mainly in the nature of refinements, such as more graceful fenders, larger steering wheels, etc.," according to the February 26, 1911, *Des Moines Register and Leader*. It described the Spaulding cars as the Grinnell automaker prepared to attend the 1911 Des Moines Automobile Show. The show was, in truth, a coming-out party for the Iowa automaker, which during the entire year availed itself of every opportunity to put itself in the public spotlight.

At the auto show, held at the Des Moines

4.9 A 1911 Spaulding 30. (GHM)

4.10 A Spaulding runabout, apparently a 1911 model. (SHSI)

4.11 Two unidentified men pose with a 1911 Spaulding. (MSS)

Coliseum, Spaulding Manufacturing displayed three cars inside and two demonstrator cars outside, one a five-passenger Spaulding 40 touring car "with body of Spaulding blue and gear of battleship gray. The other is a handsome touring car finished in green." Inside was "a three passenger, 30 horse-power roadster, silver gray body and running gear with Spanish leather trimming. Alongside of it is shown a five-passenger, fore-door [four-door] touring car, 30-horsepower, cream body and running gear and special tan trimming. The doors are equipped with lever locks," the *Grinnell Herald* said.

"The third inside car is the pride of the Spaulding force. It is the chassis of a 40-horsepower car, finished in black enamel and nickel. From stem to stern it is a beautiful example of the automobile builder's art. The model has natural wood wheels, the transmission and the bottom of the motor crank case are flaked, the steering gear is nickeled and equipped with a black walnut handle. . . . The front of one cylinder has been cross sectioned for better exhibition of the piston working," the *Herald* said.[11] Preparing the cutaway chassis took five months and cost more than $5,000, according to the *Des Moines Register and Leader*.

Fads and Freaks Need Not Apply

In a pre-show Des Moines ad blitz strong on geometric references, the company promised "A Square Deal" and asserted that its familiar diamond-shaped logo, long associated with its carriages, now also "Signifies Motor Car Quality." (See figs. 4.12 and 4.13.) "For eight years we have studied the motor car development. By eliminating the fads and freak elements and building every part on tried and true principles, we have evolved the simplest and most reliable car that can be built."

In 1911, the company also revealed its intended market by advertising that its cars were "Built In Iowa For Iowa People." Possibly due to the Iowa company's impressive showing at the Des Moines auto show, Governor Beryl F. Carroll ordered a Spaulding 30. "As usual the Governor has shown good judgment and is true to Iowa products," said the *Grinnell Herald,* which also noted that at least one state lawmaker was also driving a Spaulding car.[12]

The Iowa Publishing Company of Des Moines used Spaulding cars during a 1911 Iowa road-mapping project. The Grinnell manufacturer created an even bigger splash when one of two Spaulding 30s turned in a perfect score on the driving portion of a 650-mile "Little Glidden" tour of Iowa.

"As it is an Iowa work we are preparing and we are getting our support from Iowa people, we have been anxious to get an Iowa made auto that we could bank on and that would compare in every respect with any other auto," explained M. Huebinger of Iowa Publishing. It perhaps helped that N. C. Towne, also with the Iowa Publishing

4.12 Displaying the Spaulding diamond logo, this decorated car is pictured in the *Spaulding Model H* 1914 catalog. (SHSI)

4.13 The diamond logo adorned even this Spaulding hubcap.

4.14 Floyd E. Eichhorn piloted the No. 11 Spaulding car in the June 1911 650-mile Iowa Little Glidden tour. (SHSI)

Company, was Ernest Spaulding's father-in-law, and in mid-1910 had purchased the second Spaulding 30 touring car turned out by the factory.

"Inquiry developed the fact that the Spaulding was the machine answering this description and after some correspondence, we came to Grinnell and were pleased to find the Spaulding people glad to co-operate with us. It affords the auto company a chance to exhibit under the best conditions just what an admirable machine they have. . . . The Spaulding factory is turning out only first class machines and in time will be one of the largest factories of the kind in the West," according to Huebinger.

The mapmakers used a five-passenger Spaulding 30, painted steel gray and "gaily decorated with Grinnell pennants and illustrated signs" on an 800-mile trek across the Transcontinental and River-to-River routes in Iowa "over roads more often muddy than not," said the May 30, 1911, *Grinnell Herald*. "The car behaved perfectly and won words of praise from those who rode in it."[13]

Cold Drinks, Sandwiches, and Cigars

Spaulding Manufacturing Company entered two of its Spaulding 30 cars in the 650-mile Little Glidden tour of Iowa that began June 19, 1911. Thirty cars entered the event, sanctioned under American Au-

tomobile Association rules as a shorter version of the well-known Glidden Tours, in which contestants are rated by how well they adhere to a schedule and by how well their cars stand up.

On the first day of the four-day tour, both Spauldings "reached Grinnell on time to the minute, both in perfect condition," the *Grinnell Herald* reported. The check-in station at Grinnell, one of 70 towns on the tour, was at the Spaulding factory, where "cold drinks, sandwiches and cigars were handed out to the dust-grimed contestants."

At the end of the swing through central and northern Iowa, Floyd Eichhorn, driver of the No. 11 Spaulding (see fig. 4.14), was given a perfect road score. Driver Charles Cratty in Spaulding No. 12 was docked one point because his car lost its radiator cap.

A technical committee later tested and penalized each car for mechanical flaws. Eichhorn would have lost just one point for a loose nut except for a mixup on a brake test. Drivers had 50 feet in which to stop their cars from 20 miles per hour after their front wheels crossed a designated line. Eichhorn mistakenly waited to brake until his rear wheels crossed the line. Denied a chance to repeat the test, he lost five points. "Otherwise the car was in splendid shape, and the technical committee, while commenting on the good condition of both, laid

special stress on the remarkable fuel consumption record of 22 miles to one gallon of gasoline," the *Grinnell Herald* said.

The overall winner of the 1911 Iowa Little Glidden tour was a Cadillac with perfect road and technical scores, but the newspaper noted that many of the cars were docked a total of between 30 and 150 points. "As the Spaulding cars were the only Iowa made entries in the run, and made such a fine showing as compared with the more costly, eastern-made brothers, they were given great ovations at every turn along the route," the *Herald* said. Despite the brake-test fiasco, the company reaped a public-relations bonanza, as "the event has received publicity in all the motor serials and newspapers of the country," according to the *Des Moines Register and Leader*.[14]

Agencies, Anyone?

The *Grinnell Herald* published a "partial list" of people who bought 1911 Spaulding cars, excluding those sold by "the Texas agency." The list contained 52 names, including those of 29 Grinnellians. Other Iowans had purchased all the rest of the cars but two, as one Spaulding went to Minnesota and another went to Washington state. "The stock of the 1911 Spaulding cars is pretty well closed out and all the efforts of the factory will soon be bent on the new 1912 model," the August 15, 1911, *Grinnell Herald* said in printing the list of buyers.

Late in the year, the city got a scare when rumors began circulating that the automobile factory would move to the South. Fred Spaulding denied the rumors, which he said resulted from an item published in a recent issue of Chicago-based *Farm Implement News*. "Mr. Spaulding said, however, that the rumor had evidently traveled widely as the company was in receipt of fully 100 letters from cities desiring to urge their claims as good factory locations," the *Herald* said.[15]

Mappers for the American Automobile

Association drove through Grinnell in a Chicago-made Staver roadster in October 1911. They "were escorted out of town by Roy Shepherd, driver, and Dr. O. F. Parish, president of the Grinnell Automobile and Good Roads Association, in one of the new 1912 model Spaulding 40's, which ran like a dream all the way to Newton and back. The Staver had more than it could do to keep up," the *Grinnell Herald* said.[16]

To compare car production with the workings of an engine, 1911 represented the Spaulding company's compression

4.15 Two unidentified women in a 1912 Spaulding four-door. (SHSI)

4.16 A company publicity photo for the 1912 four-door Spaulding. (LB)

4.17 Outside the factory, workers cover a 1912 Spaulding before loading it into a Rock Island boxcar. (SHSI)

stroke that made possible 1912, a year of ignition, explosion, and power. With little warning, the company in April announced it would test an electric half-ton delivery truck and, if successful, possibly add such a commercial car to its automobile lineup. Later in the year, a new Spaulding dealer in Los Angeles placed a 300-car order. In late 1912 when the factory began in earnest to manufacture its 1913 models, production workers were regularly earning overtime pay, and the company was in the enviable position of having its first 400 cars already under contract.

"For the first time they [the factory] are allowing responsible agents to distribute their product," the *Grinnell Herald* said just two weeks into 1912. Spaulding's Iowa agents or distributors eventually included those in Des Moines, Grinnell, Hampton, Muscatine, New Sharon, Ottumwa, Spirit Lake, and Tama. Its out-of-state dealers included those in Los Angeles and San Diego; Omaha, Nebraska; and Fort Worth, Texas. There is no known record of all Spaulding dealers, but there were likely many others.

New 1912 Model 40 Is Low-Slung Car

The big-engined five-passenger Spaulding 40, or Model E, touring car of 1912 (see figs. 4.15, 4.16, and 4.17) cost $1,650 for the four-door touring body and $1,600 for the optional "touring" or "pony tonneau" bodies. A roadster body was also available, but "practically all cars will be equipped with fore [four] door bodies," the *Grinnell Herald* confided early in the year.

The local press and national trade journals alike were treating the Spaulding 40 as a new car. But almost a year earlier, at the early 1911 Des Moines auto show, the Grinnell manufacturer had displayed a five-passenger Spaulding 40 touring car. Its advertising in advance of the auto show also promoted both the "Spaulding 30 and 40."

"There is a departure in the style of frame on the 40," the *Grinnell Herald* noted. "It has a double kick-up and an insweep. The kick-up in front allows a good height and clearance to the motor, while the kick-up in the rear permits a wide opening to the springs while the body set in the hollow in

the center is low, thus bringing down the center of gravity and making in outline a low-lying car. The [front] insweep permits of turning in a short radius."

The Spaulding 40 used a Rutenber engine, a bore and stroke of 4⅛ x 5¼ inches, with cylinders cast individually rather than in pairs or as a block. For 1913, Spaulding switched to a bigger block-cast Buda engine. The 3-speed transmission in the Spaulding 40 was mounted in the middle of the frame. The new large car dispensed with the usual sheet-metal "sod pan" slung between its front frame rails because the Rutenber engine had an enclosed flywheel, the *Grinnell Herald* revealed. In the 1912 Spaulding 40, "there will be optional Goodrich or Diamond tire equipment, and an optional special equipment of electric lighting outfit for all cars and models."[17]

The Spaulding 30 touring car cost $1,500 as a CP model with a planetary transmission or $1,550 as a CS model with a more modern selective transmission. Otherwise, the CP and CS were nearly identical, as previously. Prices varied for the optional three-passenger roadster and four-passenger pony tonneau bodies. The factory defended its prices with a new slogan for 1912: "You Pay a Little More But You Pay Less Often." Its 1912 advertising also asked, "Can You Beat It?"

Truck Experiment Hardly Electrifying

The company in late April announced it would begin sales of Spaulding light delivery wagons and half-ton trucks within three or four weeks, according to the *Grinnell Herald*:

This new departure will be evidenced the first of the week when a half-ton truck equipped as a delivery wagon will appear on the streets of Grinnell, doing the work of the Co-Operative Delivery Co. The machines will have the appearance of an ordinary delivery wagon, but the motive power will be furnished by electricity instead of horsepower. . . . It will be operated purely on

trial and . . . the experience derived from the use of the car on the streets of Grinnell will give valuable data to use in getting the new line before the public.

In addition, the newspaper said, "An ingenious contrivance has been provided by which the wagon body can be removed and a tonneau put in its place, making it possible to use the vehicle both for business and pleasure. That, it is thought, should prove popular with the farmers." The electric truck experiment apparently failed to yield the valuable data the Spauldings were seeking. There was no further mention of trucks until Spaulding Manufacturing Company added a gasoline-powered truck to its 1913 line.

In late July, when Ernest Spaulding and other officials of the River-to-River Road Association drove to Omaha, they did so in a very early 1913 Spaulding 40. In fact, the car was apparently a prototype, as the *Grinnell Herald* indicates that full-scale production of 1913 models did not begin until August. By August, the prototype 1913 model had covered "nearly 5,000 miles, or nearly the mileage of an ordinary owner running two seasons. This mileage has been covered with the wonderful record of no material replacements or adjustments whatever."

Some of that mileage was added when Ernest Spaulding and the other highway officials drove to Omaha to meet "the dusty autoists of the Denver Chamber of Commerce Sociability Run" and later escorted them east to Grinnell.[18] Spaulding was undoubtedly mindful of his speed upon reaching home; he and factory driver Roy Shepherd in May had admitted their guilt and paid a $7.50 fine for speeding in town.

Californians Buy 300 Spauldings – Not!

Late in the summer of 1912, the factory received its largest single order to date from a new agent in Los Angeles, who was selling the Spaulding car exclusively. The headline in the August 27, 1912, *Grinnell Herald* summed up the news: "300 Spaulding Cars Go to California." Agent C. G. Aldrich wanted the cars delivered in the fall of 1912 and early spring of 1913.

A 1917 list of California automobile registrations numbers slightly more than 100,000 cars, according to California automotive historian William Lewis. Researchers who pour through registration lists from this time period believe many cars stayed on the road from six to 10 years, Lewis said. So if Aldrich sold 300 Spaulding cars in California in late 1912 and early 1913, many – if not most – of them would still have been registered in 1917.

Four Spauldings were on the 1917 list – owned by residents of Hollywood, Redondo Beach, San Francisco, and South Pasadena. There were five, possibly a few more, on a 1912 California registration list, Lewis said. "If the *Herald* item had said 30, I might buy it. But 300 units is pure hogwash," he said.[19]

Nevertheless, the Spaulding car had a few faithful followers in California. "Have just returned from a thousand mile trip in southern California with the Spaulding '40,' and am very pleased to inform you that it created a sensation wherever I went," Lewis Culler, a clothier from Redondo Beach, wrote to the Grinnell factory on November 15, 1913. "On the great hill climb at Riverside where they all go into low, I had no difficulty at all in going to the top on intermediate, and if the curves were not so short so a person could get any run for it, I believe I could make it like snuff on the high. I was in perhaps twenty towns and at every town some one wanted to get the agency for it," said Culler, who also wanted to get the agency for it. He was one of the four Californians who had Spaulding cars licensed in 1917.

"The sand and hill work that my Spaulding Car had done is almost unbelievable," Culler wrote in another letter. On a trip, he encountered a Winton 6-cylinder car stuck in sand in middle of the road. Culler backed up 50 feet, then accelerated and steered his

4.18 A Spaulding 40 conquers Potato Knoll near Belmond, Iowa. (SHSI)

Spaulding off the road in second gear to try to pass the stranded Winton.

"Well, she took it like a bird and threw sand about ten feet high but came through with flying colors," said Culler. With a rope between the cars, Culler's Spaulding pulled the Winton for half a mile until they reached solid ground.

"Then the owner of the car, who had a licensed chauffeur, looked the Spaulding over and said '———, what is the use of having a six when you have to be pulled out with a four.' When I told him I had never had a wheel in my hand before handling the Spaulding and had only driven her 5,000 miles, he could hardly believe it."[20]

Spaulding Tames 'Tater Terror

Of greater interest to Iowans, a Spaulding touring car made automotive history at Belmond, Iowa, by climbing Potato Knoll (see fig.4.18), "a freak formation in the center of a corn field without any track or roadway leading up its side," the 1914 Spaulding catalog relates.

"The Spaulding climbed this incline with [a] full load of passengers on both low and intermediate gears and afterwards made the same climb with driver only, on high gear. These are feats which no other car has ever accomplished and which few have ever dared to attempt and show very con-

clusively that this car will easily perform any hill climbing which the ordinary user will ever have occasion to attempt." The company did not say when it accomplished this feat.

Surviving photos also show Ernest Spaulding climbing the steps of the Iowa State Capitol in Des Moines (see fig.4.19), in another event that apparently got little play in the hometown newspaper. The photo shows Spaulding at the left-hand steering wheel of what looks to be either a 1913 or 1914 Spaulding. His daughter, Miriam Simms, says most of the six men in the car were officers of the association that promoted the east-west highway through Grinnell, the River-to-River Road. The passengers include the Spaulding cross-state recordholder, Harold "Hal" Wells, and C. B. Kurtz, superintendent of Spaulding Manufacturing's motorcar department.

Spaulding Manufacturing apparently followed its splashy debut at the 1911 Des Moines auto show by visiting the late-summer 1911 Iowa State Fair. But the automaker "has decided not to send an exhibit to the state fair this year," reported the August 23, 1912, *Grinnell Herald*. The company, instead, "will have them at some of the smaller fairs in this vicinity."

In the auto races at the Grinnell fairgrounds that August, Dr. P. L. Talbott in his Spaulding car placed second behind a Ford in a two-mile "novelty race," which required drivers to stop their cars and engines at half-mile intervals before continuing on their way. But Talbott was apparently racing on his own, without factory sponsorship.

"A Big Motor Car Year"

Spaulding Manufacturing began its 1913 production in August 1912, looking forward to a promising year. The factory had started work on the 300-car California order that turned out to be wishful thinking. The California order and the firmer orders from nearby agencies meant that "in the last two weeks 400 of the 1913 output have been contracted for," the *Grinnell Herald* reported in late summer. The pace was just as frantic near the end of the year. "Thirty men are employed and they are working until 10 o'clock every night in the effort to meet the contracts for automobiles which the company has ahead."[21] It was no wonder

4.19 A 1913 or 1914 Spaulding climbs the steps of the Iowa State Capitol Building. H. W. Spaulding's granddaughter, Miriam Spaulding Simms, identifies the occupants as Ernest Spaulding, driving; Hal Wells, front-seat passenger; and in the rear seat, from left, Factory Superintendent C. B. Kurtz, Fred Claiborne, unidentified, and Simms's Uncle George L. Towne. (LB)

4.20 A 1913 Spaulding 40, photographed on the Mississippi River bridge at Lyons, Iowa. (SHSI)

that Spaulding officials, in the words of the *Herald,* "are convinced that 1913 will be a big motor car year."

Equipped with an electric self-starter, a larger 4-cylinder engine from a different maker, new left-hand steering, deep seat cushions, and cleaner lines, the Spaulding was "most classy in appearance" for 1913 (see fig. 4.20), an exciting year for the young company. Officials of the Panama-California Exposition drove a Spaulding touring car from California to Washington, D.C., to map the best route for motorists who would drive to the 1915 exposition. Spaulding also introduced its Model T light express truck.

Another new model, the 1914 Spaulding "Sleeper" car, received flattering attention in many national trade journals upon its introduction in the second half of 1913, and was just as popular locally. Capping off the year with the granddaddy of publicity stunts, the Grinnell company grabbed state-wide headlines by sending a Spaulding "stock chassis" across Iowa on the River-to-River Road, winning the cross-state speed mark and setting what was claimed to be a world's dirt-road speed record.

Thinking Big, Spaulding Drops Small Car

For 1913, "the small model has been dropped and the large one continued," *Automobile* magazine noted. Dropping the Spaulding 30 and its optional 2-speed planetary transmission allowed the Grinnell manufacturer to focus on its bigger and more expensive – $1,875 for 1913, up from $1,650 in 1912 – Spaulding 40. Dubbed the

Model G for this year, the Spaulding 40 retained its 3-speed sliding-gear transmission.

Spaulding Manufacturing Company also dropped the Rutenber 4-cylinder engine it used in its 1912 Spaulding 40 and adopted a larger Buda engine, which it would use until it quit making autos in 1916. "The famous Buda, Model 'T' . . . is a 40 H.P., 4¼ x 5½ [bore and stroke], four cylinder, 'Enbloc' motor," the 1914 Spaulding catalog explained. "The highest grade construction is used throughout, which results in smooth and powerful action and great durability." Made in Harvey, Illinois, the Buda Model T had three crankshaft main bearings, enclosed valves and valve lifters, and a sight gauge for checking the oil level. Hinting at the speed of their big car, the company's advertisements said "1913 Spaulding Forty Goes Like 'Sixty.'"

Three changes did much to produce the cleaner lines of the Spaulding 40, the only model produced until the 1914 Spaulding Sleeper arrived during the summer of 1913. First, the switch to a left-hand steering wheel moved the gearshift lever — on the models equipped with a 3-speed sliding-gear transmission — from outside on the right side of the car to the center of the front passenger compartment. Second, Spaulding designers moved the spare tire from the right running board to the rear of the car, "so that with the left-hand steer and center control there is ready egress to the front seat from either side, and the clean-cut lines of the car are not marked by extra unsightly attachments," the *Grinnell Herald* said. The third way the Spaulding company produced the clean lines of the 1913 car was by placing tools "under the flooring of the car, doing away with the cumbersome tool box on the running board which is seen on most cars. The running board is left entirely clear."

As a result, "its deep and roomy low lying appearance, together with its deep upholstering of fine grained leather and clean running board, makes the car most classy in general appearance." The car's deep upholstery (see fig.4.21) came from "11-inch

4.21 This undated factory photo is identified as Spaulding Manufacturing's "Auto Trim Room," probably 1915 or 1916. (SHSI)

4.22 1913 Spaulding Model T gasoline truck, photographed outside the auto factory. (SHSI)

Turkish tilted spring cushions, making it ride like a rocking chair." The company promoted its 1913 Gray & Davis electric self-starter as simpler than many others since it had only four wires attached to it and weighed just 38 pounds. Still, the starter was powerful enough to "drive the car two miles without the aid of gas motor," Spaulding advertising claimed. The car also had electric lights and an electric horn.[22]

In 1912, when auto manufacturers rushed to embrace the new self-starter, Spaulding was there – though not first in line. Its first 1912 cars did not have starters. By April 1912, the company's ads proclaimed that the Spaulding was equipped with an unidentified brand of electric self-starter, very possibly the Gray & Davis model used in 1913.

Trucks Receive "No Special Effort"

In August 1912, the Spaulding Manufacturing Company announced that its 1913 lineup would also include a three-quarter-ton gas-powered truck (see fig.4.22), which was exhibited at the 1912 Grinnell Fair late in the summer. "The truck business is one that must be reckoned with in [the] future. The Spaulding truck can be used with pneumatic or cushion tires, has a double chain drive, thirty-horsepower motor and large roomy body. It is the ideal wagon for light delivery of all kinds," according to the *Grinnell Herald*.

The 2,300-pound Spaulding Model T truck carried a chassis price of $1,000 but sold for $1,100 when equipped with an express body. Except for being chain-driven and having optional 34 x 4 inch pneumatic or solid tires, the truck was similar in many ways to the company's shaft-driven touring car, but with a 115-inch wheelbase that was 5 inches shorter than the car. Though the 1913 Spaulding cars had switched to left-side steering, the Spaulding Model T truck retained a right-side wheel, according to a photograph and statistics in the March 1913 *Automobile Trade Journal*. The Spaulding Model T truck had a cargo space of 54 x 108 inches with box sides 24 inches high, a 35-mile-per-hour top speed, a Schebler carburetor, and 11-inch road clearance.

In the *Grinnell Herald* of October 29, 1912, the Spaulding company ran an ad titled "Different Styles of Spaulding 1913 Trucks," picturing three of its chain-driven trucks. The photo quality is poor, but, curiously, all three of these trucks have hand-operated horns on the left, meaning they have left-hand steering. One open-cab truck has a covered cargo area and open sides. The second looks like a low-box pickup, offering no protection to either the driver or the cargo area. The third has an open-side cab for the driver and an uncovered cargo area surrounded by a low guard rail. But the third truck has no hood, meaning the driver is most likely perched high over the engine, or else the engine is in the middle of the frame.

If Spaulding's truck production remained low, it was because the company's 30 employees were so busy trying to fill automobile orders. "The company will be taxed to its utmost to get out the orders now on hand so no special effort is being made just now for the development of the motor truck business for which there is a very tempting field," the *Grinnell Herald* said in December 1912. That explains why the Spaulding truck plans went unmentioned thereafter in the local newspapers.[23]

Spaulding's Wood–Van De Verg distributor in Los Angeles won some publicity for the Iowa car during February 1913. The *Los Angeles Evening Herald* indulged the local Spaulding dealer by printing an account of "one of the hardest tests of hill climbing ability to which an automobile was ever subjected." A 1913 Spaulding 40 with a full load of passengers "was driven up a 25 percent grade off Sunset boulevard," according to the account. "The difficulty of the test

was intensified by the fact that the street has recently been macadamized and the surface, not having had time to set, offered poor footing for the machine.

"The big Spaulding, however, never faltered, but with its motor barking savagely, threw stones and gravel into the air as it sped to the top of the hill." Consequently, the Spaulding "is rapidly winning popularity among automobile buyers," said the Los Angeles daily, "and all indications point to a record-breaking sale of the new cars during the coming season."[24] The 1913 Los Angeles city directory lists a Ross A. Wood and a Nathaniel Van De Verg as partners in the Wood–Van De Verg Auto Company that ran the Spaulding hill-climbing test.

Spaulding for "Gigantic $80,000 Logging Trip"

In August 1913, a month during which the *Grinnell Herald* revealed that a Spaulding would race across the state, the newspaper also informed its readers of a "Spaulding for Trip across Continent."[25] A group of San Diego businessmen, headed by "prominent automobile man" Robert P. Cooper, chose the Iowa car "on account of the Spaulding, by test of power, endurance and speed, having surpassed all others and more than measured up to the requirements," the 1914 Spaulding catalog noted.

The trip organizers planned to drive the

4.23 A card distributed to promote the San Diego–New York trek of the Spaulding company's "Official Exposition Car." (SHSI)

4.24 A section of movie film showing the Spaulding transcontinental car on Roosevelt Dam, Arizona. (SHSI)

Spaulding touring car to New York to compile a route book for motorists who wanted to drive to San Diego for the Panama-California Exposition, an international fair planned for the city's Balboa Park in 1915. It was Southern California's version of San Francisco's bigger Panama-Pacific International Exposition of 1915, both held to celebrate the opening of the Panama Canal. Joining Cooper for "this gigantic $80,000 logging trip" were W. E. Macarton and Lawrence Jasmin, according to a Spaulding 1914 catalog.

The transcontinental explorers also planned to make motion pictures (see figs. 4.23 and 4.24) during their planned six-month journey, the *Grinnell Herald* said. "The moving pictures will be in the nature of advertising matter for the exposition and will be exhibited all over the United States," the *Herald* said. "Incidentally the Spaulding car will be in the forefront of all these pictures." The car itself was in the nature of advertising matter for its manufacturer, as a sign painted on the left side clearly labeled it as "Spaulding/Official Exposition Car/Made

– Grinnell Iowa." The expedition left San Diego in August 1913.

"Primarily the object of the trip is to boost the San Diego Exposition and the across-continent highway, every foot of which will be photographed by a big moving picture machine attached to the front of the car," a Spaulding 50 model, according to the August 9, 1913, *San Diego Union*.

If accurate, the newspaper's mention of a Spaulding 50 suggests that the Grinnell factory may have equipped the transcontinental car with an extra-powerful engine for the trek. If the automaker had come out with a Spaulding 50 model this early, it wasn't advertising the fact. Only for its 1915 model year did it begin advertising a regular-model Spaulding 50.

The films made on the transcontinental trip "are to be shown in moving picture houses all over the United States, graphically visualizing the national highway, which terminates at San Diego. The pictures will later be published in the form of a photographic map," or book, the *Union* said.

The three men had formed the Pacific-Atlantic Film Company, according to the San Diego newspaper. Cooper was president and Jasmin secretary. The general manager, Macarton, was "a former newspaper man and has had experience in the moving picture business. A short time ago he made a similar trip from Denver to Mexico City." The 1913 Los Angeles city directory lists Macarton as president of an "Ocean to Ocean Highway Motion Picture Co."

According to the West Coast newspaper, the planned route of the transcontinental Spaulding was from San Diego to Phoenix, through New Mexico, including a stop at Albuquerque, "then over the Santa Fe trail to La Junta, Colo., through Kansas to Kansas City, Mo., to St. Louis, Indianapolis, Wheeling and Washington, and from there to Philadelphia and New York."

"A flag containing the Exposition colors, red, green, yellow and white, will be carried on the car, as will a large number of pennants boosting San Diego and its Exposition," the San Diego newspaper said. In an article previewing the "novel publicity scheme under the auspices of the Exposition management," the *Union* said the Spaulding car would leave San Diego August 17, 1913.

Plowing through Snow
Where Packards Can't Go

Just before setting off, the Spaulding car escorted a delegation of Indiana-made cars out of the Panama-California Exposition grounds, the travelers wrote in a letter to the factory. "Motion and still pictures were made of the procession with the Spaulding car leading, covered with the Spaulding banners and flying the American and Panama-California Exposition flags. This was our official start from San Diego and 500 pictures were distributed by the exposition publicity department to newspapers all over the country, with a thousand word news story about our tour."

The coast-to-coast travelers were "warmly welcomed" and "wined and dined" upon arriving in Phoenix after shooting 2,000 feet of movie film en route, the *San Diego Union* reported. "The party stopped in Phoenix to develop the film already taken. From Phoenix they will show the film exposed in this city and en route in every town in which they stop until they reach Kansas City. From here they will cut out the logging films and show only the San Diego city and Exposition films. They will pass through 700 cities and towns en route to New York and will give a show in each one. In each place they distribute Exposition advertising matter. The next stop of any consequence is Albuquerque."

Along the route, the mapping crew often cabled the news of its progress to Spaulding factory: "Have arrived at Albuquerque N M covering over 14 hundred miles from San Diego over rough mountains grades deep sand and other rough roads," R. P. Cooper

said in a September 2, 1913, telegram, and reported no problems with the car. In a follow-up letter, Cooper said: "We are exceedingly enthusiastic over the showing of your car and are telling everybody that no other car at any price could stand the strain and do work as good as the Spaulding and in making this statement we do so in good faith."

The leader of a group that was logging a southern route for the American Automobile Association warned the Panama-California car of trouble ahead. "He told us that we would never make the 'Mammoth Wash,' which is a desert of deep sand between Brawley, Cal., and Yuma, Ariz.," Cooper wrote. The AAA mapping car had bogged down in the sand a few days earlier, forcing the party to walk 20 miles before flagging down a train headed for Yuma. They hired a mule team to rescue their car.

An unrelated account also written in autumn 1913 described the same hazard: "The dreaded Mammoth Wash, a stretch of deep shifting sand almost a mile in length[,] is bound to prove a stumbling block for a number of ambitious pilots, as a car will sink clear to the axle, if the wheels are shoved over out of the beaten track," according to *Automobile* of October 23, 1913.

"Of course, we came to a standstill on the 'Mammoth Wash' grade, but let just enough air out of the casings [tires], also tied the rear casings with gunny sacks and stretched canvas in front of the rear wheels and came over the grade of deep sand in fine order," Cooper wrote. Loaded with equipment, the Spaulding 50 weighed 5,000 pounds, he said.

"We are not having any trouble in getting the papers to mention that we are making our trans-continental tour in a 'Spaulding' car," Cooper wrote in a later letter. By mid-November 1913 the exposition party had exposed 72,000 feet of movie film and hoped to shoot 40,000 more before reaching New York, said the *Morning Review* of Greensburg, Pennsylvania.

"I am writing you to let you know the success we are having with the Spaulding car in plowing through snow from one to three feet deep," Cooper wrote in a letter dated November 13, 1913. "We came from Pittsburgh, Pa., to Greensburg, a distance of 20 miles and ours was the only automobile that was able to come through. Even a Packard car could only go part way. We got a fine motion picture of the Spaulding car in about three feet of snow where it seemed to be as well contented as on a paved street." The Spaulding had traveled 4,201 miles from San Diego to Greensburg and, according to the *Morning Review,* "they have not even had so slight an accident or mishap as to require the tightening of a single nut on the car."

The expedition members would use their motion-picture film "to secure endorsements of governors, and prominent officials and to present them to President [Woodrow] Wilson and congress in a strong effort to have the highway which has been logged built with aid from the national government," the *Grinnell Herald* said.

"The Spaulding made its hard journey without the slightest accident, through sand and deep snow to the city of Washington, where President Wilson and Secretary [of State William Jennings] Bryan gave the tourists a hearty welcome and were presented with letters from governors of various states and an electric button to start the Exposition," the factory said in its 1914 catalog. "The Official Spaulding is doing yeoman work at this time on its homeward trip, pioneering a route to the world's exposition through the sunny south."

"Go Hunting, Fishing or Camping"

At the 1913 Iowa State Fair in Des Moines, the Spaulding company introduced what it variously called its "Sleeper," "Sleeping Car," "Spaulding Pullman," or "Tourist Sleeping Car."[26] (See fig.4.25.) Spectators crowded around the company's novel live display in which actors played "a company of campers just settling down for the night, with the sleeper all ready for use," reported the August 15, 1913, *Grinnell Herald.* "The car will be fitted up with every conceivable equipment for the camper's comfort and convenience and the display will doubtless be one of the most attractive of the fair."

The automaker had apparently sold at

4.25 Phantom view of the Spaulding Sleeper, introduced in the second half of 1913. (SHSI) least a few Sleeper models well before the start of the late-summer 1913 State Fair, however. A buyer from Brooklyn, Iowa, bought a Sleeper and still had time to take it on a long three-state trip before writing a July 29, 1913, letter of endorsement to the factory:

Have just returned from a 1150 mile tour in the "Spaulding Sleeper" through parts of Illinois, Indiana and Iowa. She behaved splendidly, and came through with an almost perfect score. Every where I stopped the machine created considerable interest, and in every case the comment was favorable. It averaged 15 miles per gallon of gasoline for the entire trip, the highest record being 19 miles and the lowest 12. I don't know whether this is a very good performance or not, but considering the fact that the machine was new and stiff at the start, with an inexperienced driver, I do not think it is extravagant.

"This car will be popular with motor car travelers, and makes an excellent vacation car, saving hotel bills, and giving the greatest comfort in the stifling summer weather," noted the November 1913 *Automobile Trade Journal*. "Among the further appointments of the Spaulding Pullman are a complete set of toilet articles, electric lights in the top for reading and cigar lighter."

The Spaulding Sleeper "has all the appearance of a regular machine" because it was a regular touring car with a $100 addition that brought "'all the comforts of home' to the touring motorist," the Grinnell factory said in its 1914 catalog. The Sleeper could be "converted into a sleeping compartment within a few minutes by lowering the back of the front seat onto a line with the [front and back] seat cushions, thus making a very comfortable bed. This arrangement is proving invaluable to summer tourists as it not only saves the expense of stopping at hotels but affords much more comfortable and convenient night stops in the extreme hot weather. Furnished with reading lamp in top of bow over tonneau." Two knurled-head bolts held the front seat-back upright.

The new model was "the only Sleeping Car in the World made by a manufacturer in quantities," the company advertised. "You Can Eat, Sleep and Ride with All the Comforts of Home." The Spaulding Sleeper "makes up like a Pullman and is touring car and hotel combined," according to a three-frame comic strip that ran in one series of Sleeper ads. Frame three shows a broken bed in a dilapidated room to illustrate vividly that the Spaulding Sleeper "solves the most disagreeable question of touring—the hotel." The factory therefore urged prospective buyers to "Take A Vacation This Summer. Go Hunting, Fishing Or Camping In A Spaulding Sleeping Car."

The Sleeper on display at the March 1914 Des Moines Automobile Show had "quickly adjusting curtains . . . so that the occupants need not leave the car to attach curtains," according to the *Des Moines Register and Leader,* which continued:

As a special equipment, the Spaulding Sleeper may be equipped with an air mattress which covers the whole bed which is six feet in length. The air mattress is blown up by a motor driven tire pump attached to the motor. When deflated, this air mattress occupies but one cubic foot of space. On the running board may be attached a fire less cooker, which allows the traveler to eat, sleep and ride, independent of hotels or cafes, making a great saving on the pocketbook and at the same time insuring all of the comforts of home. The Spaulding Manufacturing company believes this to be the latest word in motor car completeness and comfort and will be a boon to the long-distance tourist or the business man taking his summer outing."

Spaulding Sleeper cars also carried an "inspection light which is magnetic and will adhere to any metal surface on the car. For instance, in case of a puncture at night it may be set on the under side of the fender and will give light to the tourist directly upon the tire to be replaced."

Though how many Sleepers the Spaulding company sold is an open question, its Iowa dealers sold sleeping cars one and two at a time along with the regular Spaulding

4.26 Hal Wells in the mud-covered Spaulding racer. This undated company photo apparently shows the car after Wells "hit mud and then more mud" during his first cross-state attempt. (SHSI)

4.27 Onlookers line the street as Wells speeds through Grinnell during his record-setting 1913 run. (SHSI)

4.28 Hal Wells at the wheel of the Spaulding racer. His passenger is probably either mechanic Jerry Eiler, injured in Wells's first attempt at lowering the trans-state record, or mechanic L. T. Boyd, who accompanied Wells on his successful run. Grinnell's Congregational Church is the backdrop (SHSI).

40, according to reports carried in the *Grinnell Herald*. But a "notable boom in the sale of Spaulding 'sleeper cars'" came in July 1915 when the Davis Motor Car Company of Ottumwa, Iowa, bought 25 on contract.

Wells Gets Set for Fast Driving

Grinnell Herald Editor W. G. Ray had a personal as well as a professional interest in Spaulding company, having purchased a 1913 Spaulding car earlier in the year. "Just happening to step into the Spaulding factory," he wrote in late August, "we discovered a brand new car in process of construction, and learned it is to be the Spaulding racer. It is not yet completed but is far enough along to show that it is to be a racing beauty. Seats for two with a reserve gasoline tank for long-distance runs.

"The body is to be orange and black, and has painted on the hood, 'The Spaulding Car,' 'River to River Road.' . . . Hal Wells, of Des Moines, who expects to do some fast driving in the car, is in the city today, giving it a little personal inspection," Ray said in the first published reference to the Spaulding racer.[27] Also known later as the "Spaulding Special," "Spaulding Flyer," or "Spaulding Scout," depending on which Iowa newspaper you read, the lightweight two-passenger wooden body on a stock chassis (see color plate 3 and figs. 4.26, 4.27, and 4.28) would captivate Iowans and supercharge the Spaulding's image.

Wells, a frequent flyer on the road between Chicago and Des Moines, set three speed records on that route during the first seven months of 1911. On July 20, 1911, Wells took to the open road in a "Wells roadster" that was apparently built by his father, Jesse O. Wells, who accompanied him on the trip. Hal Wells survived a broken brake rod and "many miles of mud" west of Chicago to shave 21½ minutes off the Chicago–Des Moines record, according to the *Des Moines Register and Leader*.[28]

That contest had attracted no less a personage than Harry B. Staver, president of

the Staver Motor Company of Chicago. While attempting to lower the Chicago–Des Moines mark in June 1911, Staver had crashed his Staver car down a 15-foot bank into the Skunk River south of Ames, Iowa. He finished well off the pace after two teams of horses pulled his car from the water.[29]

One of Henry Spaulding's two sons, Ernest, was most likely the driving force behind the Spaulding racer's high-speed run over Iowa's River-to-River Road. The highway passed through Grinnell and Des Moines to follow the Rock Island railroad tracks in connecting two river towns – Davenport on the Mississippi and Council Bluffs on the Missouri. Ernest Spaulding was the first president of the River-to-River Road Association and was an Iowa trustee of the newly formed Coast-to-Coast Highway Association.

"My dad [Ernest] wanted good roads and he fought for them," his daughter, Miriam Simms, said in an interview. As late as 1919 or 1920, Ernest Spaulding would drive the Spaulding racer as a personal car, said Simms, who remembers taking a ride in the racer with her father on a pleasure trip to Des Moines.

Surprisingly, Ernest Spaulding, as purchasing agent of the motorcar department, was the only one of the three Spauldings who had formal day-to-day involvement in the automobile branch of the business. A 1913 letterhead shows the other two Spauldings listed only under the carriage-making branch: Henry as sales manager and Fred as purchasing agent. The superintendent of the motorcar department was C. B. Kurtz. After Spaulding Manufacturing ceased making cars, Cyrus B. Kurtz returned to his hometown of Cleveland, where he made about 250 Kurtz Automatic autos from 1920 to 1924. The cars were named after a semi-automatic transmission that Kurtz patented, according to the Standard Catalog of American Cars, 1805–1942.[30]

"Mud and Then More Mud"

Setting a cross-state record would bring glory to both the automobile factory and to the River-to-River Road. Oskaloosa businessman Don McClure drove an Oakland roadster across Iowa in 10 hours 42 minutes to set the existing record on a competing dirt highway. McClure drove the White Pole Road, also called the Great White Way, and was challenged by Pete C. Petersen of Davenport on the rival River-to-River Road. Both left Davenport at the same instant early on December 28, 1912. On the slightly shorter Great White Way, McClure passed through 23 towns while Petersen encountered 39, according to the Grinnell Herald's reckoning. "The River-to-River road is 346 miles and the Great White Way 321 long but drivers raced on equal terms," the January 2, 1913, Automobile noted. By taking a cutoff from Exira to Elk Horn, Wells lowered the distance to 337.8 miles.

After an accident in which he lost a tire and crashed into a fence near Ortonville, and delays of 20 minutes at two railroad crossings, Petersen finished 36 minutes behind McClure, who had lost an hour fixing a broken gas line. Some River-to-River Road boosters grumbled afterwards that Petersen's Pope-Hartford was no match for a speedy Oakland, but it was no salve to defeat.

During his first attempt to capture the title in October 1913, Hal Wells skidded into a ditch near Ladora on the east leg of the route. The Grinnell Herald theorized that a flat tire at 55 miles per hour caused the wreck. Regardless, the crash shattered the car's right front wheel. "Mechanician Jerry Eiler was thrown violently out and when he finally picked himself up found himself on the other side of the barb wire fence, twenty feet or so away," the Herald said. Temporary repairs to the wheel allowed the racer to limp along until it met a relief party dispatched from the Grinnell factory. L. T. Boyd replaced Eiler in the mechanic's seat.

Wells then traveled at a "hurricane rate" until reaching Walnut in western Iowa, with an hour and 41 minutes in which to travel the 45 miles to Council Bluffs at McClure's 1912 pace.

"And right then the car hit mud and then more mud. It had been raining all day. There was no hope. So Driver Wells pulled up and saved energy and gasoline for another run," the *Grinnell Herald* said. Nonetheless, the Spaulding factory wrote Wells a congratulatory letter, to which he replied: "I would like to have you express my appreciation to both Eiler and Boyd for their invaluable assistance, and trust that Eiler's shake up has done him no permanent harm. They both should be given credit for the nerve they exhibited in riding with one almost a total stranger to them."

Train Passengers "Take Great Enjoyment"

Sitting in the Spaulding racer, Wells posed for press photographers in Des Moines on November 13, and then left for Davenport. He would launch his second cross-state attempt the following morning. Despite rumors that Great White Way backers would put up their own racer, Wells and factory mechanic L. T. Boyd were uncontested when they left the Mississippi River town heading west at 6:37 A.M. sharp. At the start, they were 22 to 35 minutes behind the Rock Island No. 17 fast mail train, according to conflicting newspaper reports.

A designated observer telephoned the *Des Moines Evening Tribune* to report that the car rocketed through West Liberty at 60 miles per hour. A later report said Wells bolted through Iowa City at 8:03 A.M. "without a shadow of hesitation," the *Des Moines Tribune* said. But while "tearing through Marengo at 8:56, Wells dropped a card bearing the message that one of his rear springs was broken and asked that the Spaulding factory at Grinnell be notified," the Des Moines newspaper said. Wells broke the spring near the spot where his racer crashed into a ditch

during its first attempt, but he was nevertheless able to keep running at top speed.

"When I arrived at the Spaulding factory at Grinnell," Wells told the *Des Moines Capital* afterward, "I found the big side door open and dashed inside. The door was closed to keep out the crowd. Fifteen men jumped at the car and in thirteen minutes it was equipped with a new spring." Just west of Grinnell near Kellogg, Wells and Boyd lost five more minutes when their reserve gas tank broke loose and began pounding the car. Boyd yanked off the tank and left it by the roadside.

"The loss of this tank forced me to stop later at Exira and telephone to Walnut for more gasoline. I would have gained about seven minutes but for this accident," Wells recalled. Despite the delays, Wells beat the Rock Island mail train into Des Moines by 10 minutes. "After catching up with the train the passengers took great enjoyment in the efforts of the . . . Spaulding roadster to pass them. For many miles it was neck and neck, but Wells finally pulled ahead and left the train behind," the *Des Moines Register and Leader* said.

Wells's "fearsome pace," "terrific speed," and "mad speed," among other descriptors, amounted to a 39-mile-per-hour average over the 337.8-mile route. If that seems mild today, consider that Wells was sharing the narrow dirt road with horse-drawn wagons and buggies. Cross-state record holder Don McClure said his run the previous December would have been faster but for "an accidental turning over of a buggy" that was trying to clear the way for him, "which caused us to stop dead still, and get out and get back in the car and start again."

In addition, the highway meandered through some 45 towns, over hills and train crossings and around sharp curves, as even its backers admitted. "It is true that the road is hilly and lacks the natural advantages of the Iowa Trans-Continental Route," wrote the editor of the Belle Plaine newspaper, "but it is a shining example of what intelligent road work will do even under adverse conditions."

A writer who chronicled a 1911 transcontinental trip made by 12 Indianapolis-built Premier autos was less inhibited in his criticism of a bad stretch of the River-to-River Road west of Avoca. "For the next 12 miles the cars traveled over what is famed as the washboard road, because of its series of low hills ranging from one-quarter to a half mile in length, but with grades which run as high as 20 degrees." This compared to grades that only once exceeded 27 percent during the Premier caravan's climb over the Sierra Nevada.[31]

Crossings Cleared, Cows Diverted

Officials of the River-to-River Road Association, however, had the entire road dragged before Wells's run and tried to eliminate other road hazards, as the editor of the *Altoona Herald* reveals. "The *Herald* office was called about eleven o'clock [the day of the race], by Bert N. Mills, of Des Moines, secretary of the River to River Road Association, and asked to report Mr. Well's [*sic*] passing here so that the railroad crossings could be cleared."

Fred Claiborne of the Leachman-Claiborne garage in Des Moines was appointed to meet Wells for a gas and oil stop at Eighth and Grand "but decided to go east and meet the racer," the *Des Moines Capital* said. "He met Wells at the top of the hill near the interurban crossing south of Grandview park. Claiborne arrived just in time to divert the course of about 100 head of cattle which were being turned into the main road. This piece of luck no doubt saved Mr. Wells several minutes."

Because of the lunchtime traffic in Iowa's largest city, "every precaution to prevent any accident was taken by the department of public safety when Wells passed through Des Moines at 11:44 o'clock," the *Evening Tribune* said. "Patrolmen were stationed on nearly every corner. The Northwestern

[railroad] crossing in East Des Moines was held open for him. The fire chief's car was used to clear the way through the more congested district."

Fire Chief William Burnett spotted Wells coming down the Grand Avenue hill and "he turned his big car loose," according to an account in the December 1913 *Motorist* magazine, published in nearby Omaha. "He was four or five blocks ahead of the Spaulding car and his siren screeched a warning as he sped up the street at the rate of sixty miles an hour [many newspapers said 50 miles per hour]. Wells was on his heels in a twinkling. At West Eighteenth street the two were so close together that bystanders held their breath for fear some accident would happen for they were going at a terrific rate of speed. The street was absolutely clear. Both cars went up the West Grand Avenue hill like a flash and near the top the racing car swerved around the Fire Chief's machine as though it were standing still."

Wells later recalled: "I did not know that arrangements had been made for the chief's auto to pilot me but supposed there was a fire and dodged in behind the car to get a free road. I soon discovered they were clearing the road for me and hung on to their car until I reached West Grand when I dashed around them. I noticed my father in a car on the Avenue but did not take time to stop and visit."

"A Little Matter of 84 Miles an Hour"

The Spaulding racer ate up the miles on the west leg of the highway, saving nine miles and "no less than twenty-four turns" by taking the Exira cutoff, reported the *Nonpareil* of Council Bluffs. "There were times when the trip became more in the nature of a flight; only the hilltops were touched. It is seven miles from Waukee to Adel, and according to verified time and compared watches, he made the trip in just five minutes — a mere little matter of eighty-four miles an hour" on that straight, downhill stretch. In light of such speeds, the auto-maker stretched the bounds of believability when one of its later ads asserted "our driver was instructed to play safe, not run for time, but to beat the former record."

The weather – "ideal all day, though a tri-fle chilly" – turned into sleet at Council Bluffs, where Wells raced up to the *Non-pareil* office at 3:51 P.M. to stop the clocks at 9 hours 14 minutes. The new mark, which beat Don McClure's record by 1 hour 28 minutes, included 33 minutes of down time: 13 minutes for a new spring at Grinnell, 5 minutes to remove the spare gas tank at Kel-logg, 5 minutes for gas in Des Moines, 4 minutes for gas at Guthrie Center, 2 min-utes at Exira to phone ahead for gas at Wal-nut, and 4 minutes at Walnut to take on gas.

"The Spaulding car in which I made the race yesterday worked beautifully and I did not have a minute's loss from tire trouble," Wells told the *Des Moines Capital*. "I do not believe any driver ever made such great dis-tance on a dirt road at such speed without some tire trouble," he said. Photos showing the car with three spare tires strapped on the back suggest Wells was most certainly expecting trouble. "After I left the *Nonpareil* office in Council Bluffs, and started for the Spaulding garage at Omaha I ran upon a nail and had a puncture," Wells said.

The *Nonpareil* said Wells beat the Rock Is-land mail train to Council Bluffs by 27 min-utes. Doing so, according to the *Newton Daily Journal*, "is going faster than the ordinary man wants to ride in a car over country roads." On the subject of trains, the *Grinnell Herald* couldn't resist observing that "Mr. Wells beat all previous time in an Iowa road race by a time so fast that Mr. McClure's rec-ord reads like a train on a branch line alongside a limited speeder."

Record "Worth More Than 100 Racing Victories"

"The car Mr. Wells drove was a Spaulding stock car with a racing body," the *Des Moines Capital* said, though the *Newton Daily Journal* writer wondered "if it is true that it was a stock car."

Yes, it is true, and "we will guarantee to duplicate this same car to any customer at the regular price," the factory claimed in its 1914 catalog. Spaulding did make at least one copy of its famous racer. The *Grinnell Herald* reported that the Spaulding com-pany's 1915 Iowa State Fair display included "one Scout, the duplicate of the one in which Wells made the trans-state record." The automaker proudly displayed the real thing at the March 1914 Des Moines Auto-mobile Show.

"We feel that the making of the . . . world's record on a dirt road by an abso-lutely regular stock chassis, spells more for the merit of the Spaulding Car than a hun-dred triumphs on a prepared race track by a freak car which bears no resemblance in any way to the product of the manufacturer," the automaker said. "The dirt road is the kind of road the ordinary purchaser will travel and the regular chassis of the manu-facturer is what he will get to travel the dirt road with."

In a letter to the factory after his first mud-shortened run, Wells sang the praises of the Spaulding. "I want to tell you that you build an automobile, and you don't have to prove it. I admit it. If the general public were as thoroughly convinced of that fact as I am your car would need no further adver-tising. In a run such as I recently made, the slightest hitch in the working of the car gives the driver a certain amount of worry, but I wasn't even annoyed, and such a per-fect working piece of mechanism as can stand up and do such consistent good work under such an enormous strain is nothing short of marvelous," Wells wrote.

The *Newton Daily Journal* writer who ques-tioned whether the Wells car had a stock chassis said he had his reasons. Wells cov-ered the distance from Newton to Des Moines in 56 minutes; Elmer H. Maytag held the record of 54 minutes on that stretch – but needed a Velie racer to accomplish the feat, the *Journal* reported. Ironically, Maytag – son of the automobile and washing-machine manufacturer – set the record while driving a scout car that led racer Pete Petersen into Des Moines during Petersen's 1912 race against Don McClure, who was driving on the rival White Pole Road.

After the cross-state victory, Wells said he wouldn't try it again unless another driver lowered his mark. Would previous champion Don McClure attempt it? "I cannot say whether I will run again," McClure told a Des Moines newspaper. "Mrs. McClure is very much opposed to me racing."

Wells's cross-state record was still standing in 1916, when Spaulding Manufacturing ceased car production, trumpeting the racer's victory in its advertising to the end. Hal Wells in 1914 built a touring car with a cyclops headlight, wire wheels, no windshield, and a single door centered along each side of the car. The Wells car also had a 4-cylinder engine with a 5⅛-inch bore and 4-speed Warner transmission. Wells apparently never intended to go into production with it.

A description of the Wells-built car in the October 15, 1914, *Motor Age* identifies Wells as director of the River-to-River Road Association, a fitting position for someone who did so much to publicize the highway. Having mastered flying along dirt roads, Wells later took actual flying lessons at the Curtiss School of Aviation. His 1913 cross-state mark was finally beaten by a Packard. But on October 11, 1916, Wells shaved 1 hour 24 minutes off his own previous time when he drove an 8-cylinder Cadillac and four passengers over the same River-to-River Road to regain the record.[32]

1914 Cars See Minor Improvements

It appeared that the factory would add an auto-pulled road drag to its line of 1913 products. That summer, the factory made two experimental road drags to find a model that would stay on the ground without bouncing when pulled behind a car or truck at 10 or 15 miles per hour. The drags gave "entirely satisfactory results" when pulled along dirt roads behind a Spaulding test car, according to the *Grinnell Herald*. But the factory apparently failed to pursue the idea because the *Grinnell Herald* didn't mention Spaulding road drags again.[33]

"In our 1914 car the general Spaulding design has been retained, as we have found no necessity for any radical change," the company said. In contrast, *Automobile* magazine referred to the "radical body changes and minor mechanical changes" of the 1914 Spaulding 40, which advanced one letter to become the Model H.[34] (See fig. 4.29.) The factory acknowledged that the car had more comforts and conveniences than ever before:

All cars carry as regular equipment: a panatasote top, with quick acting side curtains which fold into place inside the top and a dust cover for protection when the top is down: a sixty mile Warner speedometer, driven from the propeller shaft of the car which eliminates the dirty and unsightly construction of the front wheel drive; a double action rain vision and ventilating windshield; toe and robe rails; combination, double bulb electric head lamps; electric tail lamp with license number holder; rebound straps [shock absorbers] on rear springs; electric horn; tool kit; jack; tire pump; etc. In other words, this amounts to absolutely a complete outfit necessary for comfort and convenience on a long distance tour.

Automobile magazine noted that "streamline has been the word in Spaulding body design and this has been worked out more successfully this year than ever before. The cowl arrangement has helped this considerably and the placing of one gasoline tank in the rear and another in the cowl has augmented this."

Beginning in 1914, the company moved the gas tank from under the front seat to between the rear frame rails, which "permitted of the use of an 11-inch cushion in the front, the same depth cushion being used in the rear," *Automobile* noted. Another practical advantage of the switch, *MoTor* magazine added, is it "allows a good, roomy toolbox to be installed under the front seat." Such later Spauldings used low air pressure from an engine-driven pump to force gas from the main tank to the 2-gallon cowl tank, from whence it flowed by gravity to the Holley Model H carburetor. The air pump could also fill tires.

The bodies of the 1914 Iowa-made cars were "made complete in [the] new Spaulding body plant from carefully selected lumber and heavy sheet steel," the 1914 Spaulding catalog said. "Special treatment of steel prevents all possibility of rust. All posts re-enforced with bar steel to sill. Stream line, curved sides and back, concealed hinges, inside door handles and instrument board give most stylish appearance."

"Any Color You Want as Long as It's . . ."

The 1915 Spaulding 40, still using a 4-cylinder Buda engine, "is continued with a number of improvements chief among which are the placing of the rear springs underneath instead of over the axle and the fitting of a body with more graceful lines," according to a review in the December 31, 1914, *Automobile*. "Aside from these changes the car is practically the same as before," and was also available as a Sleeper model.

The 1915 Spaulding 50 was a surprisingly thrifty car given its large Buda 4-cylinder engine, the same model retained from the previous year. The *Grinnell Herald* in July 1915 published a signed affidavit from a Spaulding 50 owner who claimed he drove 83.7 miles – partly in Des Moines city traffic – on 4.25 gallons, for an average of 19.7 miles per gallon.

As early as mid-May 1915, the automaker's Grinnell agent was advertising the Spaulding 50 car. Since Ernest Spaulding was president of Hawkeye Motor Sales Company, it's a safe bet that the ads were accurate. Whether the factory considered the car a 1915 or a very early 1916 model is an open question, however. The Spaulding company advertised its 1916 Spaulding 50 as its Model H, the same letter designation it had used since 1914. The unidentified 4-cylinder engine in the Spaulding 50 had a bore and stroke identical to that of the Buda

4.29 A 1914 Model H, illustrated in a Spaulding poster. (GHM)

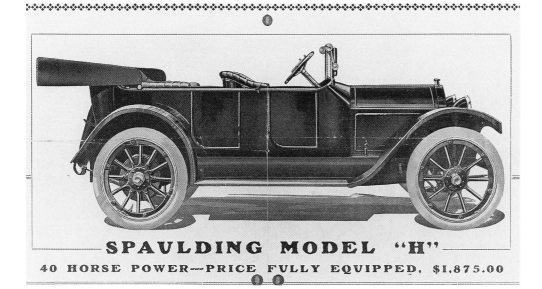

SPAULDING MODEL "H"

40 HORSE POWER---PRICE FULLY EQUIPPED, $1,875.00

engine used in the Spaulding 40s. It appears that Spaulding Manufacturing changed the name of the car and little else.

By 1916, the Iowa automaker was advertising a new one-man "silk mohair" top. But while "it has plenty of power and high-class components," *Motor Age* magazine said, the 1916 Spaulding – like those of 1915 and 1914 – "has been changed only in minor detail." It was, however, available also in a roadster model and in the Sleeper body style that the company introduced in late 1913, the magazine said.[35]

If the body style had become standard, so had its color. The Spauldings liked to paint their cars dark blue. (See fig.4.30.) As early as 1911, the *Grinnell Herald* referred to a "Spaulding blue," but press accounts also mention Spaulding body colors of "silver gray" and "steel gray" – perhaps different descriptions for the same color – as well as green and cream. The Hal Wells car was much brighter, painted orange and black. Henry Spaulding drove a red Spaulding car, recalls his granddaughter, Miriam Simms. The factory took a "special light blue car, with Spanish trimmings" to the 1915 Iowa State Fair.

Spaulding car paint was a "Twenty-one Process Finish, Spaulding deep blue, with fine stripe," the factory said in a 1914 "Announcement" sheet. "The hood and fenders and all skirts and mud splashers are finished by the enamel process," the 1914 catalog said. "This gives them not only a very fine appearance but one that will last indefinitely, is not affected by the heat of the motor, the destructive action of mud and water and which it is almost impossible to damage by accidental collision, if not too severe."

"Made in Iowa" Used as a Slur

The 1914 Spaulding car came with a one-year warranty, excluding tires and rims, that gave company officials wide latitude in honoring any claims. The company's warranty, printed in its catalog, said it would replace a part that, "under normal use and service, appears to us to have been defective in material or workmanship." Far-flung owners paid freight costs to ship a damaged item back to Grinnell for inspection and to receive a replacement. It was also up to owners to either install their own parts or hire a mechanic, both of which were risky because if a Spaulding car was "repaired outside of our factory, our liability under this warranty shall cease."

In his essay "Why Michigan," historian

4.30 The Spaulding factory's "Auto Paint Room," probably 1915 or 1916. (SHSI)

4.31 An artist's drawing of a streamline-cowl Spaulding, perhaps a prototype of the new $750 Spaulding 30 for 1916. (SHSI)

4.32 A 1915 ad for the new, low-priced Spaulding 30 and 50 models. The car pictured is an older Spaulding Sleeper. (Aug. 27, 1915, *Grinnell Herald*)

NEW
SPAULDING
THIRTY
$750.00

NEW
SPAULDING
FIFTY
$1,250.00

On account of our larger production and better facilities we are enabled to make this tremendously low price on these two beautiful and powerful models.

Home People Have Purchased More Home Cars Than All Other Makes Added Together—WHY?

Because the Home product has proved the best value. Like the Spaulding Vehicle, it costs a little more first cost, but when you figure it, it outwears two or more cheap cars, which is your best purchase, when at the same time you are fostering Home Industry and getting

HOME   FACTORY   SERVICE.

REMEMBER THE LITTLE HOME CAR PUT UP A CROSS COUNTRY WORLD'S RECORD IN 1913 THAT STILL STANDS.

BUY IN GRINNELL, YOU'LL KEEP GRINNELL ON THE MAP.

SPAULDING   MANUFACTURING   COMPANY

John B. Rae says "a remarkable concentration in time and place of a group of individuals . . . [with] exceptional entrepreneurial and technical talent" propelled Detroit by 1915 to "unmistakably and unchallengeably Motoropolis."[36] Whatever the reasons behind its rise, Detroit posed a great threat to small Midwestern manufacturers. To defend itself, the Spaulding company boasted of its own stable 40-year history as a vehicle manufacturer in Grinnell, Iowa – a much better record than those compiled during the short, often scandal-riddled, careers of many big-city car companies:

We feel that in the past some of our competitors have tried to influence the buyer by an inverse argument. They have said "O yes, the Spaulding! That car is made in the WEST, MADE IN IOWA," etc., trying to carry the inference that anything not "Made in Germany," New York, or Detroit was wholly out of consideration. We are now certainly glad they did put forth this argument, for in the era of doubt of the financial solidarity of the car manufacturer, the known inability of a defunct manufacturer to supply repairs, the slogan "MADE IN THE WEST" or "MADE IN IOWA" used against us as a slur comes back upon them like a mighty "BOOMERANG," and the MAN FROM THE WEST finds he may better see the financial solidity of his manufacturer, and get better "FACTORY SERVICE" talking face to face with the manufacturer of the "CAR THAT IS MADE IN THE WEST."[37]

In most of its advertising for 1915, the last full year of Spaulding car production, the company tried to build its "home" patronage by using such slogans as "Home Folks Buy Home Cars," "See The Home Car First," "Nothing Stops The Home Car," and "Spaulding Home Car Always Brings You Home."

Desperate Factory Chops Prices

From 1913 to 1915, the Spaulding company concentrated on turning out primarily Spaulding 40 touring cars, which in 1914 were advertised at $1,875. The Grinnell company also made a Spaulding 50 model

in 1915 but apparently didn't advertise its price that year. By August 1915, however, the automaker began a dramatic appeal to the low-price market by advertising a new small 1916 Spaulding 30 (see fig. 4.31) for $750, half the price of the last Spaulding 30 it made in 1912 and just $10 more than the Model T two-door sedan, Ford's most expensive 1916 model. The 1916 Spaulding 50 was also substantially discounted at $1,250. (See fig. 4.32.)

A photo in the January 18, 1916, *Grinnell Herald* shows the new Spaulding 30 to be a sleek, modern-looking touring car. The factory's final advertising slogan, "Spaulding Cars First Because Spaulding Cars Last," may have been true for the cars but not for the car factory.

If the company had been healthy, the price of its cars would have reflected their quality and hand-built origins. Photographs from inside the Spaulding factory, after all, show the lack of any assembly line, high-speed or otherwise. Spaulding cars were bigger, heavier, stronger, more powerful, and more luxurious than the lightweight Fords, and would normally have been priced accordingly. As if staged to demonstrate the difference between the two cars, a Ford and a Spaulding crashed at a bridge approach near Grinnell. "The lighter Ford was naturally most damaged," the *Grinnell Herald* recounted. "The left front wheel was smashed, the radiator crushed in, the axle sprung, the windshield demolished and the body dented and twisted." The Spaulding suffered a bent fender and springs, "a burst tire and a wrenched wheel," the paper added.[38]

"On account of our larger production and better facilities we are enabled to make this tremendously low price on these two beautiful and powerful models," was the Spaulding company's public justification for its price chopping. But there is little evidence to suggest that the company was able to cut its assembly time enough for production to rise accordingly.

The Grinnell automaker was apparently feeling the pinch from local dealers who were selling such lower-price cars as the Ford, Saxon, and Studebaker. In a January 1916 *Des Moines Register* ad, the company warned that "we have but a limited number of cars uncontracted," perhaps an indication that the factory wanted to rid itself of its last batch of cars and had no plans to make more.[39]

An Ominous Announcement

In part because of a rising new star among local industries – aviator Billy Robinson's Grinnell Aeroplane Company, in which Henry Spaulding was an investor – the local press turned its attention away from Spaul-

ding Manufacturing Company in 1915 and 1916. Exactly why the Spaulding family discontinued auto production therefore went unrecorded in the local news columns. By all appearances, Spauldings were still popular cars in Iowa. For instance, son Ernest Spaulding's Hawkeye Motor Sales Company sold four Spaulding cars on July 20, 1915, "to claim central Iowa's high record one day's sales for cars of medium price," the *Grinnell Herald* reported.[40] The company also had a generous five-car display at the Iowa State Fair in September 1915.

But in an ominous-sounding "To The Public" ad that ran in the March 10, 1916, *Grinnell Herald,* the Spaulding company announced: "We are now prepared to do Repair Work on All Kinds of automobiles, at our Motor Car Plant, corner of Fourth Avenue and Spring street. We also solicit your work of Repainting, Trimming, Remodeling of Bodies or Rebuilding of Tops." In its new capacity, the company would have a tow truck "constantly in readiness to haul in your car." Spaulding was out of the automobile business.

A Joplin, Missouri, collector owns the one Spaulding car known to exist – a 1913 Spaulding touring-car chassis and Buda engine, including the radiator with the Spaulding diamond emblem, hood, and other body parts, but without the body and original wheels.

To handle its anticipated larger volume of repair work, the company said, it would close its repair garage attached to Grinnell's Colonial Theatre and transfer its garage mechanics to the roomier auto factory. To complete the transformation into a king-size service station, the company advertised that it would test and charge storage batteries and carry "a full line of automobile accessories, tires, oils, and gasoline."

Next Product: Manure Spreader

In an article just three weeks later, the *Grinnell Herald* reveals that the factory, far from idle, had begun producing a new machine designed to pave the way for more automobiles – though apparently not for any new cars bearing the Spaulding diamond. For the factory's new machine was "a combined excavator, self-loading and self-dumping wagon and manure spreader, all combined in one under the name of 'The Self Loader,'" an invention of Robert Shedenhelm of Ladora.

"Its inventor claims . . . it furnishes the easiest and speediest way of building smooth roads, grading, leveling, building levees, shallow drainage ditching, straightening water courses, inoculating soil for alfalfa, hauling fertile soil on unfertile ground, cleaning feed lots, spreading manure, and like uses. It seems a machine of great possibilities, and it has been turned out with the usual Spaulding care," the newspaper said.[41] The Spaulding company put a Self Loader, but no cars, on display at the summer 1916 Iowa State Fair.

By mid-1917, the graders were "being sold in larger quantities than [the] factory can turn them out," a Grinnell newspaper reported. In January 1918 during World War I, the Spaulding company began nationally advertising its Liberty knitting needles. "The factory now has facilities for turning out 1,400 needles an hour and can double and triple this figure if necessary to keep up with demand," the Grinnell press reported.

Later reports indicate the Spaulding carriage factory received a wartime U.S. government order to produce between $100,000 and $200,000 worth of parts for "wagons, ambulances, etc., such as poles, shafts, single trees, double trees, neck yokes and the like." The company also contributed to the war effort with a May 1918 order to make 4,000 packing crates for the air tanks that pilots used in high-altitude flying.

Spaulding tapped the burgeoning postwar truck market and by summer 1920 was "turning out work at an amazing rate" with orders to deliver 60 carloads of truck bodies and cabs by early 1921. "The Herring Motor Company is one of the largest users of Spaulding cabs and bodies. This company will receive 1,000 jobs before February 1 at its distributing warehouses in Kansas City, Omaha, Sioux Falls and Des Moines," the local paper reported. The Spaulding plant had to introduce a 10-hour day in April 1924 to keep up with orders.

Ford Trucks Get Spaulding Bodies

In May 1925, the Spauldings announced they had contracted with the Chittenden-Eastman Furniture Company of Burlington, Iowa, to build 525 frames per week for sofas, wing chairs, and straight chairs. Spaulding's truck and cab production continued unabated, however, at a pace of 75 carloads for the first quarter of 1925. Noting this Midwestern production capacity, Ford Motor Company in June 1925 ordered 3,000 Spaulding stake bodies for Ford trucks. (See fig.4.33.) Fred Spaulding immediately set out for Jackson, Mississippi, to get two trainloads of yellow pine lumber for the Spaulding dry kilns quickly enough to begin delivering Ford bodies in six weeks' time.[42]

Henry Ford tried to buy Spaulding Manufacturing, but Henry Spaulding refused, according to his granddaughter, Miriam Simms. "I've heard it all my life that Grandpa would just have no part of it," Simms said. "The story is he [Spaulding] didn't think too much of him [Ford]. He was too independent to go in with anybody."

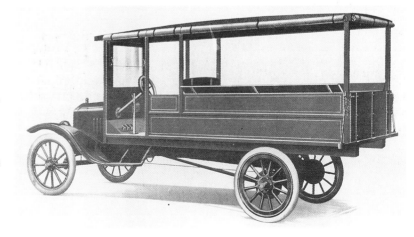

4.33 An undated catalog illustrates a Spaulding body made for Ford Model T trucks. (GHM)

It was perhaps because the independent Henry Spaulding didn't want to satisfy stockholders that he never incorporated the business, Simms speculates. Orders evaporated in the late 1920s as automakers in Detroit and elsewhere began building their own truck bodies and cabs. The Spauldings were forced out of the business in a receivership action, losing most of what they owned, Simms recalls. "That's what cleaned us out and we lost everything but what was in the women's names."

Henry Spaulding "left the manufacturing field in 1928 and retired," according to his obituary in the *Des Moines Tribune*. In fact, no Spauldings were among the officers elected during a January 1928 Spaulding Manufacturing Company board of directors' meeting. Simms said Henry Spaulding apparently still had some money after the collapse of the business, but that her own father, Ernest Spaulding, was left in relative poverty, and her Uncle Fred Spaulding was forced to open up his large Grinnell home as a tourist hotel after the plant closed.

The Eggleston Compartment Coach Company bought the Spaulding factory compound in 1929 to make buses. Its other products included a large "parlor funeral coach" pulled by a Douglas tractor truck made in Omaha.[43] The various buildings in the Spaulding complex survived the Eggleston venture, a shoe factory that moved in during the mid-1930s, and a variety of other businesses over the years. Some of the buildings were still standing in the 1990s.

Durable Spaulding "An Honest Car"

Henry Spaulding's *Des Moines Tribune* obituary dismissed Spaulding cars as being "too heavy . . . and [they] did not meet popular demand," a false claim often echoed in retrospective articles about Spaulding cars. According to a variety of customers' testimonial letters, the car was durable, powerful, and thrifty. The cross-state record run proved the car's speed, and the San Diego–New York mapping adventure demonstrated its durability.

By most accounts, the car was popular in its limited market, and could scarcely have been otherwise to have survived six years against intense competition. Despite having West Coast and Southwest dealers, the company sold most of its cars to Grinnell-area buyers, who found driving a Spaulding as natural as breathing.

In April 1915, the factory published a list of 123 "Well Satisfied Home Owners of The Home Car," later noting that "Home People Have Purchased More Home Cars Than All Other Makes Added Together – WHY? Because the Home product has proved the best value. Like the Spaulding Vehicle [carriages and wagons], it costs a little more first cost, but when you figure it, it outwears two or more cheap cars, which is your best purchase, when at the same time you are fostering Home Industry and getting Home Factory Service."

When the factory was making cars, "many business men and prominent citizens of Grinnell were driving Spauldings," noted a retrospective article. "Local support for the enterprise was good but the car did not 'catch on' over a wider field and its production was ultimately discontinued."

Perhaps the biggest reason behind the demise of the Spaulding automobile was simply the advent of the mass-produced low-priced car. "The coming of automobiles into general use proved the undoing of their enterprise," was the neat summary offered in the *Annals of Iowa* history magazine. A 1949 Grinnell newspaper historical piece paid the Spaulding car perhaps the greatest compliment of all. The car venture ultimately folded, the article acknowledges, but "like everything that the Spauldings built, it was an honest car, honestly constructed of honest materials."[44]

Moon of Missouri

An Aggregation of Well-Tried-Out Constructions

5

Despite an engineering department that played follow-the-leader, the Moon Motor Car Company of St. Louis enjoyed a reputation for making well-designed, often innovative, and – especially in the 1920s – fashionable automobiles. The cars named after founder Joseph W. Moon had well-finished bodies, deep cushions, and rich finishes.

The automaker eagerly borrowed ideas from other cars, especially as the nationwide demand for automobiles prompted Moon and other builders to buy more parts from suppliers. Moon used its advertising to take the sting out of the term "assembled car," asserting that "every man who has read the catalogues of even two or three makes of cars knows that practically every make of car today is an 'assembled car' – and has been for years."[1]

Joseph Moon, who in 1905 started building cars after nearly 25 years in the carriage-making business, was fervent about the Moon's design. So he recruited Peerless designer Louis P. Mooers to create the early Moon cars, which used a Mooers-designed overhead-valve 4-cylinder engine. The car sold well to Midwestern farmers, many of whom undoubtedly owned or had owned Moon carriages. Moon cars proved themselves on race tracks, endurance runs, and hill climbs. In late 1907, as Moons began selling on the East Coast under the name Hol-Tan, one of the St. Louis cars became the first U.S. entry in the monumental New York-to-Paris race.

Moons had aluminum bodies in 1907, and were leaders with closed bodies in 1908 and self-starters in 1909. In 1916, Moon Motors helped pioneer the use of dual-cowl bodies in America and experimented with a canvas-and-leather body in 1928. Under Stewart McDonald's control after Joseph Moon's death in 1919, the company became one of the first U.S. automakers to adopt four-wheel hydraulic brakes and balloon tires. The St. Louis company made an early switch to straight-8 engines and was among the first to export autos fully assembled, rather than crated.

From 1913 through World War I, Moon produced a line of light and heavy trucks that found buyers as far away as California. Joseph Moon's philosophy of quality over quantity held annual production to under 2,500 cars. A new era dawned under McDonald's stewardship. With McDonald's emphasis on wealthier car buyers – who undoubtedly appreciated the Rolls-Royce radiator that Moon copied in 1919 – production figures rose impressively from 2,466 in 1920 to 10,271 in 1925, when Moon Motor Car Company became the 24th largest U.S. automaker. The company's agencies and distributors – as many as 700 – eventually sold cars in 47 countries.

Then, as competition sharpened and bigger companies gobbled up smaller ones, McDonald and Moon Motors made a series of costly mistakes. First, the Diana, a dramatic sales success upon its introduction in 1925 as a Moon companion line, had serious – and expensive – engine flaws that weren't corrected in time to save Diana's reputation. McDonald crippled sales further by sweeping out the Moon distributor network and, in its place, setting up factory branches to route cars to Moon dealers. Even as sales dwindled to 3,001 in 1928, Moon Motors persisted in trying to be all things to all buyers by offering three models and 25 body styles.

Buyers eyed Moon's next offering, the Windsor in 1929, with some understandable suspicion – even more justified because company layoffs had depleted the engineering staff. For all his willingness to experiment in some areas, McDonald showed reluctance in borrowing money, thus hampering the company's growth. Factory equipment deteriorated. As if the company needed more trouble, Moon Motors even managed to anger Windsor Castle by illegally replicating the crest of the Prince of Wales on the Windsor's radiator. Despite its advertised 80-mile-per-hour top speed, the Windsor saw sluggish sales.

In 1929, during the St. Louis automaker's worst production year since World War I, the company was so desperate for work that it considered manufacturing cotton pickers under contract. So when Eastern promoter Archie Andrews offered Moon officials the chance to buy patent and production rights to a new front-wheel-drive car called the Ruxton, it seemed that happy days were just around the corner. But when Andrews secretly bought a majority share of Moon stock, ousted the old guard, and installed

5.1 Joseph W. Moon, 1915. (NAHC)

his own officers, the Moon company of the early days was gone. The new Moon venture, so undercapitalized that it ran partly on the force of Andrews's strong personality, faced intimidating odds.

"A Horse, Bridle, and Saddle"

Born in March 1850 in Brown County, Ohio, the son of Alva and Delila (Sewell) Moon, Joseph W. Moon (see fig.5.1) grew up on his father's farm and, like his younger brother, John Corydon Moon, attended country public schools, according to several accounts. The boys' formal schooling thus apparently went no further than the eighth grade. By the time Joseph Moon began making cars, the Moon name had been "a household word in the Middle West for several generations, as the family first became famous prior to the Civil War, as manufacturers of the first rifled shoulder gun placed on the market," according to an article based on the auto factory's press release.[2]

"When they were 21, they were given a horse, a bridle and a saddle, and they were off on their own," Mrs. Grace (Moon) Ferriss, Joseph Moon's daughter, said in a 1977 interview. Moon rode into business as a photographer for four years. "Later he became a buggy salesman and after traveling for some years with an Eastern firm, came to St. Louis in January, 1882, to enter business." With his brother John, he formed the Moon Bros. Carriage Company, which by 1888 was turning out 5,000 carriages a year. Opposed to letting John's father-in-law buy a stake in the business, Joseph Moon in 1893 sold his half-interest to his brother and left to set up the Joseph W. Moon Buggy Company. According to one account, the two brothers scarcely talked to one another again.[3]

As early as 1902, when he attended a carriage makers' convention in Detroit, the emerging motor metropolis, Joseph Moon contemplated making horseless carriages. In April 1905 he set up an automobile department in his buggy factory. "The Joseph W. Moon Buggy Company, of St. Louis, has almost completed its first automobile," reported the August 3, 1905, *Motor Way* magazine. The *Horseless Age* magazine of two months later mistakenly called him "James Moon" but said the buggy factory bearing his name was "erecting a building 140 x 120 feet in floor plan, and three stories high, adjoining their present plant, which will be used as an automobile factory."[4] Though developed as the "Hercules" automobile, the car that Joseph Moon shipped to the January 1906 New York auto show had been renamed the Moon Model A five-passenger touring car with a "King of Belgium" side-entrance body. It was advertised as a product not of the buggy company but of the new, still unincorporated, Moon Motor Car Company.[5]

Hub and Nub of Moon's Philosophy – Service

Joseph Moon capitalized on his buggy-building experience as he set out to sell his factory's new product. "The oldest designer and the oldest builder of automobiles have been at the business but a few years," he noted in a 1911 ad. "Unless you have many more years experience in machinery – knowledge of materials – the factor of safety

– accuracy – all that goes into fine machinery – what can you depend on?" Moon was seldom quoted directly in the press – even in his own factory's press releases. In a rare exception, Moon gave the local *St. Louis Post-Dispatch* his reaction to a 1916 car order from Copenhagen, Denmark:

It is most peculiar that in these orders from far-off places, as a rule, the buyer has little or no negotiation with the company and no personal contact whatever. It would be rather interesting to analyze where the buyer received his knowledge and confidence in the particular make of car, so much so as to order them shipped to him from a point many thousand miles distant, and leave it entirely to the manufacturer to see that the goods are put up and shipped exactly as he desires, without any recourse whatever.[6]

Joseph Moon was more prominent in the company's advertising from 1910 to 1912, when the ads carried his photo and a short talk about how his cars were constructed.

By turn-of-the-century standards, Moon was a rich man. A 1900 St. Louis taxpayers' directory put the value of Joseph Moon's real estate and personal property – excluding savings, investments, and other income – at just over $40,000.[7] A careful and conservative manager, as befitting his Republican affiliation, Moon believed in satisfying every customer, even if it meant remaining a small manufacturer. A sense of Joseph Moon's approach to the automobile business emerges from his advertising comments on the $1,500 Moon 30 of 1910: "This car costs more to produce – and it represents more money all the way through, even to the high-grade attachments, than others; more really than is necessary – but the service it gives is what counts – and service is the hub and the nub of the automobile proposition."

The company's early advertising message is neatly summarized in one 1911 ad: "Joseph W. Moon is more interested in the reputation of the Moon car than he is in the profit on any individual car. And the car must be perfect even at the sacrifice of all profit on it before it leaves the factory." He also favored overbuilding his cars. Of the 1912 Moon 40, said to develop 46 actual horsepower, Joseph Moon said: "Buyers have no reason to expect our steering and transmission gears, universal joints or back axles to be any stronger than the motor's horsepower — yet we guarantee them for 60 horsepower. . . . The Moon policy invariably delivers more than the buyer expects or pays for." Further, Joseph Moon declared, "My policy is just this — make a small profit on each car and sell a lot of them. That's why I'm selling this $3,000 car [1913 Moon 48] for $1,985."[8]

Sick for a year and bedridden for a month, the 68-year-old Moon died February 11, 1919, from what his obituary called "hardening of the arteries," or arteriosclerosis. Stewart McDonald (see fig.5.2) succeeded his father-in-law as president and guided the company through the turbulent 1920s with a different emphasis and business philosophy.

Moon Hires "Green Dragon" Creator

Joseph W. Moon built cars and carriages (see fig.5.3) practically side by side during the early years. A Sanborn fire-insurance map from 1909 shows the buggy company occupying less than half of a U-shaped brick factory building at 4401–31 N. Main Street, also called First Street. The company sometimes listed its North St. Louis address as Main and Cornelia streets, but at other times rounded the street address to 4400 N. Main. The other leg of the "U" and the union of the two legs was occupied by the various departments of the Moon Motor Car Company, including a small corner office, areas for wheel painting, body painting, and, on the second and third floors, "painting" of an unspecified nature — possibly automobile chassis. The auto factory also included a first-floor machine shop, second-floor assembly room, and third-floor upholstering and cabinet shops. An elevator carried cars between levels.

5.2 Stewart McDonald. (SLML)

5.3 A Moon three-spring phaeton, as pictured in a 1911 Joseph W. Moon Buggy Company catalog. (CWB)

Jos. W. Moon Buggy Co.

Early Moon designer Louis P. Mooers – who designed Peerless cars in Cleveland up to and including the 1906 models – was made Moon supervising engineer and factory manager in time to design the 1907 Moon Model C. It was a coup for Moon: Mooers was to engines what Thomas A. Edison was to electricity. While such pioneer U.S. automakers as Auburn, Cadillac, Oldsmobile, and Packard were still making 1-cylinder cars, Mooers for the Peerless car and George Weidely for the Premier "led the way to multi-cylinder engines," according to a history of the American automobile engine. "Their two-cylinder power units were built in considerable numbers and proved both powerful and reliable."[9]

For Peerless, Mooers in 1904 designed the 60-horsepower Green Dragon racer that was piloted by Barney Oldfield, who made a name for himself driving Henry Ford's famous 999 racer to a mile-a-minute record the previous year. Mooers was "the man who made it possible for Barney Oldfield to secure and still hold all world's circular track records from 1 to 50 miles with his Green Dragon," according to the Moon company.[10]

The trade press raved about Mooers's Moon designs. "In the details of the Moon Model C, Mooers gave free rein to his fancy, and introduced a great number of improvements of such obvious novelty and value as to sharply differentiate this Moon Model C touring car from others of its class and price . . . thus giving this 1907 Moon touring car a distinct individuality of its own," *Cycle and Automobile Trade Journal* said. Mooers designed most parts of the new car, including the axles, universal joints, and engine. The engine's valve action "is an original Mooers design, a single horizontal beam and single cam serving to work two valves."[11]

An Aggregation of Well-Tried-Out Constructions

Before signing on at Moon, Mooers traveled abroad – reportedly for four months – to study European automobile design with an eye toward starting his own company in the United States. Unable to secure financing, he went to work for the Moon Motor Car Company, bringing with him an appreciation for foreign methods. *Motor Age* suggested that, in designing the 1907 Moon, Mooers

has almost strayed from the beaten paths of custom and what many consider motor rectitude, yet a scrutiny reveals all of them to be tried constructions, if not well known at home then acknowledged abroad. The designer has in this menu card made a few selections not widely followed in America. . . . The upswept frame has two or three other American devotees and boosts of a large clientele abroad. . . . The arched rear axle has been known since the days of Mooers' association with the Peerless company and has a limited European following. Welch and one or two other makers have exploited the overhead camshaft and stick to it. Valves in the cylinder heads have been talking points with many makers since Dugald Clark declared it is the only place for them and since the 2-mile-a-minute Darracq with its valves so located set a world's mark on the Florida sands. One rocker arm for two valves was brought out on Fiat racing cars 2 years ago and since then has received recognition at the hands of Pope-Toledo and De Luxe makers. . . . Carrying the radiator in rear of the front axle is a chip from the Mercedes workshop. All told, then, the new Moon car, although looking at first glance to be a combination of new features, is but an aggregation of well-tried-out constructions, constructions, however, that are not old, that are not radical, but that have been tried and found successful.[12]

After just two years at Moon, "L. P. Mooers, the designer of the Moon car, has severed his connection with the company," the April 15, 1908, *Horseless Age* said in a terse one-sentence announcement. It is unclear exactly why Mooers left Moon. Still unable to secure the financial backing to produce his own car, Mooers went to Geneva, Ohio, to design the Ewing taxicab. A patent search reveals Mooers received patents for two carburetors and a differential–rear axle mechanism he designed for Peerless, but no patents for his Moon designs.

Moon Joins Round-the-World Race (Almost)

Like most automakers of the day, Moon earned bragging rights by entering its first cars in a variety of early endurance runs and other events. But Moon – actually a Moon derivation named the Hol-Tan – is perhaps most famous for being the first American car to enter what many historians call the greatest automobile race of all time – and then backing out.

"First we convinced Boston we were right when we established their track record for a standard touring car," read a Moon Motor Car Company ad in the January 1908 *Cycle and Automobile Trade Journal*. "New York was convinced when our car was selected to be used in the race from New York to Paris – 'around the world route.'" The "our car" was actually a Hol-Tan, as Moon Motors had arranged for the Hol-Tan Company of New York City to sell 1908 Moon cars to Easterners as Hol-Tans.

In late December 1907, the Hol-Tan was still the only official American entry, "though the Franklin, Thomas, and some others have been considering the advisability of competing," the *New York Times* said. The *Times* joined *Le Matin* of Paris as sponsors of what would become a six-month race across the snow-covered United States, by ship across the Pacific to Siberia, and then across Asia to Paris.

"We have carefully considered the question in all its details, and have come to the conclusion that we are entertaining no dream in endeavoring to show that an American built machine can successfully accomplish the rigors of a tour of this sort," said Harry Fosdick, Hol-Tan Company vice president and Boston agent. "Of course I cannot say absolutely how we will equip our car. While the engine will be exactly similar to those used in the regular stock machines, the frame, of course, will be strengthened. The wheels will be heavier and contain more spokes than customary. The wheel base will undoubtedly be shortened, and the car placed on higher wheels, so as to get a higher clearance." The Hol-Tan was "the regulation runabout with a special body designed by the Moon Company in St. Louis to fit it for this race," the *New York Times* said in January 1908. "The motor will be unchanged, but the designers have a number of special ideas which they will embody in it to protect it and make its work easier. A special body will be attached to it so that supplies and implements may be carried readily. This body is also designed to facilitate rough work."[13]

With just three weeks left to go, "The Hol-Tan Company has not decided on the driver who will handle its car," the January 22, 1908, *Times* reported. Hol-Tan officials then missed a January 23 meeting that the *New York Times* organized to familiarize American drivers with the race route. Whatever the reason, the company failed to appear at Times Square February 12 for the start of the Great Race. Moon was in company, however, with the likes of Corbin, Franklin, Maxwell-Briscoe, Reo, Studebaker, and White – American entries who expressed an interest and then backed off, partly because of the 1907 financial panic, according to Dermot Cole's *Hard Driving: The 1908 Auto Race from New York to Paris*. A gamble on glory was an expensive proposition: The E. R. Thomas Company of Buffalo, New York, spent $100,000 to see its winning Thomas Flyer through to the end.[14]

Hill Climbs, Economy Contests, Speeding Tickets

In other areas, the Moon company in early 1908 boasted of winning Chicago's "big Algonquin Hill Climbing Contest against a large field of all priced motor cars. The Pacific Coast was convinced when we won the Los Angeles Economy Contest – taking five passengers over 199 miles of mountain roads on 10½ gallons of gasoline."[15] Driver Phil Wells finished second in his class and two-fifths of a second behind the leader in a 1909 Algonquin Hill Climb, driving a stock roadster he borrowed from Earl J. Moon, son of the company president. Billy Delno piloted a Moon racer to a fourth-place finish in a 102-mile AAA-sanctioned race at Tucson, Arizona, on January 9, 1915.

During a late-summer "Munsey Historic Tour" through Vermont in 1910, a factory-entered Moon car driven by R. M. Upton received a nearly perfect road score. The car lost one point "for cleaning sand from its gear quadrant" and lost another point "when the jarring and swinging necessary to make 20 miles an hour rendered 1 minute's repair work necessary on the rear fender." The car lost 197 points on a technical examination afterward, however, to place 20th in scoring among the 23 finishers.[16]

In January 1909, a Moon Model C driven by W. J. Morgan and L. A. Phillips set off from Kansas City, Missouri, to blaze a trail to Denver. They hoped to land a spot on the route of that summer's Glidden Tour, the annual national reliability contest. Instead, they almost died in a blizzard. "For 2 days and nights they withstood the wind and snow. They protected themselves as well as possible with blankets and furs until the snow drifted entirely over the car. On the morning of the third day, after the storm had somewhat abated, they were rescued by farmers," and then resumed their journey to Denver, *Motor Age* said.

"Did you hear of the 'Moon Scout' car on its recent run to Denver, through mud, water, snow and ice, over the hubs for over four-fifths of the way?" the company asked in an ad. "A searching examination showed the car to be mechanically perfect when it reached its destination. This shows our car construction is right, our power plant is right, our whole car is right."[17]

5.4 This stripped 1908 or 1909 Moon saw action as a race car. (NAHC)

The year 1910 was a particularly active one for Moon cars in races, reliability contests, and hill climbs. (An early Moon racer is pictured in fig.5.4.) The Moon's Omaha, Nebraska, agent attempted a 24-hour nonstop run. He drove a Moon for 23 hours 15 minutes "without engine or car stopping for a single instant or the making of a single repair or adjustment during the entire run," the agency later advertised. According to *Motor Age,* the 479-mile run ended only when a tire blew out. "Most of the time was spent on the down town streets, an average speed of 20.8 miles per hour being maintained. Thirty gallons of gasoline were consumed, an average of 15.9 miles per gallon, and 6 quarts of oil, an average of 79.8 miles per quart."

At the September 1910 Algonquin Hill Climb in Chicago, a Moon placed first in the division for stripped-chassis cars with engines displacing 300 cubic inches or less. Overall, it finished 11th out of 55 hill-climb contestants. At the Algonquin climb that was held in June 1911, however, three Moon cars finished well off the pace in their respective divisions. Elsewhere in Chicago during June 1911, a Moon received a perfect score in a 248-mile two-day Chicago endurance contest held annually by rival Chicago auto clubs.

Late in 1910, a Moon competing in a

1,347-mile 48-hour reliability contest near Oakland, California, placed ninth among 10 gasoline-powered finishers. A Mitchell and Velie received perfect scores. The Moon, however, was penalized 762 points for broken springs and because the driver made carburetor adjustments and replaced a spark plug.

In mid-October 1910 racing at Kansas City, Phil Wells won a five-mile stock-chassis contest and a 10-mile handicap race. Also in mid-October at the Sioux City, Iowa, track, Wells – who traveled with two Moon racers – won five-mile races in two different classes based on engine size.

Late in October 1910 at Dallas, Wells piloted a Moon racer to a second-place finish in a 50-mile race for stock-chassis cars, behind the winning Cutting car and ahead of a Cole. At the three-day Dallas meet, Wells also placed second in a 10-mile open-class race and second in a one-hour open-class race that was halted prematurely when he wrecked his Moon. "P. Wells, driving a Moon, went through the fence on the forty-sixth mile of this race, and was seriously

though not fatally injured," *Motor Age* recounted.[18]

"Word has just reached the Moon Motor Car Co. . . . which shows that Eagle Rock Mountain near Los Angeles, Cal., has been climbed for the first time by an automobile and that car was a Moon 6-40," reported the November 1914 *Auto Review*. "The car was driven by L. C. Buxton, California distributor of the Moon. The accomplishment was one which required nearly as much skill on the part of the driver as it did snap, reserve power and faultless braking system in the car." Even a junked Moon car could stand up and deliver, learned Joseph L. Tackaberry of Webster Groves near St. Louis. From a salvage yard in 1917, he rescued a 1912 Moon (see fig. 5.5) that had been stripped of its first and second gears in an earlier life as a racer. After cleaning up the car and fitting it with a commercial body for hauling, "recently Tackaberry was arrested by a county constable for driving his 'wreck' at 55 miles an hour. He claimed that the gas throttle was only half open then. The car is still without its first and second speed gears."[19]

5.5 A 1912 Moon touring car. (JAC)

"Fashionable Clientele" Buy "Hol-Tan" Moons

Some 1908 model Moons were sold in the East by the Hol-Tan Company, which had previously imported Fiats from Italy and in 1908 would also import Lancias. The Hol-Tan Company "selected our factory product to replace the Fiat and to be sold to their fashionable clientele in New York, Boston and Philadelphia – precisely the same customers to whom they have been selling their high priced imported motor cars," the Moon company advertised. It sounded as if the Hol-Tan Company of its own volition dropped Fiats to sell Moons. In fact, one account contends Fiat revoked Hol-Tan's agency in late 1907 as the Italian automaker prepared to begin producing American Fiats in New York state.[20]

The St. Louis automaker promoted Moons and Hol-Tans in the same ads, making it abundantly clear that the Hol-Tan Company was simply marketing Moon cars under another name. Hol-Tan organizers E. R. Hollander and G. P. and C. H. Tangeman lent part of their last names to their company title. Importers of Fiats since 1902, they were promoting themselves by 1906 as Fiat's "sole American agents," with sub-agencies in Boston and Philadelphia. Starting at $3,000, the Hol-Tan cars were a large step down from the 50-horsepower Fiat touring car that the Hol-Tan Company advertised for $9,500 in May 1907. Its *New York Times* ads also show that the Hol-Tan firm was still selling both Fiats – perhaps the last of its inventory – and Hol-Tans in late January 1908.

"Over half of the [Moon] factory's output of this car for this season has been purchased by the Hol-Tan Co. of New York and will be sold under the name of Hol-Tan," the *Auto Review* said. No figures are readily available to contradict or support the magazine's production claim. The trade press in November 1907 announced that the Hol-Tan Company would sell two styles of 1908

Moon cars. "It is intended to follow foreign practice to a certain extent in marketing the cars, the bodies being supplied by Locke, Quinby and Demarest, in many cases, to the purchaser's order." The Moon Model C with a 110-inch wheelbase thus became a Hol-Tan Standard, equipped with either a touring body or a two-passenger roadster body having rumble seats for up to two additional riders. No special bodies would be fitted to the $3,000 Hol-Tan Standard. The Hol-Tan Special, on the longer 121-inch wheelbase of the Moon Model D car, would share the Model D's $3,750 price if ordered with a touring body. It would cost more when fitted with a special-order limousine or landaulet body. "The Model D is a large seven-passenger car, and was especially constructed to meet the demands of the New York trade, who like an extra long wheel base," the *Auto Review* said.[21] Both Hol-Tan models would use the same Moon 4-cylinder engine.

The Hol-Tan Company did advertise a $4,000 "Hol-Tan Coupe Town Car," which suggests it carried a custom body. But despite the plans of the Hol-Tan Company, some – perhaps most – of the renamed cars were fitted with stock Moon bodies and, except for the name, were Moons. In January 1908, the Hol-Tan Company did make a small splash with a benzol fuel test. "Joseph Tracy, the well-known automobile engineer and driver, is making the tests for the Hol-Tan Company in a Hol-Tan car, including a run from New York to Philadelphia and return, in which this new fuel is to be used exclusively."[22] By 1909, Hol-Tan was again acting solely as an auto agency. Moon historian Carl W. Burst III said he was unaware of any surviving Hol-Tans.

Moon Motors a Family Affair

Joseph Moon called his venture the Moon Motor Car Company throughout 1906 but didn't incorporate until October 2, 1907, when he became president of a fledgling motorcar company with a net worth of $40,000. Half of the stockholders were longtime officers of the Joseph W. Moon Buggy Company, which "continued to manufacture buggies and carriages in gradually diminishing numbers until 1916, when the manufacture of horsedrawn vehicles was abandoned, and the great buggy and carriage manufacturing plant of the company was enlarged and thoroughly equipped for the manufacture of automobiles."[23] Three of the auto company's six shareholders were officers of the buggy company, and two of the three officers were or would become in-laws: Stewart McDonald, who married Moon's daughter, Grace, became vice president and general manager; Alfred F. Moberly, who in 1893 married Joseph W. Moon's sister, Myra, became treasurer; and George H. Schelp became secretary. Other shareholders were Henry W. Klemme, Burch C. Hopkins, and Louis F. Whitelock. In 1922, Moon still had fewer than 300 stockholders. By March 1924 there were 3,000, and two-thirds of the investors owned Moon cars, the company estimated.

L. F. Goodspeed, George F. Heising, and George H. Kublin, who would become chief engineer for the Auburn Automobile Company, were Moon chief engineers at various times. After leaving Moon in 1915, Goodspeed helped engineer the Roamer car, a short-lived auto bearing his own name, and the Checker.

Joseph Moon's sons, Earl Joseph and Stanley Alva Moon, went into the family business, both designing some cars. Over the years Stanley Moon held such titles as general sales manager, secretary, and vice president. Earl Moon (see fig.5.6) – at various times the advertising manager, city sales manager, Eastern sales manager, and vice president – in 1925 was promoted. In his new post as body style and equipment engineer, he would give "particular attention to the finish, upholstery, color scheme and refinements of Moon cars. He has returned to this country after several years in

Europe, where he specialized in interior decoration and studied European motor car body design."[24]

Moon Motors was first a member of the Chicago-based American Motor Car Manufacturers' Association. Late in 1909, however, the company joined the Association of Licensed Automobile Manufacturers, which licensed automakers to build cars under the Selden patent. The patent holder claimed a licensing monopoly until 1911, when Henry Ford won a court case to limit the scope of the Selden patent. Moon Motors re-incorporated as a Delaware corporation on July 5, 1917, a move attributed to an increasingly influential vice president, Stewart McDonald.[25]

"A Good Dollar-Value Car"

Though Moon can claim few technical breakthroughs, the factory did succeed in its mission of distilling into a single car the best – or at least the most popular – designs and styles of other cars, American and European. And it did so for 1924 models at an announcement price as low as $995, meaning Moon also broke new ground in produc-

5.6 Earl J. Moon. (SLML)

5.7 Lockheed brakes looked like this on the Series A models for 1924, the first year Moon offered hydraulic brakes. (FLP)

ing a luxury car for the medium- to low-price market. In retrospect, the Moon car is regarded as among the most solid and luxurious of cars that were assembled largely from components manufactured outside their own factories. Historians generally view Moon's imitating tendencies as the sincerest form of flattery.

"Borrowing a design from another automaker was typical of an approach that made Moon by the 1920s one of the best known of what was termed an 'assembled' car," says automotive historian George S. May. With a radiator copied from Rolls-Royce, the 1919 Victory model Moon, in particular, "was a good-looking, well-made, though assembled, machine," according to *The Complete Encyclopedia of Motorcars, 1885 to the Present.* The St. Louis company "developed few automotive firsts," according to a December 1953 *Motor Trend* feature. "But Moon was quick to grab at good features and incorporate them into its own cars. . . . Let the record be clear that the Moon was invariably a good dollar-value car." *The Standard Catalog of American Cars, 1805–1942* says "despite being an assembled automobile, the Moon was a fine, well-built car" that was quick to adopt technical innovations. A well-known California collector of Moon and Diana cars, the late Harry Hastings, wrote that Moon products sported a distinctive look that they lost only late in the 1920s, when they "followed the new trend of looking very much like the rest of the American cars of the period."[26]

In starters, brakes, and engines, Moon was at the head of the class. The automaker in 1908 experimented with a magneto self-starter it would install on some of its 1909 models. Moon "has brought out a car with a new self starting arrangement, consisting of a Bosch high tension magneto, the armature of which can be disengaged from the crank shaft and spun . . . so as to produce a spark for igniting the residual charge remaining in one of the cylinders from the previous operation. As soon as one explo-

sion has taken place the magneto automatically drops into gear again." But starting a car with such a device, "invented by the engineers of the company," was a gamble because an air-fuel charge begins seeping away the moment an engine stops. Moon Motors thoughtfully continued to equip its cars with hand-crank handles.[27]

Moon joined Colby, Everitt, Hudson, Pullman, and Westcott in offering the Disco acetylene starter on its cars for 1912, the year of the self-starter. The 1912 New York auto show saw 14 kinds of mechanical, 13 acetylene, seven electric, six compressed-air, two gasoline, and one exhaust-gas starters. The Disco acetylene starter injected a charge of acetylene gas into the proper cylinder, then "the spark is turned on, thus igniting the explosive mixture and starting the motor," as *Automobile* described it. Moon announced it would use the new Wagner electric starter on its 1913 cars. The 12-volt Wagner motor turned an engine at 70 rpm and, once it started, automatically disengaged. "After the car has reached a speed of approximately 8 miles an hour, the electric motor, which now acts as a generator, commences to recharge the storage battery."[28] Moon switched to a Delco electric starter for 1914.

Ever Heard of a Moon Frame Sagging?

By 1924, Moon was offering the new low-pressure balloon tire and had joined the small number of U.S. automakers that had adopted four-wheel Lockheed hydraulic brakes. (See fig. 5.7.) Even a year later in May 1925, just 29 makes were using Lockheed brakes, according to a Lockheed ad. Moon was in company with such well-engineered cars as Chrysler, Duesenberg, Peerless, and Stutz. "The old mechanical brakes had to go," Moon claimed in an ad. "They are not safe enough for modern traffic strains."

Though the company used a 4-cylinder Rutenber in 1906 models, Louis Mooers's

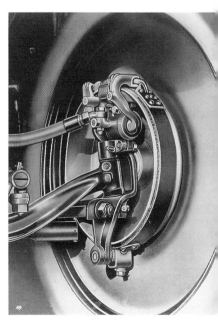

forthcoming overhead-valve 4-cylinder engine put Moon at the vanguard in engine
design. After Mooers's departure, engineer
George Heising designed and the Moon
plant built a 30-horsepower 4-cylinder engine with a T-head valve arrangement. It
was a more traditional design than the
Mooers engine, but proved to be a very reliable engine for the Moon company. The automaker added a Heising-designed
6-cylinder engine in 1913, making Moon
slightly late in shifting to the 6-cylinder engine. In order to produce cars fast enough
to meet demand in 1912 and 1913, Moon
used some 4-cylinder engines made by Continental Motors of Muskegon, Michigan.
The 1914 season marked the passing of the
Moon-made engine except for a few later
Moons in which buyers specifically ordered
a Heising 4-cylinder engine. Domestic
models thereafter used Continentals, including the Continental straight-8 that
Moon adopted in mid-1925 for its 1926 Diana, a new Moon companion car. Duesenberg in 1920 became the first U.S. car with a
straight-8 engine. Continental and other
engine makers followed suit but, even so,
Moon was among the select first few cars to
use a straight-8.[29]

A search of U.S. patent indexes turned
up only one patent attributed or assigned to
the Moon Motor Car Company – Patent No.
1,420,990, granted June 27, 1922. Julian S.
Friede of St. Louis invented for the Moon
company an air-tight cushion with an adjustable vent to vary its firmness. Moon has
also received some unearned credit for innovation. An error in May and December
1924 *Automobile Trade Journal* articles
sparked the persisting false assertion that
Moon pioneered left-hand drive autos in
America. Moon cars actually made the
switch with many other U.S. automakers in
1913.

"Moon engineers were among the first to
discover that about 90 per cent of all noises
that develop in a motor car – the rattles,
raps and squeaks – may be traced to the
frame construction," a factory sales catalog
claimed. Though its body construction
evolved from wood to aluminum to steel,
Moon Motors always used steel frames, beginning with a frame of cold-pressed steel
on its 1906 car. But while many early automakers were using straight frames, the
1907 Moons exhibited at a New York show
joined B-L-M and Frayer-Miller as the only
American automobiles with drop frames.[30]

5.8 Chassis drawing of a 1913
4-cylinder Moon 48. (Sept. 26,
1912, *Automobile*)

5.9 A Moon chassis, identified
as a 1928 Six-72 model. (FLP)

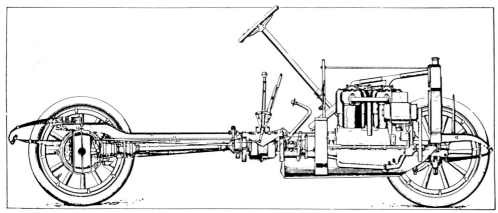

628   THE AUTOMOBILE   *September 26, 1912*

Fig. 1—Moon four-cylinder model 48 chassis showing arrangement of drive and control used on all three models

Moon Adds a Six to Its Line for 1913

The 3½-inch downward bend in the Moon frame just in front of the rear axle allowed a lower center of gravity. The Moon frame also narrowed toward the front to allow for greater front-wheel movement, and thus a shorter turning radius.

"I want you to notice the Moon Frame. I never heard of a Moon's sagging," Joseph W. Moon commented in a 1912 ad. "Hot riveting is used throughout the frame construction" of 1913 Moons (see fig.5.8), *Automobile* said. "The cross-members of the frame are all gusetted heavily to prevent racking strains,"[31] and the factory claimed the frame of its 48-horsepower 1913 car was overbuilt to withstand the weight and twisting strains of a 70-horsepower engine. By 1922 the frames had four cross members; a molded gusset plate at the rear of the frame added stiffness and protected the gas tank. (See frame detail in fig.5.9.)

Choice of Bodies: Wood, Aluminum, Fabric

In the best carriage-making tradition, Joseph Moon in 1906 fitted his first cars with wooden bodies, dashboards of pressed steel backed by wood, and hoods and fenders of sheet iron. According to its catalogs and ads, the small factory used hand-formed aluminum bodies over a wooden framework for 1907, 1908, and perhaps half of 1909, and then cut costs in 1910 by switching to bodies that were "built of sheet steel over wood and steel frames." Moon actually phased in the use of steel during 1909. Bodies were made of sheet aluminum, according to a 1909 catalog and Moon ads, but the December 17, 1908, *Automobile* reveals that "both fenders and hood are of aluminum-coated steel, which insures permanent retention of the paint and finishing varnish." One restorer

says the entire body of his 1909 Moon car was made from aluminum-coated steel.

In 1910, Moon cars had fenders "constructed of heavy sheet steel, and the space between them and the body, as well as that between the running board and the body, is closed, thus protecting the car and occupants from splashing mud." (See fig.5.10.) To wealthy customers who wanted to use their 1910 Moons in comfort both winter and summer, the automaker for $4,250 would sell a Model 45 "equipped with both enclosed body and touring body," a catalog claimed. The April 9, 1908, *Automobile* pictures a closed car – rare in that day and even in 1918 accounting for just 10 percent of U.S. auto production – over the cutline: "Designer E. J. Moon in 1908 Limousine Moon Car."[32]

As it did with other parts, Moon Motors eventually turned to suppliers for bodies. In 1914, for instance, it ordered bodies – made "after designs of Ladis Lewkowicz" – from the Convertible Automobile Body Corporation of New York, described in *Horseless Age* as a new company that was also filling orders for Cadillac, Case, E-M-F, Ford, Locomobile, Packard, and Simplex. Boat-shaped bodies were becoming popular in 1916, noted the fashion-conscious *Vanity Fair* of November 1915, which used a Moon car to illustrate the trend. Concealed door hinges, a deep cowl and instrument panel, wide 22-inch doors, and concealed locks were features of the 1916 Moon Six-30. Besides the slanting windshield of the 1917 Six-43 (see fig.5.11), "the most distinctive visible feature of this new five-passenger car is the handsome double-cowled body – Delaunay-Belleville type," said a Moon ad.[33]

Moon and other automakers presented dual-cowled bodies – in which a cowl board separated a car's front and rear passenger compartments (visible in fig.5.12) – at the 1916 auto shows. "So well has this design been received by the public that we believe by the end of 1917 every car of any moment will have followed our lead in the adoption

of this double-cowled body," Moon Motors predicted.[34] Perhaps the quintessential Moon body design, the post–World War I 1919 Victory model (see fig.5.13) had a beveled top body line and a sharp-edged radiator – a Rolls-Royce look-alike that Moons displayed through the 1928 model year.

A description of the Six-40 sedan tells how Moon bodies were made in 1922: "The body super-structure is built of hard wood, with all joints screwed and glued. The body panels are of 20 gage steel and are flanged by mechanical means, eliminating the use of solder. . . . The roof is made of light bows

5.10 A 1910 Moon with a victoria top. (JAC)

5.11 Ad for the 1917 Moon Six-43. (September 1916, *Auto Review*)

5.12 This retouched photo shows a 1917 Moon touring car. (FLP)

5.13 A 1919 Moon 6-cylinder Victory touring car. The *St. Louis Globe-Democrat* identified the three Moon officials as Edward Beecher, "advertising counsol," at the wheel; Sales Manager Fred H. Rengers in the front seat; and Export Manager E. H. Serrano in the back. (FLP)

and slats covered with wadding and waterproof top material." Recognizing by 1923 that "roofs have been responsible for most of the noise and rumble of closed cars," Moon Motors began using a roof in which "each intersection of bow and slat is very carefully and securely fastened to prevent any movement. The quiet roof on the Moon sedan is one of its best features."[35]

For its 1924 cars, Moon ordered 10,000 closed-car bodies from the Pullman Company of Chicago, "which confines its activities along this line to but two motor car manufacturers, namely, Packard and Moon." For its open cars, Moon used Victor tops, also used by Chevrolet, Durant, Ford, and Star. In 1924 Moon offered a Six-58 "Salamanca" with a special body by Rubay, and in 1925 ordered 6,000 Murray bodies.[36]

In 1928, Moon Motors put out at least one and likely several Six-60 sedans with a canvas-and-leather body (see fig.5.14), apparently the work of Kenneth L. Childs. Apperson, Auburn, Chrysler, Dodge, Hudson, Marmon, and Moon "did build a few" Childs bodies for show cars and special dealer orders, according to a history of fabric car bodies. As the August 13, 1927, *Automobile Topics* described it, the Moon fabric body used a foundation of "expanded metal" mesh over a framework of maple or fir:

Over this expanded metal is placed a couple of layers of cotton wadding which serves not only as a padding and to give smooth appearance when finished but also as a deadener for sound and an insulator against heat and cold. A heavy canvas is then stretched tightly over the wadding to force it into the openings of the metal in order to prevent any possibility of its shifting or changing position and to make a true surface for the leather cloth which forms the outer covering. In the next step the leather cloth is drawn tightly over the body and securely tacked in place and is so sectionized that the exterior of the body is composed of a number of separate panels [to make repairs easier].

The unusual durability of fabric construction is due beyond a doubt to its extreme flexibility which permits it to weave with the chassis much the same as a sapling will bend before a wind that would break a more rigid obstacle. A fabric-paneled body is much lighter than a composite or all-steel body and by reducing the weight of the superstructure of the car the center of gravity is automatically lowered thus making the car infinitely safer.

5.14 A 1928 Moon Six-60 sedan with a fabric-and-leather body. (FLP)

The 1928 Moon fabric sedans were painted "a two-color combination of deep Woodland green and soft, lustrous French gray – hood, cowl and belt being finished in green while body panels, upper structure, top and disc wheels are in gray. Upper and lower aluminum body mouldings are set off with black welt."[37]

"How Brave the Colors"

Blues, greens, and reds were time-tested Moon colors, and the cars were as comfortable as they were eye-catching. Because of the double-spring construction in the seat cushions of the first Moon in 1906, "it is claimed that no amount of jolting can make them 'strike bottom,'" *Horseless Age* said. The 1906 Moon had a "light derby red finish." The tone of its ads and press releases suggests Moon Motors was proud of its upholstery, which was leather exclusively until World War I, when options were offered. Thereafter, Moon upholstered its roadsters and other open cars in leather while many Moon closed cars came in broadcloth, corduroy, mohair, or other weaves, often brightly colored and certainly cheaper than leather, but less durable.[38]

Moon touring cars had hand-buffed black leather in 1909, and "the standard color is a dark blue body with French gray running gear," according to the trade press. The next year, 1910, cream-colored running gear and wheels set off the dark blue standard body color. But at the 1910 St. Louis auto show, Moon Motors exhibited cars that were also painted black, blue, green, and red. At 1912 auto shows, Moon showed a gray roadster. Its display at the 1913 New York auto show included "a racy looking speedster in gray and black, a torpedo in dark green and red stripes and gear with brown leather upholstery, a touring type in green and a five passenger touring machine in blue with white stripes."

"Many upholsterers in the Moon plant served with the founder back in the days before the Moon automobile was dreamed of," claimed a factory catalog. Moon in July 1913 received "the largest hide that has ever been imported into the United States," *Motor Age* reported. "The hide contains 87½ square feet. It measures 11 feet in its greatest length and the greatest width is 9 feet. The hide came from France where the largest hides in the world are produced today." Adorning one 1914 Moon was not French but "Brown Dutch leather upholstery" and a black body, in marked contrast to the "exquisite blue interior" of a 6-cylinder 1914 Moon coupe.

Moon's 1916 standard colors were "a gunmetal, a gray and a black." Spanish leather, alternately described as buff or tan in color, remained the standard Moon interior. Why tan? "With Spanish leather the color is natural; therefore, there is no dye to sweat out and soil light clothes. Dust and dirt are instantly visible and may be quickly removed. It does not require polishing nor scuff up as badly as black leather," explained a 1920 factory catalog.

The 1919 Victory model seven-passenger sedan had an interior of "gray Chase cloth." In 1922, the Six-40 two-door sedan was trimmed in heavy broadcloth. Its companion brougham model was "trimmed in silk-finished blue broadcloth, and the two doors have large pockets similar to an opera bag and are lined with blue silk." The brougham also had blue silk roll-up curtains and blue carpet. Brewster green and maroon were standard 1917 body colors. The 1918 Six-36 open touring sedan had a royal blue body and black running gear. Perhaps to celebrate the Allied defeat of Germany to end World War I, Moon said that for the 1919 Moon Victory models "dealers can give purchasers any color option they want without extra cost."

A seven-passenger 1920 Moon was "painted in 'Mist-o'-Marne' with nickel trimmings." Another 1920 Moon body style had

5.15 The 1923 Moon Six-40 Tourlux offered a solid California top with removable side windows for summer driving. (FLP)

5.16 Texas Governor Miriam A. "Ma" Ferguson at the wheel of her 1925 Series A Moon roadster. The Texas Capitol Building in Austin is the backdrop. (FLP)

5.17 A 1926 Moon cabriolet roadster interior. (FLP)

a California top – a solid top, with the glazed windows removable for summer driving – of "marine blue leather to match the color of the car." (Fig. 5.15 pictures a California top on a 1923 model.) The automaker paid as much attention to its use of color in its advertisements (see color plate 4), noting that in 1921 "ours was the only color advertising of automobiles to appear throughout the year in *The Saturday Evening Post*." Moon Motors raved about the bright finish of its 1922 Moon touring car: "How brave the colors – Versailles blue and silver. Amongst the sober-hued traffic of the crowded thoroughfares it looks as would a French Chasseur riding down 'Main Street.'"

Blue – including "Versailles blue," "royal coach blue," and "marine blue" – "lake maroon," and "milori green" were among Moon colors for 1923 and 1924. The 1923 Six-58 seven-passenger sedan was finished in dark blue with dark blue broadcloth upholstery. The 1924 Six-58 Salamanca with a special Rubay body had a gray broadcloth interior and "is finished in coach medium with gold striping." The automaker an-

nounced in April 1924 that it was using Duco finishes on all its Series A cars. "Moon is using what might be termed a 'super-Duco' system of finishing their cars," commented *Motor Age*. "After the cars are finished in the regular Duco way, Moon applies a coat of finishing varnish, producing a high lustre finish." The 1925 cabriolet roadster had "brown striped mohair upholstery to match the two-tone tan finish." The 1925 Series A Moon two-door sedan also sported two-tone paint: "Duco gray satin finish up to the belt line, with black above. A black molding extends across the top of the cowl and along the sides of the car." The Series A roadster (see fig.5.16) played its Duco gray finish against upholstery of blue Spanish leather.

The new 1925 four-door sedan was upholstered in "high grade corduroy" while the De Luxe two- and four-door 1925 sedans had blue-gray mohair. The Moon also experimented with a variety of upholstery fabrics: a dull blue Royal Cord fabric in 1926 De Luxe sedan models (see fig.5.17 as an example of 1926 interiors), perhaps

others, and Mo-Tex, "a special new automobile fabric," in 1927 enclosed cars. Roadster interiors ranged from the "steel-gray Morocco grain leather" of the 1927 to the "pigskin yellow" of the 1929 new standard Six-72 roadster, which was available in "Chinese red and black; green and fawn, and blue and straw – these colors being set off by ivory door panels."

Faster Than 60 – If You Dare!

In 1914, Moon Motors had the St. Louis inspector of weights and measures confirm a fuel consumption of 15½ miles per gallon for the new Moon lightweight six. The automaker claimed 21 miles per gallon for its 1915 4-cylinder Four-38, 18 for the Six-40, and 16 for the bigger Six-50. Moon's $1,000 new 1918 Six-36 light 6-cylinder car averaged 25 miles per gallon "on a test made last week to DeSoto, Mo., and back, which is forty miles, over the toughest hills in the West." An ad for the 1927 model claimed "you can get 22 miles to the gallon of gasoline from the long-stroke motor of the '6-60.'"[39]

Moon Motors occasionally mentioned the top speed of its cars. Surprisingly, it changed little – at least in the telling – from 1908, when Moon and Hol-Tan cars would do "sixty miles an hour and as easy riding as a swing," to 1927. The 1920 Moon Six-48 was slower than its 1908 ancestor, if we are to believe advertised claims that "the high-speed motor accelerates from the pace of a walk to 45 and 50 miles an hour with lightning-like rapidity and without a single false vibration." The four-bearing crankshaft and pressure-fed oiling system in the 1925 Moon meant "you can hold your speedometer at 50 to 60 – or better if you dare – without vibration." Of its 1927 Jubilee Six-60 model (see fig.5.18), Moon advertised: "You can shoot its speed from 5 to 25 in 7¾ seconds and then up to 60 miles an hour."[40]

Making "Jos. W. Moon Commercial Cars"

As early as summer 1911, the Rapp & Moller Carriage Company of St. Louis finished a hearse on "a Moon '45' chassis which has a special lighting system." Rapp & Moller, which built the hearse for a local under-

5.18 A 1927 Moon Jubilee Six-60 roadster. Oliver Life, Moon's advertising manager, and an unidentified Moon employee. (FLP)

5.19 A variety of 1913 Moon commercial cars. (May 1913, *Auto Review*)

taker, apparently bought the chassis from Moon, which otherwise had little to do with the finished product. Still, it represented one of the earliest press mentions of a Moon used as a commercial car.[41]

In October 1912, the *Auto Review* announced that the J. W. Moon Buggy Company "has embarked in the manufacturing of commercial motor cars." Truck production was carried out under the auspices of the buggy company, rather than the car company. "They have set aside a large area in their big factory for the truck department. During the past month they have turned out a number of 3,000-lb. trucks, a number of which they have already sold. They are also bringing out a 1,000-lb. light delivery car." Moon began advertising that it was offering its cars with "special bodies for special purposes, such as light delivery, ambulances, etc."

Its line of special bodies included hearses, as the buggy factory that autumn took a local mortician's order for "one of the most elaborate automobile hearses." By November 1912, the Moon plant was hard at work on 25 Model A half-ton-capacity trucks that would sell for $1,100 with open bodies or $1,200 with panel bodies. This truck had a 4-cylinder engine with a 3½ x 4-inch bore and stroke; 3-speed transmission; Bosch high-tension magneto with fixed spark; Holley carburetor; 112-inch wheelbase; pneumatic 32 x 3½-inch tires, front and rear, with solid tires optional; and equipment that included three kerosene lamps, horn, tool kit, jack, and tire pump. The automaker soon shortened the name of its new "Jos. W. Moon Commercial Cars" to simply "Moon Commercial Cars." (See fig. 5.19.)

November 1912 saw Moon ship three of its 1½-ton Model B trucks with panel-delivery bodies to a buyer in Oakland, California. "They are booking some very encouraging and profitable orders every week," said the *Auto Review,* also noting that several Moon 1½-ton trucks went to St. Louis businesses. In January 1913 the buggy company announced a price hike of $50 on its Model A

half-ton truck, to $1,150 for an open body and $1,250 for a panel-top body. Sales were apparently brisk enough to allow Moon in mid-1913 to raise prices further – to $1,450 for the open body and $1,600 for the panel body. The shaft-drive Model A light delivery car had a top speed of 30 miles per hour and a 44 x 72-inch cargo area. "The open delivery body is furnished regular [*sic*] with windshield, two seats and sideboards. The rear seat is easily removed, converting it from a pleasure car into a delivery," a trade

MOON Commercial Cars

Model A
Delivery Car
Pneumatic Tires
Carrying Capacity
1000 lbs.

Model A With No. 20 Body
Price $1450.00

Model A With No. 21 Panel
Body Price $1600.00

Model B Truck
Solid Tires
Carrying Capacity
3000 lbs.

Model B No. 4 Body. Price $1950.00

Model A Delivery Car with Panel Top Body is most suitable for Grocery, Laundry, Florists and many other lines requiring a closed body car.

Model B Truck is constructed to meet the rigid requirement of truckings

You Can Use Moon Trucks to Advantage in Your Business.

Model B With No. 6 Body, $2000.00

The Moon Truck and Light Delivery Cars are Built for Service

Various Styles of Bodies Can be Furnished to Suit the Requirements

Model B Truck No. 5 Body, $2050.00

Dealers write us for Agency Proposition and Catalogue.

JOS. W. MOON BUGGY COMPANY
Main and Douglass Streets   SAINT LOUIS, MISSOURI

journal related. Converted to a delivery car, the vehicle looked like a tiny pickup truck with a shallow box on back. Model year 1913 was thus "the first year the Moon company has shown or made any trucks for sale," according to the February 13, 1913, *Motor Age* magazine. As with pleasure cars, Moon delivery cars switched to left-hand steering wheels on 1913 models.

The 1½-ton Moon Model B truck as exhibited at the early 1913 Chicago auto show had chain drive, a 125-inch wheelbase, solid tires, a 4-cylinder Continental 3¾ x 5¼-inch engine, a 48 x 104-inch cargo space, and a top speed of 18 mph. The cost was $1,900 for a covered express body. In 1915, Moon offered its Model B heavy truck in two wheelbase sizes – 125 and 140 inches – though both were rated for a 1½-ton hauling capacity. For its 1918 models, the company "proposes later to put out a two-ton Moon truck for commercial use," according to one account. Moon Motors contracted to build 300 trucks for the U.S. Army in autumn 1918. But the official end of World War I on November 11, 1918, probably meant the cancellation of that order. There is scant evidence to suggest that Moon truck production continued after the war, though the annual *Moody's Industrials* through 1922 described the company as making both automobiles and motor trucks. It appears no truck production records survive.

"Favorably Known the World Over"

To get his car before the public, Joseph Moon had his second-year cars displayed at the biggest and best auto shows – in New York, Chicago, San Francisco, and Boston. (See fig.5.20.) Moon Motors hit the 1912 auto-show circuit with a stripped chassis fitted with an electric motor that turned a cutaway engine, transmission, and rear axle. "Small electric lights" and glass covers allowed observers to see "all the internal workings of the automobile, exactly as each part operates under road conditions."[42]

Cadillac was the "Standard of the World." Ford was "The Universal Car." Maytag was "The Hill Climber." But Moon swam against the tide by offering not one but a variety of advertising slogans over the years. Thus Moon billed its 1906 auto as "The Car You Will Eventually Buy," "The best that brains and experience can build or money can buy," and "Just the Car You've Been Wishing For!" Its 1907 product was "The Most Up-To-Date Car In America." Potential buyers of 1909 were treated to this jingle: "Nature Provides a great deal – but to enjoy it, you need the Moon." The 1910 "Car of Merit" evolved into "The Character Car" of 1912, an uninspired slogan that may have precipitated the dry spell to follow. "Then along comes a Moon!" was tried in 1917, and in 1919 readers learned "the low cost of

5.20 Moon's display at New York City's 1910 Grand Central Palace auto show included a stripped chassis, center. (NAHC)

5.21 Actress Clara Bow perches on the hood of a 1924 Moon Series A car. (MHS)

driving the Moon car is the final verdict in its favor." In addition, the automaker said in 1919, "Its Price is an Appeal to Your Reason." In the early 1920s, Moon built "Modern Motor Cars," "The Success of the Year," and "The car of proven units." During this period and later, Moons were also "Favorably Known the World Over." In the mid-1920s the automaker again appealed to the public's sense of reason with this slogan: "From A Thinking Automobile Manufacturer – To The Thinking Automobile Buyer."[43]

Moon also shied away from the testimonial ads that some automakers used so frequently. A collection of 250 Moon ads contains only about half a dozen testimonials – all from 1908, when Moon issued "a pamphlet of some exceptionally strong testimonials from users of Moon cars." A tepid testimonial from F. S. Taggart of St. Louis, owner of a two-year-old Moon, appeared in an April 16, 1908, *Automobile* ad: "Will say that I have used this car almost daily, rain or shine . . . [and] the car has given me but very little difficulty. There is nothing broken or worn out on the machine as yet and I consider it in almost as good condition to-day as when I first got it."[44]

Moon Motors printed a disclaimer under photos in its 1919 ads: "Photographs of Moon Cars Are Not Retouched." Surviving photographs – both snapshots and advertising photos – show a variety of celebrities posing by Moon cars, including silent-screen sensation Clara Bow (see fig.5.21), the "'It' Girl," as well as slugger Babe Ruth (see fig.5.22) and "stage and screen star" Ann McKay, who appeared in silent movies. The female models posing with cars in factory publicity photos – which used various St. Louis landmarks as backdrops – were often from Moon Motors' clerical staff. The automaker also promoted its cars through its own magazine. *Moon Motor News* "is one of the best house organs that has come to our notice in some time," the April 1912 *Auto Review* said, discussing the house organ's 11th issue. "It is attractively gotten up

and places the features of Moon cars before the reader in a concise form." Later, the Moon in-house magazine would have such names as *The Moon Crescent, The Silver Shell,* and *Moon Aerotype News.* Artwork showing its cars in opulent settings made Moon's 1920s ads beautiful as well as avant-garde.

Moon got a gigantic gift of free publicity when R. E. Madsen, "who is seven feet ten and one-half inches high, making him one of the tallest, if not the tallest man in the world," bought a Moon Six-66 car from dealer W. C. Tolifer at Sapulpa, Oklahoma, the November 1917 *Auto Review* reported. "The photograph taken shows him standing behind the car with its top raised, and he is writing his name on the 'dotted line' on the top of the top. This was such an unusual event that the Universal Animated Weekly has photographed it and is showing it as one of the odd events of the everyday world."

E. L. Cord: A "Hotshot" Moon Salesman

The numbers are hard to pin down, but Moon clearly had a sizeable dealer network.

As it opened its 1910 model year, the automaker ran an ad listing its 38 agencies in 20 states plus the District of Columbia. Larger cities with Moon dealers included Los Angeles, San Francisco, Denver, Atlanta, Chicago, Des Moines, Boston, Minneapolis, Omaha, New York (see fig.5.23), Cincinnati, Oklahoma City, Pittsburgh, Providence, Nashville, Houston, and Milwaukee. Texas had the most agencies with eight, followed by Illinois with seven, Nebraska with three, and Kansas and Missouri with two apiece.

Even with this relatively modest dealer network, the Midwestern automaker's cars were beginning to appear in distant states.

A list covering New England auto registrations for the first three months of 1913 reveals that 38 Moon cars and one Moon truck were registered in Massachusetts and that seven Moon cars were registered in Connecticut. Michigan had seven Moon cars registered during January and February 1915. A search through a Connecticut registration list published in June 1915 uncovered 15 Moons, ranging from 1912 to 1915 models. Colorado owners registered 29 Moons in the first half of 1915, and Vermont showed two Moons registered in 1918.[45]

By late 1923, *Motor Way* claimed, Moon

5.22 Slugger Babe Ruth with a 1927 Moon Six-60. (FLP)

5.23 A 1911 or 1912 Moon at the New York City agency. (JAC)

had 500 U.S. dealers. The *New York Times* counted Moon distributors in 55 cities, representing 700 dealers. *Moody's Industrials'* 1925 edition says Moon cars "are sold through 73 distributors in principal cities of the United States." A 1929 factory catalog claimed 82 distributors and 598 dealers. Poor 1929 sales apparently prompted many dealers to abandon ship: After acquiring the St. Louis automaker in February 1930, New Era Motors issued a press release saying its Ruxton car "will be distributed by 375 Moon dealers."

Probably the most prominent Moon salesman was Errett Lobban Cord. Later, as president of the Auburn Automobile Company, he achieved fame for introducing the Cord automobile and guiding the Duesenberg through its glory years. But in the early 1920s, Cord was "the hotshot salesman of Moon cars for Chicago's Quinlan Motor Company," where he "learned to festoon the cars, already among the more sharply styled, with accessories and extra nickel trim. Though this cost him little, it allowed Cord to charge another $300 per car," earning him a $30,000 annual salary and allowing him to save $100,000. When Cord in 1924 went to Auburn, Indiana, to revive the flagging Auburn company, he remained faithful to his Moon credo. "A little stylish nickel plating and some flashy repainting, and the unsold Auburns began to sell," according to a history of the Auburn company. In St. Louis, another man, John D. Perry Lewis, achieved a measure of fame before he became a Moon dealer in September 1912. At age 20 in spring 1893, Lewis drove "the first horseless carriage that ever was driven over the streets of St. Louis," an electric car he built himself.[46]

During an annual convention, Moon invited its distributors to St. Louis for several days of merrymaking, seasoned with just a splash of business. The 100 distributors who attended the November 1923 convention were put up at the Hotel Statler, and during the four-day meeting were treated

to a hotel luncheon and a "dinner and smoker." Finally, on the last day, the distributors ate a buffet luncheon at the Moon plant, "after which the real business of the convention began and manufacturing and merchandising policies and plans were discussed," an account said.

President Stewart McDonald, Sales Manager Fred H. Rengers and Assistant Sales Manager Neil E. McDarby "gave the distributors opportunity to express themselves fully and frankly regarding the manufacturing, distributing and advertising of Moon cars for 1924[,] and on various important matters Mr. McDonald called for a vote of the distributors and their decisions were recorded. New models, body types and closed car upholstery were discussed at this session," according to *Auto Review*. At such conventions, claimed the May 1924 *Automobile Trade Journal*, "No change of policy is put into effect unless supported or agreed to by distributors representing a majority of the factory output."

At the closing banquet that night, the car salesmen huddled in a strategy session with Los Angeles distributor Don P. Smith, who presented his formula for selling Moon cars:

We have seven salesmen in the company's employ, all on a salary and commission basis, and one chief requirement we make is that they ride three white-collar men each day. We then send literature and sales letters to them and many sales have been made as the result of this plan. Each salesman is instructed to invite persons waiting for street cars, who look as though they could afford an automobile, to ride to their destination in the salesman's car. This affords good opportunity to demonstrate the car and as the salesman turns in the passenger's [sic] names we are provided with a very good mailing list.[47]

The factory, which used these conventions to get contracts for Moon cars, also entertained distributors before many large annual auto shows.

Moon Outsells Cadillac, Essex, Reo

On January 4, 1926, Stewart McDonald announced that the Moon company would set up factory branches in such large cities as Atlanta, Chicago, Kansas City, Milwaukee, New York, Philadelphia, and San Francisco. The factory branches would channel cars directly to agencies, thus eclipsing Moon's distributors. Moon acquired its Chicago and Milwaukee distributors and began negotiating to buy out its New York distributor, press accounts reveal.

The experiment lasted less than 18 months. Income data from *Moody's Industrials* shows that two-thirds of Moon Motors' nearly $1 million deficit in 1926 can be attributed to the $624,060 loss recorded by Moon's "subsidiary selling companies" – that is, the factory branch houses. *Moody's* also reports that the branch houses lost $187,000 in 1927 before the company reinstated its distributor network. In May 1927, Moon "returned to merchandising its cars through distributors and dealers instead of maintaining branches in several of the larger cities which were closed."[48]

During the first five months of 1923, Moon Motor Car Company claims, it sold 535 Moon cars "in Chicago territory," to beat Cadillac (459), Essex (416), Reo (345), Packard (301), Oakland (279), and Oldsmobile (221), and nearly three dozen other nationally known automakers. Curiously, Chevrolet and Ford are missing from the list. Chicago was extraordinary because Quinlan Motor Company – home of super salesman E. L. Cord – was Moon's best-selling distributor in 1923. In U.S. metropolitan "style-centers" during 1924, "figures show that Moon actually outsold a number of makers whose total volume of production is greater than Moon's," the company claimed. In Minneapolis and Hennepin County, Minnesota, Moon tied with Oakland in selling 18 cars during August 1924. It was a far cry from first-place Ford with 472 sales or second-place Buick with 119, but it was good enough to beat Hudson, Chrysler, Packard, Cadillac, Hupmobile, Lincoln, Jordan, and other well-known makes.[49]

Moon was courting upper-class buyers by copying the Rolls-Royce radiator, draping its cars with comforts, and creating some of the most stylish automobile ads of the Roaring Twenties. This all tended to boost sales in big cities, where the largest distributors were concentrated. "In 1923 each of the three largest [Moon] distributors sold more cars than the entire factory output of 1919," the May 1924 *Automobile Trade Journal* claimed. But Moons also sold well in the Midwest, West, and Southwest. It could be that early Moon buyers simply remained faithful to a car that had served them well.

"The company has had an unusually good Western business, incidentally selling more cars in the State of Texas than in any other section of the country," the July 1, 1909, *Automobile* reported. In 1914, "a canvass of the territory shows that during the past year Iowa has been the best sales section, and as to individual cities Philadelphia and Brooklyn have proven exceptionally good territory," according to *Motor Age*. The St. Louis factory's strong ties to the Midwest were especially evident by 1915, when exactly half the Moon sales were to buyers "who have owned one to three Moon cars previously."

Another reason that Moon cars sold well in the western half of the United States was that "freight charges from St. Louis to all of the West and South are much less than that on cars shipped from the East," President Stewart McDonald said in early 1919. "We are to our customers 'home folks,' and the man in Missouri or Arkansas, or Iowa, or Kansas, or Texas, or Mississippi, who breaks an axle or 'jims' a transmission can get his duplicate parts from St. Louis in one or two days, where he must sometimes wait weeks to get them from an Eastern factory."[50]

Moons Sell in 47 Countries

Early in 1908, its third production year, Moon chanced to export one car when C. H. Turner of Honolulu, Hawaii, a former Peerless owner, bought a Model C and shipped it home. "Mr. Turner selected a Moon car for the reason that his old car, which was designed by Louis Mooers, gave such good service. This is but the beginning of the Moon Company's export campaign," the *Auto Review* said.[51]

The October 1911 *MoTor* magazine ran a photo of "A Moon Car in Wellington, New Zealand." Early in 1912, *Auto Review* reported "Moon cars are now being driven in all the countries of Europe, in Australia and South Africa." During the next year or so, the Moon factory "received several offers from automobile dealers in different cities of England to handle Moon cars," which were up to three times more powerful than English-made autos. In spring 1913, Moon set up a Melbourne, Australia, agency. A journal reported in February 1916 that the automaker "recently made a shipment of Moon cars from St. Louis to Denmark." Some 1916 Moons went to South America; a distributor in San Juan, Puerto Rico, bought 55 Moon cars between May and November 1916. Moon shipped 42 cars to Germany in 1924, some six years after World War I, prompting Moon's distributor in Cologne, Germany, to observe "this foreign business presages the improved economic conditions in Germany and resumption of buying of American-made automobiles." Moon products were eventually "represented and sold" in 47 foreign countries.[52]

By 1927, Belgium, England, Germany, and Holland were among countries that regularly imported the St. Louis cars, which until that year were shipped in crates. But Moon adopted a new arrangement beginning with a January 5, 1927, overseas shipment, taking a cue from travelers who had successfully shipped their personal autos overseas uncrated. The new plan called for

Mississippi River barges to take uncrated Moon and Diana cars from the St. Louis municipal docks to New Orleans, where they would be transferred to oceangoing ships. (See fig.5.24.) Other automobiles would be sent uncrated in railcars for overseas shipment from New York, Export Director E. H. Serrano told the *St. Louis Globe-Democrat*.

Under the new arrangement, Moon and Diana cars for export are driven aboard ship at New York under their own power and are lashed to the deck floor as in standard shipping practice on uncrated goods. This plan will effect a big savings eventually for the car buyer overseas, since it eliminates the usual heavy crating expenses and the handling charges necessary under the old plan. In addition to this the expense of assembling the car, which formerly was shipped "knocked down" upon arrival at the dealers' showroom, is removed. The car thus arrives at its destination virtually ready to deliver or to show to the prospective buyer. . . . The new plan has aroused much interest among prospective dealers in Europe and elsewhere. Last week we closed a contract for a new distributor at Tokyo, Japan, and recently added a large distributor at Manila, Philippine Islands.

Eleven months after Moon's first overseas shipment of complete cars, the *New York Times* would report that "several of the big manufacturers" – including Erskine and Studebaker – were experimenting with exporting uncrated autos.[53]

Moon Motor Car Company apparently so inflated the production figures in its press releases that there are still questions today about how many Diana, Moon, Windsor, and Ruxton cars the factory produced. *Moody's Industrials* – formally known as *Moody's Manual of Investments* – is among the most reliable source of production figures. Succeeding editions of *Moody's Industrials* regularly revised earlier production figures downward, presumably as more independent information became available. *Moody's* 1930 edition contains many such revisions,

5.24 Moon and Diana cars being loaded onto Mississippi River barges. (NAHC)

and puts Moon Motor's peak production at 10,271 in 1925. Thus from being the 47th largest U.S. automaker in 1920 it advanced to 24th place in 1925, *Automotive Industries* said. Since 1970, Carl W. Burst III, grandson of the 1928–1930 Moon president and a Moon chronicler, has tracked the whereabouts of remaining Moon cars. He says he believes about 100 survive in countries throughout the world but is unaware of any pre-1909 Moons. Surviving Moons have been identified in such countries as Australia, the Canary Islands, Egypt, Great Britain, Holland, India, Mexico, New Zealand, Norway, and South Africa.

"The Latest Improved Machinery"

Moon Motors in 1910 was using a "special form of multiple-spindle drill . . . to bore cylinders without resetting." A February 29, 1912, *American Machinist* feature pictures a different multiple-spindle machine at work on a Moon crankcase. The Gardam machine, fitted with at least nine bits, is drilling "holes for the vertical-pump shaft," using a jig that was also used for drilling the 12 cylinder-base holes in each crankcase. Other illustrations show Garvin and Brown & Sharpe millers smoothing flat edges on Moon's cast-aluminum lower crankcase covers; a Garvin duplex miller simultaneously finishing flat surfaces on the exhaust and intake sides of four twin-cylinder castings; and other machines or jigs for finishing engine hangers, for boring camshaft and crankshaft bearing holes in crankcases, and for drilling and reaming 10 tappet guides in one operation.

By autumn 1912, the factory had equipment to ensure that its gray-iron pistons "are all interchangeable, being made on automatic piston machines which turn them out in quantities," *Automobile* reported. The magazine also revealed that Moon was making engine valves of one-piece chrome nickel steel, cast-iron valve seats, tappet and valve guides of phosphor bronze, and drop-forged I-beam connecting rods with "exceptionally strong and heavy" four-bolt lower bearing caps. The Moon engines had crankshafts of solid steel, heat treated, and "the grinding work on this part of the motor has a very small limit of tolerance, accuracy within .0005 inch being required by the inspection department." The drop-forged Moon camshafts – finished to the same tolerances as the crankshafts – were "given a double heat treatment under a secret process," and cast in one piece, including the cams and a oil pump drive gear. "The unit construction is more expensive, but the advantage claimed is greater silence owing to the impossibility of parts working loose."[54]

John Yost, Moon factory superintendent, was on hand in March 1913 when the E. R. Thomas Company of Buffalo, New York, makers of the Thomas car, auctioned off "jigs, fixtures," and a variety of "extremely high grade, modern machinery," trade journals reported. "With this added machinery the Moon Company will be in a position to immediately increase their output." The Moon factory "is equipped with the latest improved machinery – scarcely a machine is

older than two and one-half years," Joseph Moon claimed in a 1913 catalog. But the "extremely high grade, modern machinery" of the Moon plant was just a memory by the late 1920s. William J. Muller, the last president of Moon Motors, saw the factory in 1929 and was unimpressed. "The Moon plant was very old, not very suitable for building automobiles."[55] Despite a steadily increasing annual output through 1925, the Moon factory was never equipped with a fully automated assembly line.

Until the factory acquired its Duco paint-spraying system in 1924, Moon cars were painted by hand. "Every Moon body must spend thirty days in the paint shop," according to a 1920 factory catalog. "No forced processes are used in the enameling. Eighteen coats of paint are applied with the finest of camel's-hair brushes. Each coat is rubbed down by hand with pumice. Then it is ready for the finishing varnishes. This laborious process is the only way to get the Moon's elastic and lustrous finish, as glowing as mahogany furniture."[56]

Moon Motors subjected its cars – in the early years, its own engines, as well – to a variety of rigorous tests. As early as October 1908, the *Auto Review* reported that "the Moon Company has a private track on the race course of the Old Fair Grounds on Grand avenue, which they use for testing their 1909 cars." One catalog pictures two Moon cars kicking up dust as they race past an empty two-tier grandstand at the "private testing track."

Engines got tested on a dynamometer that the factory installed late in 1909. Before the road-testing stage, testers would also run each Moon-built engine "by belt drive for many hours to wear in the bearings and prepare it for test under its own fire," *Motor Age* said.

When the motors under fire have been tested for a number of hours at varying speeds, they are given a rough dynamometer test, which gives the testers exact information as to the power which each individual motor will develop. It will thus be possible, if the number of a motor is given at any future time, to tell exactly what that particular motor did on the test board. At the end of the dynamometer test each motor is taken down and each part examined by inspectors to determine whether it has been performing its work properly. Motors that stand inspection are then reassembled and delivered to the chassis assembly department to be fitted to chassis for road testing.

The engine-testing department in 1912 weaned itself from the factory's main power plant, which previously supplied the energy to run belt drives for the engine wearing-in sequence. "Now each motor which is being tested under its own power drives another motor through the wearing-in period," according to *Motor Age*.[57]

The factory conducted one notable experiment to make sure its soft tops would protect passengers from the elements. "In order to test the waterproof qualities of the mohair used in the tops of Moon cars, the Moon Motor Car Co., of St. Louis, has kept a bag made of it filled with water for the past 2 years. Not a drop ever has leaked through this material," even though the bag was refilled as water evaporated, the trade press reported.[58]

In "Pet Test," Moon Rises over Calvary Hill

Moon engineers tested new models by racking up hundreds of miles on the dirt highways of Missouri and nearby Illinois. "A trip of 678 miles in a [new 1915] Moon Four-38, in which one-half gallon of oil was used, was made this week by Chief Engineer [L. F.] Goodspeed of the Moon Motor Car Co., who made a trial run in the new model to Moline, Ill., from St. Louis and return," *Automobile* magazine reported. "Goodspeed drove the car 172 miles in two days he was in Moline, showing its paces. On the trip to Moline an average speed of 20 miles per

hour was maintained and the gasoline mileage was 21 miles to the gallon of fuel."

The standard practice by 1925 was to give every new Moon car – not just the prototypes – a road test before shipping it on to a dealer. "And when we say 'road test' we mean road test. Not a casual run down the loading platform – but a work-out on the open road, taking things as they come."[59]

Moon introduced a new $995 1927 model aimed at the low end of the medium-price market – a light 6-cylinder car called the Six-60 Jubilee Moon, in belated honor of Moon's 20 years as an automaker. "The hill climbing ability of this new Moon car is especially interesting," according to a *Motor Age* writer. "The pet test in St. Louis is up Calvary Hill which starts up steeply at right angles to a car line paved with rough cobble stones. There is also quite a bump at the bottom so that it is nearly out of the question to get much of a start. At the time this test was made there were two cars on the hill, one apparently stuck and the other laboring. The Jubilee Moon sedan swung into the turn, went up on high with three passengers, passing the other two cars and reached the top going approximately 15 m.p.h. The car was then turned around and went down again, passing the two cars, still laboring painfully upward."[60] With the introduction of its new Six-60 Jubilee, Moon was also constructing a one-level 50-by-150-foot building to house its final-test department.

St. Louis, already an undisputed shipping center, was growing into one of the country's premier automotive centers. The St. Louis–based *Auto Review* in 1913 claimed the city held fourth place in U.S. auto production. By 1930, St. Louis was, or had been, home to dozens of automobile manufacturers, who produced such makes as Dorris, Gardner, St. Louis, and Victor cars; Eureka and Success motor buggies; Darby, Eagle, and Traffic trucks; and Robinson and Webb fire engines. Accordingly, Moon felt less compulsion to justify its Midwestern location than did automakers in Grinnell, Iowa; Topeka, Kansas; Luverne, Minnesota; or Lincoln, Nebraska.

The Moon company also rarely acknowledged the competition it felt from Detroit and the East. But the *Auto Review* went to bat for its hometown industry, saying that shipping cars from St. Louis "means a marked saving in freight to the ultimate buyers of such a car in St. Louis territory, and it really means an invisible addition to the profit of the dealer because freight per automobile from St. Louis to the surrounding territory will be from $15 to $35 per automobile less than if shipped from an eastern manufacturing center."

"The geographical location of St. Louis makes it a logical distributing point for automobiles for the West, Southwest, South, Central East and North," the St. Louis Chamber of Commerce concurred. "Freight costs per automobile are lower to these districts than on shipments from Detroit, Cleveland or Indianapolis and the time of delivery is much shorter. The saving in freight is sufficient to give to the dealer practically an increased profit of five per cent."[61]

Factory Grows to 700,000 Square Feet

To the brick structure housing both his buggy and motor works, Joseph Moon added a fourth floor in 1912 (see fig.5.25), the same year the automaker "installed a considerable amount of costly new machinery in its rear axle department," according to *Auto Review*. "Special machinery is required to manufacture the Moon rear axle, which is of the full-floating type and enclosed in a one-piece crucible steel housing. The large increase in Moon business has made it necessary to add to the equipment of the factory so as to make it possible to produce many more cars per day. The Moon rear axle department is now equipped to turn out a new rear axle every twenty minutes."[62]

5.25 Artist's drawing of the Moon factory, about 1912. (*Moon Motor News*)

The motor company in 1917 "acquired title to a city block already equipped with factory buildings adjoining the main plant at Main and Cornelia Streets," according to a factory press release. "The machinery for the new buildings has been bought and will be installed at once." The automaker, in fact, moved into adjoining space left vacant with the closing of the Joseph W. Moon Buggy Company. By 1924, Moon had purchased, leased, or built five other St. Louis buildings. This allowed the factory to grow from 225,000 square feet in 1922 to 500,000 square feet by 1926, and 700,000 square feet by 1928, according to press reports and *Moody's Industrials* manuals. Prompted by its Diana and Moon sales, the company constructed a new final-test department, bought a large adjacent warehouse, and enlarged its research department.

"The mechanics in the Moon factory are largely of German descent," Vice President Stewart McDonald told *Auto Review* in 1913. "I believe that there is not a field in which the German-American mixture is a better one than in manufacturing. German-American workmen are very exacting."[63] The company employed some 1,000 workers in 1926, when there were seven engineers for Moon and Diana cars, but business fell off in the late 1920s. *Moody's Industrials'* 1930 edition put Moon's employment at 350.

Early Moon "Not an Assembled Proposition"

In 1909, the Moon was known as "a distinct production – not as an assembled proposition – a product of the Moon engineers – the Moon designs and the Moon shops." One reason for making cars from scratch was so "we do not have to wait for the parts manufacturers to catch up with public demand, but immediately develop what is needed and employ it in our models," the company said. In spring 1914 Moon "installed three large and modern enameling ovens in its plant so that the sheet metal parts of machines can be made in St. Louis instead of Detroit and other cities as heretofore has been the case," *Motor Age* said.[64] The plant did eventually shift to outside body producers, though in late 1926 it was planning to again build its own bodies. The company also retired its own engines and most other components after the 1913 model year, turning instead to suppliers.

Suppliers themselves reinforced Moon's view that every U.S. automaker was building an "assembled" car, and frequently ran ads to boast of how many cars carried their parts. Thus we learn, for instance, that such big names as Chalmers, Dodge, Hudson, Mitchell, and Reo joined Moon in buying Stanweld wheels; Buick, Kissel, National, Overland, and Studebaker joined Moon in buying Stewart vacuum tanks; and Cadillac, Peerless, and Thomas joined Moon in buying Timken axles.

Moon Engineers Have "Higher Work"

Moon Motors was on the bandwagon as early as 1914 when Joseph Moon said "a car is a collection of units – no matter who makes those units or who builds them into a car – it is no better than its weakest unit; and likewise if all the units represent the best of their kind and are built into a car by real builders (not hit or miss assemblage) that

car must be the best car of its kind." By 1921 the company was advertising "Moon's Ten Proven Units," which are "well known by mechanics and garagemen everywhere – even in the smallest villages. And where is there a leading city that hasn't well established parts and service stations for Delco, Continental, Timken and the other Moon units?" asked an August 1921 ad.

"Moon long ago freed itself from any false pride about making its own engines. We have higher work for our engineering talent than to keep them working over engines that can be built better and at lower cost by the engine specialist." Additionally, Moon's practice was such that "you're not going to find this design changed on you. Your investment in a Moon Car is safe from the artificial depreciation due to forced style changes."[65]

Thirty percent of 1925 U.S. auto makes were assembled, claims *Classic Car* magazine. Almost none were left a decade later. When auto demand was high, small, undercapitalized companies were able to assemble cars and compete regionally or even nationally, though many had weak or nonexistent dealer networks. "Unable to afford the engineering expertise so necessary to remain at the cutting edge of technology, such makers were quickly left behind," *Classic Car* concluded.[66]

When Joseph Moon died in February 1919, son-in-law Stewart McDonald succeeded him. McDonald, a Cornell University engineering graduate, spent five years apiece working for the Chicago & North Western Railway in Chicago and for a St. Louis insurance company. One biography says he got his first experience with autos in 1904, selling National, Pungs-Finch, and Royal cars for a St. Louis agency. In 1912 he became vice president and general manager of the motor company. He was president from Joseph Moon's death until 1928, when he became Moon chairman and the presidency passed to Carl W. Burst.

"The growth of the business to its present size has been entirely taken care of from earnings," the *New York Times* said in May 1922, when Moon issued 60,000 shares of ⌐ck through a Chicago–New York syndi⌐te. In a 1926 press release to trade journals, Moon asserted it was "in the strongest financial position in its history, there being no bonded indebtedness, no notes outstanding and no obligations of any kind against the company except the regular current liabilities." This very reluctance on McDonald's part to borrow money or issue bonds actually inhibited growth and left the company chronically undercapitalized, according to an article written by Burst's grandson, Moon historian Carl W. Burst III, and by Andrew D. Young.

Spurred on by the dramatic popularity of the postwar Moon Victory model, designed under his direction, McDonald aimed the cars toward wealthier urban buyers, forsaking the Midwestern farmers for whom Joseph Moon produced cars. McDonald began paying more attention to a car's paint and upholstery to the neglect of its mechanical soundness, frequently over the strident objections of Moon's engineering staff, Burst and Young contend. Moon ads during McDonald's 1919–1928 tenure rarely talked about the car's mechanical underpinnings, because McDonald believed well-to-do buyers "felt nothing but contempt for a motorcar's greasy vitals," the writers say.[67]

Though hard to estimate the amount of confusion it caused buyers, Moon Motors had an annoying tendency to announce new body styles throughout the year. Thus in the 1920s the company typically announced its new cars in the fall, usually open-car designs, and only later would begin fitting its autos with closed bodies, as they became available. Similarly, the company made a policy of changing model names almost every year, despite only minor design and mechanical changes. McDonald patterned Moon after General Motors, trying to ap-

peal to such a wide range of buyers that in 1928 – when Moon Motors made just 3,001 cars – the automaker offered three models in 25 body styles, at prices ranging from $995 to $2,295. More than likely, this approach overwhelmed rather than impressed customers. And most business planners would agree that Moon should have abandoned the strategy once its sales began slipping.

"Women Can't Shut Their Eyes to It"

When Moon Motors announced one of the first American cars with a straight-8 engine, McDonald at first withheld vital details about it. On the eve of the 1925 New York auto show, he told 150 Moon dealers at the Biltmore Hotel little more than "Moon soon would be on the market with an eight-in-line" to sell for less than $2,000.[68] Just three weeks later, before the Chicago show, McDonald quoted a price of less than $1,700.

McDonald formed a subsidiary – with the same officers as Moon Motors – to market the new car, and ads claimed it was "built by the Moon Motor Car Company for the Diana Motors Company." Introduced in July 1925 as a 1926 model with engineering claimed to be 10 months ahead of the competition, the new Diana was billed as "the Light Straight '8,'" packing a 73-horsepower engine capable of accelerating from 5 to 25 miles per hour in 6½ seconds. For the Diana, Moon Motors claimed a top speed of 77 mph and up to 17.2 miles per gallon, though perhaps not simultaneously. "Diana is right," asserted a July 18, 1925, *Saturday Evening Post* ad. "Indianapolis proved it. In the 500-mile race the first ten cars to finish were all Light Straight Eights." The company's reports of brisk Diana sales were reflected by a 1925 balance sheet showing a $562,828 surplus on record gross revenues of $12.7 million.

Diana – Artemis in Greek mythology –

5.26 A 1927 Diana hood ornament. (FLP)

5.27 Diana radiator emblem.

5.28 Sales Manager Fred H. Rengers in a 1927 Diana sedan. (FLP)

5.29 A 1927 Diana Palm Beach Special roadster. (FLP)

was the Roman goddess of hunting and the moon, thereby a suitable mythological figure to grace the radiator of a Moon companion car. (See figs. 5.26 and 5.27) Because Diana also protected young creatures, maidens, and women in childbirth, it was an ideal name for a car that Moon Motors would sell mostly to women. Women buyers outnumbered men "15 to 4," Moon claimed in one Diana ad. "Tamed, harnessed, under the thumb – easy to start, steer, park and stop – Diana Eight's appeal to women is irresistible. They can't shut their eyes to it, can't disregard it. Diana was engineered for women to drive. And here are results they sense, see, feel and want."[69]

In the Moon tradition – though perhaps unintentionally in this instance – Diana was actually a borrowed name. In late 1919, the Charles A. Balton Engineering Corporation of Buffalo, New York, proposed to manufacture a "Diana, The Fastest Of Them All." Balton guaranteed that his 4-cylinder 187-horsepower Diana could propel the car over 100 miles per hour, but was unable to secure financing to go into production.[70]

Overheating Diana "A Lemon"

Moon's Diana, "The Easiest Steering Car In America," was priced in July 1925 at $1,895 for the roadster and phaeton, $1,995 for the standard four-door, $2,095 for the cabriolet roadster and deluxe two-door brougham, and $2,195 for the deluxe four-door. In 1927 (see fig.5.28), newly dubbed "The Advanced Straight Eight," Diana included a Palm Beach Special (see fig.5.29) that sported red wire wheels, a royal blue body, and brass trim – including headlamps, radiator shell, deck rails, and step plates. Diana ad copy assumed the shape of a Grecian vase. Automotive writers said Diana borrowed its radiator from the Belgian-made Minerva. Designer Howard "Dutch" Darrin even remembers Moon President Stewart McDonald looking over a new Minerva body in the Paris-based Hibbard and Darrin design studio. But Moon Motors would allow only that "the radiator is essentially from a foreign motif" that is "exclusively a Diana design."[71]

The Diana body of the "latest European

Arrowhead design" was finished in "two-tone Double Duco (tested by violet rays)," an ad claimed. The arrowhead pattern – pressed into the body metal and hood (as in fig.5.30) – was wide at the cowl but tapered to a point just behind the hood ornament of Diana shooting an arrow at the sky. A number of Diana ads display a closeup view of a Diana ornament with a bounding greyhound at her feet; but the same ads show cars having ornaments with only the Diana figure, and factory photos confirm the use of this simplified ornament design. Later, Pierce-Arrow introduced a helmeted archer hood ornament, first offered as an option on the 1928 Series 81 Pierce-Arrows.

The Diana's "composite steel" body of metal over a wood framework allowed for thin roof pillars – "visibility increased 53%!" – and the Diana, unlike all-steel bodies, was so quiet that "at 71 miles an hour you can hear your watch tick," the company contended.[72]

Those claims aside, and despite styling and a hood ornament that many car collectors relish today, "Diana was a lemon," according to Moon historian Carl W. Burst III. Problems with Diana's Continental engine included defective piston rings and a poorly placed water pump that caused overheating. Perhaps for this reason, a 1927 Diana factory catalog played up a 30-day endurance run in which a Diana roadster was driven 15,094 miles through Wisconsin and upper Michigan.

Early in the 1920s the Maxwell, long a de-

5.30 Hood design of a 1926 Diana Arrowhead phaeton. (FLP)

5.31 A 1929 Moon Eight-80 Aerotype sedan. (FLP)

pendable car, was also plagued by serious engineering problems. The company responded by recalling the cars for free repairs and then introducing an improved model it called the "Good Maxwell," but it still had trouble winning back customers.

Moon also took steps to correct the Diana's mechanical problems, but nonetheless paid unusually high warranty claims of nearly $65,000 for the 1925 calendar year and $56,000 for 1926. By contrast, warranty claims totaled $23,850 in 1924.[73]

The damage to the reputation of Diana and its maker was at least as severe. In April, Moon felt compelled to cut prices $200 to $300 on its various Diana body styles, though it claimed its reasons for doing so were "gratifying" Diana advance orders and the gradual absorption of Diana tooling expenses.

The company had other problems that year. It was also faced with "compulsory payment of an old war claim in which the government demanded the immediate payment of approximately a half million dollars, but which was settled for less," said *Automotive Industries*. The war debt – details are lacking, but it apparently stemmed from Moon's World War I production of Navy guns, sights, and shells – eliminated what

would have been a 1926 net profit of $125,421, the journal said. After paying 40 consecutive quarterly dividends, Moon in the last quarter of 1926 missed its dividend due to what the company called "a sharp downturn in earnings."[74]

The other drain on Moon's treasury in 1926 and 1927 was its failed experiment with big-city branch houses. Because of Diana's marred reputation and its own financial problems, Moon Motors dropped its Diana line early in the 1928 model year. Moon historian Carl Burst III says he has identified 19 remaining Dianas, some four or five of which are little more than parts.

Stewart McDonald, who was planning the Diana when he saw designer Howard "Dutch" Darrin in Paris, called on Darrin to design a replacement for the Diana. The resulting Moon Aerotype (see fig. 5.31) – "taken from the finest development in aircraft practice" – had a different front, though it had many parts in common with the Diana. The Hibbard and Darrin shop did design work for the world's leading automakers, including General Motors and Stutz in the United States. McDonald, "a little shocked" at Darrin's $1,000-a-day fee – Darrin said it would be unethical to charge Moon less than he charged GM – gave Dar-

rin permission to make his trip to St. Louis unusually short. Darrin recalled his Moon experience this way:

Two or three days wasn't very long, but I thought perhaps I could give him some outside lines and then his staff could fill in the body draft. That way he would get away for about $3,000 which pleased him no end. When I arrived at the plant Friday morning he had everything ready, drawing materials, instruments and so on, and I plunged to work. About noon they wheeled in my lunch on a tray. I immediately went to Mr. MacDonald's [sic] office and said, "Look, in France we take two hours for lunch. Now what's the nicest restaurant the farthest away from the factory? If you will loan me a car I think I can make it back here in two hours." He was rather aghast, but he gave me the car, and I took off. Actually I was pulling his leg. To make up for lunch, I stayed 'till two in the morning working on the plans and was able to finish the job in three days as agreed upon. Some people may remember this car as "the Moon with the Hispano-Suiza radiator."[75]

Windsor Skirts a Royal Roadblock

Moon Motors' next experiment came with the Windsor in 1929 and 1930, for which it formed the paper company, the Windsor Corporation. "In the past few years the Prince of Wales, Britain's Royal Ambassador to the world at large (and for whom this car is named), has visited the British Dominions, the Argentine and Chile, China and Japan, the Philippines and our own United States," said a Windsor factory catalog. "His globe-trotting record undoubtedly exceeds 100,000 miles – a record you may duplicate now at the wheel of the Windsor White Prince, the hundred-thousand-mile car, and America's smartest turnout."

Another factory promotional piece quotes a *New York Times* account of a London banquet at which the American ambassador toasted the Prince of Wales as "The White Prince," for his "pure mind, a gentle

disposition, a sweet nature, a glorious spirit of honesty and truth, courage beyond measure, and a heart of gold."[76] Not so imbued with the same traits, Windsor Castle in England was upset to learn that the Windsor cars carried reproductions of the Prince of Wales's crown and three-plume crest. (See fig.5.32.)

Not for long. On March 2, 1929, the British Department of Overseas Trade sent a telegram – preserved in the Royal Archives at Windsor Castle – to the British Embassy in Washington, D.C.: "It is important that no motorcars bearing this mark should be imported into either the United Kingdom or any part of the British Empire where the Prince's feathers are legally protected but it would be far more satisfactory if mark could be discontinued altogether."

In response, the Windsor Corporation on March 27 wired the British Embassy in Washington: "In designing new radiator emblem we have eliminated crown and plumes substituting therefor [sic] in profile a lion on a black background (stop) On the bottom of name plate the word Windsor (stop) We sincerely think nothing offensive but would like your opinion as to suggested

5.32 Moon Motor Car Company got into trouble with Windsor Palace for the unauthorized use of the Prince of Wales's crown and three-plume crest.

5.33 A 1929 Windsor White Prince roadster. (JAC)

5.34 A 1929 Windsor White Prince, identified in this factory photo as a petite sedan. (MHS)

design by wire if possible." The British Embassy apparently did approve the design, as Moon Motors adopted a revised Windsor emblem similar to the one it described in the telegram.

If Diana was the car for women, the Windsor was the car for young motorists. "It's the Windsor White Prince, dashing, distingue, devil-may-care. Every inch an aristocrat, every inch a thoroughbred. And the youth of America doffs his cap," claimed a Windsor catalog. "Truly, here is style, distinction and charm worthy of the spirit of Youth."

At the January 1929 New York auto show the St. Louis automaker displayed two nearly identical Windsor White Prince models: the Eight-92, equipped with a Warner Hyflex 4-speed transmission, and the Eight-82, which had a 3-speed transmission. The models shared a Continental 15S model straight-8 engine that was finished in black enamel with chrome fittings. The engine's 3 x 4¾-inch bore and stroke displaced nearly 287 cubic inches, developed 85 horsepower, and propelled the Windsor White Prince to 80 miles per hour. The two models shared a 125-inch-wheelbase "dreadnaught" frame, 7 inches deep, with "tubes at front and rear holding the frame rigid at both ends. Five tubular cross members insure rigidity and eliminate 'body weave.'"[77] The cars were similar in many other ways. Prices ranged from $1,795 to $2,345 for the six body styles: brougham victoria, cabriolet, roadster (see fig. 5.33), five-passenger petite sedan (see fig. 5.34), five-passenger sedan, and seven-passenger sedan.

Low with Sweeping Fenders

In describing the White Prince, the February 1929 *Automobile Trade Journal* said "the bodies are low hung and long, the appearance of length being further emphasized by long horizontal louvers and . . . long sweeping fenders and molding treatment. The radiator shell is quite unusual. The raised beading, one at the forward edge of the shell and another at the rear, are chrome plated, while in between, the shell is finished in the same color as the hood." The journal also observed that the "bodies are of composite manufacture to Hibbard Darrin design," since the cars were patterned after the Moon Aerotype models that Howard

"Dutch" Darrin designed.[78] The single remaining Moon car, the Six-72 (see fig.5.35) carried the same equipment and body but had a conventional chrome-plated radiator shell, as well as a 6-cylinder engine.

Moon Motors early in 1929 halted U.S. sales of the Moon automobile, a marque that was both an industry pioneer and 24-year veteran. It transformed the Moon Six-72 into a Windsor Six-72 for domestic sale but would continue to export Moon cars. By early February 1929, the company had opened "display rooms for White Prince sixes and eights" in New York City and in March reported on the addition of a Six-72 Windsor roadster. In April the Windsor Corporation brought out the White Prince Six-77, the re-badged Moon car with a 4-speed transmission, with prices ranging from $1,545 to $1,895 for six body styles. Another Windsor model was the Six-69, which used a Continental 6-cylinder engine less powerful than that used in the Six-72 and Six-77. In spring 1929 the company cut Windsor prices $50 for all but the seven-passenger sedan. The 1930 Windsors came out as Eight-85, the 3-speed model, and Eight-92, the 4-speed version, virtually identical to the 1929 cars. The Six-69 and Six-75 made up the 1930 Windsor 6-cylin-

der line. The Windsor died with the Ruxton, another new vehicle, and with the Moon company itself in 1930.

Moon historian Carl W. Burst III says he has identified 24 surviving Windsors, of which 15 are 8-cylinder models. Joe Egle of Kansas City, Missouri, a car collector and Windsor enthusiast, has owned several of the cars. The Windsor's 80-mile-per-hour advertised top speed is understated, Egle said. "It's the best-handling '29 model car I've ever driven. I've had Lincolns and Cadillacs and Packards and they're all trucks by comparison. The only time it ever shows any weakness is – it has single-action shocks, and if you try to stop on a washboard road the axles will bounce." The Windsor's heavy Warner 4-speed transmission also makes for truck-like shifting, Egle said.[79]

Moon Motors' Final Fling

In 1929, when the Ruxton was a new car in search of a factory, the Moon company was in search of anything it could make and sell. Windsor sales were so bad that the Moon factory built prototypes of a new cotton picker. The Ruxton, a low front-wheel-drive car of the future, looked to be an ideal grand finale for a decade in which anything

5.35 A 1928 Moon Six-72 royal cabriolet coupe. (FLP)

5.36 Ruxton promoter Archie Andrews demonstrates his car's pull-out gearshift lever. The shifting linkage ran to the front of the engine, where the front-wheel-drive transmission was mounted. (FLP)

seemed possible. The Moon-Ruxton pairing could have been a match made in heaven. It wasn't.

Moon traded a minority share of its stock for the patents and rights to produce the Ruxton. But the Ruxton promoters, organized as New Era Motors, stealthily bought up more Moon stock. Once New Era President Archie M. Andrews and his cohorts controlled a majority share, they wrested away control of the Moon company from President Carl Burst and the Moon old guard, prompting a confrontation at the Moon factory in St. Louis, over which Andrews prevailed. The Moon company and the Ruxton car weren't so fortunate.

The Ruxton story, however, starts in 1926, when experimental engineer William J. Muller got permission to build a front-wheel-drive prototype. Muller worked for the Edward G. Budd Company of Philadelphia, which hoped to interest one of the established automakers in producing the car using Budd-made bodies.[80]

If a front-wheel-drive car seemed a novel idea in the 1920s, it shouldn't have. Before 1500, Italian inventor Leonardo da Vinci drew plans for a vehicle that "clearly had front drive," according to a history of front-drive cars. Widely regarded as the first self-propelled land vehicle, Nicolas Cugnot's 1769 steam wagon was front drive, as was a series of racing cars that Walter Christie built beginning in 1904. The Bateman Manufacturing Company of Greenloch, New Jersey, put out a few Frontmobiles in 1917–1918, and Ben E. Gregory of Kansas City, Missouri, made some experimental front-drive cars – including a race car – from 1920 to 1922. Race-car-builder Harry Miller also embraced front-wheel drive in the mid-1920s, and the Cord L-29 was based upon his patents. Muller was first with his Ruxton prototypes, but the Cord reportedly beat the Ruxton into production. Some U.S. commercial vehicles were using front-wheel drive; European passenger cars had embraced the idea years earlier.[81]

While William Muller worked in the Budd factory on the mechanics of his experimental car, Budd designer Joseph Ledwinka crafted its modernistic body. Faced with a budget of just $15,000, Muller modified a 6-cylinder Studebaker engine and a Warner transmission to fit his new car. Even so, they had spent $35,000 by autumn 1928, when they finished a four-door sedan prototype on a 130-inch wheelbase.

F. Schumacher "created and loomed" the fabrics, said a New Era press release, "while color effects are from Josef Urban, stage designer and decorator of the New York Casino in Central Park." Urban's splashy paint scheme used on some Ruxtons consisted of horizontal bands of colors progressing from light at the top of the car to dark on the bottom. "It looked like hell to me, but then I'm not one much for styling," Muller wrote in a 1969 article.

Griffin Replaces Question Mark

When Wall Street financier and promoter Archie Andrews (see fig.5.36), a member of the Budd board of directors, saw the car, he wanted it, and the Budd company grudgingly turned the project over to Andrews. Muller delivered the prototype un-

named car – its grill medallion was a question mark – to Andrews's Park Avenue office in February 1929 and took the promoter on a test drive through New York's Wall Street area. Later that day, Andrews and William V. C. Ruxton, a member of the New York Stock Exchange governing committee, met to plan the car's future "during a very socially convivial evening – of which neither of them probably remembered very much," Muller recalls. Anticipating Ruxton's investment in the project, Andrews named the one-time mystery car – "Dolphin" had also been considered as a name – the Ruxton. Instead of a question mark, a griffin – the monster of Greek mythology, having a lion's body and eagle's wings – was on the grill, hubcaps, and elsewhere. The hood ornament looked like a griffin wing.

Andrews's first stop was at Hupp Motor Car Corporation, where he was also a director. Hupp President DeBois Young agreed to make the Ruxton car, using many Hupmobile parts. The deal later fell through simply because "a lot of people in the Hupp group just didn't like Archie Andrews," Muller claims. So in April 1929 Andrews formed New Era Motors. Andrews was president; Muller, vice president; Stanley Nowak, treasurer; and F. E. Welsh, secretary. J. E. Roberts was general manager, and sales manager was Fred D. Peabody, former assistant general sales manager for Hupp Motors.

The board of directors included William Ruxton; Fred W. Gardner of the Gardner Motor Company, St. Louis; and metallurgist C. Harold Wills, the former Ford chief engineer whose own Wills Sainte Claire Motor Company – and the like-named cars it made – folded in 1927. Though a consultant on the Ruxton production prototype, Wills "didn't really do too much," Muller claims. And not only did Ruxton fail to invest in the project, he later sued Andrews over a $50,000 stock subscription and disassociated himself with the Ruxton car.

After sending Muller back to Phila-

delphia to prepare a production Ruxton sedan prototype, Andrews and Fred Gardner in about June 1929 arranged for Gardner Motor Company to produce the Ruxton in St. Louis. Gardner's assistant chief engineer spent some time with Muller as Muller finished the production prototype. But just as Muller prepared to begin sending production material to the St. Louis factory, Gardner backed out of the deal. Russell E. Gardner, Jr., whose father founded Gardner Motor Company, said in a 1977 interview that the deal fell through because Andrews failed to supply the money he promised.[82]

Following that disappointment, a lawsuit over a supplier's driveshaft units delayed construction five or six months, Muller said. By about August 1, 1929, however, Muller had finished his production prototype. He meshed a backward Continental Model 18S 100-horsepower straight-8 engine with an unusual worm-gear-and-wheel differential of his own design. The car's transmission and differential were also one unit. (See fig.5.37.) To move the engine forward for greater front-wheel traction – also to prevent an unusually long hood and cramped

5.37 In the front-wheel-drive Ruxton, the transmission and differential box mounted in front of the engine. (FLP)

5.38 A Hupmobile, left, dwarfs the new Ruxton, a low, front-wheel-drive car. (FLP)

5.39 Actress Claire Windsor poses beside a Ruxton town car. (FLP)

5.40 A Ruxton rumble-seat roadster. (JAC)

passenger compartment – Muller split the transmission. He put the reverse and first gears in front of the differential and the second and third gears behind it, which shortened the driving gear by about a foot.

Because the front-drive car didn't need clearance for a drive shaft and rear axle, it sat about 10 inches lower than most cars. At 63¼ inches tall, "so low is the Ruxton that one of average height standing on the ground may look over the top," the *New York Times* said. (See figs. 5.38, 5.39, and 5.40.) The Ruxton dispensed with running boards because passengers could step into the car without them. While early Ruxtons had ordinary round headlamps, later cars were equipped with sinister-looking cat's-eye Woodlite headlamps.

Andrews, meanwhile, made a deal to swap Ruxton production rights and assets of New Era Motors for stock in the Marmon Motor Car Company. Terms called for Marmon to build Ruxtons in Indianapolis, but the deal collapsed a day later with the stock-market crash of late October 1929, Muller said. "After that, there would be some talk – but little action – about Jordan and Stutz getting into the Ruxton picture. And Peerless too. But they were all in a bad way," Muller said. Plans to build Ruxtons at the Sunbeam plant in England also led nowhere, he said.

Desperate Moon Eyes Taxicabs, Aviation

Even before the stock-market crash, Moon Motors was also in a bad way. In a frighteningly steep slide since producing almost 10,300 cars at a $562,828 profit in 1925, Moon Motor Car Company built just 1,333 autos in 1929. Accordingly, the company turned in losses of $148,000 in 1927, $338,000 in 1928, and $277,000 in 1929, according to *Moody's Industrials*. Spring 1929 was the apparent low-water mark for Moon; President Carl Burst began looking at any proposition that might keep the factory busy.

In April Burst announced "that his organization will manufacture a large fleet of taxicabs for the Diamond Cab Co. of New York," *Automotive Industries* reported. Also in April, the company was planning to enter the aviation field, according to *Moody's Industrials*. The taxicab and aviation deals apparently fell through. But less than a month later, Moon company officials "announced plans for the manufacture of 'a newly-perfected mechanical cotton picker' at the rate of about 30,000 per year, with an annual sales value of $15,000,000 and calling for employment of some 1800 additional men," according to a St. Louis newspaper. During its first day of production in August, Moon reportedly made five machines under contract to the American Cottonpicker Corporation, and scaled back its production estimate to 20,000 cotton pickers for 1930. Despite such claims, some former Moon employees have suggested that the factory never made more than one or two prototypes of the cotton picker.[83]

About a month after the stock-market crash, former Moon President-turned-Chairman Stewart McDonald met with Archie Andrews in New York City and talked him into making a loan to Moon Motor Car Company. McDonald wrote to his brother-in-law, Stanley Moon, saying he would come up with money to save the Moon company if Stanley would help him divorce Grace Moon. "We found this letter in the Moon safe at the factory later," William Muller asserts. McDonald "got [Carl] Burst to come to New York and the loan was handed over," said Muller, who by the end of 1929 had moved all the Ruxton tooling to the Moon factory. After a two-year separation, Grace, contending desertion, divorced McDonald in May 1930.

Published accounts fail to mention any direct loan from New Era to Moon. Reports of the plan, however, indicate that Moon would exchange 150,000 shares of its stock to acquire "all Ruxton patent rights, granted and pending, plant equipment, engineering data and finished and unfinished

cars." Moon would also issue an extra 100,000 shares on the open market at not less than $5 a share. The resulting $500,000 would finance production of the Ruxton. Moon's New York Stock Exchange application indicates that along with Ruxton licenses it acquired $763,000 in New Era assets. In a November 24, 1929, announcement, Moon officials said they would supplement the 8-cylinder Ruxton with a line of light 8- and 6-cylinder front-drive cars at lower prices. A February 24, 1930, New Era press release said these new models would appear "in the two-thousand-dollar class," compared to a price of $4,000 to $4,500 for the original Ruxton models.

At the January 1930 New York automobile show, the Moon Motor Car Company's display consisted of three Windsors and two Ruxtons, "a stock roadster, done in two tones of green after a color motif originated by Josef Urban, and a standard five-passenger sedan," the *New York Times* said.

How Andrews bought up the extra 100,000 Moon shares to control the company is unclear in light of a February 22, 1930, *Automobile Topics* account. The magazine said "Moon Motors received permission to list 100,000 more capital shares on official notice that they have been sold to bankers for a price of not less than $5 a share and that they are outstanding in the hands of the public." But as soon as he made his deal with Moon, "Andrews was busy buying up Moon stock on the market," Muller said in his 1969 retrospective article. After Moon failed, reports surfaced of a Moon stock-manipulation scheme involving an Eastern syndicate in charge of selling the 100,000 Moon shares. The syndicate could have been Andrews's source, though his name wasn't mentioned in a January 16, 1931, *New York Times* account of the stock fraud.

"New Officials Crawl through Windows"

A February 23, 1930, *New York Times* story said New Era Motors had acquired a "substantial interest" in Moon — later revealed to be 239,400 of 350,000 outstanding shares. The company name would henceforth be Moon-Ruxton, though Andrews said he planned no change in personnel.

Despite Andrews's control of Moon, "nobody there relished the idea of his sitting on the board of directors," Muller said. So Andrews called a special stockholders' meeting for April 7 "over the protests of the officers and old directors, at which it was voted to increase the number of directors from seven to fifteen, the Easterners obtaining the additional eight and with it apparent control of the company," the *New York Times* reported. Meeting again on April 12, the eight new directors voted to oust Moon President Carl Burst and the other old-guard Moon officers. "Each side contends the other failed to live up to its agreement in connection with the transfer of the Ruxton rights," the *St. Louis Globe-Democrat* noted. "It is said to be the contention of the Moon interests that no change in management ever had been contemplated."

The new Moon-Ruxton officers were thus William J. Muller, president; Helm Walker and J. E. Roberts, vice presidents; Frederic E. Welch, treasurer; and R. P. Kilwitz, secretary. They brought in Fred W. Ayres, formerly of Oakland and Pontiac, as general manager in charge of production, the June 1930 *MoTor* magazine reported.

A smooth transition it wasn't. "New Officials Crawl Through Windows to Obtain Moon Control," is the headline over the *St. Louis Globe-Democrat*'s story on the factory confrontation. Elected Saturday in New York, Moon's new officers appeared at the door of the St. Louis factory on Monday morning, April 14, only to discover that "armed representatives of the old officers" were barricaded inside the factory:

The new officers immediately sought and obtained a temporary restraining order. . . . Accompanied by a Deputy Sheriff and a squad of policemen, they returned to the plant. Still the group behind the door refused to open, though the Deputy informed them of his identity and told them of the court order. The Sheriff then crawled through a window. Policemen boosted the new officers and their attorney, S. Mayner Wallace, over the windowsill and the defenders were ordered out. They went without further trouble. Those who had resisted the new regime included, besides several old employes, an operative of a private detective agency. They told the Sheriff they had been instructed to open the door to no one.[84]

Some retrospective histories contend that the old officers, including Moon President Carl Burst, were among the defenders. In the *Globe-Democrat* version, however, the new regime charged that Burst and his old officers were communicating with Moon employees from "their places of hiding or retreat, believed to be somewhere in the city."

The old guard tried a variety of legal remedies — they failed in their attempt to declare the special stockholders' meetings illegal — but were silenced for good on July 29, 1930, when a judge in St. Louis "granted a permanent order restraining former officers from interfering with operations of the firm." For its part, New Era also filed a number of lawsuits, one claiming that former Moon officers overestimated Moon's inventory by $491,000.

Kissel Shutdown Dooms Moon-Ruxton

Even before Andrews installed his own officers at Moon, the press was awash with rumors of new deals pending. One popular report was that Stutz would move from Indianapolis to St. Louis in a three-way merger with Gardner and Moon-Ruxton. That didn't happen, but Gardner and Moon-Ruxton on March 31, 1930, announced the cost-cutting consolidation of their engineering and sales forces. Moon and Gardner remained separate companies, however. The combined departments would market Ruxtons, Windsors, and Gardners, including a new Gardner front-wheel-drive model that appeared at the 1930 New York and Chicago auto shows. Gardner's new model didn't get past the prototype stage, however. Due not to Moon-Ruxton's problems but because of its own financial difficulties, Gardner in 1931 voluntarily liquidated at a profit to stockholders.

Andrews struck a deal with the Kissel Motor Car Company of Hartford, Wisconsin, for Kissel to make complete Ruxtons as well as transaxles for Ruxtons built in both Hartford and St. Louis. Like Gardner and Moon in St. Louis and many other small independent automakers across the country, the Kissel company was financially strapped. According to *The Classic Kissel Automobile* book and other sources, Andrews forwarded $100,000 of $250,000 in new financing he promised Kissel President George Kissel. Under their agreement, Kissel would make Ruxton transaxles and also build 1,500 Ruxtons annually and a specified number of Kissels, or else forfeit

control of the Kissel company in exchange for New Era preferred stock.

The Kissel factory "was a nice one, far superior to what we had at Moon," Muller recalls. "I had visions of moving all our manufacturing apparatus up there – earlier I had shipped them transmission tools – and we had tentatively made arrangements with a big warehouse company to take over the Moon plant."

Since 1929, New Era press releases had promised that full-scale Ruxton production was weeks away. Finally, in a dateline June 16, 1930, story from St. Louis, *Automotive Industries* reported that "the first Ruxton to be built entirely in the factory of the Moon Motor Car Co. here came off the assembly line last Monday and production will be speeded up gradually. Dealer shipments started during the week. The initial models are a roadster, sport touring car, five-passenger sedan and a cabriolet." (See fig.5.41.)

There followed a slowdown of news re-

5.41 This photo, dated for release to the press after June 15, 1930, was accompanied by the announcement that "quantity production of the Ruxton is now under way." But the photo was staged. The only Ruxtons are the foreground car and the one behind it; the rest are Windsors. (JAC)

ports about Ruxton production. The *St. Louis Globe-Democrat* reported that E. H. Serrano, Moon-Ruxton director of exports, on August 29, 1930, placed a seven-minute telephone sales call to Buenos Aires, Argentina. Even at $76, it saved time and cost half what it would have cost to cable, and because of the call "an order was secured for a carload of Ruxton cars."

On September 19, 1930, George Kissel announced that Andrews, who claimed the depressed stock market left him unable to raise the money, had never come through with his promised additional $150,000. The Wisconsin manufacturer was virtually penniless. Thus George Kissel endorsed a friendly receivership action, effectively preventing Andrews from taking over the Kissel factory for Ruxton production.

"Since we had so much of our tooling up there, the Ruxton was doomed too," Muller said. Out of money, the St. Louis factory closed its manufacturing department November 10, 1930, with a stock of just 30 Ruxtons on hand, a St. Louis newspaper reported. On application of a stockholder who claimed the Moon-Ruxton company had already begun liquidating assets to pay creditors, a judge on November 15 named a temporary receiver. The company had $1.2 million in assets, $205,000 in direct liabilities, and $492,000 in material commitments, including the $17,971 it owed Continental Motors for engines. Solvent on paper, Moon-Ruxton nonetheless had no money with which to conduct business. New Era Motors filed a voluntary bankruptcy petition two weeks later on November 28, 1930, with assets of $317,793 and liabilities of $855,976.

Moon's Legal Tangles Unraveled . . . in 1966

Moon Motors, which began by making 1906 model cars, died outright. The Kissel company, which began by making 1907 cars, reorganized and survived making outboard motors and other products until its 1944 sale to West Bend Aluminum. Even after the passing of these two automotive pioneers, the trauma and turmoil refused to end for Moon.

In New York in early 1931, the Bureau of Securities and state attorney general were investigating five men who allegedly defrauded investors of $1 million. The five suspects – Leonard J. Rollnick, William L. Jarvis, Charles S. Rich, and two unnamed men – "acquired control of 100,000 shares of Moon Motors, partly by purchase and partly under option," reported the January 16, 1931, *New York Times*. The men faced charges of arranging fictitious sales to inflate Moon stock from about $5 per share in November 1929 to $15 per share in April 1930. The five men then allegedly induced a publication called *Wall Street Era* to recommend Moon stock, after which "many thousands of shares of the stock were dealt in daily by men named in the order." The *New York Times Index* lists no follow-up articles on the Moon stock-fraud investigation.

Chief Engineer Herman Palmer estimated that Kissel assembled 26 Ruxtons, according to *The Classic Kissel Automobile* book. Some automotive historians say the total Ruxton production was as high as 500 or 600 cars. Other guesses are much lower. Reporting on New Era's bankruptcy filing, the November 29, 1930, *New York Times* went so far as to say the Ruxton "has never been placed on the market, though working models have been made." Other sources argue for a figure somewhere between such extremes.

"The frequently quoted production figures of 200 to 300 models are sheer nonsense," Hank Wieand Bowman concludes in a December 1953 *Motor Trend* feature about the Moon-Ruxton venture. Carl Burst III, a Moon historian and grandson of Moon President Carl Burst, agrees, contending the Moon factory under Andrews's control repeatedly assembled, then disassembled, Ruxtons for a series of publicity photographs purportedly showing production in full swing. Burst, a Ruxton owner, says the number of Ruxtons made was closer to 60.

Jack Donlan, also a Ruxton owner and enthusiast, puts the total figure at between 125 and 150 Ruxtons. Specifically, he says New Era made 10 prototype Ruxtons in Philadelphia, Kissel-Ruxton produced about 25 in Wisconsin, and Moon-Ruxton assembled 75 cars – perhaps as many as 100 – in St. Louis. This production estimate is confirmed by the serial numbers of surviving Ruxtons, Donlan said. The highest serial number is less than 140, and the car so numbered was among the last few that were assembled under orders from the Moon-Ruxton receiver in St. Louis, he said.

Donlan puts the number of surviving Ruxtons at 19, including 11 sedans, seven roadsters, and one phaeton. *Automobile Quarterly* pictures five surviving Ruxtons. Thus the auto that debuted as a question mark bowed out as a mystery car.[85]

Epitaph: "A Manufacturer of Prestige Autos"

Many retrospective articles paint Archie Andrews – who went on to head Hupp Motors until his ouster in 1935, and who died in 1938 – as a fast-talking con artist. "Toward the end he got pretty desperate and became a rather rough sort of person," even though he was a likeable man, said Ruxton designer and Moon-Ruxton President William Muller. "Whenever one of his high-powered attorneys would say, 'Mr. Andrews, you can't do that. It's illegal,' Andrews would reply, 'What the hell do you think I pay you for. You're the one who's going to tell me how to make it legal.'"

An example of accounts kinder to Andrews, the *Standard Catalog of American Cars, 1805–1942* says "the machinations of Archie Andrews in attempting to bring the Ruxton to life were often monstrous, [but] it seems evident he was genuinely interested in the Ruxton as a car, which tends to make

its story just a little bit sad." Like Moon-Ruxton creditors and stockholders, Andrews also suffered financially, as his A. M. Andrews Investment Corporation claimed it lost $293,000 in the Moon-Ruxton failure. On New Era's bankruptcy petition, Andrews claimed he lost $77,200 of his own money in the Moon-Ruxton collapse.

Moon Motors showed that a small company could live through three of the most turbulent decades of the American automobile industry. Some 607 manufacturers started building cars after Moon did, but by 1929 only 36 independent companies were still in business, the factory claimed in a 1929 catalog. Though its technical innovations were negligible except during the Louis Mooers years, Moon Motors took advantage of an unprecedented demand for automobiles in the 1920s. Buying its engines and other components from suppliers, the St. Louis company built a solid, even luxurious, car and offered a large number of standard and special body styles. It studied other cars and freely borrowed new ideas that improved the appearance, comfort, or design of its own vehicles. Moon's low- and medium-range prices made its cars a good buy from the rural Midwest to large cities across America, as well as in nearly 50 other countries. Moon Motors designed the "Easiest Steering Car In America," an attractive automobile especially for women. It followed the Diana with the Windsor White Prince, an appeal to the youngsters of the late 1920s.

Yet after 26 years of making cars, Moon Motors ultimately failed for several reasons. The company neglected to thoroughly test its new Diana model, with disastrous results for both the company's treasury and reputation. Stewart McDonald reversed Joseph Moon's philosophy of putting a car's engineering ahead of its appearance. Though Moon Motors was a leader in adopting hydraulic brakes and balloon tires, mechanically its 1920s cars showed signs of mediocrity. Offering as many as 25 body styles a year further undercut Moon's attempt to maintain its quality standards. The company stumbled financially by setting up factory branches in its biggest markets as a way to bypass distributors. Moon was also bucking a trend toward a smaller number of larger automobile manufacturers – mostly centered in Detroit.

Moon's four-story main factory plus two adjoining one-story buildings sold for $72,500 on August 13, 1935. Its new owner, the Cupples Company, planned to use the former auto plant for making wooden matches. The final distribution of Moon assets was tied up in court until late January 1966, when a judge ordered that the remaining $25,938 be divided among 355 creditors, who received payments ranging from seven cents to $2,107. The Moon Motor Car Company's main factory building was demolished in 1978.

"Moon Motor Car Co. was once a manufacturer of prestige automobiles," began a 1965 St. Louis newspaper article about the legal haggling over Moon's remaining assets.[86] As a manufacturer "more interested in the reputation of the Moon car than he is in the profit on any individual car," Joseph Moon would have considered such offhand praise a fitting epitaph.

Notes

Chapter 1, Great Smith of Kansas

1. Llewellyn Kiene, *The Story of Two Brothers*, 1905, p.15. This and all other Smith factory publications mentioned in this chapter, except for *Instruction Book and Parts Price List, 1909–1910*, are held by the Kansas State Historical Society.
2. Much of the biographical information in this section is from Kiene, *The Story of Two Brothers*, except as noted.
3. *Where Smith Automobiles Are Made*, 1905 factory catalog, p.10.
4. U.S. Department of Commerce, Patent and Trademark Office, *Official Gazette*, Sept. 1, 1885, p.1120, Patent No. 325,635, and Sept. 8, 1885, p.1229, Patent No. 326,062. The Kansas Museum of History, Topeka, has a Clement Smith harp that it dates to between 1885 and 1895. It has 43 strings, a spruce soundboard, and a body of maple and maple veneer.
5. John B. Rae, *The American Automobile Industry* (Boston: Twayne Publishers, 1984), p.18.
6. Motor Vehicle Manufacturers Association (MVMA), *Automobiles of America: Milestones, Pioneers, Roll Call, Highlights*, 4th ed. (Detroit: Wayne State University Press, 1974), p.13.

7. *Topeka Daily Capital*, "Terry Stafford Quits the Smith Company," Dec. 29, 1907, p.5, and "Topeka's First 'Gas Wagon,'" Feb. 23, 1919.
8. *Topeka State Journal*, "Snap Shots" column, June 8, 1900, and July 9, 1900; and *Topeka State Journal*, "Only Automobile in Topeka, and Its Inventor and Builder, Terry Stafford," Aug. 11, 1900.
9. *Topeka State Journal*, Aug. 11, 1900; *Kansas Portraits*, 1985 feature on Terry Stafford, collection SP 906 K13 kp, Kansas State Historical Society; plus *Topeka Daily Capital*, "50 Years Ago Automobiles Were F.O.B. Kansas," Aug. 24, 1952, and "Early Topeka Car Not Made in Single Shop," May 20, 1962.
10. Clement Smith, *Catalogue-Treatise upon the Automobile*, 1906, vol.1, p.8.
11. *Topeka Daily Capital*, "Are Many Enthusiastic Automobile Owners Here," Feb. 28, 1909, p.1 of auto section.
12. John Ripley, "The Lesser Smiths, the Great Smith and the Stafford," *Bulletin* of the Shawnee County Historical Society, December 1959, p.39; and Beverly Rae Kimes and Henry Austin Clark, Jr., *Standard Catalog of American Cars, 1805–1942*, 2d ed. (Iola, Wisconsin: Krause Publications, 1989), p.610.

13. *Merchants Journal*, "Ten Automobiles Bought by the Parkhurst-Davis Mercantile Company for the Use of Their Traveling Salesmen," Aug. 30, 1902, pp.12–13. All the information for this section comes from the *Merchants Journal*, except as noted.
14. Author's interview with Ron Carey, Sept. 3, 1991.
15. *Automobile and Motor Review*, blurb under "New Enterprises," Nov. 22, 1902, p.24.
16. *Topeka Daily Capital*, "Industrial Development of Topeka Attracting Attention . . . Smith Company Turning Out Topeka Made Automobiles," March 22, 1903, p.10; and John Ripley, "Their First Order a Whopper," *Bulletin* of the Shawnee County Historical Society, November 1972, pp.16–18.
17. *Topeka Daily Capital*, March 22, 1903, p.10, which put the cost of the new local factory at $7,000. The Nov. 22, 1902, *Automobile and Motor Review* says $2,000.
18. *"Veracity" Automobiles, 1904*, 1st and 2d eds. All subsequent quotations and information about the 1904 Smith cars come from these two catalogs unless noted otherwise.
19. *Topeka Daily Capital*, March 22, 1903, p.10; Ripley, "The Lesser Smiths," p.38;

and *1911: The Great Smith*, factory catalog, unpaged.

20. *Topeka Daily Capital*, "Topeka Looms Up As a Motor Town," April 17, 1904, and "$50,000 Addition/Smith Automobile Co. Plans Big Improvement," Nov. 4, 1904, p.6.

21. *"Veracity" Automobiles, 1904*, 2d ed., p.19.

22. MVMA, *Automobiles of America*, p.26; and Kimes and Clark, *Standard Catalog*, p.551.

23. *Instruction Book: Great Smith Cars, 1909*, p.3.

24. MVMA *Automobiles of America*, pp.31–32; *"Veracity" Automobiles, 1904*, 2d ed., p.18; and Smith, *Catalogue-Treatise*, vol.1, pp.36–37.

25. Vol. 66, Charter #284, corporation charter for Smith Automobile Company, Kansas State Historical Society; Incorporation Certificate No. 18746 and amendments, Smith Automobile Company, Missouri Secretary of State's office, Corporation Division; Kiene, *The Story of Two Brothers*, p.20; and *Motor Way*, "New Interest in Kansas Company," Oct. 26, 1905, p.16.

26. Unless otherwise noted, this and much of the other information about 1905 Smith cars is drawn from two factory catalogs, *March Brochure, 1905*, and *Where Smith Automobiles Are Made*.

27. *The 1907 Great Smith Car*, factory catalog, p.3.

28. *The 1907 Great Smith Car*, p.12; and Smith, *Catalogue-Treatise*, vol.1, p.41.

29. Author's interview with Harold Irwin, April 11, 1991; and Barney Hackney, *Horseless Carriage Gazette*, "Story of the Great Smith," July–August 1958, p.42.

30. Factory details come from the 1905 Smith Auto catalog *Where Smith Automobiles Are Made*; *Topeka Daily Capital*, "Automobiles Are Built in Topeka, Kan./A Visit to the Great Smith Factory," June 21, 1908, p.16; and Smith, *Catalogue-Treatise*, vol.1, p.44.

31. *Topeka Daily Capital*, "Topeka Automobilists Plan Long Distance Run to Colorado," March 26, 1906, p.5.

32. *Where Smith Automobiles Are Made*, p.8; and Smith, *Catalogue-Treatise*, vol.1, p.1.

33. *Topeka State Journal*, Nov. 11, 1902, Jan. 8, 1910, and Feb. 19, 1910; and *Topeka Daily Capital*, March 22, 1903, April 17, 1904, Aug. 18, 1907, June 21, 1908, and Dec. 11, 1910.

34. *Topeka Daily Capital*, June 21, 1908, p.16.

35. *Topeka Daily Herald*, "Topeka Cars in the East/A Smith Machine Running in the City of Brotherly Love," July 22, 1905, p.3.

36. MVMA, *Automobiles of America*, pp.29, 46–47; *Advance Sheet of 1907 Great Smith Car*, unpaged factory catalog; and Smith, *Catalogue-Treatise*, vol.1, p.12.

37. Quotations and information about the design and construction of the early Smith 4-cylinder cars come from Smith, *Catalogue-Treatise*, vol.1; *Advance Sheet of 1907 Great Smith Car*; *The 1907 Great Smith Car*; and *The Great Smith Car: Tenth Annual Catalog*, 1908, unless otherwise noted. The same catalogs are also the primary sources for the upcoming description of the blacksmith shop.

38. Smith, *Catalogue-Treatise*, vol.1, pp.4–5, 31.

39. *Smith Auto Company Catalogue of Automobile Accessories, Supplies and Parts*, 1906, p.43; *The 1907 Great Smith Car*, pp.16–19; *The Great Smith Car*, 1908, p.17; and *Instruction Book: Great Smith Cars, 1909*, p.8.

40. Smith, *Catalogue-Treatise*, vol.1, p.40; and *The 1907 Great Smith Car*, p.19.

41. Smith, *Catalogue-Treatise*, vol.1, pp.21–22, 28, 31; and *The 1907 Great Smith Car*, p.16.

42. *Topeka Daily Capital*, Jan. 1, 1906, p.3, and March 26, 1906, p.5.

43. *Topeka Daily Capital*, "Topeka Autos in New York," May 15, 1906.

44. The following information about 1906 Smith autos is from Smith, *Catalogue-Treatise*, vol.1.

45. *Motor Age*, "Smith Automobile Co.–Smith," Dec. 6, 1906, p.64; and *Automobile*, brief, Dec. 6, 1906, p.757.

46. *The 1907 Great Smith Car*, p.10; and *Cycle and Automobile Trade Journal*, "The 'Great Smith' 1907 Touring Car," January 1907, p.102b.

47. Information about the 1907 Great Smith autos comes from *The 1907 Great Smith Car*, *Advance Sheet of 1907 Great Smith Car*, and *The Great Smith Car: Tenth Annual Catalog*, 1908, except where otherwise noted.

48. *Topeka Daily Capital*, "Best Automobile in Kansas Is Made in Topeka," Aug. 18, 1907, p.8.

49. MVMA, *Automobiles of America*, p.38; *Cycle and Automobile Trade Journal*, January 1907, p.102b; and *Topeka Daily Capital*, Aug. 18, 1907, p.8.

50. Smith, *Catalogue-Treatise*, vol.2, p.19, and vol.1, p.46; and *Instruction Book and Parts Price List, 1909–1910*, p.11.

51. Llewellyn Kiene, *In the Valley of the Kaw: An Account of a Little Journey in a Great Smith Automobile*, 1907.

52. *Advance Sheet of 1907 Great Smith Car*, unpaged.

53. *Topeka Daily Capital*, "Terry Stafford Buys the Mulvane Garage," July 17, 1908, p.10:4; and Milton F. Perry, "A Report on Harry S. Truman's Stafford Car, 7/8/74," 7 pp., held by the Harry S. Truman Library, Independence, Missouri.

54. *Automobile* ad, Nov. 7, 1907, p.129.

55. From *The Great Smith Car: Tenth Annual Catalog*, 1908.

56. An account of the race, and Mathewson's participation in it, can be found in Dermot Cole, *Hard Driving: The 1908 Auto Race from New York to Paris* (New York: Paragon House, 1991).

57. *Denver Post*, "10,000 See Mathewson Win Big Auto Race," May 31, 1908, p.1; *Motor Age*, "Denver Race Is Won by Thomas-Detroit," June 4, 1908, p.20; and *Topeka Daily Capital*, "Great Smith in Denver Race," June 2, 1908, p.7.

58. *Denver Post*, "20,000 People See a

Youngster Win 295 Mile Race," Sept. 8, 1908, p.11:1; and *Motor Age,* "Thomas Flyer Wins Road Race at Denver," Sept. 10, 1908, pp.4–5.

59. *San Diego Union,* "Great Auto Run Made by Renton," June 22, 1908, p.6:2; *Motor Field,* photo and cutline, August 1908, p.28; *San Diego Union,* "Finish Record Run with White," May 23, 1908, p.5:3; *San Diego Union,* "Round-Trip Record Is Broken by White Steamer," May 24, 1908, p.13:2; *San Francisco Call,* "Breaks a Road Record," Sept. 24, 1908, p.13:7; and *Motor Age,* "Another Rambler Record," Dec. 31, 1908, p.97:3.

60. *Lincoln Daily Star,* "Autos Again on Their Way," Sept. 22, 1909, p.7:1; *Motor Age,* "Big Field of Cars Start in Kansas' Reliability Run," Sept. 23, 1909, p.5:2; *Omaha World-Herald,* "Kansas City Autos Speed into Omaha," Sept. 23, 1909, p.2:3; and *Motor Age,* "Cadillac and Franklin Kansas City Winners," Sept. 30, 1909, p.15:2.

61. *"Pike's Peak or Bust" – But We Didn't Bust, We Climbed It in a Great Smith Car,* factory catalog based on a reprinted January 1909 *Motor Field* article, "At the Top."

62. *Scientific American,* unheadlined blurb about John Brisben Walker's Pikes Peak climb, Sept. 22, 1900, p.188:1; Ray Amundsen, *Horseless Carriage Gazette,* "Pike's Peak Conquered in 1901 by Locomobile Steamer," Winter 1952, pp.42–43; *Automobile,* "To the Summit of Zebulon Pike's Peak," Oct. 10, 1907, p.506:1; and *Motor Age,* "Brush Climbs Pike's Peak," Sept. 3, 1908, p.30:1, and "Brush Climbs the Peak," Sept. 17, 1908, p.9:3.

63. *Topeka Daily Capital,* "Great Smith Up Pikes Peak," Oct. 28, 1908, p.6.

64. The two sources for this section are a Smith factory booklet, *Six-Day Non-Stop Run Demonstrating the Dependability of the "Great Smith,"* 1910; and the *Dallas Daily Times Herald,* "Great Smith Stands Test," May 22, 1910, p.21.

65. *Topeka Daily Capital,* "100 Great Smith Cars Go to Lone Star State," May 15, 1910, p.29:1, and a blurb, no headline, on the Wyoming sale, p.29:3; and Alberta Wilson Constant, *Those Miller Girls!* (New York: Thomas Y. Crowell Company, 1965).

66. *Horseless Age,* item in "Minor Mention," Sept. 29, 1909, p.359; *Topeka State Journal,* "Big Auto Deal: Grand Rapids Capitalists Get Smith Company," Jan. 8, 1910; *Automobile,* brief, Jan. 13, 1910, p.138; *Motor Age,* "May Get Great Smith," Dec. 30, 1909, p.109:2; Kimes and Clark, *Standard Catalog,* 2d ed., p.1313; and Association of Licensed Automobile Manufacturers (A.L.A.M.), *Hand Book of Gasoline Automobiles,* 1911, "Smith Automobile Company," pp.272–73.

67. *Topeka State Journal,* "To Work 300 Men," Feb. 19, 1910, p.15, and "Receiver Named," Nov. 24, 1910; *Topeka Daily Capital,* "Receiver for the Smith Auto Co.," Nov. 25, 1910, p.12, "No Receiver for Smith Co.," Dec. 1, 1910, p.7, and "Appoint Receiver for Smith Auto Co.," Dec. 2, 1910, p.1.

68. *Topeka Daily Capital,* "Smith Co. Will Continue to Run," Dec. 3, 1910, p.10, and "Will Take Over Smith Auto Co.," Dec. 11, 1910, p.1; and *Motor Age,* "Smith Company Reorganized," Dec. 22, 1910, p.17:2.

69. *1911: The Great Smith,* unpaged.

70. *Motor Age,* "Smith Plant May Move," Sept. 21, 1911, p.40:2; *Motor World,* "Engraver Purchases Great Smith Plant," Jan. 11, 1912, p.289; *Topeka State Journal* ad, Feb. 17, 1912, p.5; *Automobile,* "The Westerner, a New Make," April 18, 1912, p.959:2; *Motor Age,* "Smith Plant for Sale," May 23, 1912, p.11:3; *Topeka Daily Capital,* "Smith Auto Plant Is Sold for $27,500," May 30, 1912, p.2; and *Automobile,* "Smith Automobile Plant Sold," Sept. 5, 1912, p.509:1.

71. *"Veracity" Automobiles, 1904,* p.1.

72. *Where Smith Automobiles Are Made,* p.6.

73. *Topeka Daily Capital,* Dec. 11, 1910, p.1.

74. *Motor Vehicle Register, 1905–1907,* for Nebraska, microfilm RG002 at Nebraska State Historical Society; William Kent, *Horseless Carriage Gazette,* "1914 Oregon Automobile Registration," July-August 1992, p.15; and *Automobile,* "21,826 Cars and Trucks in Colorado," July 22, 1915, p.172.

75. *Where Smith Automobiles Are Made,* p.12.

Chapter 2, Luverne of Minnesota

1. Information in this section and in the following section about the carriage business comes from several sources, including Arthur P. Rose, *An Illustrated History of the Counties of Rock and Pipestone, Minnesota* (Luverne, Minnesota: Northern History Publishing Company, 1911); Trygve M. Ager, *Minneapolis Tribune,* "'Big Brown Luverne' Makers Now Turn Out Fire ———— [Engines or Trucks]," Sept. 17, 1950; and an undated article from the *Rock County Star-Herald* (Luverne, Minnesota) titled "Leicher Bros. Who Teamed Up to Build Buggies, Now Make Fire Trucks Here/Men Who Started Building Buggies over 50 Years Ago Recall Early Day Vehicles." From this point on, I'll identify these sources in the text, where necessary, rather than through additional endnotes.

2. From author's interviews with Ann Hollaren, Sept. 5, 1991, and Sept. 25, 1991, and with Jim Leicher, Oct. 14, 1991, and Jan. 3, 1992. Their subsequent remarks come from these interviews.

3. *A Few Facts about Luverne Automobiles and the Company That Makes Them,* 1912. I will draw on this booklet again, as well as on five other pieces of factory literature: the 1907 automobile catalog; *1910 Luverne Automobiles,* full-line catalog; *Condensed Information Regarding Luverne Automobiles,* 1912, specifications booklet; *Detailed Description and Specifications of the 1913 Big Brown Luverne Four and Six Cylinder Motor Cars,* booklet; and *Important Information Regarding the Big Brown*

Luverne Six Cylinder Motor Cars, 1914, instruction manual.

4. Don Spavin, *St. Paul Pioneer Press Pioneer Pictorial* magazine, "Minnesota Auto Was Sensation in '14," March 15, 1953.

5. The *Rock County Herald* showed its keen interest in the automobile factory by writing frequent reports on the company's activities. In addition, the automaker began running weekly *Herald* ads in 1908. This has left a valuable historical trail but makes it impossible to cite the hundreds of articles and ads that I drew upon for this chapter. Hereafter I will indicate general sources – whether it is a *Herald* ad or an article – in the text and use endnotes only for additional information.

6. Letter to author from Chuck Rhoads, Nov. 3, 1992.

7. *Rock County Herald,* "Many New Cars Now Being Built by Luverne Automobile Co./Factory at Full Capacity," Feb. 28, 1908, p.1:6.

8. Harold E. Glover, *Antique Automobile,* "Minnesota's Big Brown Luverne," November-December 1969, p.27.

9. From articles about lamps in *Motor Age,* Dec. 30, 1909, pp.78–79; Feb. 10, 1910, pp.42–43; and Feb. 2, 1911, p.50.

10. Beverly Rae Kimes, *Automobile Quarterly,* "Wouldn't You Rather Be a Buick?" vol.7, no.1 (Summer 1968), p.84.

11. *Horseless Age,* "Ferro Eight-Cylinder V-Type Engine," Jan. 20, 1915, pp.97–98.

12. Victor W. Page, *The Modern Gasoline Automobile: Its Design, Construction, Maintenance and Repair* (New York: Norman W. Henley Publishing Company, 1913), pp.430–31.

13. *Worthington (Minnesota) Daily Globe,* "Luverne Car Factory Was Well Known," May 9, 1958.

14. *Motor Age,* "Building Four-Cylinder Power Plant," June 19, 1913, p.38; and *Automobile Trade Journal,* "The Luverne Electric Starting Unit Power Plant," November 1914, p.119.

15. A May 9, 1958, *Worthington (Minnesota) Daily Globe* article gives the speed roadster's bore and stroke as 7½ x 9 inches. That represents a piston displacement of more than 800 cubic inches, well over the 500-cubic-inch limit that was imposed in 1911 and lowered twice to stand at 300 cubic inches by 1915, Jim Hoggatt said in a letter to the author.

16. *Buffalo (New York) Commercial,* "Powerful New Automobile to Be Built Here," Nov. 6, 1919; article from an unidentified Buffalo, New York newspaper, "A New Buffalo Product," April 18, 1920; author's interview with Denyse Kraud, Jan. 2, 1992; Charles A. Balton, *Buffalo Commercial,* "The Car of Tomorrow," April 22, 1920; and a Charles A. Balton Engineering Corporation stock prospectus.

17. Thomas A. McPherson, *American Funeral Cars & Ambulances since 1900* (Glen Ellyn, Illinois: Crestline Publishing, 1973), p.33.

18. *Rock County Herald,* "Local Items" brief that summarizes the *Minneapolis Tribune* stories, Sept. 27, 1912, p.7:6.

19. Reprint of *Deadwood (South Dakota) Herald* article in *Rock County Herald* ad, Sept. 26, 1913, p.1:1.

20. *Belle Fourche (South Dakota) Post* article reprinted as a brief in "Local Items" section of *Rock County Herald,* Feb. 10, 1911, p.10:4.

21. Bill and Doris Whithorn, "Photo History of Chico Lodge," circa 1981, p.10.

22. *Rock County Herald,* "Luverne Cars Make Big Hit," Feb. 23, 1912, p.1:6; and *Minneapolis Sunday Tribune,* quoted in *Rock County Herald* ad, Feb. 13, 1914, p.1:1.

23. *Automobile,* "New Agencies Established during the Week," Nov. 28, 1912, p.1141; and William Kent, *Horseless Carriage Gazette,* "1914 Oregon Automobile Registration," July–August 1992, p.15.

Chapter 3, Patriot of Nebraska

1. This biographical information comes from newspaper articles, Lincoln city directories, interviews with descendants, a variety of records, and two unpublished autobiographies by Hebb's son, Grainger: "The Life of Arthur Grainger Hebb [Jr.]," January 1975, 5 pp., and pp.13–38 of a longer untitled autobiography. Subsequent Grainger Hebb comments are drawn either from these two autobiographies or from his letters dated July 5, 1986, and December 2, 1986, on the subject of Patriot trucks. The number of active accounts in Hebb's feed, grain, and fuel business comes from *Motorist,* "Home and History of the Patriot Truck," June 1919, p.36.

2. *Sunday State Journal,* Lincoln, "Romance in Auto Business/Lincoln Has Something of the Kind in the Rise of the A. G. Hebb Auto Company," April 8, 1917, p.7A of auto show number; and *Motorist,* June 1919, p.36.

3. *Lincoln Daily Star* ad, June 22, 1913, p.3.

4. *Sunday State Journal,* April 8, 1917, p.7A of auto show number.

5. *Sunday State Journal,* April 8, 1917, p.7A of auto show number.

6. Author's interview with F. Pace Woods, Sr., January 4, 1991.

7. Patriot Manufacturing Co., *Quality Patriot Bodies for Chevrolet,* a small catalog showing a line of Patriot bodies made especially for Chevrolet trucks and included as one section of a data book titled *Chevrolet Sales Data: A Hand Book of Sales Information for Chevrolet Salesmen,* published by Chevrolet Motor Company, 1925.

8. *Lincoln Sunday Star,* "Havelock to Get Big Auto Plant," Feb. 17, 1918, p.10; and *Havelock Post,* "Havelock Secures Location for Large Auto Truck Factory," Feb. 14, 1918, p.1:5.

9. *Lincoln Trade Review,* "Business and Trade News," Feb. 16, 1918, p.4; and *Lincoln Sunday Star,* "New Hebb Factory

Now in Operation," Sept. 1, 1918, p.11.

10. *Havelock Post* ad, April 11, 1918, p.5.

11. Author's interviews with Charles William Jones, Feb. 1, 1991, and April 4, 1991. Subsequent information attributed to Bill Jones also comes from these interviews.

12. *Lincoln Sunday Star* ad, Feb. 17, 1918, p.11; *Havelock Post* ad, April 11, 1918, p.5; and *Lincoln Sunday Star* ad, March 3, 1918, p.11.

13. Much of the biographical information in this section comes from a file at the Nebraska State Historical Society, RG13, #951, "Bureau of Securities – Patriot Motor Co. – Advertising," and from the *Havelock Post*, "Prof. L. R. [*sic*] Seaton Joins Hebb Company," Aug. 21, 1919, p.1.

14. *Lincoln Sunday Star* ads, April 7, 1918, p.9, and April 14, 1918, p.10.

15. Letter to the author from Lillis Grassmick, manager-curator of the North Platte Valley Historical Association, Gering, Nebraska, Jan. 10, 1991.

16. *Sunday State Journal*, "New Auto Factory at Havelock," May 12, 1918, p.13B; and *Havelock Post*, Aug. 21, 1919, p.1.

17. *Motor World* ad, Oct. 2, 1918, p.83; and *Commercial Car Journal* ad, June 15, 1918, p.151.

18. *Commercial Car Journal* ad, June 15, 1918, p.151.

19. Item titled "Former Factories of the 'Hebb Quality Bodies'" in collection RG13, #951, Nebraska State Historical Society.

20. "Machine Shop Department," 3-page document in RG13, #951, Nebraska State Historical Society.

21. *Havelock Post*, Feb. 14, 1918, p.1:5; ad, April 11, 1918, p.5; and "Havelock Wants Big Tractor Meet," Feb. 14, 1918, p.1.

22. *Lincoln Sunday Star* ad, Feb. 17, 1918, p.11; *Lincoln Trade Review* ad, March 16, 1918, p.7; *Sunday State Journal*, May 12, 1918, p.13B; and *Lincoln Trade Review*

ads, April 27, 1918, p.15, Aug. 31, 1918, p.1, and Sept. 30, 1918, p.7.

23. *Lincoln Trade Review*, "Business and Trade News," Aug. 3, 1918, p.5.

24. *Lincoln Trade Review*, "Business and Trade News," Sept. 14, 1918, p.5.

25. Specifications – from sources too numerous to cite individually – come from articles and ads in local newspapers and national trade journals, annual specifications issues of *Automobile Industries* and other journals, and annual reference guides.

26. James A. Wren and Genevieve J. Wren, *Motor Trucks of America: Milestones, Pioneers, Roll Call, Highlights* (Ann Arbor, Michigan: University of Michigan Press, 1970), pp.85, 87.

27. *Patriot Trucks: Three Popular Sizes* and *Patriot Farm Trucks*, undated Patriot Motors sales folders, collection RG13, #951, Nebraska State Historical Society.

28. *Lincoln Sunday Star*, "Trucks Enable Cut in Hauling Cost to Farmer," Aug. 31, 1919, p.4 of "Ship by Truck" special section.

29. *Havelock Post*, "Havelock Fire Truck to Be a Fair Exhibit" and "New Consolidated School Districts May Use Modern Transportation Vehicles," Aug. 28, 1919, p.1.

30. Hebb Motors Company, *A Little Journey to the Home of Patriot Trucks* (Lincoln, Nebraska: 1919).

31. Hebb Motors in 1918 "merged" with the E. Children Sons Manufacturing Company of Council Bluffs, makers of "the famous Badger Cultivator" and other agricultural equipment, according to an undated article in a "Council Bluffs Business and Industry" vertical file at the Council Bluffs Public Library. Hebb Motors, which actually owned a 95 percent interest in the Council Bluffs company, renamed Badger Manufacturing, would later buy it outright.

32. The 1919 softbound picture book, *A Little Journey to the Home of Patriot Trucks*, describes a 200-ton press; but an early

1920 company tool inventory lists the largest press as having a 20-ton capacity.

33. *Motor World*, "Patriot Trucks Made in Two Models," Nov. 27, 1918, p.29.

34. Motor Vehicle Manufacturers Association (hereafter MVMA), *Automobiles of America: Milestones, Pioneers, Roll Call, Highlights*, 4th ed. (Detroit: Wayne State University Press, 1974), p.72.

35. *Lincoln Sunday Star*, "Trucks Enable Cut in Hauling Cost to Farmer," Aug. 31, 1919, p.4 of "Ship by Truck" special section.

36. Author's interview with Aaron Johnson, Dec. 6, 1991.

37. W. E. de B. Whittaker and P. A. Barron, *Automobiles of the World: An Encyclopedia of the Car* (London: The Aeroplane and General Publishing Co., 1921).

38. Wren and Wren, *Motor Trucks of America*, p.80.

39. Author's interview with Isabelle Lampshire, Dec. 5, 1990. Later comments attributed to her are also from this interview.

40. *Lincoln Trade Review* ad, April 27, 1918, p.15; and *Motor Age* ad, Jan. 23, 1919, p.280.

41. *Lincoln Daily Star*, "Hebb Announces a New Truck/Engineers Worked Hard and Long on New Three-Quarter Ton Product," Aug. 31, 1919, p.6 of "Ship by Truck" special section.

42. *Havelock Post*, "Orders Booked for 3000 Patriot Trucks," Jan. 30, 1919, p.1; "Details of Good Will Values," financial spreadsheet, and document giving biographical information about company officials, both in collection RG13, #951, Nebraska State Historical Society; and a Patriot promotional piece, Nebraska State Historical Society.

43. "Details of Good Will Values," RG13, #951, Nebraska State Historical Society.

44. Manufacturer's letter to stockholders, May 8, 1920, and letter from motor-company attorney Fred C. Foster to the Nebraska Bureau of Securities, March 15, 1920, both in RG13, #951,

Nebraska State Historical Society.

45. "Exhibit T," company financial documents, filed in RG13, #951, Nebraska State Historical Society.

46. *Motor Age* ad, Dec. 25, 1919, p.82.

47. *Literary Digest* ad, March 6, 1920, p.74.

48. These testimonials are from a variety of company ads, promotional pieces, and newspaper articles, 1919 and 1920.

49. *Patriot Performance*, undated Patriot Motors Company sales catalog, in MS3733, Standard Securities Corporation, Nebraska State Historical Society.

50. From numerous local newspaper articles; author's interviews with Charles William Jones, Jan. 30, 1991, and April 4, 1991; and Charles William Jones, *The History of the Standard J-1 Airplanes from 1919 through 1922 at Lincoln, Nebraska*, 5 pp.

51. From a dozen *New York Times* articles, including "Kansas Banks Burdened," Nov. 16, 1920, p.1:2; "Farmers' Union Urges Strike by Producers," Nov. 19, 1920, p.18:1; "1,085 Failures Set November Record," Dec. 4, 1920, p.18:8; "Surplus of Labor Not Serious Yet," Dec. 5, 1920, sec. 2, p.1:6; "More Idle Men in Detroit," Dec. 7, 1920, p.2:5; "Billions Tied Up by Cancellations," Dec. 23, 1920, p.22:2; and "Ford Motor Plant to Stay Shut Another Month," Dec. 29, 1920, p.15:4.

52. The Patriot Motors letters quoted in the next few paragraphs are part of collection MS3733, Standard Securities Corporation, Nebraska State Historical Society.

53. MVMA, *Automobiles of America*, p.72.

54. *Lincoln Star*, "County Slashes Assessment of Havelock Plant," July 18, 1921, p.1.

55. *Havelock Post*, "Referee Confirms Sale Hebb-Patriot Motor Co.," June 30, 1921, p.1.

56. *Lincoln Sunday Star*, "New Corporation to Make Patriot Trucks Is Formed," Aug. 7, 1921, p.1.

57. *Lincoln Sunday Star*, "Patriot Sales Record Advance," April 8, 1923, p.2 of autoshow special section.

58. Letter to author from Kenneth Latimer, Jan. 7, 1987.

59. Author's interview with Betty Witham, Dec. 28, 1990.

60. Author's interview with Marion Garcia in late November 1990.

61. *Lincoln Trade Review* ad, April 17, 1920, pp.12–13.

62. "Investors: The Last of the Issue of Hebb Motors Co.," undated Standard Securities Corporation newspaper ad, in collection RG13, #951, Nebraska State Historical Society.

Chapter 4, Spaulding of Iowa

1. Much of the biographical information for this section comes from *The History of Poweshiek County, Iowa* (Des Moines: Union Historical Company, 1880), p.927; an untitled article from an unidentified Grinnell newspaper, Aug. 18, 1881, Spaulding clip files, Grinnell Historical Museum; *Grinnell Herald*, "Senator Spaulding As Others See Him," Feb. 10, 1911, p.2:4, reprint of a *Des Moines Tribune* "Little Jaunts to the Statehouse" column; *Grinnell Herald*, "Grinnell's Foremost and Most Constructive Builder," Nov. 24, 1931, p.3:3; *Des Moines Tribune*, "Illness Fatal to Spaulding," Jan. 21, 1937; *Grinnell Herald-Register*, "'There Were Giants in Those Days': Senator Henry W. Spaulding, One of the Builders of Grinnell, Passes Away at the Ripe Old Age of Ninety Years," Jan. 21, 1937, p.1:8; *Annals of Iowa*, vol.20, no.8, Third Series (April 1937), p.636; and Grinnell Herald-Register, *Grinnell – A Century of Progress* (Grinnell, Iowa: Grinnell Herald-Register, July 1954), pp.84–85.

2. Author's interview with Miriam Spaulding Simms, Oct. 11, 1991. Her subsequent comments are from this interview.

3. *Grinnell Herald* "Spaulding Mfg. Co. May Make Autos," June 11, 1909, and "Spaulding's Auto Plans Progressing," Aug. 17, 1909; and "Correspondence, Motor Vehicles," SVI 224, collection at the State Historical Society of Iowa, Des Moines.

4. *Grinnell Herald* "Spauldings Busy on Auto Plant," Oct. 5, 1909, and "Work Is Resumed on Auto Factory," Jan. 25, 1910, p.1:1. A November 1911 Sanborn fire-insurance map disagrees with the Jan. 25, 1910, article on the location of the various motorcar departments. The accounts agree that cars were painted on the third floor, but the Sanborn map says autos were assembled on the second floor and stored on the first, while the *Grinnell Herald* article says the opposite.

5. *Grinnell Herald*, "Glidden Tour Path Finder in City," April 5, 1910, p.1:7.

6. Information about specifications, testing, and other activity relating to 1910 Spaulding cars is from *Grinnell Herald*, Oct. 5, 1909; *Grinnell Herald*, "Grinnell's Newest Industry," April 15, 1910, p.1:3; unnamed Grinnell newspaper, untitled brief, May 17, 1910, Spaulding clip files, Grinnell Historical Museum; *Motor Print*, "The Spaulding 'Thirty,'" June 1910, p.24; *Grinnell Herald*, "First Finished Spaulding Car Makes Its Debut," June 10, 1910, p.2:5; *Register and Leader*, "New Iowa Car Built in an Attractive Style," June 26, 1910, p.3:2 of society-automobile section; *Grinnell Herald*, "An Open Letter to the People of Grinnell and Vicinity," June 27, 1911, p.2:4; and *Model 'H' Spaulding*, 1914 factory catalog.

7. Alice Huyler Ramsey, *Veil, Duster, and Tire Iron* (Pasadena, California: Castle Press, 1961), pp.50, 55.

8. Articles about the new factory and its employment levels are from *Grinnell Herald*, "Excavation at Spaulding Plant," Aug. 5, 1910, p.2:3, and "Spaulding Motor Cars Are Popular," Dec. 24, 1912,

p.1:4; and *Grinnell Herald-Register*, "The Story of a Pioneer Enterprise," Sept. 10, 1936.

9. *Grinnell Herald*, "Sen. Spaulding Is Placed on Good Committees," Jan. 13, 1911, p.2:2.

10. *Grinnell Herald*, "Terribly Hurt in Auto Accident," Aug. 26, 1910, p.1:4, "Italian Hurt in Auto Accident Is Doing Well," Aug. 30, 1910, p.2:2, "Spaulding Tester Narrowly Escapes," Dec. 30, 1910, p.2:3; and *Grinnell Register*, "Another Auto Turns Over," Jan. 2, 1911.

11. *Grinnell Herald*, "Spauldings Strong at the Auto Show," March 7, 1911, p.1:6.

12. *Des Moines Register and Leader* ad, Feb. 26, 1911, p.2:3 of "Automobile Number"; and *Grinnell Herald*, "Governor Carroll Is to Drive a Spaulding Auto," March 28, 1911, p.3:5.

13. Unidentified Grinnell newspaper, untitled brief, May 11, 1911, from Spaulding clip files, Grinnell Historical Museum; and *Grinnell Herald*, 'Will Travel in Spaulding Car," May 16, 1911, p.1:4, "Spaulding Car Starts on Journey," May 23, 1911, p.1:7, and "Spaulding Car Home from Trip," May 31, 1911, p.2:6.

14. *Grinnell Herald*, "Spaulding Car Will Take Part in Little Glidden," June 6, 1911, p.1:6, "Little Glidden Tour Comes Monday/Two Spaulding Cars Are in the Lists," June 16, 1911, p.2:2, "Little Glidden Tourists Pass," June 20, 1911, p.1:3, "Spaulding Car Has Perfect Score on Road," June 23, 1911, p.2:5; and *Des Moines Register and Leader*, "Little Glidden a Great Success," June 25, 1911, p.6:1.

15. *Grinnell Herald*, "Spaulding Factory Stays Right Here," Oct. 31, 1911, p.2:2.

16. *Grinnell Herald*, "Are Logging Trans-Continental Route," Oct. 10, 1911, p.2:4.

17. *Grinnell Herald*, "Spaulding Auto Factory Is Busy," Jan. 16, 1912, p.2:4.

18. *Grinnell Herald*, "Will Make 1–2 Ton Motor Trucks," April 26, 1912, p.1:5, "1913 Spaulding Forty," Aug. 30, 1912, p.1:6, and "Denver Autoists Find a Friendly Greeting Here," July 2, 1912, p.2:3.

19. Letter to author from William Lewis, who had research assistance in California from Jeff Minard and Jim Valentine, Jan. 6, 1992.

20. Lewis Culler letter in Collection SP286, Spaulding Manufacturing Company Correspondence, State Historical Society of Iowa, Des Moines; and *Grinnell Herald*, "To Log the River to River Road . . . Spaulding Car Receives Endorsement from California," Jan. 30, 1914, p.1:3.

21. *Grinnell Herald*, Aug. 30, 1912, and Dec. 24, 1912.

22. Most of the technical information about the 1913 models comes from *Automobile*, "Spaulding – Drops Small Model," Jan. 9, 1913, p.135; *Grinnell Herald*, Aug. 30, 1912; and *Grinnell Herald* ad, Feb. 14, 1913, p.4:5.

23. *Grinnell Herald*, Aug. 30, 1912, and Dec. 24, 1912; and *Automobile Trade Journal*, "Spaulding Gasoline Commercial Cars," March 1913, p.265.

24. *Grinnell Herald*, "Spaulding '40' Undergoes Hill Climbing Test," Feb. 21, 1913, p.1:5, reprint of *Los Angeles Evening Herald* article.

25. These sources provided information about the transcontinental Spaulding: *Grinnell Herald*, "Spaulding for Trip across Continent," Aug. 5, 1913; *San Diego Union*, "Autoists to Boost Exposition and National Road," Aug. 9, 1913, p.11:1, "Auto Trip to Gotham Will Advertise Fair," Aug. 15, 1913, p.2:2, "1915 Auto Party Warmly Welcomed," Aug. 21, 1913, p.5:2; *Grinnell Herald*, "After Auto Route to Big Exposition," Sept. 12, 1913, and "More Good Words for Spaulding Car," Sept. 30, 1913; *Automobile*, "Many Entries for Los Angeles–Phoenix," Oct. 23, 1913, p.796:1; *Grinnell Herald*, "The Transcontinental Spaul-ding," photo and cutline, Nov. 14, 1913, p.2:4, and "Through Snow As If on Paving/Spaulding Trans-Continental Car Triumphs over Hard Sledding in the East," Nov. 21, 1913; 1914 Spaulding catalog; "Correspondence, Motor Vehicles SVI 224," State Historical Society of Iowa, Des Moines; and undated clipping of a letter by R. P. Cooper, from a Grinnell newspaper, Spaulding clip files, Grinnell Historical Museum.

26. The following are among my sources of information for the Spaulding Sleeper car: *Grinnell Herald*, "Spaulding 'Sleeper' at the State Fair," Aug. 15, 1913, p.1:6; *Automobile Trade Journal*, "Pullman Sleeping Car on Wheels," November 1913, p.136; *Des Moines Register and Leader*, "Feature Tourist Sleeper Model/Spaulding Factory Builds Iowa Car of Special Interest to Autoists," March 8, 1914, p.4:1 of auto-show edition; *Des Moines Register and Leader* ad, March 8, 1914, p.4:3 of auto-show edition; *Automobile*, "Wants Hunting Body with Bed," July 16, 1914, p.125; *Grinnell Herald*, "Spaulding 'Sleepers' Prove Popular; Twenty-Five Sold on Contract," July 13, 1915, p.1:4; *Grinnell Herald* ads from March 26, 1915, March 30, 1915, April 9, 1915, April 13, 1915, April 16, 1915, June 15, 1915, and June 18, 1915; 1914 Spaulding catalog; and Collection SP286, Spaulding Manufacturing Company Correspondence, State Historical Society of Iowa, Des Moines.

27. Articles about the race include *Des Moines Register and Leader*, "Cross-State Race Boost for Roads," March 2, 1913, p.12:1 of auto-show number; *Grinnell Herald*, "Spaulding Racer Is after the Record," Oct. 10, 1913, p.1:1, "Spaulding Racer after the Record," Oct. 14, 1913, p.2:2, "Mud Drives Back Spaulding Racer," Oct. 17, 1913, p.1:1, and "Hal Wells Likes the Spaulding Car," Oct. 24, 1913, p.2:3; *Davenport Democrat and Leader*, "Wells Again Makes Dash

across State," Nov. 14, 1913, p.15:2; *Des Moines Capital*, "Hall Wells Is Dashing across Iowa to Break Trans State Auto Record," Nov. 14, 1913, p.1:1; *Des Moines Evening Tribune*, "Through Des Moines at Top Speed," Nov. 14, 1913, p.1:1; *Grinnell Herald*, "Spaulding Racer Makes Trial Today," Nov. 14, 1913, p.2:5; *Newton Daily Journal*, "They Sure Were Going Some," Nov. 14, 1913, p.1:3; *Council Bluffs Nonpareil*, "Wells Establishes New Cross State Road Record," Nov. 15, 1913, p.1:6; *Davenport Daily Times*, "Wells Sets New Road Record," Nov. 15, 1913, p.10:3; *Des Moines Capital*, "M'Clure Undecided Whether He Will Try for New Mark" and "Wells' Fast Race," Nov. 15, 1913, p.1:5; *Des Moines Register and Leader*, "Wells Makes New Cross State Time," Nov. 15, 1913, p.1:1; *Newton Daily Journal*, "Hal Wells Makes Record Trip across the State," Nov. 15, 1913, p.1:3; *Davenport Democrat and Leader*, "Breaks Record in Run across State," Nov. 16, 1913, p.17:1; *Newton Daily Journal*, "E. H. Maytag Holds Record from Newton to Des Moines," Nov. 17, 1913, p.1:3; *Grinnell Herald*, "Hal Wells Makes a Great Run," Nov. 18, 1913, p.1:4; *Marengo Republican*, "Makes New R. to R. Record," Nov. 19, 1913, p.1; *Altoona Herald*, "Makes New Auto Record," Nov. 20, 1913, p.1:4; *Grinnell Herald*, "How the Spaulding Set World's Record," Jan. 30, 1914, p.1:4, partial reprint of December 1914 *Motorist* article; and Collection SP286, Spaulding Manufacturing Company Correspondence, State Historical Society of Iowa, Des Moines.

28. Beverly Rae Kimes and Henry Austin Clark, Jr., *Standard Catalog of American Cars, 1805–1942*, 2d ed. (Iola, Wisconsin: Krause Publications, 1989), p.1479; and *Des Moines Register and Leader*, "Wells Cuts Chicago Mark," July 23, 1911, p.3:1 of automobile section.

29. *Des Moines Register and Leader*, "Ditched on the Last Lap," photo and cutline,

June 25, 1911, p.6:2 of automobile section.

30. Kimes and Clark, *Standard Catalog of American Cars*, p.795.

31. *Grinnell Herald*, "Belle Plaine Editor Speaks Well of R. to R. Road," Aug. 20, 1912, p.1:8; and *Automobile*, "The Record of a Transcontinental Trek – II," Feb. 22, 1912, John Guy Monihan, p.531:2.

32. *Motor Age*, "Builds an Unusual Touring Car," Oct. 15, 1914, p.32; *Automobile*, "Unique Car Built by Iowan," Oct. 29, 1914; and *Grinnell Herald*, "Wells Breaks Record," Oct. 13, 1916, p.2:5.

33. *Grinnell Herald*, "Road Drag Drawn by Automobiles," Feb. 13, 1914, p.1:1.

34. *Automobile*, "Spaulding Radically Refines Bodies," Jan. 1, 1914, p.81; 1914 Spaulding catalog; and *MoTor*, "The Spaulding 'Forty,'" December 1913, p.87.

35. *Grinnell Herald*, "19.6 Miles on One Gallon of Gasoline/Affidavit," July 23, 1915, p.3:5; and *Automobile*, "Spaulding Has Special Body," Dec. 30, 1915, p.1192.

36. John B. Rae, "Why Michigan," in *The Automobile and American Culture*, edited by David L. Lewis and Laurence Goldstein (Ann Arbor: University of Michigan Press, 1983), p.4.

37. 1914 Spaulding catalog.

38. *Grinnell Herald*, "Autos Crash near Bear Creek Bridge," July 7, 1914, p.1:5.

39. *Grinnell Herald* ad, Aug. 27, 1915, p.2:1; and *Des Moines Register* ad, Jan. 16, 1916.

40. *Grinnell Herald*, brief, July 23, 1915, p.3:6.

41. *Grinnell Herald*, "Spaulding Manufacturing Company Is Putting New Machine on the Market," March 31, 1916, p.1:2.

42. Unidentified Grinnell newspaper articles, "Work Now Booming," July 16, 1920, "Orders for Truck Bodies Coming In," April 18, 1924, and "Ford to Grinnell/Spaulding Manufacturing Co. Get

Large Contract to Build Stake Bodies," July 23, 1925; all from Spaulding clip files, Grinnell Historical Museum.

43. Unidentified Grinnell newspaper articles, "Bus Factory Starts Nov. 15," Sept. 3, 1929, "Plans Complete for Manufacture of Funeral Coach," Oct. 25, 1929, and "Eggleston Co. Brings Families to Grinnell," Nov. 19, 1929; all from Spaulding clip files, Grinnell Historical Museum.

44. *Grinnell Herald* ad, Aug. 27, 1915, p.2:1; and clipping from unidentified newspaper, "The Spaulding Car Was Once Manufactured in Grinnell," photo and cutline, Aug. 23, 1949, Spaulding clip files, Grinnell Historical Museum.

Chapter 5, Moon of Missouri

1. *Saturday Evening Post* ad, March 29, 1924, p.120.

2. *Automobile*, "Explaining the Patronym of the Moon," April 16, 1908, p.553.

3. *St. Louis Globe-Democrat Sunday Magazine*, "Of Moons and Dachshunds: The Early St. Louis Cars," July 17, 1977; *St. Louis Globe-Democrat*, "Joseph W. Moon, Motor Car Company President, Is Dead," Feb. 12, 1919, p.1:4; and Carl W. Burst III and Andrew D. Young, *Automobile Quarterly*, "The Moon in All Its Phases," vol.25, no.4 (1987), p.396.

4. *Motor Way*, item in "The Industrial Side" column, Aug. 3, 1905, p.21; and *Horseless Age*, entry in "Minor Mention" column, Oct. 4, 1905, p.405.

5. Burst and Young, "The Moon," p.396; and *Cycle and Automobile Trade Journal*, "Moon 1906 Model A," January 1906, p.97.

6. *Automobile* ad, Nov. 9, 1911, inside front cover; and *St. Louis Post-Dispatch*, "Moon Cars Shipped to Far Off Denmark," Feb. 6, 1916, p.3S:3.

7. Office of the St. Louis Assessor of Revenue, *St. Louis Taxpayers' Directory* (St. Louis: 1900).

8. *MoTor* ad, October 1910, p.56; *Auto-*

mobile ad, Oct. 12, 1911, inside front cover; *Automobile* ad, May 25, 1912, inside front cover; and *MoTor* ad, October 1912, p.139.

9. Jan Norbye, *Automobile Quarterly*, "Survey of the Gasoline Engine," vol.5, no.1 (Summer 1966), pp.87–88.

10. *Automobile* ad, April 11, 1907, p.106.

11. *Cycle and Automobile Trade Journal*, "The Moon Model C Touring Car," May 1907, pp.69–70.

12. *Auto Review*, "Three Models of Moon Cars for 1908," March 1908, p.44; and *Motor Age*, "Motor Car Development," March 28, 1907, p.12.

13. *New York Times*, "Auto Race to Paris to Start Feb. 15," [but actually started Feb. 12], Dec. 21, 1907, p.1:5; and *New York Times*, "Believe American Will Win Big Race," Jan. 26, 1908, sec. 1, p.1:1.

14. Dermot Cole, *Hard Driving: The 1908 Auto Race from New York to Paris* (New York: Paragon House, 1991), p.21.

15. *Cycle and Automobile Trade Journal* ad, January 1908, p.53.

16. *Motor Age*, "Progress of Munsey Historic Tour," Aug. 25, 1910, pp.10–11, and "Maxwell Declared Munsey Tour Winner," Sept. 1, 1910, pp.20–23.

17. *Motor Age*, "Glidden Scouts Busy," Feb. 11, 1909, p.41:1; and Moon ad in *Official Program: Third Annual Automobile Show, March 8 to 14, 1909, Convention Hall, Kansas City, Mo.*, p.42.

18. *Omaha Daily News* ad for Sweet-Edwards Automobile Co., March 27, 1910, p.7D:5; and numerous articles in *Motor Age*: "Non-Motor Stop Run," April 7, 1910, p.31:1, "Algonquin Climb Proves True Hill Test," Sept. 22, 1910, pp.1–7, "Table Showing Relative Time Standing Morning, Afternoon and Finish in Algonquin Climb," June 15, 1911, p.8, "Cherry Circle Again Wins Team Match," June 22, 1911, p.6:1, "Sensational Reliability in California," Dec. 1, 1910, p.5:1, "Sioux City Results," Oct. 20, 1910, p.10:1, "Kansas City Results," Oct. 20, 1910, p.10:2, and "Three Days

of Racing at Dallas," Nov. 3, 1910, p.14:1.

19. *Auto Review*, "Made 55 Miles in 'Junk Pile,'" September 1917, p.16.

20. *Cycle and Automobile Trade Journal* ad, January 1908, p.53; and Beverly Rae Kimes and Henry Austin Clark, Jr., *Standard Catalog of American Cars, 1805–1942*, 2d ed. (Iola, Wisconsin: Krause Publications, 1989), p.682.

21. *Auto Review*, brief, December 1907, p.27, and "Three Models of Moon Cars for 1908," March 1908, p.44.

22. *Auto Review*, "Hol-Tan Car Makes Successful Test in Using Benzol for Fuel," January 1908, p.20.

23. North St. Louis Business Mens Association, *Who's Who in North St. Louis* (St. Louis: 1925), p.168.

24. *Motor World*, "Moon Made Company Engineer," March 5, 1925, p.38.

25. Burst and Young, "The Moon," p.402.

26. George S. May, "Moon Motor Car Company," in *The Automobile Industry, 1896–1920*, edited by George S. May (New York: Facts on File, 1990), p.337; G. N. Georgano, ed., *The Complete Encyclopedia of Motorcars, 1885 to the Present*, 2d ed. (New York: E. P. Dutton, 1973), p.494; Hank Wieand Bowman, *Motor Trend*, "New Light on the Moon," December 1953, p.25; Kimes and Clark, *Standard Catalog*, p.953; and Harry Hastings, *Western Collector*, "Saga of the Moon," October 1963, p.4.

27. *Horseless Age*, "Minor Mention," Dec. 9, 1908, p.850.

28. Motor Vehicle Manufacturers Association (MVMA), *Automobiles of America: Milestones, Pioneers, Roll Call, Highlights*, 4th ed. (Detroit: Wayne State University Press, 1974), p.54; *Automobile*, "Explosive Gas Starters," Jan. 4, 1912, p.33; and *Automobile*, "Moon Adds a Six to Its Line for 1913," Sept. 26, 1912, p.630.

29. MVMA, *Automobiles of America*, p.70.

30. *17 Individual Features*, 1920, Moon factory catalog; and *Horseless Age*, "A Comparison of Foreign and American Cars at

the Show," Dec. 19, 1906, p.887.

31. *Automobile* ad, Feb. 29, 1912, inside front cover; and *Automobile*, Sept. 26, 1912, p.631.

32. *Horseless Age*, "Descriptions of New Vehicles and Parts," Feb. 23, 1910, p.297; *The Moon Motor Car*, 1910, factory catalog; and MVMA, *Automobiles of America*, p.67.

33. *Horseless Age*, "To Build Convertible Bodies," Jan. 21, 1914, p.102; and *Saturday Evening Post* ad, July 8, 1916, p.40.

34. *Automobile* ad, June 29, 1916, p.92.

35. *Automotive Industries*, "Moon Develops Sedan for Its 6-40 Model," June 15, 1922, p.1354; and *Automobile Journal*, "The Moon Sedan," February 1923, p.26.

36. *Automobile Trade Journal*, "News of the Trade in Brief," March 1924, p.94; *Auto Review*, "Moon Sales Indicate Strong Winter Demand," November 1923, p.16; and Burst and Young, "The Moon," p.408.

37. Rolland Jerry, *Automobile Quarterly*, "The Fabric Body and How It Flexed," vol.14, no.3 (1976), p.311; and *Automobile Topics*, "Flexible Body Is a Moon Coach Feature," Aug. 13, 1927, p.25.

38. I culled information on colors and upholstery from scores of articles, ads, automobile guides, and factory literature – too many to cite specifically. Sources include articles and ads in *Auto Review*, *Automobile*, *Automobile Manufacturer*, *Automobile Topics*, *Horseless Age*, *Motor Age*, *Motor World*, *Saturday Evening Post*, and *Vanity Fair*.

39. *Auto Review*, "Moon's New Light Car," September 1917, p.2; and *Motor Age* ad, Aug. 5, 1926, p.65.

40. *Motor Age* ad, Dec. 5, 1907, p.223; *Motor Life* ad, May 1920, p.22; *Saturday Evening Post* ad, April 25, 1925, p.212; and *Motor Age* ad, Aug. 5, 1926, p.65.

41. Information for this section about Moon trucks came from *Auto Review*, July 1911, p.38, October 1912, p.23, November 1912, pp.31–32, December 1912, p.28, and January 1913, p.29; *Mo-*

tor Age, Oct. 3, 1912, p.36, Feb. 13, 1913, p.26, and Sept. 26, 1918, p.33; *Automobile Trade Journal,* March 1913, pp.255 and 387, and a July 1913 ad, p.307; and the St. Louis Chamber of Commerce *Bulletin,* "St. Louis Growing As 'Auto' Manufacturing Center," Oct. 1, 1917, p.3.

42. *Auto Review,* "News from Manufacturers," February 1912, p.100.

43. Moon slogans were drawn from 1906–1929 ads and factory literature.

44. *Auto Review,* "Latest St. Louis News," April 1908, p.33; and *Automobile* ad, April 16, 1908, p.99.

45. *New England Auto List and Tourist Containing Complete List of All Automobiles* (Boston: Auto List Publishing Co., 1913); *Automobile,* "37,990 Michigan Licenses in 2 Months," April 8, 1915, p.633:1; *Connecticut Motor Register* (Hartford, Connecticut: State Publishing Co., June 1915); *Automobile,* "21,826 Cars and Trucks in Colorado," July 22, 1915, p.172; and J. H. Valentine, *SAH Journal* (Society of Automotive Historians), "What Vermonters Drove in 1918," November–December 1992, p.7.

46. Kimes and Clark, *Standard Catalog,* p.66; Michael G. H. Scott, *Old Cars News & Marketplace,* "1936 Auburn Model 852: Cord Shot the Moon," Aug. 29, 1991, p.5; and *Auto Review,* "Six-Cylinder Types" (feature on Lewis), March 1913, p.29.

47. *Auto Review,* "Moon Distributors in Convention," December 1923, p.10; and *Automobile Trade Journal,* "Moon Records Real Achievement," May 1924, p.50.

48. *New York Times,* "Moon Alters Sales Plan," Jan. 5, 1926, p.42:3; *Automotive Industries,* "Moon Co. Acquires Quinlan Motors Co.," Jan. 14, 1926, p.78, and "Moon Closes Out Factory Branches," May 28, 1927, p.821.

49. Ad titled "Moon Popularity in the East," magazine title and date unknown; *Saturday Evening Post* ad, Feb. 21, 1925, p.135; and *Automobile Trade Journal* ad, November 1924, p.57.

50. *Automobile,* brief, July 1, 1909, p.36; *Motor Age,* "Outlook Seen through St. Louis Eyes," May 14, 1914, p.23; *Automobile* ad, Dec. 30, 1915, p.259; and *St. Louis Post-Dispatch,* "1919 Moon Feature on Victory Light 6," Feb. 16, 1919, sec. 4, p.5B:3.

51. *Auto Review,* "Latest St. Louis News," January 1908, p.39.

52. *Auto Review,* brief, February 1912, p.39, brief, January 1913, p.40, and brief, February 1916, p.26; *New York Times,* "Germans Order 42 Autos Here," March 28, 1924, p.25:8; and *Roadsters for 1929: Moon-Aerotype,* factory catalog.

53. *St. Louis Globe-Democrat,* "Moon Motor Ships Car to Europe without Cratings," March 13, 1927; and *New York Times* "Motor Cars Are Being Shipped Abroad on Their Own Wheels," Dec. 18, 1927, sec. 9, p.17:1, and "550 Uncrated Autos Shipped; Make Up Ship's Entire Cargo," Dec. 30, 1927, p.39:2.

54. *Automobile,* photo and cutline, Oct. 6, 1910, p.569; *American Machinist,* "Moon Motor Car Jigs and Fixtures," Feb. 29, 1912, pp.330–32; and *Automobile,* Sept. 26, 1912, pp.628–29.

55. Maurice D. Hendry, *Automobile Quarterly,* "Thomas!" vol.8, no.4 (Summer 1970), p.432; *Auto Review,* brief, May 1913, p.17; *Moon Cars 1913,* factory catalog; and William J. Muller, *Automobile Quarterly,* "Do I Remember the Ruxton? Boy, Do I Remember the Ruxton!" vol.8, no.2 (Fall 1969), p.195.

56. *17 Individual Features,* 1920 factory catalog.

57. *Motor Age,* "Moon's New Testing System," Dec. 26, 1912, p.47.

58. *Motor Age,* "Testing Motor Tops," Jan. 16, 1913, p.76; and *Motor Print,* brief, February 1913, p.56.

59. *Automobile,* "New Moon Uses 1 Gallon Fuel Each 21 Miles," Aug. 13, 1914, p.333; and *Saturday Evening Post* ad, March 29, 1924, p.121.

60. *Motor Age,* "Jubilee Moon Six-Sixty," Aug. 5, 1926, p.19.

61. *Auto Review,* "Moon's New Light Car," September 1917, p.2; and St. Louis Chamber of Commerce *Bulletin,* Oct. 1, 1917, p.3.

62. *Auto Review,* "Moon Motor Car Co. Installs New Machinery," December 1912, p.29.

63. *Auto Review,* "Moon Likes German Mechanics," September 1913, p.7.

64. *MoTor* ads, September 1909, p.8, and August 1910, p.29; and *Motor Age,* "Moon Making Sheet Metal Parts," May 14, 1914, p.41.

65. *Automobile* ad, Aug. 6, 1914, p.67; and *Saturday Evening Post* ads, Aug. 13, 1921, p.68, and March 29, 1924, p.121.

66. Karl S. Zahm, *Classic Car,* "The Remarkable History of Two Assembled Classics," March 1988, p.22.

67. *New York Times,* "Moon Motors Stock Offer," May 24, 1922, p.26:5; *Accessory and Garage Journal,* "Great Motor Concern Is Evolved from Buggy-Making Business," June 1926, p.35; and Burst and Young, "The Moon," p.404.

68. *Automotive Industries,* "Moon Entertains 150; New Model Coming," Jan. 8, 1925, p 83.

69. *Saturday Evening Post* ads, July 18, 1925, p.148, and Aug. 15, 1925, p.132.

70. Charles A. Balton Engineering Corporation stock prospectus and stationery; *Buffalo Commercial,* "Powerful New Automobile to Be Built Here," Nov. 6, 1919; and an article from an unidentified Buffalo, New York, newspaper, "A New Buffalo Product," April 18, 1920.

71. *Leadership! Diana: The Light Straight "8,"* 1926 catalog.

72. *Saturday Evening Post* ad, April 10, 1926, p.187; Marc Ralston, *Pierce-Arrow* (San Diego: A. S. Barnes & Company, 1980), p.167; and *Saturday Evening Post* ad, May 29, 1926, p.168.

73. *St. Louis Globe-Democrat Sunday Magazine,* July 17, 1977, p.10; *For 1927: Diana,* factory catalog; Burst and Young, "The Moon," p.413; and from a factory memo

Burst cited in an interview with the author, April 9, 1992.

74. *St. Louis Globe-Democrat*, "Diana Prices Reduced $200 to $300 Per Car," April 10, 1927; *Automotive Industries*, May 28, 1927, p.821; and *New York Times*, ". . . Moon Omits Declaration," Jan. 6, 1927, p.40:3.

75. Howard "Dutch" Darrin, *Automobile Quarterly*, "Disaster Is My Business," vol.7, no.1 (Summer 1969), p.63.

76. Factory catalogs, *The White Prince of Windsor* and *America's Smartest Motor Car: Windsor White Prince*, both undated.

77. *Windsor – White Prince Models*, undated factory brochure.

78. *Automobile Trade Journal*, "White Prince Is Moon's Latest," February 1929, pp.69, 74.

79. Author's interview with Joe Egle, March 31, 1992.

80. For the Ruxton section, I drew upon more sources than I can cite directly. They include 100 articles from *Automotive Industries* and other trade journals and from the *New York Times*, *St. Louis Globe-Democrat*, and *St. Louis Post-Dispatch*. All of William J. Muller's recollections come from his *Automobile Quarterly* article, vol.8, no.2 (Fall 1969), pp.191–96. Equally valuable was an accompanying article in the same edition of *Automobile Quarterly*, "Ruxton: A Superb Automobile That Never Had a Chance," by Jeffrey I. Godshall, pp.178–90. Other sources include several Ruxton promotional pieces and press releases held by the Free Library of Philadelphia. Besides press accounts, the two main sources for

the involvement of the Kissel Motor Car Company is Val V. Quandt, *The Classic Kissel Automobile* (Hartford, Wisconsin: Kissel Graph Press, 1990), and Gene Husting, *Automobile Quarterly*, "The Kissel Kaper," vol.9, no.3 (Spring 1971), pp.318–41.

81. Most of this information comes from the *New York Times*, "Front Drive Car Began Long Ago," June 9, 1929, sec. 9, p.18:6; Harvey B. Janes, *Automobile Quarterly*, "Front Wheel Drive," vol.1, no.4 (Winter 1962–1963), pp.372–81; and Kimes and Clark, *Standard Catalog*, pp.630–31.

82. *St. Louis Globe-Democrat Sunday Magazine*, July 17, 1977, p.10.

83. *St. Louis Globe-Democrat*, May 8, 1929; but Moon historian Carl Burst conducted interviews years ago with former Moon employees. According to their accounts, the Moon plant made one or two prototypes of a cotton picker that used a vacuum system. Tests revealed that the new machine was considerably slower than field laborers, so it never went into production, Burst said.

84. *St. Louis Globe-Democrat*, "New Officials Crawl through Windows to Obtain Moon Control," April 15, 1930.

85. Author's interview with Jack Donlan, April 26, 1992; and *Automobile Quarterly*, "Five of the Five Hundred: A Portfolio," vol.8, no.2 (Fall 1969), pp.196–205.

86. My source is an article pasted on a 3 x 5 card at the St. Louis Public Library. Card has no headline or page reference, but article is from Dec. 11, 1965, *St. Louis Post-Dispatch*.

No. 761,857.

PATENTED JUNE 7, 1904.

C. SMITH.
SPRING BRACE.
APPLICATION FILED SEPT. 17, 1903.

NO MODEL.

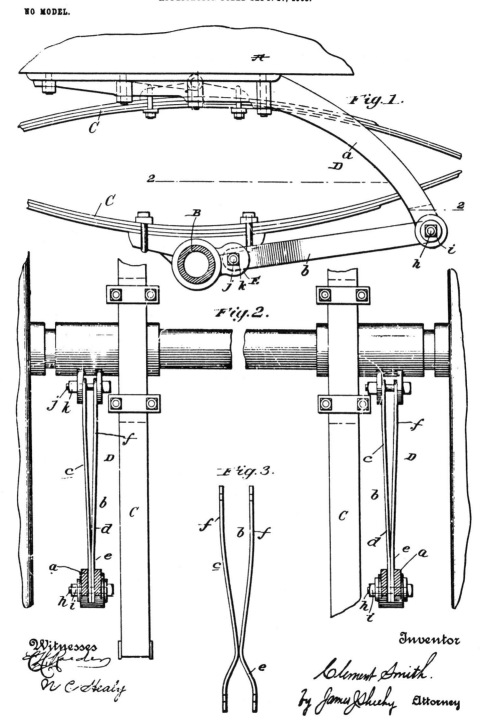

Fig.1.

Fig.2.

Fig.3.

Witnesses

Inventor

Clement Smith.

By James J Sheehy Attorney

Appendix 1: *Smith Specifications Table*

ABBREVIATIONS:

Engine Position:
us/amid = under seat, amidships
us/rear = under seat, rear
Carburetor:
King FF = Kingston float-feed
Scheb = Schebler
Scheb FF = Schebler float-feed
Smith FF = Smith float-feed
Differential:
BL/SG = Brown-Lipe/spur gear
Drive:
c = chain
s = shaft
Ignition:
B/s = Bosch-Splitdorf
DC = dry cells
M = magneto
SB = storage battery
Split = Splitdorf
Starting:
crank-F = crank, front
crank-RS = crank, right side
Steering:
RT = tiller, right side
RW = wheel, right side
Transmission:
P-2 = 2-speed planetary
Prog-3 = 3-speed progressive

FOOTNOTES:

1. Information in the 1903–4 Veracity section comes from the 1904 Veracity catalogs. The information, presumably, also applies to 1903 models.
2. Until midyear 1906, prices were $2,500 for the Side Door Tonneau and $2,300 for the Side Entrance Surrey.
3. Adding a second rumble seat raised the 1908 runabout's price $50 to $2,700. The 1908 touring car, which the automaker also called its Side Door Tonneau, cost $2,775 with headlamps and a top, or $2,787 with a top, dust cover, side curtains, and a front storm curtain.
4. New Smith Automobile Company owners apparently hoped to use this low price in 1912 to clear out the few cars remaining.
5. All are water-cooled 4-cycle engines; the horsepower ratings are the automaker's.
6. According to the January 1907 *Cycle and Automobile Trade Journal,* Smith Automobile Company sold a "few" early 4-cylinder engines that were underpowered with a 4 x 4 bore and stroke, but then increased the dimensions to 4 1/2 x 5.
7. All tires are pneumatics, 1902–12.
8. *1902:* dark green was the original color of the car bought by Canadian collector Ron Carey. *1903–4 models:* rich red running gear, outlined in black; lighter red on panels, seat, and fenders, also outlined in black; white pinstripe on wheels and panels; flat black on radiator. *1905 2-cylinder Surrey:* imperial blue body with black striping; yellow running gear with black striping; solid blue frame. *1905 2-cylinder runabout:* same as for 1904. *1907 touring car:* 3 options – rich red with black and gold stripes, gear and all; lake body with lighter red belt panel and gear, striped black & gold; and Smith Auto green with coach-green belt, panels and running gear, and black and gold striping. *1908 touring car:* rich red, chassis and all, with black and gold stripes. *1908 runabout:* gray with blue and gold leaf stripe. *1911:* automobile red or Richelieu blue with cream running gear.
9. Smith Automobile Company made its own worm-and-sector steering gear.
10. The automaker replaced the Veracity tiller with a steering wheel in mid-1904.
11. A Stewart 60-mile-per-hour speedometer was an accessory for 1909–10 Great Smiths, and a factory ad put the top speed at 60. Great Smith owner Harold Irwin says his 1910 car came with papers indicating a factory driver test-drove it at 57 miles per hour.
12. From 1903 to 1912, the automaker used its own semi-automatic transmissions, which could be shifted without using the clutch pedal.
13. A partial list of slogans: *1905 2-cylinder models:* "All the way from Topeka, Kansas, U.S.A." *1905–6 4-cylinder models:* "The Handsomest Car in America." *1907:* "Makers of the World's Greatest $2500 Car." *1908:* "Isn't It Great?" *1909:* "Equal to the Occasion." *1910 and later:* "An Individual Car," "No Road Too Rough – No Hill Too Tough," and "A Western Car for Western Roads."

Sources: articles and specification tables in national trade journals and local newspapers, and factory ads and literature.

table begins next spread

Year	Model/ Price	Engine/ Bore & Stroke/ hp [5]	Engine Position	Wheelbase (inches)	Wheels (inches) [7]	Weight (lbs.)	Color	Carburetor	Differential
1902 Smith	Runabout $1,300	2 cyl opposed/ 4 x 5/ 8 hp	US/rear	78	34 x 3	1,400	[8]		
Veracity[1] 1903–4	Runabout $1,250	2 cyl opp/ 4½ x 5/ 10 hp	US/rear	78	34 x 3	1,390	[8]	King FF	BL/SG No.2
1904 Veracity	Observation Car $1,500	2 cyl opp/ 5½ x 5½/ 18 hp	US/amid	78	34 x 3½	1,800	[8]	King FF	BL/SG No.9
1905 Smith (2 cyl)	Runabout $1,250	2 cyl opp/ ?/ 10 hp	US/rear		34 x 3½	1,390	[8]	King FF	BL/SG
	Surrey $1,600	2 cyl opp/ 5½ x 5½/ 18 hp	US/amid	98	34 x 4	"about" 1,900	[8]	King FF	BL/SG
1905–6 Smith/ Great Smith (4 cyl)	Side Door Tonneau $2,600 [2]	4 cyl/ 4½ x 4½/ 40 hp [6]	hood	98	34 x 4	2,100		Scheb	
	Side Entrance Surrey $2,400 [2]	4 cyl/ 4½ x 4½/ 32 hp [6]	hood	98	34 x 4	2,000		Scheb	
1907 Great Smith	Touring Car $2,500	4 cyl/ 4½ x 5/ 45 hp	hood	107	34 x 4	2,458	[8]	Smith FF	BL/SG
1908 Great Smith	Runabout $2,650 [3]	4 cyl/ 4½ x 5/ 45 hp	hood	110	36 x 4	2,100	[8]	Smith FF	
	Touring Car $2,650 [3]	4 cyl/ 4½ x 5/ 45 hp	hood	110	34 x 4	2,500	[8]	Smith FF	
1909 Great Smith			hood					Smith FF	
1910 Great Smith	Cruiser $2,650	4 cyl/ 4½ x 5/ ?	hood	115	option: 34 x ? or 36 x ?			Scheb FF	
	Runabout	4 cyl/ 4½ x 5/ ?	hood	110	"			Scheb FF	
	Toy Tonneau	4 cyl/ 4½ x 5/ ?	hood	110	"			Scheb FF	
	Touring Car	4 cyl/ 4½ x 5/ ?	hood	110	"			Scheb FF	
1911 Great Smith	Cruiser $2,500	4 cyl/ 4½ x 5/ ?	hood	115	option: 34 x 4 or 36 x4	2,500	[8]	Scheb FF	
	Tourabout $2,250	4 cyl/ 4½ x 5/ ?	hood	110	"	2,450	[8]	Scheb FF	
	Toy Tonneau $2,500	4 cyl/ 4½ x 5/ ?	hood	114	"	2,500	[8]	Scheb FF	
	Touring Car $2,650	4 cyl/ 4½ x 5/ ?	hood	114	"	2,600	[8]	Scheb FF	
1912 Great Smith	Model 45 $1,400 [4]	4 cyl/ 4½ x 5/ 45 hp	hood	115	34 x ?				

Year	Model	Drive	Gas Capacity/ Cruising Range	Ignition	Starting	Steering [9]	Top Speed (mph)	Transmission [12]	Slogan
1902 Smith	Runabout	C			crank-RS	RT	16–20	P-2	
Veracity[1] 1903–4	Runabout	C	?/100M	DC	crank-RS	RT/RW [10]	22–30	P-2	
1904 Veracity	Observation Car	C			crank-RS	RT/RW [10]	30	P-2	
1905 Smith (2 cyl)	Runabout	C		DC	crank-RS	RW		P-2	[13]
	Surrey	C		DC	crank-RS	RW	35–40	P-2	[13]
1905–6 Smith/ Great Smith (4 cyl)	Side Door Tonneau	S	15g/225M		crank-F	RW		option: P-2 or Prog-3	[13]
	Side Entrance Surrey	S	15g/225M		crank-F	RW		"	[13]
1907 Great Smith	Touring Car	S	15g/225M	DC, SB	crank-F	RW		Prog-3	[13]
1908 Great Smith	Runabout	S		DC,SB	crank-F	RW		Prog-3	[13]
	Touring Car	S		DC,SB	crank-F	RW		Prog-3	[13]
1909 Great Smith		S	15g/200M	DC, SB	crank-F	RW	[11]	Prog-3	[13]
1910 Great Smith	Cruiser	S		DC, Split M	crank-F	RW	[11]	Prog-3	[13]
	Runabout	S		DC, Split M	crank-F	RW	[11]	Prog-3	[13]
	Toy Tonneau	S		DC, Split M	crank-F	RW	[11]	Prog-3	[13]
	Touring Car	S		DC, Split M	crank-F	RW	[11]	Prog-3	[13]
1911 Great Smith	Cruiser	S	20g	DC, B/S M	crank-F	R		Prog-3	[13]
	Tourabout	S	25g	DC, B/S M	crank-F	R		Prog-3	[13]
	Toy-Tonneau	S	20g	DC, B/S M	crank-F	R		Prog-3	[13]
	Touring Car	S	20g	DC, B/S M	crank-F	R		Prog-3	[13]
1912 Great Smith	Model 45	S		M	self-starter	RW			[13]

THE "LUVERNE THIRTY"

The simplest and most reliable Car in existence.

Four Cylinder Motor   --   Contact Drive

This Cut shows a top view of the Running Gear or Chassis of our "Luverne Thirty" Model, and below we give a description and explanation of same.

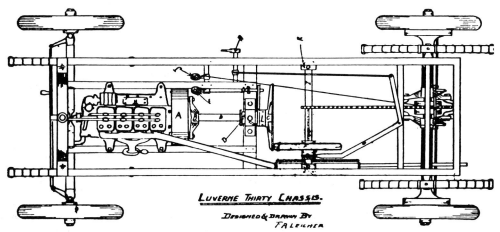

LUVERNE THIRTY CHASSIS.
DESIGNED & DRAWN BY
F A LEIHER

The Motor shown at front end of Car is a 30 H. P.

Four Cylinder Rutenber Motor.

Fly wheel of Motor is marked letter A.

Connected to this Fly Wheel, by a Sliding Socket, is Shaft marked B, and attached to Shaft B is a Disc marked C.

Now when the Motor is running, the Shaft B and Disc C revolve with the Motor. By pressing forward on Foot Pedal, marked E, the Disc and Shaft are moved a slight distance away from Motor and the Disc comes in contact with the Drive Wheel marked F, which is a wheel with a Wood Fibre Rim. This Drive Wheel F is fitted on a Sliding Key in the Cross Shaft, marked I, so that as the Drive Wheel revolves the shaft must also revolve. On this Shaft is keyed a Sprocket, connecting by roller chain to rear Axle, consequently the act of pressing forward on Foot Pedal E immediately starts the car in motion, and by releasing the pressure on this Foot Pedal E the contact between Disc C and Drive Wheel F is broken, and the car stops.

To get different speeds; the drive Wheel F is slid on Shaft I to any position required.

As shown in Cut Drive Wheel F is placed for highest speed, as it is in contact with the outside edge of the Disc C. By pulling back on Hand Lever H, this Drive Wheel F is slid towards the center of the Car, and the nearer to the center, the slower the car is driven and the greater the power.

When Drive Wheel F reaches the exact center it does not revolve at all. As it is slid on past the center, it begins to revolve in the opposite direction, and thus drives the car backwards.

Luverne Automobile Company

Luverne, - - - Minnesota

Appendix 2: *Luverne Specifications Table*

Engine:
Beav = Beaver
Cont = Continental
Rut = Rutenber
Engine Position:
amid = amidships
UFS = under front seat
Wheels and tires:
s = solid tires
Carburetor:
Ray = Rayfield; Scheb = Schebler
Clutch:
D = disk; MD = multiple-disk
Differential/rear axle:
F = floating; SF = semi-floating
Drive:
C = chain; S = shaft
Axle, front:
I = I-beam; IF = I-beam forging
T = tubular
Gas tank location/capacity:
UFS = under front seat
Ignition:
DC = dry cells; JS = jump spark
M = magneto
M/batts = magneto and batteries
SB = storage battery
Springs:
E = elliptic; ½ E = half-elliptic
¾ E = three-quarter elliptic; F = front; R = rear
Starting:
E = electric
P = pneumatic
Steering:
LW = left wheel
RW = right wheel
Transmission:
P-2 = 2-speed planetary
S-3 = 3-speed selective

table begins next spread

FOOTNOTES:

1. The friction-drive 1909 Luverne Thirty was so short-lived that the company never advertised complete specifications for it; it probably shared most specs with the shaft-drive Thirty.
2. Later raised to $1,650.
3. Horsepower ratings are the automaker's.
4. But *Motor Age* for Feb. 24, 1910, puts the 540 and 740 engine size at 4 1/2 x 4 1/2.
5. National auto journals variously reported the wheelbase as 128 and 130 inches for 1914 and 1915, and 130 and 132 inches for 1917.
6. Many national auto journals listed two wheel sizes for 1914 and 1917.
7. The February 1912 *MoTor* lists the "chassis weight" – minus the body – of these four Luverne models.
8. For all models, from the 1907 Luverne catalog: "Automobile yellow running gear with black fine lines. Aluminum on metal parts. Brewster green on body with gold fine lines. Genuine gold leaf ornamentation."
9. Dark brown or dark blue.
10. Battleship gray.
11. Brakes: *1907* (from Luverne catalog): Model A – "Foot brakes on differential. Emergency foot brakes on transmission. Emergency hand lever brakes on rear hubs." Models B and C: "Foot brakes on differential. Emergency foot brakes on transmission." *1908:* brakes on differential and transmission. *1909:* Models A, B, C, and D (from March 1909 *Cycle and Automobile Trade Journal*) – "internal brakes on rear hubs; slow speed and reverse, and brakes are operated by pedals and high gear by lever." Luverne Forty: "internal and external brakes on rear hubs; foot pedal operates brakes and clutch, hand lever operates brake and change speed gear." Luverne Thirty shaft-drive (Luverne ad): "internal and external brakes on rear hubs, operated by foot pedal and hand lever." *1910–14:* external contracting and internal expanding brakes, both on rear hubs.

12. Clutch: *1907* (from Luverne catalog): "tapered metal type" for all models. *1909:* Models A-D: tapered metal-to-metal cone clutch. Luverne Thirty shaft-drive: bronze lining with cork inserts and an aluminum cone clutch. Luverne Forty: multiple-disk, running in oil.
13. Differential/rear axle: 1907: Brown-Lipe spur-gear differential on a Weston-Mott axle. *1909:* Models A-D – live rear axle on roller bearings. 1916: Weston-Mott axle.
14. Drive: *1904, 1906, and 1908* – documentation is lacking but these autos undoubtedly shared the chain drive of other models for these years.
15. Solid steel, 1 ⅜ inches square.
16. Ignition: *1909:* the Model A also carried a storage battery, says February 1909 *MoTor*. *1912:* the 540 used dry cells, not a storage battery, according to the February 1912 *MoTor*. *1913:* a factory catalog says the 760 used a Bijur electric generator; the February 1913 *MoTor* said the 760 used both a storage battery and dry cells. *1916:* the Dec. 30, 1915, *Motor Age* says the 760 used a Splitdorf-Aplco starter-generator.
17. Springs: The Jan. 1, 1917, *Motor Age* doesn't specify if the 1917 Luverne used semi-elliptics on the front, rear, or both.
18. Starters: Published reports and the automaker's own literature are rife with conflicting information on Luverne's self-starters. *1912:* electric and pneumatic, unspecified brands. *1913:* 540 – no mention of a self-starter; 550 and 740 – pneumatic; 760 – Bijur electric (factory literature), but other sources say Gray & Davis. *1914:* Kellogg pneumatic. *1915:* auto journals list Jesco and Jones electric. *1916:* Splitdorf-Aplco electric. *1917:* Bosch electric.

Sources: articles and specification tables in national trade journals and local newspapers, and factory ads and literature.

Year	Model/ Price	Engine/ Bore & Stroke/ hp [3]	Engine Position	Wheelbase (inches)	Wheels/Tires (inches)	Weight (lbs.)	Color	Brakes	Carburetor	Clutch
1904	Surrey	?/ ?/ 10 hp								
1905	Surrey	2/ ?/ 10 hp	UFS							
	Touring	2/ ?/ 16 hp								
1906	Runabout $650	?/ ?/ 10 hp								
	Surrey $1,000	?/ ?/ 20 hp								
	Touring $1,350	?/ ?/ 20 hp								
1907	Model C-Runabout $1,000	2/ 5 x 5/ 20 hp	amid	78	3 x 30	1,600	[8]	[11]	Scheb	[12]
	Model B-Surrey $1,000	2/ 5 x 5/ 20 hp	amid	94	34 x 2-S	1,700	[8]	[11]	Scheb	[12]
	Model A-Touring $1,250	2/ 5 x 5/ 20 hp	amid	94	32 x 3 1/2	1,850	[8]	[11]	Scheb	[12]
1908	Model C-Runabout $650	2 / ? / ?						[11]		
	Model B-Runabout $700	2 / 4 x 4 1/2 / 14 hp		84	30 x 3			[11]		
	Model A-Touring $1,250	2 / 5 x 5/ 20 hp		98				[11]		
1909	Model C-Surrey $800	2/ 5 x 5/ 24 hp	body	84	32 x 3 1/2	1,600		[11]		[12]
	Model B-Touring $900	2/ 5 x 5/ 24 hp	body	100	32 x 3 1/2	2,000		[11]		[12]
	Model D-Runabout $750	2/ 5 x 5/ 24 hp	body	100	32 x 3 1/2	1,550		[11]		[12]
	Forty $2,000	Rut 4/ 4 1/4 x 5/ 40 hp	hood	108	34 x 4	2,650		[11]		[12]
	Model A-Touring $1,250	2/ 5 x 5/ 24 hp	body	100	32 x 3 1/2	2,250		[11]		[12]
1909	Thirty friction-drive [1]	Rut 4/ ?/ 30 hp								
1909	Thirty shaft-drive $1,400	Rut 4/ ?/ 30 hp	hood	108	32 x 3 1/2	2,100	onyx brown	[11]		[12]

Year	Model	Differential/Rear Axle	Drive	Front Axle	Gas Tank Loc./Capacity	Ignition	Springs	Starting	Steering	Transmission
1904	Surrey		[14]						RW	
1905	Surrey		C					crank	RW	
	Touring		C					crank		
1906	Runabout		[14]					crank		
	Surrey		[14]					crank		
	Touring		[14]					crank		
1907	Model C-Runabout	[13]	C	[15]	UH/12g	JS,DC	1/2 E	crank	RW	P-2
	Model B-Surrey	[13]	C	[15]	UH/12g	JS, DC	1/2 E	crank	RW	P-2
	Model A-Touring	[13]	C	[15]	UH/12g	JS, DC	1/2 E	crank	RW	P-2
1908	Model C-Runabout		[14]					crank		
	Model B-Runabout		C				E	crank		
	Model A-Touring		[14]					crank		
1909	Model C-Surrey	[13]	C	T	UH/15g	JS, DC	F-E, R-E	crank	RW	P-2
	Model B-Touring	[13]	C	T	UH/15g	JS, DC	F-E, R-E	crank	RW	P-2
	Model D-Runabout	[13]	C	T	UH/15g	JS, DC	F-E, R-E	crank	RW	P-2
	Forty	F	S	I	US/15g	Simms-Bosch M, DC	F-1/2 E, R-E	crank	RW	S-3
	Model A-Touring	[13]	C	T	UH/15g	JS, DC [16]	F-E, R-E	crank	RW	P-2
1909	Thirty friction-drive [1]		C					crank	RW	friction
1909	Thirty shaft-drive		S			M	F-E, R-E	crank	RW	S-3

Year	Model/Price	Engine/Bore & Stroke/hp[3]	Engine Position	Wheelbase (inches)	Wheels/Tires (inches)	Weight (lbs.)	Color	Brakes	Carburetor	Clutch
1910	530/$1,400	Rut 4/ 4 x 4/ 30 hp	hood	110	32 x $3\frac{1}{2}$	2,200	onyx brown	11		MD
	535/$1,600	Beav 4/ $4\frac{3}{8}$ x $4\frac{3}{4}$/ 35 hp	hood	120	32 x $3\frac{1}{2}$	2,600	Brewster green	11		MD
	540/$2,000	Rut 4/ $4\frac{1}{2}$ x 5/ 40 hp[4]	hood	120	34 x 4	2,600	Brewster green	11		MD
	740/$2,250	Rut 4/ $4\frac{1}{2}$ x 5/ 40 hp[4]	hood	120	34 x 4	2,800	Brewster green	11		MD
1911	530/$1,350	Rut 4/ 4 x 4/ 30 hp	hood	110	32 x 4			11	Scheb	MD
	740/$2,500	4/ $4\frac{1}{2}$ x 5/ 40 hp	hood	122	36 x $4\frac{1}{2}$			11	Scheb	MD
1912	260/$2,750	Rut 6/ $4\frac{1}{8}$ x $5\frac{1}{4}$/ 60 hp	hood	130	36 x $4\frac{1}{2}$	2,200 [7]	9	11	Scheb	MD
	460	6/ $4\frac{1}{8}$ x $5\frac{1}{4}$/ 60 hp	hood	128	36 x $4\frac{1}{2}$	2,200 [7]		11	Scheb	MD
	540/$1,850	Beav 4/ $4\frac{3}{8}$ x $4\frac{3}{4}$/ 40 hp	hood	124	34 x 4	2,500 [7]	10	11	Scheb	MD
	545/$2,000	Beav 4/ $4\frac{1}{8}$ x $5\frac{1}{4}$/ 45hp	hood	124	36 x 4		9	11		MD
	750/$2,600	Rut 4/ $4\frac{3}{4}$ x 5/ 50 hp	hood	128	36 x $4\frac{1}{2}$	2,600 [7]	9	11	Scheb	MD
	760/$2,850	Rut 6/ $4\frac{1}{8}$ x $5\frac{1}{4}$/ 60 hp	hood	130	37 x 5		9	11		MD
1913	540/$1,850	4/ $4\frac{3}{8}$ x $4\frac{3}{4}$/ 40 hp	hood	128	36 x 4	3,250	Luv. brown	11		MD
	550/$2,500	6/ $3\frac{3}{4}$ x 5/ 50 hp	hood	128	36 x $4\frac{1}{2}$	3,450	Luv. brown	11		MD
	740/$2,000	4/ $4\frac{3}{8}$ x $4\frac{3}{4}$/ 40 hp	hood	128	36 x $4\frac{1}{2}$	3,350	Luv. brown	11		MD
	760/$2,850	6/ $4\frac{1}{4}$ x $5\frac{1}{4}$/ 60 hp	hood	128	37 x 5	3,650	Luv. brown	11	Scheb	MD
1914	760/$2,500	Beav 6/ 4 x 5/ 60 hp	hood	128/130 [5]	37 x 5 or 36 x $4\frac{1}{2}$ [6]	3,700	dark Luv. brown w/ light brown trim	11	Ray	MD
1915	760/$2,500	Beav 6/ 4 x 5/ 60 hp	hood	128/130 [5]	36 x $4\frac{1}{2}$	3,600			Scheb	D
1916	760/$2,500	Beav 6/ 4 x 5/ 60 hp	hood	130	36 x $4\frac{1}{2}$				Scheb	D
	2-passenger roadster $2,250		hood	130	36 x $4\frac{1}{2}$				Scheb	D
1917	Model 17 $1,500 [2]		hood	130/132 [5]	35 x $4\frac{1}{2}$ or 36 x $4\frac{1}{2}$ [6]				Scheb	D
	760/$2,500	Cont 6/ $3\frac{3}{4}$ x $5\frac{1}{4}$/ 60 hp	hood	130/132 [5]	35 x $4\frac{1}{2}$ or 36 x $4\frac{1}{2}$ [6]				Scheb	D

Year	Model	Differential/ Rear Axle	Drive	Front Axle	Gas Tank Loc./ Capacity	Ignition	Springs	Starting	Steering	Transmission
1910	530	SF	S	T	15g	Bosch M, JS, DC	F-E, R-E	crank	RW	S-3
	535	SF	S	I	15g	Remy M, JS, DC	F-1/2 E, R-E	crank	RW	S-3
	540	SF	S	I	15g	Bosch M, JS, DC	F-1/2 E, R-E	crank	RW	S-3
	740	SF	S	I	15g	Bosch M, JS, DC	F-1/2 E, R-E	crank	RW	S-3
1911	530	SF	S			Bosch M, JS, DC	F-1/2 E, R-3/4 E	crank	RW	S-3
	740	SF	S		US/15g	Bosch M, JS, DC	F-1/2 E, R-3/4 E	crank	RW	S-3
1912	260	F	S	IF		JS, Bosch M, SB	F-1/2 E, R-E	E/P [18]	RW	S-3
	460		S			JS, Bosch M,SB	F-1/2 E, R-E	E/P [18]	RW	S-3
	540	F	S	IF		JS, Bosch M, SB [16]	F-1/2 E, R-E	E/P [18]	RW	S-3
	545	F	S	IF		JS, Bosch M, SB	F-1/2 E, R-E	E/P [18]	RW	S-3
	750	F	S	IF		JS, Bosch M, SB	F-1/2 E, R-E	E/P [18]	RW	S-3
	760	F	S	IF		JS, Bosch M, SB	F-1/2 E, R-E	E/P [18]	RW	S-3
1913	540	F	S	IF		M/batts	F-1/2 E, R-E	[18]	LW	S-3
	550	F	S	IF		M/batts	F-1/2 E, R-E	P [18]	LW	S-3
	740	F	S	IF			F-1/2 E, R-E	P [18]	LW	S-3
	760	F	S	IF	US	JS, Remy M, DC [16]	F-1/2 E, R-E	E [18]	LW	S-3
1914	760	F	S		UFS/24g	JS, Bosch M, DC	F-1/2 E, R-E	P [18]	LW	S-3
1915	760	F	S		US/20g	JS, DC, Bosch M	F-?, R-E	E [18]	LW	S-3
1916	760	F [13]	S			JS, Bosch M [16]	F-?, R-E	E [18]	LW	S-3
	2-passenger roadster	F [13]	S				F-?, R-E	E [18]	LW	S-3
1917	Model 17		S			Bosch M	1/2 E [17]	E [18]	LW	S-3
	760		S			Bosch M	1/2 E [17]	E [18]		S-3

K. W. GILLESPIE.
BODY HOIST.
APPLICATION FILED APR. 10, 1918.

1,277,907.

Patented Sept. 3, 1918.
2 SHEETS—SHEET 1.

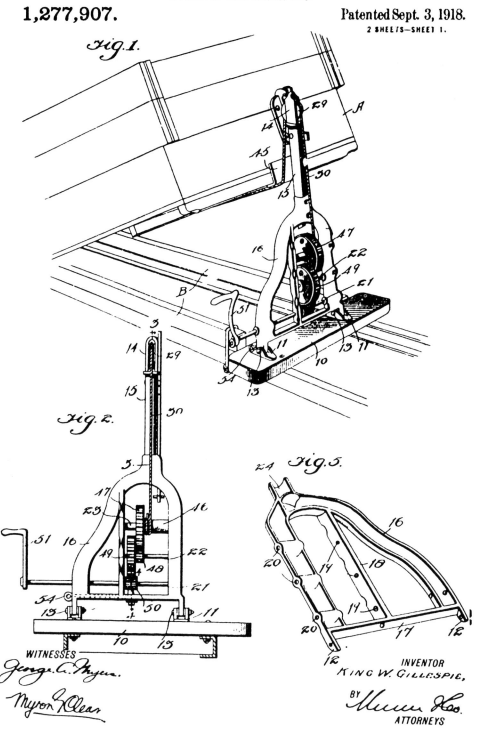

Fig.1.

Fig. 2.

Fig. 5.

WITNESSES

George A. Myers.

Myron L. Clear

INVENTOR
KING W. GILLESPIE,

BY

ATTORNEYS

Appendix 3: *Patriot Specifications Table*

table begins next spread

ABBREVIATIONS:

Engine:
Cont = Continental
Hink = Hinkley
Wheels:
F = front
R = rear
Carburetor:
Strom = Stromberg
Strom FF = Stromberg float-feed
Clutch:
B & B = Borg & Beck
DP = dry plate
MD = multiple-disk
P = plate
SDP = single disk plate
Cooling:
C = cellular radiator
P = pump
T = tubular radiator
TS = thermosiphon
VT = vertical-tube radiator
Differential:
IG = internal gear
W = worm gear
Drive:
S = shaft
Front axle:
I = I-beam
DF = drop-forged
Gas tank:
US = under seat
Ignition:
IS = ignition system
M = magneto
Split = Splitdorf
Starting:
E = electric
Transmission:
BL = Brown-Lipe
S-3 = 3-speed selective
S-4 = 4-speed selective

FOOTNOTES:

1. Price is for the chassis only; the body was extra.
2. At midyear, prices were lower: $1,950 for the Lincoln and $2,750 for the Washington.
3. The horsepower formula is unspecified.
4. Hebb Motors' early ads, in June 1918, list a 4 1/8 x 5 1/4 Continental engine for the Washington model.
5. Sources vary considerably on tire sizes offered in 1918. These are the most common sizes listed.
6. Pneumatic tires, measuring 35 x 5 front and 38 x 7 rear, where a $300 option for the 1919 Lincoln.
7. In 1920, optional pneumatics were 35 x 5 front and 38 x7 rear for the Lincoln ($300) and 36 x 6 front and 42 x 9 rear for the Washington ($550).
8. For all three 1920 models, the standard body color was a brewster green with a yellow stripe.
9. The 1918 Lincoln was advertised early as having a worm-drive rear axle but Hebb Motors soon switched to an internal-drive rear axle.
10. Atwater-Kent distributor with a generator that charged a storage battery.

Sources: articles and specification tables in national trade journals and local newspapers, and factory ads and literature.

Year	Model/ Price [1]	Engine/ Bore & Stroke/ hp[3]	Wheelbase (inches)	Wheels (inches)	Weight (lbs.)	Color	Carburetor	Clutch	Cooling	Differential
1918	Lincoln $2,150 [2]	Cont "N" 4/ 3$_{3/4}$ x 5/ 22.5 hp	135	F- 34 x 3$_{1/2}$ R- 34 x 5 [5]	3,400		Strom FF	B&B, SDP	VT, TS	Russel IG [9]
	Washington $3,150 [2]	Cont 4/ 4$_{1/2}$ x 5$_{1/4}$/ 27.2 hp [4]	156	F- 34 x 4 R- 34 x 7 [5]	4,600		Strom	B&B, DP	VT, P	Empire W
1919	Lincoln $2,150	Cont "N" 4/ 3$_{3/4}$ x 5/ 22.5 hp	135	F- 34 x 3$_{1/2}$ R- 34 x 5 [6]	3,400		Strom M-1	B&B, SDP	T, TS	Russel IG
	Washington $3,150	Cont "C4" 4/ 4$_{1/8}$ x 5$_{1/4}$/ 27.2 hp	156	F- 34 x 4 R- 34 x 7	4,600		Strom M-2	B&B, P	T, P	Empire W
1920	Revere $1,875	Cont "N" 4/ 3$_{3/4}$ x 5/ ?	129	F and R- 34 x 4$_{1/2}$	2,800	[8]	Strom FF	B&B, SDP	C, TS	Empire W
	Lincoln $2,450	Hink 4/ 4 x 5$_{1/4}$/ ?	140	F- 34 x 3$_{1/2}$ R- 34 x 5 [7]	3,900	[8]	Strom FF	Covert, MD, DP	C, P	Empire W
	Washington	Hink 4/ 4$_{1/2}$ x 5$_{1/2}$/ ?	156	F- 36 x 4 R- 36 x 7 [7]	5,200	[8]	Strom FF	Covert, MD, DP	C, P	Empire W

Year	Model	Drive	Front axle	Gas Tank Loc./ Capacity	Ignition	Springs	Starting	Top Speed	Transmission
1918	Lincoln	S			Bosch IS	1/2 E	crank		Covert S-3
	Washington	S			Bosch IS	1/2 E	crank		BL S-4
1919	Lincoln	S	I, DF	US/20g	Bosch M		crank	18 mph	Covert S-3
	Washington	S		US/20g	Bosch M	1/2 E F & R	crank	14 mph	BL S-4
1920	Revere	S	I, DF	US/20g	10	1/2 E	Bijur E		S-3
	Lincoln	S	I, DF	US/20g	Split M	1/2 E			Covert S-4
	Washington	S	I,DF	US/20g	Split M	1/2 E			Covert S-4

Appendix 4: *Spaulding Specifications Table*

ABBREVIATIONS:

Engine:
Rut = Rutenber
Carburetor:
Ray = Rayfield
Scheb = Schebler
Gas Tank:
FR = frame, rear
UFS = under front seat
US = under seat
Ignition:
DC = dry cells
M = magneto
Starting:
E = electric
SS = self-starter
Transmission:
P-2 = 2-speed planetary
S-3 = 3-speed selective

table begins next spread

FOOTNOTES:

1. The horsepower ratings are the automaker's.
2. Buda Model T engine.
3. Colors: *1910* – dark blue. *1911* – during the March 1911 Des Moines auto show, the automaker displayed a gray-and-cream Spaulding 30 and a "Spaulding blue" 40 model. *1913 and 1914* – dark blue. *1915* – dark blue; the Spaulding company also displayed a "special light blue car" at the 1915 Iowa State Fair.
4. A low-pressure pump forced gas from the main tank to a 2-gallon tank in the cowl. From there, it flowed by gravity to the engine.
5. Ignition: *1912* – Sources suggest the Spaulding 40, Model E, was available with either a Bosch magneto or a Remy combination magneto, used for ignition and lights. *1913* – *Motor Age* of Jan. 9, 1913, says the Spaulding 40, Model G, used an Eisenmann magneto, but the March 1913 *Automobile Trade Journal* lists ignition as a "Gray & Davis system."
6. Spaulding introduced an unspecified self-starter in late winter 1912.

Sources: articles and specification tables in national trade journals and local newspapers, and factory ads and literature.

Year	Model/Price	Engine/ Bore & Stroke/ hp [1]	Wheelbase (inches)	Wheels (inches)	Weight (lbs.)	Color	Carburetor	Gas Tank Loc./ capacity	Ignition	Starting
1910 Spaulding 30	C or CS $1,550	4/ 4 x 4/ 30 hp	112	32 x 3½		[3]		UFS/15g	DC, M	crank
	D or CP $1,500	4/ 4 x 4/ 30 hp	112	32 x 3½		[3]		UFS/15g	DC,M	crank
1911	30 or C CS touring $1,550 CP touring $1,500	4/ 4 x 4/ 30 hp	112	32 x 3½		[3]		US	DC, M	crank
	40 or D Touring $2,500	4/ 4½ x 5/ 40 hp	112	34 x 4		[3]		US	DC, M	crank
1912	30 or C CP $1,500 CS $1,500	4/ 4 x 4/ 30 hp	112	32 x 3½	2,100		Scheb	13g	Renny M, DC	crank/ SS [6]
	40 or E Touring $1,650	Rut 4/ 4⅛ x 5¼/ 40 hp	117	34 x 4	2,200		Scheb	13g	[5]	crank/ SS [6]
1913	40 or G $1,800	Buda 4/ 4¼ x 5½/ 40 hp [2]	120	36 x 4		[3]	Scheb	US	[5]	Gray & Davis E
1914	Sleeper H	Buda 4/ 4¼ x 5½/ 40 hp [2]	120	36 x 4	3,300	[3]	Holly "H"	FR/20g [4]	Simms M, DC	Entz E
	Spaulding 40 H $1,875	Buda 4/ 4¼ x 5½/ 40 hp [2]	120	36 x 4	3,300	[3]	Holly "H"	FR/20g [4]	Simms M, DC	Entz E
1915	Sleeper H or 40 $1,730	Buda 4/ 4¼ x 5½/ 40 hp	120	36 x 4		[3]		FR		Entz E
	40 or H $1,680	Buda 4/ 4¼ x 5½/ 40 hp	120	36 x 4		[3]		FR		Entz E
1916	30 $750	4/ 3¼ x 5/ 30 hp	110					cowl		
	50 or H $1,250	Buda 4/ 4¼ x 5½/ 50 hp	120	36 x 4			Ray		Simms M	Entz E

Year	Model	Steering	Transmission
1910 Spaulding 30	C or CS	RW	S-3
	D or CP	RW	P-2
1911	30 or C CS touring CP touring	RW	CS S-3 CP P-2
	40 or D touring	RW	S-3
1912	30 or C, CP, CS	RW	CS S-3 CP P-2
	40 or E	RW	S-3
1913	40 or G	L	S-3
1914	Sleeper H	L	S-3
	Spaulding 40 H	L	S-3
1915	Sleeper "H" or 40	L	
	40 or H	L	
1916	30	L	
	50 or H	L	S-3

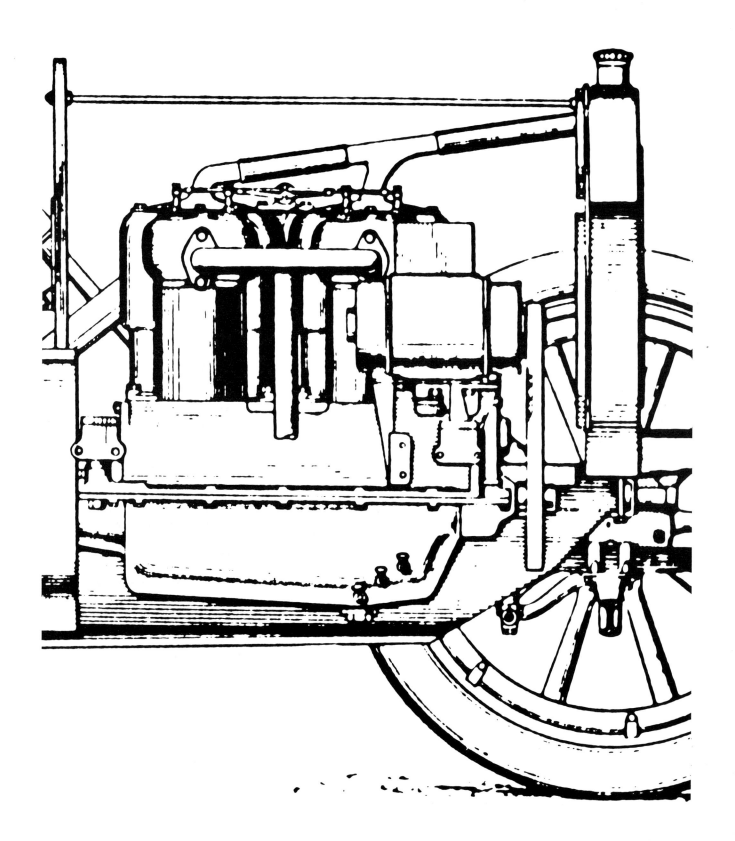

Appendix 5: *Moon Chronicle*

KEY:

cyl. = cylinder
hp = horsepower
limo = limousine
pass. = passenger
std. = standard
trans. = transmission
vs. = versus
w/ = with
w/o = without

table begins next spread

1906 Model

A

Body style

5-pass. touring

Technical details

Leather-faced multiple-disk clutch

3-speed sliding-gear trans.

Rear shock-absorber straps

Steering knuckle arm placed behind front
 axle for protection

Body & appearance

Wooden body

No front doors

Moon-made top

Underbody frame-width tool box

Luggage under rear seats

Engine

Rutenber 4-cyl. w/Hill precision oiler

Lever or pedal controls throttle

1907 Model

C

Body styles

Limo, "semi-racer"/runabout, 5- & 7-pass.
 touring

Technical details

Louis P. Mooers designs multiple-disk oil-
 bath clutch

New 4-speed sliding-gear trans.

Drop frame & triangular rear-axle brace
 rods

Body & appearance

Aluminum body

Smoother hood w/o louvers

1st Moon curved-top radiator

Mahogany dash

Engine changes

Mooers's 4-cyl. T-head engine w/overhead
 valves & camshaft

1 exposed cam & rocker arm per cyl.

Cyls. cast in pairs

3-bearing crankshaft

Governor maintains speed despite hills

Flywheel fan cools radiator

Ad claim

"All unnecessary parts are eliminated, and
 . . . the best features of European and
 American cars have been considered and
 adopted after they had been simplified"

1908 Models

5-pass. C & 7-pass. D. Cars sold in East as Hol-Tans

Body styles

Limo, roadster, touring

Technical changes

Minor

Body & appearance

Minor changes

Engine changes

Magneto supplements low-tension ignition

Sealed gears for timer, magneto, water pump

"Knife switch" contacts for spark plugs

Ad claim

"The First Car [Hol-Tan] to Enter the Famous Race Around The World, New York to Paris"

1909 Models

5-pass. C & 7-pass. D

Body styles

Landaulet coupe, limo, runabout, touring, "Town Car Brevetti" (enclosed back compartment), toy tonneau

Technical changes

Higher 3-speed gear ratio

Trans. gears pitched to reduce breakage & noise

Enlarged brake surfaces

Body & appearance

Open-grate running boards act as foot scrapers

Cork linoleum covers floorboards

Some models have cowled dash

Engine changes

New Moon-made magneto starter

Backup low-tension ignition system optional vs. std.

Ad claim

"Refinement that stands for increased strength and efficiency, more simplicity and greater economy in the long run is found in the 1909 Moon"

1910 Models

Moon 30 & Moon 45

Body styles

Landaulet, limo, roadster, town car, toy tonneau, touring

Technical changes

"30" has 3-speed, "45" 4-speed trans.

"30" is a lightweight "45" w/many common parts but its own expanding-band clutch

Wooden wheels "give at a certain point to prevent loosening up at the miter"

Body & appearance

Steel body

Kick-up rear-fender tailing edge

Engine changes

"45" retains overhead-valve engine

"30" gets new T-head valve-in-block design

Ad claim

Moon 45 "will offer $1,000 more real value than any other automobile upon the market"

1911 Models

30 & 45

Body styles

Coupe, 4-door, landaulet, limo, roadster, torpedo, touring, victoria

Technical changes

"30" adopts multiple-disk clutch, improved steering gear, & "200 drop forgings where malleable castings could be used"

Body & appearance

Moon adds 4-doors, torpedoes, & bodies w/smoother sides

Engine changes

Quieter, lighter, & 25% more powerful "30" engine; straighter "45" exhaust manifold

Ad claim

J. W. Moon in ad: "Let me send you my new Illustrated Analysis of Automobile Mechanism (free)"

1912 Models

30, 40, & 45

Body styles

Coupe, 4-door, limo, "raceabout"/roadster, torpedo, touring

Technical changes

Combination oil-electric lamps

Body & appearance

"40" has driver's-seat goggle box

Engine changes

Drops Mooers's engine design

"40" gets bigger version of "30" valve-in-block T-head

Some engines by Continental

New Disco acetylene starter

Ad claim

J. W. Moon in ad: "For 30 years I have personally inspected every product of my factories. Not a Moon car goes on the market until it has my O.K."

1913 Models

39, 48, & 65 (6-cyl.)

Body styles

Coupe, limo, raceabout, roadster, speedster, torpedo, touring

Technical changes

Adopts left-side steering

"65" has grade indicator

Drains keep grease off brakes

Body & appearance

Std. windshield mounts w/o struts & straps (except early models)

2 rear-mount spare tires

Engine changes

New 12-volt "Moon-Wagner" starter-generator

No crank handle

Adopts valve covers

"65" is 1st Moon 6-cyl.

Ad claim

J. W. Moon: "Right-side drive is a relic of horse-drawn vehicle precedent"

1914 Models

4-42 (4-cyl.) & 6-50 (6-cyl.)

Body styles

Coupe, "Parkway Speedster," roadster, torpedo, touring

Technical changes

Adopts pressure-fed gas system w/rear tank

4-42 has 3-speed, 6-50 has 4-speed trans.

Body & appearance

1st true streamlined hood & cowl

Clean running boards

Concealed door hinges

Crescent hood ornament appears in ads

Engine changes

"Light Weight" 6-50 uses 590-lb. 58-hp Continental

Front fan assists 4-cyl. fan-in-flywheel cooling

Delco electric starter

Engine-driven air pump

Ad claim

"Everybody wants a Six for its evenness of torque and smooth running – few can afford the big upkeep cost of the big six. The problem is solved by the 'light weight six'"

1915 Models

4-38, 6-40, & 6-50

Body styles

Cabriolet, limo, roadster, runabout, touring

Technical changes

Crucible steel lightens rear axle

Larger brakes

Brake parts cut from 50 to 22

Steering wheel has "corrugated" grip

Vacuum system draws fuel

Hotchkiss drive eliminates torque rods

Body & appearance

New slightly rounded radiator

Dash-mounted dimmer switch

All cars have speedometers

Engine changes

Beginning this year, all Moons except some exports use Continental engines

Ad claim

"We have put the largest and most famous exclusive manufacturers of motors to work to make for us the best motor"

1916 Models

6-30, 6-43, 6-44, & 6-66

Body styles

Roadster, touring

Technical changes

Non-skid rear tires

Body & appearance

New dual-cowl bodies have curving top line

Others have convex sides, rounded top edge

Adopts ammeter in dash

Offers early solid removable top

Engine changes

Moon retires 4-cyl. engines

4-30 develops 46 hp

Ad claim

50% of sales are to new buyers and "the other fifty per cent are sales to people who have owned one to three Moon cars previously"

1917 Models

6-43, 6-45 (a midyear 4-pass. club roadster), & 6–66

Body styles

Cabriolet, club roadster, coupe, sedan, Springfield sedan (1 center door per side), touring

Technical changes

Few changes under wartime material shortages & ordering delays

Adopts 2-unit "Moon-Delco" starter & generator

Body & appearance

Cars have higher radiators, narrower hoods, sloping windshields

Dual-cowl bodies available

Engine changes

Flexible exhaust pipe

Ad claim

The dual-cowl body "is destined to supplant all others in popular favor"

1918 Models

6-36, 6-45, & 6-66

Body styles

Cabriolet, club roadster, coupe, roadster, sedan, touring, victoria

Technical changes

Oil cups on spring bolts

Adjustable clutch & brake pedals

Body & appearance

New 6-36 appeals to new market w/low-priced 6-cyl.

Few other changes but Moon among 1st to unveil 1918 models

Engine changes

Priming cups

Moon co. profit

$29,872 (*Moody's* 1924)

Ad claim

New light 6-36 is "Built for the Man with the Four-Cylinder Income and Six-Cylinder Taste"

1919 Models

6-38, 6-46 Victory & 6-66

Body styles

Cabriolet, club roadster, "open sedan," sedan, touring, victoria

Technical changes

Minor

Body & appearance

Dual-cowl Victory has beveled top body line, hood louvers, Rolls-Royce radiator & hood line

Flat springs & low seats give it low-hung look

Many use wire wheels

Engine changes

Minor

Moon co. profit

$67,883 (*Moody's* 1925)

Ad claim

Victory model is "Acclaimed in the East – the one real Post-War Car"

1920 Models

6-48 & 6-68

Body styles

Coupe, roadster, sedan, touring

Technical changes

Heavier frame

Boasts of short turning radius

Body & appearance

Many cars use octagonal-shaped headlamps

Driver's-door tool compartment

Tilting steering wheel & cowl ventilators in
closed cars

Wire or disk wheels replace wood

Engine changes

Few claimed

Moon co. profit

$100,365 (*Moody's* 1926)

Ad claim

"Only the slight touch of your thumb and
index finger is necessary to shift the
gears. You can steer with the pressure of
two fingers"

1921 Models

6-42 (for export), 6-48, & 6-68

Body styles

Coupe, roadster, sedan, touring

Technical changes

Adopts many oil cups for chassis lubrication

Body & appearance

Roadster top lower

New closed-car crank-down windows

Snare-drum headlamps appear

Engine changes

Few claimed

Moon co. profit

$77,540 (*Moody's* 1927)

Ad claim

"Ten proven units demand that each and
every unit be of proven quality in the car
you purchase. Don't accept merely one
or two"

1922 Models

6-40, 6-48, & Six-68

Body styles

Brougham, coupe, roadster, sedan, touring

Technical changes

Adds own "drip-proof" windshield

6-40's new-design frame has 4 cross members

Body & appearance

Many inside storage spaces & carry-all
pockets

La Petite Sedan's front bucket seat slides
toward driver for back-seat access

Outside sun visors in most closed cars

Bodies lose beveled top accent line that
originated w/1919 Victory

Engine changes

6-40 Continental has new "Sheppard"
valve design

Moon co. profit

$619,128 (*Moody's* 1929)

Ad claim

The 6-40 was "born for those who shun the
commonplace – for those seeking individuality"

1923 Models

6-40 & 6-58

Body styles

Coupe, phaeton, roaster, sedan, Tourlux
(permanent top w/removable windows),
touring

Technical changes

Minor

Body & appearance

New "Gypsy Touring" has Pullman bed,
"complete kitchen trunk"

2 side-mounted spares on some touring
models

New cowl lights, rear-mounted removable
trunks, "silent roof"

Engine changes

Few claimed

Moon co. profit

$251,557 (*Moody's* 1929)

Ad claim

"People just naturally turn to the Moon –
it's the car they instinctively want to own
– to drive – to be seen in"

1924 Models

Series A, Series U (or U6-40), 6-50, & 6-58

Body styles

Coupe, phaeton, roadster, sedan, touring,
Tourlux

Technical changes

4-wheel hydraulic brakes optional (later
std.)

New balloon tires

Improved rear axle

Larger trans. gears

Body & appearance

Triangular-shaped corner glass in closed-
car windshields

Monogram headlamp lenses in some cars

Engine changes

Continental improves bearings, manifolds,
pistons, & tappets

Moon co. profit

$154,585 (*Moody's* 1929)

Ad claim

New low-price Series A is "Not a light six –
but a substantial man-size six with plenty
of power, speed and endurance. Large!
Roomy for five passengers!"

1925 Models

Series A, Newport, Metropolitan, & London

Body styles

Cabriolet roadster, coupe, roadster, sedan,
touring

Technical changes

New Ross cam-and-lever steering gear

Stiffer frame w/corner gussets added

Wooden wheels make a comeback

Body & appearance

Golf-bag compartment & roll-down rear
window in rumble-seat roadster

"MM" headlamp tie-bar (early) mimics
Rolls-Royce's "RR"

Headlamp switch on top of steering column

Engine changes

Few claimed

Moon co. profit

$562,828 (*Moody's* 1929)

Ad claim

"All Moon cars have six cylinders, 4-wheel
hydraulic brakes, balloon tires, patented
easy-parking steering gear, Duco finish"

1926 Models
Series A & London
Body styles
Roadster, sedan, touring
Technical changes
Hartford front shocks
Body & appearance
Deeper radiator
Wider & longer front fenders
Cover for gas tank & rear frame horns
Engine changes
Few claimed
Moon co. deficit
$971,138 (*Moody's* 1929)
Ad claim
Of 42,050 cars sold in past 6 years: "Practically all of these cars are in commission. Due to this well-known tenacity of service, Moon cars enjoy the top-notch resale market price"

1927 Models
Jubilee 6-60 & Series A
Body styles
Brougham, coupe, roadster, sedan, touring
Technical changes
Weight savings via steel stampings, plywood dash vs. solid oak
7-cross-member frame in 6-60
Wooden wheels
Body & appearance
New 6–60 has slender "safety-vision" windshield posts, 1-piece crank-open windshield, Diana-style radiator
Engine changes
Light cast-iron pistons
Crankase gases rerouted to carburetor
Moon co. deficit
$148,276 (*Moody's* 1929)
Ad claim
New Jubilee 6-60 "is compact, low, roomy, light like the European type, but adapted throughout to meet America's traffic needs"

1928 Models
6-60 & Series A (early in model year)
Then 6-62, 6-72, 8-75 (8-cyl.), & 8-80 (8-cyl.)
Body styles
Cabriolet roadster, coupe, roadster, sedan
Technical changes
Extra frame bracing
Body & appearance
Arrowhead design in hood & cowl of new "Aerotype" bodies
Radiator copies Hispano-Suiza's w/shutters
"M" in headlamp tie bar
Lower running boards
Nickel trim encircles cowl
Cowl lights
Engine changes
1st Moon-badged 8-cyl. (85 hp) has Lancaster vibration dampener, oil filter
Moon co. deficit
$338,038 (*Moody's* 1930)

1929 Models
6-62, 6-72, 8-75, & 8-80
Body styles
Cabriolet roadster, coupe, roadster, sedan, victoria coupe
Technical changes
Stanley automatic chassis lubricator
Body & appearance
Aerotype body continues
Trim gets chrome plating
Automatic windshield cleaner
Engine changes
Few claimed
Moon co. deficit
$276,626 (*Moody's* 1930)
Ad claim
"Moon Borrows from the Airplane!"

Note: Financial information comes from John Moody, *Moody's Manual of Investments and Security Rating Service* (New York: Press of Publishers Printing Co., various years).

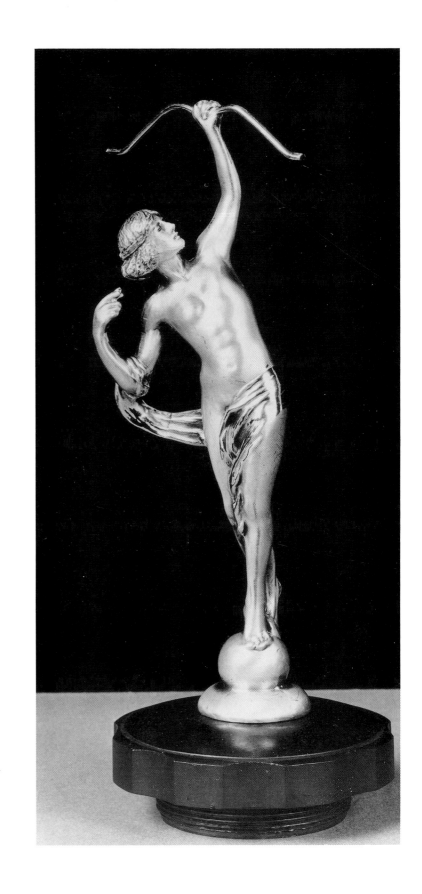

Index

Page numbers in italics refer to illustrations.